WINGS OF THE LUFTWAFFE

Flying German Aircraft of the Second World War

CAPTAIN ERIC BROWN, CBE, DSC, AFC, RN

Edited by
William Green and
Gordon Swanborough

Illustrated with cutaway
and cockpit interior
drawings by John Weal

DOUBLEDAY & COMPANY, INC.
GARDEN CITY, NEW YORK

Library of Congress Catalog Number 77-14891

Doubleday & Co., Inc. edition 1978

Copyright© Pilot Press Limited, 1977

This book, or any parts thereof, must not be reproduced in
any form without permission.

First published in Great Britain in 1977 by
Macdonald and Jane's Publishers Limited

ISBN: 0-385-13521-1

Printed in Great Britain

CONTENTS

FOREWORD

I have spent almost 10 years of my life in Germany and I count them amongst the most exciting in a life which has, for me, been crammed full of excitement. As a boy addicted to aviation, I had the extraordinary good fortune to be introduced to the exhilaration of aerobatics by that great German ace Ernst Udet and I recall with absolute clarity witnessing that famous demonstration of helicopter potential by Hanna Reitsch in Berlin's Deutschlandhalle; two events that left indelible impressions on my youthful mind and the determination to make myself thoroughly conversant with the language of this remarkably aviation-minded nation.

Subsequently, I was to return to Germany to continue my studies in the environment of the Third Reich and acquired my pilot's wings. Much has been written of the evils of this era in Germany, but to a young and impressionable foreigner the atmosphere was one of vibrant excitement and military pageantry. I was too inexperienced to sense the underlying tensions and above all I was bewitched by the tremendous aviation activity throughout the country. There seemed to be so many more powered aircraft and gliders than I had ever seen in England, and the youth of Germany was being encouraged to participate in the sport of aviation at no personal expense. To me it seemed truly an aviator's Utopia.

I haunted gliding sites at weekends, meeting many *Luftwaffe* officers who were helping to organise the feverish aviation activity that was to be seen everywhere. They took no exception to my presence and while they never offered me a flight, they seemed to gain some pleasure from trying out their English on me. For my part, watching the flying and getting aviation magazines from the clubhouses were sufficient reward. I read much of Germany's aircraft, little realising that the magazines of the day revealed no more than the tip of Germany's technological iceberg. I developed an avid desire to fly the aircraft depicted in the pages of *Der Flieger* and other German aviation publications of that time, having, of course, no concept of how completely my desire would be fulfilled or in what fashion.

World War II broke upon my life like a thunderbolt. I was bundled unceremoniously out of Germany, called up by the Royal Air Force and found myself in the Fleet Air Arm all within a couple of months. It all seemed a glorious adventure and, despite my many German friends, I entertained no misgivings about fighting Germans as long as they were in the air. My first operational posting was as a fighter pilot and while I regretted that I had had no opportunity to fly German aircraft, I consoled myself with the thought that I would soon have an opportunity to find out if they were as good as they appeared to be.

I was to be doubly fortunate – both to have the experience of aerial combat and to survive it. Fate was to be even kinder to me when I moved into the world of test flying, eventually, in January 1944, to become the Royal Navy's Chief Test Pilot at the famous Royal Aircraft Establishment at Farnborough, where I was to serve for six years and command the élite Aerodynamics Flight, always regarded as the top job in experimental test flying in Britain. During my first year at Farnborough, I built up a considerable amount of experience in flying different types of aircraft, including a half-dozen captured German types, and the RAE decided to make use of my knowledge of the German language in preparing teams of scientists that would move in to take over German installations and interrogate German technical personnel once the war was won. In retrospect, this must appear supreme confidence to have shown at that stage in history.

However, events moved swiftly, proving that this confidence had not been misplaced, and I found myself launched into the most fascinating period of my life. I visited virtually every major aeronautical installation in Germany, interrogated some of the aircraft designers whose names had become household words in Britain and the USA as well as in Germany – Messerschmitt, Heinkel, Tank – and I marvelled at some of the results of their incredible ingenuity, such as the V-1 and V-2 missiles, the Natter expendable rocket-driven interceptor, the similarly-powered Me 163 Komet, the prone-position Horten Ho IX, and many others.

During those first chaotic months after the fall of the Third Reich, the RAE sent its test pilots hither and thither throughout the British Zone of Occupation to collect examples of the *Luftwaffe*'s standard aircraft, these being flown to a central collecting point set up at Schleswig airfield, checked and then ferried to Farnborough. The pilots of the RAE's Aerodynamics Flight had the most jet experience and were therefore used to collect and ferry the more sophisticated types of captured aircraft. The fact that I was a part of the Flight and German speaking led to my being heavily employed in this task, finally being designated as Officer in Charge of German Aircraft Reception at Farnborough itself. It was thus that I flight tested every German aircraft that arrived at the RAE, selected those that I considered best retained for further test work and wrote the handling notes for the other RAE pilots who were to fly some of these aircraft and help ferry those not required at Farnborough to RAF Brize Norton for storage.

Altogether, I was to fly 55 different types of German aircraft, mostly at Farnborough, but quite a number of them in Norway, Denmark, France, Holland, Belgium, Austria and Germany itself. The very fact that these aircraft had belonged to the enemy endowed them with an aura of utter fascination and consequently I took copious notes of my impressions. It is the distillation of these notes relating to the principal ex-*Luftwaffe* aircraft that I flew that provides the content matter of the pages that follow.

When I reflect on the shambles that existed in Germany after the collapse of the Third Reich, I cannot but help marvel that so many of these captured aircraft were flown with comparatively few accidents, yet virtually no records of their life histories were available and maintenance was often undertaken by British personnel totally unfamiliar with German systems. I did at least succeed in enlisting the services of two highly skilled *Luftwaffe* technicians whom I found in Norway with an Ar 234B squadron and gave the option of an interesting tour of duty with my unit at Farnborough or an indeterminate spell as prisoners-of-war. They accepted my offer and proved completely trustworthy, extremely industrious and highly intelligent. They flew all over the Continent with me in a Siebel Si 204D, which I used as a flying workshop, inspecting ex-*Luftwaffe* aircraft before ferrying them to England. We shared some exciting experiences and maintain contact to the present day.

The following chapters were originally written as individual features for publication in AIR INTERNATIONAL and the reason for their publication collectively in book form is to provide as a permanent record an assessment by a former enemy of the characteristics of the principal *Luftwaffe* aircraft whose true capabilities are already being lost in the mythology that inevitably evolves with the passage of time; aircraft built by a nation whose aeronautical technology had advanced to such an extent that it rendered an attempt to conquer Europe appear less of a mad gamble than in fact it was. The gamble, of course, failed and the Third Reich was reduced to ashes, but phoenix-like from those ashes arose a rich legacy of aeronautical knowledge to enrich the victors and accelerate aviation progress.

Eric Brown
Copthorne
Sussex

March 1977

FOCKE-WULF FW 200C CONDOR

ON THAT late-autumn day in 1937 at Tempelhof Airport, Berlin, when Ernst Udet, Chief of the *Technischen Amt*, newly promoted to the rank of *Generalmajor* and a long-standing friend of my father, proudly showed me the first prototype of the latest of Prof Dipl-Ing Kurt Tank's progeny, I established a love-hate relationship with the supremely elegant Focke-Wulf Fw 200 Condor commercial airliner; an affair that was destined not to be consummated for almost eight years, until July 1945, when I was finally to have the opportunity to fly this æsthetically most appealing of large aeroplanes. To this moment I recall clearly the admiration that I felt for the Condor's clean lines and majestic stance as it stood on the apron in front of the Tempelhof terminal building; still very much a *versuchs* machine but its every contour holding promise of great feats.

Almost exactly four years were to elapse before I was once again to take more than a passing interest in the Condor, but by now the primary rôle of Kurt Tank's creation had translated from pacific to militant; its achievements as a commercial transport having already been overshadowed by its feats as a commerce raider. It had become, to quote wartime Prime Minister Winston Churchill, the "scourge of the Atlantic", but with all its awesome reputation and fearsome array of weaponry, the application of which had perforce been accompanied by some loss in elegance, the Condor had retained all the grace-

ful shapeliness of the prototype that had left so indelible an impression on me.

By that time, the summer of 1941, I was a young Fleet Air Arm pilot with No 802 Squadron, a Grumman Martlet unit deployed aboard the Royal Navy's first escort aircraft carrier, HMS *Audacity*, a converted German merchant vessel of 5,600 tons. Such midget carriers were really the brainchild of Churchill who saw in them part of the answer to the marauding U-boat packs that were posing a major threat to Britain's survival. The key to the steadily increasing success of the U-boat was obviously its partnership with the military version of the Fw 200 Condor which served as its eyes, shadowing Allied convoys and then acting as its *Fühlungshalter*, or contact plane, by sending out continuous D/F signals. The tactics of the Condor were controlled by the *Befehlshaber der U-Boote* (Flag Officer Submarines), no direct communication taking place between the aircraft and the submarines that it was responsible for directing.

The Condor had been given a formidable character by the Allies, who saw it as a winged Barracuda. Its auspicious success certainly entitled it to the reputation of being a voracious killer. Between 1 August 1940 and 9 February 1941, the Condors of I *Gruppe* of *Kampfgeschwader* 40 operating from Bordeaux-Mérignac, flying out across the Bay of Biscay and following an

arc around the Irish Atlantic coastline to attack targets of opportunity before landing at Stavanger-Sola or Trondheim-Værnes, accounted for 85 Allied vessels totalling some 363,000 tons. During the late summer of 1941, the *Fliegerführer Atlantik* had radically changed the Condor's rôle from commerce raider to that of U-boat co-operation, issuing instructions to KG 40 that its aircraft were no longer to initiate attacks and were to seek cloud cover when attacked, offering fight only if absolutely necessary. As Squadron Armament Officer, however, I was unaware of the fact that the Condor's activities had become any less aggressive as I performed my duty of briefing our squadron's pilots on the armament of enemy aircraft that they were likely to encounter, and the most likely to be met on the voyage to Gibraltar on which we were bound was the Fw 200.

Formidable defensive capability

In retrospect, it would seem that the intelligence brief from which I worked had been compiled with a little too much enthusiasm as it credited the Condor with capabilities that time was to reveal it did not possess. At this juncture, the improved Fw 200C-3 had made its operational début and, according to my brief, this was a veritable "flying armoury"! It could allegedly lift four 2,205-lb (1 000-kg) bombs beneath its wings and augment these with a pair of 1,102-lb (500-kg) bombs in its ventral gondola — a mighty 11,125 lb (5 000 kg), or almost as much as a Lancaster! Defensive armament certainly appeared daunting and apparently included a fixed forward-firing 20-mm cannon in the fuselage nose, a second 20-mm weapon in the nose of the gondola which fired forwards and downwards through 55 deg angle of depression and possessed a lateral

The Fw 200C-3/U2 version of the Condor (above left) introduced the Lotfe 7D bomb sight, the bulged housing of which may be seen aft of the transparent ventral gondola nose. This substantially improved the Condor's bombing accuracy. (Below) Crews of I Gruppe of Kampfgeschwader 40 parading for inspection in front of their Fw 200C-3 Condors. This Gruppe was the only exponent of the Condor over the Atlantic during its heyday.

The Fw 200C-4/U2 (CE+IB) illustrated above and the Fw 200C-4/U1 seen below were each one-off VIP armed transport variants of the Condor commerce raider, the latter having been flown at the Royal Aircraft Establishment, Farnborough. Both feature abbreviated ventral gondolas and differed solely in their seating arrangements, the U1 accommodating 11 passengers and the U2 having provision for 14 passengers.

traverse of 28 deg on each side of its central axis, a third firing aft and downwards with similar angles of movement, and a fourth in a powered turret which, rotating through 360 deg, was mounted immediately aft of the flight deck. If this array of artillery was not enough, the Condor was also credited with a 13-mm gun on a Scarff ring-type mounting firing from an aft dorsal position, a pair of 7,9-mm machine guns mounted behind sliding beam panels and two similar weapons firing through side windows.

In due course it was to be ascertained that the Condor's bomb-toting potential as indicated by this brief was greatly exaggerated — bomb load invariably being restricted to a quartet of 551-lb (250-kg) bombs for the offensive reconnaissance mission — but the defensive armament was not so far out, give or take a fixed forward-firing cannon and a pair of machine guns, and if the intelligence boys had perhaps led us to believe that the defensive capabilities of the Condor were even more awesome than they in fact were and installed armament differed somewhat from *umrüst-bausatz* to *umrüst-bausatz**, the defences of the Condor were nevertheless to be treated with the greatest of respect. We squadron pilots discussed for hours on end the best means of attacking this "winged porcupine" which apparently possessed no undefended spots.

I eventually decided for myself that the best way in was a flat attack from head on, always disconcerting for those under

attack. Moreover, such an attack would be directed at the Condor's most vulnerable items — its pilots. Thus armed each with his own pet theories, we eight pilots with our six Martlets set sail in September 1941 as escort to a Gibraltar-bound convoy, the aircraft parked on the aft end of *Audacity's* tiny flight deck which measured a mere 420 ft (128 m) by 60 ft (18 m). Since there was no hangar, the Martlets were permanently on deck and the foremost had only 300 ft (91 m) in which to take-off. The *Audacity's* maximum speed was only fourteen-and-a-half knots and so it was all very tight. This applied particularly to the landing as, with only two arrester wires, a barrier and its associated safety trip wire, the test of pilot skill in a rough sea was just about the ultimate. Quite apart from the risk involved, there was the hard fact that any accident to one of our Martlets depleted the convoy's operational air cover by one-sixth.

Our convoy soon ran into U-boat trouble, and on 20

*Factory conversion set signified by a suffix letter "U" and a numeral added to the designation and indicating an armament or other equipment change. For example, the Fw 200 C-3/U1 had an HDL 151 forward turret mounting a 15-mm MG 151 cannon in place of the low-drag Fw 19 with its single 7,9-mm MG 15 machine gun and a 20-mm MG 151 cannon in the nose of the gondola in place of the older MG FF of similar calibre, but the Fw 200 C-3/U2 reverted to the Fw 19 forward turret and, as a result of the introduction of a Lotfe 7D bomb sight, supplanted the MG 151 cannon in the nose of the gondola with a 13-mm MG 131 machine gun.

Focke-Wulf Fw 200C-4/U3 Cutaway Drawing Key

1 Starboard navigation light
2 Wing skinning
3 Starboard aileron
4 Aileron trim tabs
5 Outboard mainspar
6 Aileron control run
7 Wing ribs (centre section)
8 Wing ribs (forward section)
9 Wing dihedral break point
10 Starboard flap (outer section)
11 Starboard flap (centre section)
12 Starboard flap (inner section)
13 Wing fuel tank covers
14 Inboard mainspar structure
15 Starboard outer oil tank
16 Multiple exhaust stubs
17 Cooling gills
18 Starboard outer nacelle (angled)
19 Three-blade VDM controllable-pitch metal-bladed propeller
20 Propeller boss
21 Carburettor air intake

22 Auxiliary fuel tank (66 Imp gal/300 1 capacity) semi-recessed
23 Starboard inner nacelle
24 FuG 200 Hohentwiel search radar array (port antenna omitted for clarity)
25 Nose D/F loop
26 Nose bulkhead
27 Rudder pedals
28 Hand-held 13-mm 131 machine gun (D-Stand)
29 Lotfe 7D bomb sight fairing
30 Ventral gondola side windows (gondola offset to starboard)
31 Rear dorsal gunner's take-off seat
32 Pilot's circular vision port
33 First pilot's seat
34 Sliding windscreen panel
35 Co-pilot's seat (co-pilot also served as bomb-aimer)
36 Flight deck entry
37 Arc-of-fire interrupter gate
38 Cabin air inlet (starboard side only)
39 Hydraulically-operated Fw 19 turret mounting single 7,9-mm MG 15 machine gun (A-Stand)
40 Gunner's seat
41 Ammunition racks (A-Stand)
42 Bulkhead

43 Radio operator's rectangular vision port
44 Ventral gondola entry hatch in cabin floor
45 Radio operator's station (A-Stand gunner's station)
46 Ammunition racks (D-Stand)
47 Ammunition racks (D-Stand)
48 Ventral gondola centre section (with maximum capacity of one 198 Imp gal/900 1 armoured fuel tank or 12 110-lb/50-kg bombs)
49 Underfloor control runs
50 Cabin window stations (staggered two to port and three to starboard)
51 Underfloor structure
52 Fuselage oil tank
53 De-icing fluid reservoir
54 Aerial mast
55 Five main fuselage fuel tanks (canted)
56 Mainspar fuselage carry-through structure
57 Rear ventral gunner's take-off seat
58 Upper fuselage longeron
59 Mainframe
60 Cabin ventilators/air extractors

61 Fuselage sidewalls
62 Ammunition racks (C-Stand)
63 Second radio operator's take-off seat
64 Strengthened fuselage frame
65 Dorsal D/F loop
66 Starboard 7,9-mm MG 15 machine gun (F-Stand)
67 Beam gunners' take-off seats
68 Bulkhead
69 Dorsal aft gunner's position (B-Stand)
70 Dorsal glazing
71 Ammunition racks (B-Stand)
72 Hinged canopy section
73 MG 15 machine gun (7,9-mm calibre)
74 Rear fuselage frames
75 Starboard tailplane
76 Endplate-fin balance
77 Starboard elevator
78 Elevator hinge
79 Elevator tab
80 Tailfin front spar structure
81 Tailfin structure
82 Rudder balance
83 Rudder construction
84 Electrically-operated rudder trim tab (upper section)
85 Electrically-operated rudder trim tab (lower section)
86 Rudder post
87 Tailwheel mechanism access panel
88 Tail cone

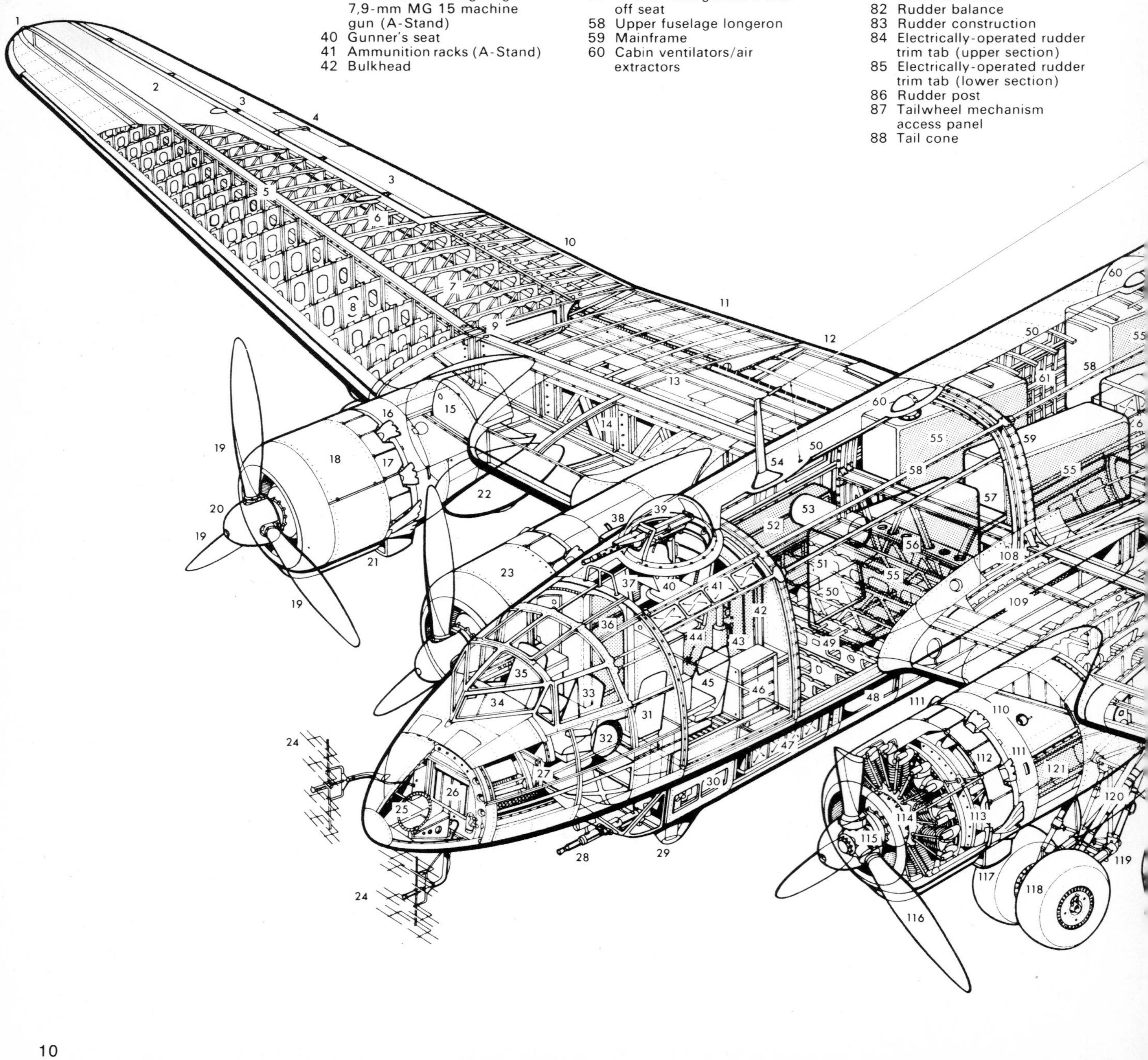

89 Aft navigation light
90 Elevator tab
91 Port elevator
92 Electrically-operated elevator tab (port only)
93 Endplate-fin balance
94 Port tailplane
95 Elevator hinge
96 Tailplane spar
97 Forward-retracting tailwheel
98 Tailwheel retraction mechanism
99 Control runs
100 Oxygen bottles
101 Aft bulkhead
102 Chute for Schwan D/F buoys, Lux light-buoys or flares
103 Port 7,9-mm MG 15 beam gun (F-Stand)
104 Ammunition racks (F-Stand) – starboard racks identical

105 Entry door
106 Aft 7,9-mm MG 15 ventral gun (C-Stand)
107 Ventral gondola side windows
108 Main fuselage/wing attachment points
109 Ventral weapons/overload fuel bay

110 Port inner nacelle
111 Multiple exhaust stubs
112 Cooling gills
113 Engine mount
114 BMW-Bramo 323 R-2 Fafnir nine-cylinder radial air-cooled engine
115 Propeller pitch mechanism
116 Three-blade VDM controllable-pitch metal-bladed propeller
117 Carburettor air intake
118 Twin mainwheels
119 Forward-retracting hydraulically-operated main undercarriage member
120 Retraction jack

121 Mainwheel well
122 Mainwheel door
123 Wing structure
124 Mainspar
125 Wing fuel tanks
126 Flap structure
127 Port flap (centre section)
128 Wing dihedral break point
129 Port outer oil tank
130 Port outer nacelle (angled)
131 Propeller boss
132 Semi-recessed 551-lb (250-kg) bomb beneath outboard nacelle
133 Position of 1,102-lb (500-kg) bomb on outboard nacelle rack (external)
134 Port underwing bomb rack
135 551-lb (250-kg) bomb
136 Pitot head
137 Wing skinning
138 Port aileron
139 Aileron trim tabs
140 Electrically-operated aileron trim tab (port only)

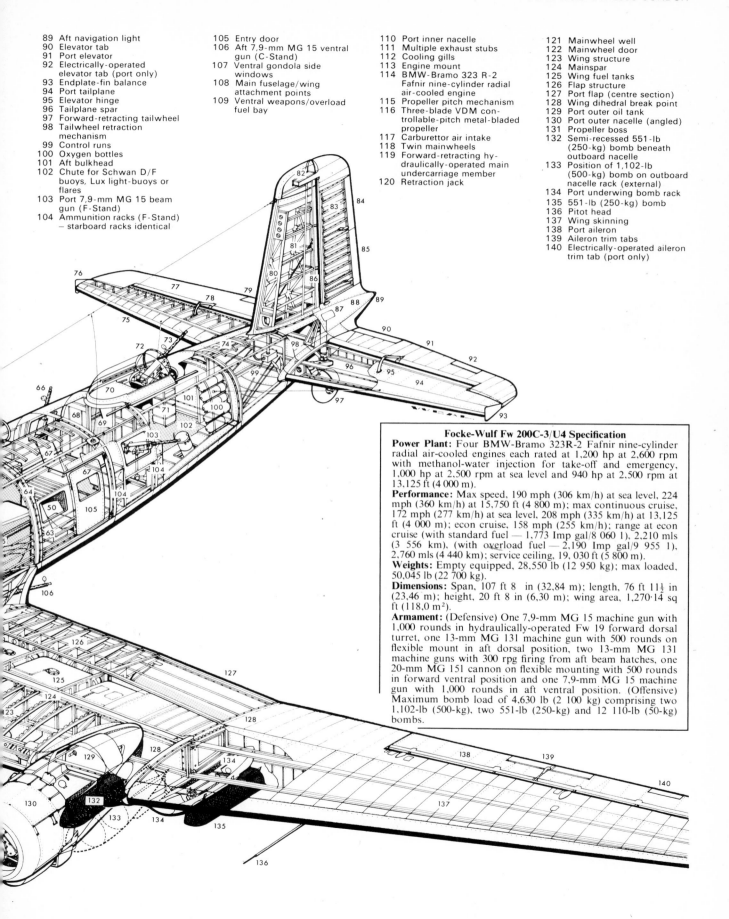

Focke-Wulf Fw 200C-3/U4 Specification

Power Plant: Four BMW-Bramo 323R-2 Fafnir nine-cylinder radial air-cooled engines each rated at 1,200 hp at 2,600 rpm with methanol-water injection for take-off and emergency, 1,000 hp at 2,500 rpm at sea level and 940 hp at 2,500 rpm at 13,125 ft (4 000 m).

Performance: Max speed, 190 mph (306 km/h) at sea level, 224 mph (360 km/h) at 15,750 ft (4 800 m); max continuous cruise, 172 mph (277 km/h) at sea level, 208 mph (335 km/h) at 13,125 ft (4 000 m); econ cruise, 158 mph (255 km/h); range at econ cruise (with standard fuel — 1,773 Imp gal/8 060 l), 2,210 mls (3 556 km), (with overload fuel — 2,190 Imp gal/9 955 l), 2,760 mls (4 440 km); service ceiling, 19, 030 ft (5 800 m).

Weights: Empty equipped, 28,550 lb (12 950 kg); max loaded, 50,045 lb (22 700 kg).

Dimensions: Span, 107 ft 8 in (32,84 m); length, 76 ft 11½ in (23,46 m); height, 20 ft 8 in (6,30 m); wing area, 1,270·14 sq ft (118,0 m²).

Armament: (Defensive) One 7,9-mm MG 15 machine gun with 1,000 rounds in hydraulically-operated Fw 19 forward dorsal turret, one 13-mm MG 131 machine gun with 500 rounds on flexible mount in aft dorsal position, two 13-mm MG 131 machine guns with 300 rpg firing from aft beam hatches, one 20-mm MG 151 cannon on flexible mounting with 500 rounds in forward ventral position and one 7,9-mm MG 15 machine gun with 1,000 rounds in aft ventral position. (Offensive) Maximum bomb load of 4,630 lb (2 100 kg) comprising two 1,102-lb (500-kg), two 551-lb (250-kg) and 12 110-lb (50-kg) bombs.

September, after a night attack which cost us three ships, our rescue vessel, prominently displaying red crosses, was detached to pick up survivors. It was then that a Condor that had apparently been shadowing the convoy could not resist the temptation offered by the lone ship, its low-level bombing run leaving the defenceless rescue vessel a mass of flame. The Condor had barely had time to close its gondola bomb doors, however, when it was bounced by two of our Martlets, flown by Sub-Lts N H Patterson and G R P Fletcher, which despatched it in a single concerted quarter attack, the entire tail-end of the fuselage breaking off.

Analysis of this first "kill" filled the off-duty hours of the pilots and produced some interesting conclusions. Firstly, as the attack had taken place 900 miles (1 450 km) due West of Brest, it was obvious that we were going to be within surveillance range of the Condor all the way from Britain to Gibraltar. Secondly, it was accepted as possible that the Condor's crew, coming out of cloud cover for a quick, low-level bombing run, might not have seen the red crosses on their target until virtually the moment of pressing the bomb release button. Thirdly, it was decided that the quarter attack by the Martlets had succeeded only because of the element of surprise, the Condor's

It was the normal practice of I Gruppe of Kampfgeschwader 40 to record the missions flown and vessels sunk on the vertical tail surfaces of its Condors. An early example of this practice is seen above left. Later in the operational career of this unit, the vessels destroyed, their tonnage and the date of their destruction were usually indicated on the rudder.

The earliest version of the Condor, the Fw 200C-1, the fifth production example of which is illustrated above, featured a raised cupola immediately aft of the flight deck mounting a single 7,9-mm MG 15 machine gun. Derived from a commercial transport, it embodied virtually no structural strengthening and the result was a number of structural failures. Some attempt to strengthen the Condor so that it could more readily withstand the strain of continuous low-altitude operational flying was represented by the Fw 200C-3 illustrated below.

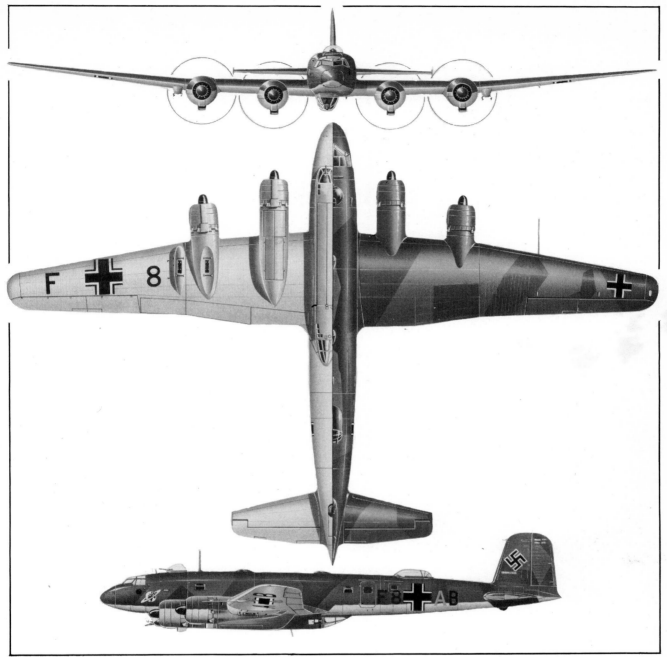

The Fw 200C-3 Condor began to reach the I Gruppe of Kampfgeschwader 40 in the summer of 1941, the example illustrated above (F8 + AB) belonging to the Geschwader Staff. At this time, I/KG 40 was operating primarily from Bordeaux - Mérignac. The style of the Balkenkreuz on the fuselage side is noteworthy as is also the size and position of the swastika on the tail fin.

crew, presumably busy assessing the results of their bombing, barely having time to open fire. Finally, the two Martlet pilots that had engaged the Condor were convinced that the concentration of their fire in the rear fuselage coupled with the evasive action being taken by the Condor's pilot who was using coarse rudder movement resulted in the tail end of the aeroplane breaking away.

With regard to the last conclusion, we did not really see that this had revealed an exploitable weak point on which to concentrate attack under normal conditions of full defensive fire from the Condor. Of course, we then had no means of knowing that we *had* quite fortuitously discovered the "Achilles Heel" of the Condor; that as a legacy of the haste with which this commercial transport had been adapted for its tasks it suffered a serious structural weakness. Virtually no structural changes had been embodied in the process of changing the Condor's

designed rôle and a structure intended for the prosaic flying at medium altitudes anticipated for an airliner could hardly have been expected to prove adequate to the strain of continuous operational flying at low altitudes for long periods and the violent manœuvres that were often to be called for when taking evasive action. There were to be many cases of rear fuselage failures during landings despite the attempt made, with the Fw 200C-3 version, to beef up the structure.

The next combat between Martlets from *Audacity* and a Condor was to be a very different affair and took place during the second voyage of the escort carrier in November 1941. This time the Condor's crew was on the alert. The Martlets again made quarter attacks but one of the Martlets was shot down during the first firing pass, succeeding only in setting one of the Condor's engines afire, although the second Martlet finally succeeded in finishing off the Focke-Wulf. This combat only

The hydraulically-operated Fw 19 forward upper turret (A-Stand) mounting a single 7,9-mm MG 15 machine gun (above) was introduced by the Fw 200C-3, and replaced the fixed raised fairing featured by earlier sub-types. A 66 Imp gal (300 l) auxiliary tank could be mounted semi-recessed beneath each outboard engine nacelle (below).

served to further my conviction that a head-on attack was the most likely to succeed with impunity to the attacker, and my chance soon came — twice in succession — to put my theory into practice.

It proved to be much more difficult than I had imagined to get into position for a head-on attack and, indeed, my first such attack was largely the result of a chance confrontation after losing my quarry in cloud. Once committed, the head-on attack is a hair-raising affair, as you close at high speed with a large aeroplane belching fire at you while you are glued to a gunsight. I was fully occupied in sighting, firing and breaking away over my target, but I can imagine that the Condor pilot must have been going through hell, sitting behind his controls just flying straight and level and praying that his gunners would swat this portly little wasp spitting venom directly at him. One such pass was enough and my lasting impressions were of the Condor's windscreen crumbling under the weight of lead spewing from my 0·5-in (12,7-mm) Brownings and of the very violent evasive action necessary to prevent collision with the monster.

The results of my second encounter with a Condor were similar, but this time I knew that there could be only one head-on attack and I was therefore more calculating in setting it up properly. Not all our attacks on Condors were by any means successful, however, for KG 40's pilots were adept in the art of using cloud cover and were masters of the technique of gently manœuvering to bring maximum firepower to bear against the attacker. Indeed, our only other success — the fourth Condor "kill" of that voyage — resulted from another head-on attack which actually ended in collision in which the sturdy little Martlet survived and the Condor did not.

The *Audacity* certainly came as a surprise packet to the *Fliegerführer Atlantik* and hit *Kampfgeschwader* 40 and its Condors the hardest blow they were ever struck. More is the pity that she was destined to have such a short life in Royal Navy service, being sunk by U-751 on her fourth convoy trip after a seven-day running battle with U-boats and their attendant Condors. The CAM ships of 1940, with their Hurricanes being catapulted into the air at the sight of a Condor, were a sign of Allied desperation, but the début of *Audacity* and the escort carriers that were to follow her marked the beginning of the decline in effectiveness of the Condor, though I finished that tour of convoy duty with a healthy respect for this commercial transport turned Atlantic marauder. It was to be said that the Condor possessed little more than a respectable endurance to commend it; that it was an improvisation forced on the *Oberkommando der Luftwaffe* by a lost gamble that the Heinkel He 177 would be available for the long-range armed reconnaissance and anti-shipping rôles. This is as may be, but Martlet

One of the last production versions of the Condor was the Fw 200C-8 which was intended specifically to carry the Henschel Hs 293A anti-shipping missile although a number of examples of this sub-type were completed for the normal maritime search rôle, one of these (Werk-Nr 256) being illustrated below.

The Condor standardised on the FuG 200 Hohentwiel search radar, the aerial array of which may be seen on the nose of this Fw 200C-8 (above and below right). The Hohentwiel was used in conjunction with a blind bombing procedure and was accurate down to a range of less than a mile.

pilots far out over the Atlantic certainly considered the Condor a formidable opponent and, improvisation or not, it certainly established an enviable record over the Atlantic for two years.

A very special Condor

I was to see only one more Condor, off the west coast of Scotland, during the war years and then, with the ending of hostilities, I was finally to have the opportunity to fly this aircraft with which I had been acquainted for nearly eight years, and a strange Condor it was — the former personal transport of the notorious SS leader Heinrich Himmler and later kept for the private use of Grand-Admiral Karl Doenitz. This particular aircraft, the sole example of the Fw 200C-4/U1 (*Werk-Nr* 137), marked a near turning of the circle as it had been built as a passenger transport, but was fully armed and embodied some *very* special features. It could accommodate a maximum of 11 passengers in two compartments, the forward compartment, which was the one intended to be used by Himmler and, later, Doenitz, featuring an armour-plated forward-facing seat, a hinged armour-plate screen for protection from beam attacks and a jettisonable escape hatch in the floor in front of the seat, so that in dire emergency the occupant of the seat would have some chance of escaping by parachute. Immediately facing this seat was a small panel carrying an airspeed indicator and an altimeter (these instruments being duplicated, incidentally, in the abbreviated gondola beneath the fuselage) and this forward compartment provided accommodation for four additional passengers. A further six passengers could be accommodated by the aft compartment, both of these compartments being finished in highly-polished light wood panelling, all upholstery being a sombre grey. Only one other such *special* Condor was built, the Fw 2000C-4/U2 (*Werk-Nr* 138), which provided accommodation for 14 passengers*.

On entering the cockpit, the layout struck me as being more

civilianised than anything that I had encountered to that time in a four-engined aircraft. It was classically arranged with all the throttles and engine instruments on a central console and the flight instruments duplicated on either side for the first and

---

* *It is of interest to recall that two pre-series Condors, Fw 200A-08 (Werk-Nr 3098) and Fw 200A-09 (Werk-Nr 3099), were completed as "special" transports, the latter being named Immelmann III and becoming the Führermaschine for the personal use of Adolf Hitler. Hitler's armoured seat housed a parachute in its upholstery and was* *mounted above a jettisonable trap, activation of a lever jettisoning the trap and ejecting the seat, the parachute being deployed automatically. This escape system was repeatedly tested on the ground, a sack loaded to 175 lb (80 kg) being used to simulate the seat's occupant, but the device was never to be used*

As a legacy of its commercial lineage, the Condor commerce raider possessed a structure inadequate to absorb the strain of continuous low-altitude operation and the violent manoeuvres often called for when taking evasive action. The result was a series of structural failures, one such, suffered by an Fw 200C-3, being illustrated above.

second pilots. The view was somewhat restricted on either side by the heavy framework of the windscreen.

The starting-up procedure was simple. There was a master fuel cock which had to be set to START, the fuselage tank group selected, four fuel pumps switched on, internal handpump primers and an advance/retard ignition lever operated and then the inertia starters could be electrically energised and engaged. The BMW-Bramo 323R-2 Fafnir nine-cylinder radials fitted to this particular Condor had what I can only describe as a reliable throb when they came to life. For warm up the master petrol cock had to be set to REISE (cruise) and the standard engine and ancillary checks made at 2,300 rpm. The aircraft was then ready to be taxied to the take-off point where the following drill had to be carried out: Master petrol cock to START (take-off); cooling gills set one-third open; airscrew pitch indicators set to 12 o'clock; flaps set to START; ailerons trimmed one division right wing low; rudder trimmed four divisions nose right; elevator trimmed neutral for light load and progressively nose heavy for increasing load; engine rev counter gauges to MOTOREN GESAMT (all engines).

Installation of the Lotfe 7D bomb sight necessitated replacement of the 20-mm MG 151 cannon in the nose of the ventral gondola by a 13-mm MG 131 machine gun in the Fw 200C-3/U2 (as seen above left). The Fw 200C-4/U1 (below) as flown at the RAE, Farnborough.

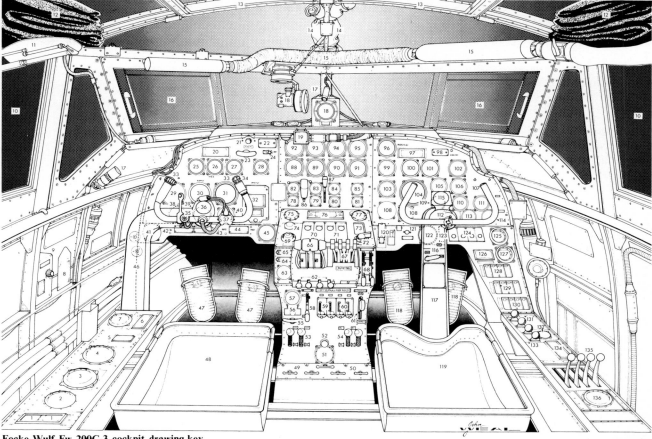

Focke-Wulf Fw 200C-3 cockpit drawing key

1 Undercarriage de-icing switches
2 Undercarriage de-icing cock
3 Suction-air throw-over switch (starboard)
4 Suction-air throw-over switch (port)
5 Instrument panel lighting switch (port)
6 NACA-cowling floodlight switch
7 Pilot's oxygen pressure gauge
8 Frequency tables
9 Radio R/T tuner
10 Fixed side panels
11 Pilot's sun visor
12 Anti-glare curtains (stowed)
13 Hinged upper canopy sections
14 Anti-glare curtains (stowed)
15 Cockpit warm air
16 Sliding (Perspex) windscreen panels
17 Cockpit illumination
18 Compass installation
19 Auxiliary lighting switch
20 Gyro-compass course indicator
21 Fuselage-flap control lamp
22 Gyro compass heating indicator
23 Fuselage flap release handle
24 Gyro compass heating switch
25 Airspeed indicator
26 Turn-and-bank indicator
27 Rate-of-climb indicator
28 Radio beacon (Navaid) visual indicator
29 Pilot's repeater compass
30 Coarse-fine altimeter
31 Artificial horizon
32 Gyro compass
33 Pilot's control yoke
34 Automatic pilot ON/OFF switch
35 Intercom switch
36 Clock
37 Illumination buttons
38 Suction – and pressure-gauge for gyro devices and automatic

pilot (partly obscured)
39 External temperature gauge (obscured by control column)
40 Coarse altimeter
41 Lateral trim indicator
42 Gyro support switch
43 Wing searchlight setting/adjustment switch
44 Wing searchlight ON/OFF switch
45 Signal lamp
46 Pilot's control column
47 Pilot's rudder pedals
48 Pilot's seat pan (seat-back deleted for clarity)
49 Fire extinguishers (port engines)
50 Fire extinguishers (starboard engines)
51 Fire extinguisher pressure gauge
52 Servo unit emergency pull-out knob
53 Fuel safety cock levers (port tanks)
54 Fuel safety cock levers (starboard tanks)
55 Parking switch activating handle
56 Directional trim switch
57 Directional trim indicator
58 Undercarriage retraction lever
59 Airscrew pitch control levers (port)
60 Airscrew pitch control levers (starboard)
61 Wing flap lever
62 Throttle locks
63 Longitudinal trim indicator
64 Directional trim emergency switch
65 Longitudinal trim emergency switch
66 Throttles
67 Supercharger levers
68 Fuel tank selectors
69 Servo unit emergency button
70 Ignition switches (port)
71 Ignition switches (starboard)
72 UV-lighting switch

73 Landing light switch
74 Master battery cut-off switch
75 Instrument panel dimmer switch
76 Undercarriage and landing flap indicators
77 Starter selector switch
78 Oil temperature gauge (port outer)
79 Oil temperature gauge (port inner)
80 Oil temperature gauge (starboard inner)
81 Oil temperature gauge (starboard outer)
82 Pitch indicator (port outer)
83 Pitch indicator (port inner)
84 Pitch indicator (starboard inner)
85 Pitch indicator (starboard outer)
86 Emergency bomb release (sealed)
87 Bomb-arming lever
88 Double manifold pressure gauges (port engines)
89 Oil and fuel pressure gauges (port engines)
90 Oil and fuel pressure gauges (starboard engines)
91 Double manifold pressure gauges (port engines)
92 RPM indicator (port outer)
93 RPM indicator (port inner)
94 RPM indicator (starboard inner)
95 RPM indicator (starboard outer)
96 RPM synchronization selector switch
97 Remote compass course indicator
98 Pitot head heating indicator
99 Airspeed indicator
100 Turn-and-bank indicator
101 Rate-of-climb indicator
102 Control surface temperature gauge
103 Coarse-fine altimeter
104 Artificial horizon

105 Cylinder temperature gauge
106 Cylinder temperature throw-over switch
107 Co-pilot's control yoke
108 Blanked-off dials
109 Cruise fuel contents gauge (part obscured by control column)
110 Starting fuel contents gauge
111 Oil contents gauge
112 Cruise fuel transfer switch (obscured by control column)
113 Starting fuel transfer switch
114 Oil transfer switch
115 Clock
116 Control locking lever
117 Co-pilot's control column
118 Co-pilot's rudder pedals
119 Co-pilot's seat pan (seat-back deleted for clarity)
120 Starter switches
121 Starter mechanism signal lamp
122 Suction – and pressure gauges for undercarriage de-icing and gyro devices (part obscured by control column)
123 Longitudinal trim switch
124 Injection valve press buttons
125 Hydraulic systems pressure gauge
126 Windscreen heating
127 Control surfaces temperature switch
128 Fuel pump switches (port tanks)
129 Fuel pump switches (starboard tanks)
130 Controllable-gill adjustment
131 Airscrew de-icing levers (port engines)
132 Hydraulics emergency-pump signal lamp
133 Airscrew de-icing levers (starboard engines)
134 Hydraulics emergency pump switch
135 Control surface de-icing levers
136 Pressure reservoir gauge

The take-off in the Condor was the most difficult aspect of its entire flight handling as it had a very strong tendency to swing to port. The technique recommended by German pilots was to open up the engines to half throttle only for about 330 yards (300 m) when the tail would begin to lift of its own accord. From this point the throttles were progressively opened up, simultaneously being manipulated differentially to counteract the swing until, after about 765 yards (700 m) run, the engines were at full power with 2,500 rpm and 1·5 *atas* of boost. The Condor then had to be allowed to fly itself off at 102 mph (165 km/h). If pulled off under that speed it veered to starboard quite strongly. Using this technique the take-off run with the aircraft in fully loaded condition was 985 yards (900 m).

After unstick the undercarriage was retracted hydraulically and this procedure took a lengthy 24 seconds during which the airspeed had to be kept below 125 mph (200 km/h). The flaps were then raised and rudder trim centralised before settling into the climb at 155 mph (250 km/h) with 2,250 rpm and 1·25 *atas* of boost. This speed was maintained up to 13,125 ft (4 000 m) and then reduced to 149 mph (240 km/h), the superchargers having been moved into high gear at 8,530 ft (2 600 m). This particular Condor could reach 28,000 ft (8 535 m) but was obviously happier at around 15,000 ft (4 570 m). Indeed, its maximum speed as we measured it at Farnborough was 250 mph (402 km/h) at 13,000 ft (3 960 m), this being some 25 mph (40 km/h) more than the production Fw 200C-3. The most economical cruising speed appeared to be 171 mph (275 km/h) at 5,000 ft (1 525 m) and with tankage for 1,760 Imp gal (8 000 l) this provided an endurance of the order of 14 hours with normal safety reserves, or a range of about 2,400 miles (3 860 km), and this could be stretched in the standard maritime reconnaissance model with overload fuel in the ventral gondola to around 18 hours — small wonder that the Condor could cover a very large area of the wartime convoy routes when operating from Bordeaux-Mérignac.

In flight the Condor proved very stable about all three axes, but any change of speed or power called for immediate trimming, the elevator and rudder trimmers being conveniently positioned on the left horn of the control column. There was a second elevator trim switch located in front of the second pilot and the aileron trim was on the first pilot's left console. The Condor certainly turned more easily to left than to right on account of engine torque but it could hardly be considered the ideal aircraft for evasive manœuvering. Its maximum permissible indicated airspeed below 5,000 ft (1 525 m) was 280 mph (450 km/h). All in all, this was the type of aircraft which, when attacked, had little option but to fly straight and level and give its heavy defensive armament a good platform for fighting off the attacker.

The all-weather equipment installed on the aircraft was good; rubber pulse de-icers on the wings and tailplane, airscrew de-icing sprays, auto-pilot and good internal heating. I flew the Condor several times in really nasty weather and found this equipment to be extremely reliable. It was not, however, the sort of aeroplane which I would have taken-off blind with equanimity.

The maximum permitted weight for landing was 41,890 lb (19 000 kg). The undercarriage was lowered in level flight below 124 mph (200 km/h) and took 10 seconds to extend fully, and the flaps were lowered at 115 mph (185 km/h). If an attempt was made to lower the flaps at anything above this speed they would creep up and not extend fully again until speed had been reduced to 109 mph (175 km/h). The approach speed was 102 mph (165 km/h) and this could be allowed to decay in the late stages until a three-pointer was made at 80 mph (130 km/h). It was important to check that the throttle friction nut beneath the throttles was loosened otherwise it was difficult to close the throttles fully and an excessive landing run resulted.

To assess the Condor's value to Germany as a war machine is not difficult because, in concert with the U-boat, it so nearly brought Britain to her knees in 1940-41, but as a fighting machine the Condor possessed all the shortcomings that were to be expected of a converted commercial airliner, a fact which only became obvious after the Allies had taken the measure of this aeroplane. Its lack of armour and the fact that all fuel lines were on the underside of the aircraft rendered it extremely vulnerable but to counter this inherent weakness it was armed to the teeth and so was defensively potent. If not the perfect lady that her lines had suggested to me that day at Tempelhof in 1937, the Condor was a thoroughly competent aeroplane, and the fact that a relatively small number of Condors created such havoc is surely a tribute to the efficiency of the adaptation of this airliner for the long-range maritime reconnaissance-bomber rôle.

An Fw 200C-3/U1 Condor seen from a fellow aircraft and presenting a view that became familiar to the fighters of the Royal Navy's escort carriers. The Condor was perhaps one of the most remarkable adaptations of a commercial aircraft for a military rôle.

HEINKEL HE 162

Easing myself into the cockpit of the tiny Heinkel He 162 for the first time on that September morning 27 years ago, I recalled the first words that I had ever read concerning this so-called *Volksjäger*, or "People's Fighter": "A tool of desperation!" That was how the British wartime intelligence report had described this oversize example of the modeller's art, and, indeed, its history seemed to have merited such a description.

The story of the *Volksjäger* had really begun with realisation on the part of the *Oberkommando* that Germany could no longer maintain an offensive posture; that the deterioration of the war situation as hostilities entered their fifth year was accelerating and that all effort should be devoted to defence. Only the *Führer* himself would seem to have been oblivious of this *moment critique* in the fortunes of his Third Reich. Hermann Göring had lost his grip on the *Reichsluftfahrt-ministerium* (RLM) and the real power had passed to the highly efficient Minister of Armaments, Albert Speer, although the *Reichsmarschall* still fronted the aviation administration. Even Hitler's blind eye to the desperate situation would appear to have been prized open, however, by the awesome destruction wreaked by the Allied bombing of late February 1944, and he had apparently raised no objection when one of Speer's inner circle men, Party Leader Otto Saur, had formed the *Jägerstab*, or Fighter Staff, to concentrate the remnants of the German aircraft industry on manufacture of fighters. In the chaos into which Germany was descending, however, the mass production of sophisticated jet aircraft such as the Me

262 on which the RLM now pinned its faith was becoming an increasingly difficult task.

The summer months of 1944 had seen the Bf 109 and the Fw 190 at a loss to counter effectively the ever-escalating low flying attacks on West German targets by the Allied air forces. Neither the edge in speed possessed by the defending fighters nor warning of the approach of low-flying intruders was sufficient to result in successful interception, and inadequate numbers precluded standing fighter patrols. Thus, the stage was set for serious consideration to be given to the most unorthodox proposal for combating the situation, and one of the most remarkable results was the *Volksjäger*; a simple

A surprisingly large number of examples of the minuscule He 162A-2 was acquired by the Allies, the example below having been photographed in Germany before transportation to the UK and that seen at the head of the page being the one in which Flt Lt R A Marks lost his life at Farnborough on 9 November 1945

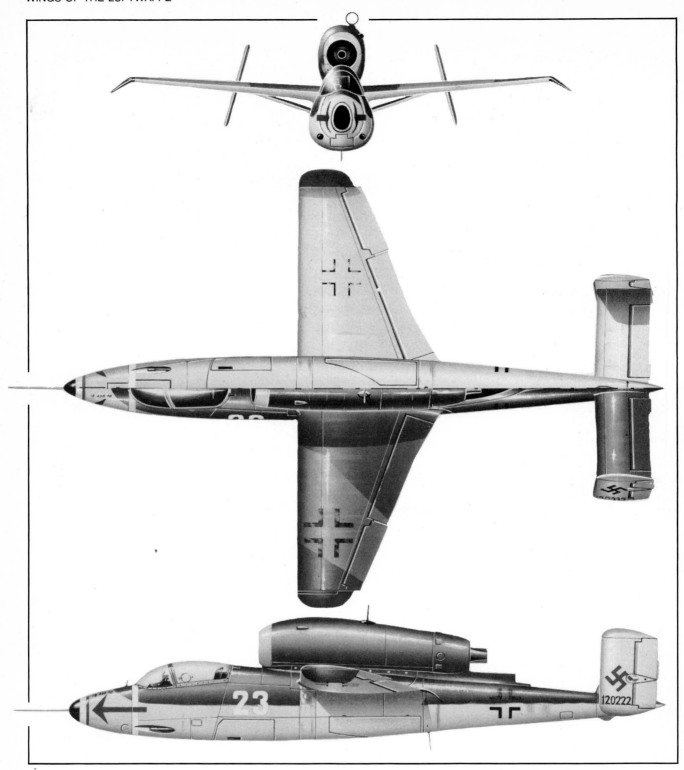

single-engined jet fighter capable of being mass produced even in the shambles to which German industry had degenerated. It was even to be proposed that boys from the Hitler Youth should receive rudimentary flying training on gliders and then be pitched headlong into the defence of Germany in this *Volksjäger*!

The scheme had, of course, its opponents, including no lesser personages than Adolf Galland, the then *General der Jagdflieger*, and eminent designers Willy Messerschmitt and Kurt Tank, but it had been forced through, and the basic

project requirement issued by the *Technischen Amt* of the RLM on 8 September 1944 had called for the following:
(a) Maximum speed at low and medium altitudes with a minimum speed of 750 km/h (466 mph) at sea level.
(b) Unassisted take-off within less than 600 m (1,970 ft).
(c) Minimum production build-up to obtain large-scale production in the shortest possible time.
(d) Extensive employment of wood for the structure.
(e) Production of the type not to interfere in any way with the manufacture of the Me 262 and Ar 234.

(f) Exploitation of dormant production capacity made available by cancellation of other production programmes.

(g) Only one turbojet to be employed.

(h) Armament to comprise two 20-mm MG 151 cannon interchangeable with two 30-mm MK 108 cannon.

(i) Radio equipment to comprise FuG 24 R/T and FuG 25a IFF.

(j) Protective armour against only frontal attack.

Twelve days after the issue of this requirement the Heinkel mock-up had been ready, and on 24 September construction of prototypes began, work on detailed drawings proceeding in parallel. The Heinkel contender in the contest had won the day partly as a result of a personal decision on the part of Otto Saur and partly because it incorporated basically simple constructional features unlikely to run into development troubles. Time was of the essence, and it was obvious that no potential problem area would be welcomed. The first prototype was flown for the first time at Schwechat on 6 December 1944 with a company test pilot, *Flugkapitän* Peter at the controls — a mere 90 days had elapsed between conception and initial flight test!

Peter was killed four days later while demonstrating the prototype in front of a large gathering of RLM, *Luftwaffe* and Party officials, and some time later I was able to see a film of this accident. The aircraft was making a low pass over the airfield when the leading edge of the starboard wing appeared to split and the upper skinning began to roll back like a carpet. The starboard aileron then broke away and the aircraft rolled out of control to crash just outside the airfield boundary. The accident was attributed to the failure of a new type wood adhesive. Initial flight testing had revealed insufficient stability around the vertical and horizontal axes, faults that had been corrected by modifications to the tail assembly, the introduction of a ballast weight in the nose, and the lowering of the wing trailing edge. Perhaps the major shortcoming was a tendency towards excessive side-slip, this resulting in the drooping of the wingtips to add another unique feature to the appearance of the little Heinkel fighter. A tendency to go into a spin at acute flying attitudes was relieved by the addition of a small strake in the V of the tail unit.

An "exciting-looking" aeroplane

The story of the abortive subsequent development and production of the Heinkel He 162, as the *Volksjäger* had been officially designated, is now well known, and in the spring of 1945, at around the time that the He 162s that had been issued to *Jagdgeschwader* 1 were standing around awaiting fuel to enable their pilots to complete their familiarisation flying or were being destroyed to prevent them falling into Allied hands, I was preparing myself to go to Germany with a team of scientists and technicians to pick up captured aircraft and

Heinkel He 162A-2 Cockpit Instrumentation Key

1	Rudder trim control	7	Throttle lever	
2	Take-off rocket jettison	8	Undercarriage operating lever	
3	Undercarriage selector	9	Port undercarriage indicator	
4	Elevator trim control	10	Ventilation/clear vision disc	
5	Take-off rocket activation switch	11	Flap manual control pump	
6	Fuel cock	12	Flap indicator	

13 Turn-and-bank indicator
14 Pitot indicator
15 Airspeed indicator
16 Firing button (A-Knopf)
17 Gun-charging button (B-Knopf)
18 Altimeter
19 One-piece windshield
20 Canopy release
21 Canopy lock
22 Revi gunsight
23 Port cannon indicator
24 Starboard cannon indicator
25 Rate of climb/descent
26 Compass
27 Oil pressure gauge
28 Jet pipe temperature
29 Fuel pressure gauge
30 Fuel contents
31 Revolution counter
32 Oxygen valve
33 Oxygen contents
34 Rudder pedals
35 Rudder pedal adjustment screws
36 Nosewheel well window (visual check)
37 FuG 24 transmit button (front of column)
38 Control column
39 Cannon blast tubes
40 Cannon forward mounts
41 Foot stirrups
41 Seat handles
43 Seat ejection trigger
44 Ejection seat
45 Canvas recoil-spring cuffs
46 Oxygen supply
47 Flare pistol holder/chute
48 FuG 25a control box
49 Starboard undercarriage indicator
50 FuG 24 (R/T) and AFN 2 (radio-navigation) control box
51 Starter switch
52 Engine setting
53 R/T socket
54 Electrics switch panel, reading from front:
Battery
Fuel pump
Weapons and gunsight
Pitot heating
Ignition
Turn-and-bank/Rocket take-off
FuG 24
FuG 25a
Starter

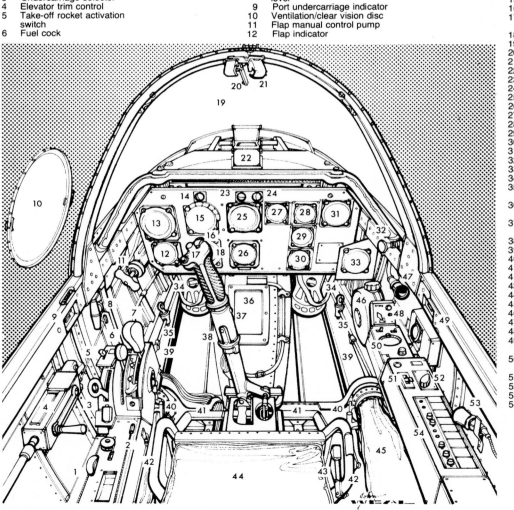

The He 162A-2 (Werk-Nr 120 222) illustrated below left, above, and by the general arrangement drawing on page 20 , was obtained at Leck and was one of three taken to the USA for test and evaluation. This aircraft, seen above after removal of the individual number "23" from the nose, was flown at Freeman Field, Seymour, Indiana, as T2-504, later being taken to Wright Field and, in 1947, presented to the Smithsonian Museum. The other He 162A-2 taken to Freeman Field (Werk-Nr 120 077) was transferred to Edwards AFB where it was flown in 1946 as T2-489 and is now displayed by the Ontario Air Museum, California. The third He 162A-2 (Werk-Nr 120 017) was taken to Wright Field for structural analysis.

get them to the UK for examination and testing. My qualifications for this job were twofold: I was German speaking and a test pilot in the Aerodynamics Flight at the RAE at Farnborough. Our plan was to check the aircraft briefly on site where found, ascertain if they were flyable, and, if so, fly them to Schleswig for a more detailed inspection before ferrying them to Farnborough. This *modus operandi* was hardly practicable with the He 162, however, owing to its strictly limited endurance of 20 minutes at sea level, although this was reportedly extended to 57 minutes up around 36,000 ft (10 970 m).

The problem resolved itself when we acquired one or two of the multi-wheeled Ar 232B transports and discovered that the He 162 could be fitted into its capacious fuselage with the minimum of dismantling.

The first He 162 that I encountered was a standard production A-series model, and I was staggered by its tiny dimensions. I was also astonished by the amount of wood that had been used in its construction, and the notes that I made at the time read: "An exciting-looking aeroplane, though not exactly beautiful. There is so much wood around that it looks as though it has been built by a modelling enthusiast. Its narrow-track undercarriage is likely to make it a handful in a crosswind. An oversize V1 on wheels!" We came across quite

a few He 162s in good condition, and selected the best for onward passage to Farnborough, but there was one major problem. The Germans had been very conscientious about destroying all documentation, and this was particularly so in the case of the airframe and engine records of virtually all the aircraft that we captured in Germany. This was not so true of pilot's notes as many *Luftwaffe* pilots had retained copies out of sentiment, but in the case of the He 162 I drew a complete blank.

The problem of "getting to know the taps" was obviously not to be simple of solution. This was equally obviously not the time to apply the RAF jet jockey's dictum of "Kick the tyres, light the fires and last man off is a sissy!" I had spent some time rooting out and interrogating well-known German aircraft designers and test pilots, but the only pilot who appeared to have actually flown the He 162 was a chap named Lohoffener who had been seconded to Heinkel from the *Luftwaffe* as a production test pilot. During interrogation Lohoffener impressed me neither with the reliability of the information that he imparted nor his experience as a pilot, but in so far as I was concerned it was a matter of Hobson's choice, and, therefore, at 10.25 hours on the morning of 7 September 1945, armed with the notes that I had made during the interrogation, I clambered into the cockpit of He 162A-2 *Werk-Nr* 120 098.

By this time, I had flown the Ar 234 and the Me 262, so I had at least some idea of German jet aircraft cockpit practice, and this was of some importance as many switches and levers, as well as certain instruments, were of standardised pattern. There was also the system colour code of yellow: fuel, brown: hydraulics, blue: oxygen, and red: emergency, and combined with that distinctive smell common to all German cockpits, this ensured that I did not feel entirely unfamiliar with the "front office" of this little fighter, which, incidentally, offered an additional home comfort lacking in the Ar 234 or Me 262, namely an ejector seat. The *Volksjäger* was deemed expendable in the crumbling Third Reich, but pilots were decidedly in short supply.

Starting involved the usual German jet system of winding up the turbine of the main engine through a petrol donkey engine while pressing a button on the closed throttle to engage fuel injection and ignition. The throttle was then moved to the idling position as the revs approached 3,000 at which point the fuel cock was opened. The donkey engine was then disengaged and the ignition button released. The BMW 003 engine was fitted with a jet orifice control which had four

(Above) An He 162A-2 that had apparently suffered the attentions of strafing Allied fighters, although the shattered windscreen and canopy suggest that a charge had already been exploded in the cockpit, presumably to prevent the aircraft falling intact into the hands of the approaching Allied forces

positions: A-H-S-F. Position A was selected for running up, and it was vital to have the ground crew check the nozzle position at this stage to ensure that it was functioning correctly. The nozzle was left in this position for taxying which proved quite easy as the brakes were very efficient. The efficiency of the brakes was important since they had to be applied a lot during taxying, the rudders being completely ineffective at such low speeds.

Caution had to be exercised in handling the throttle in order to avoid overheating, although the BMW 003 was better in this respect than the Jumo 004. View from the cockpit was perfect, although the non-adjustable seat was too low if a British-type seat parachute was used. At the runway threshold

(Above right) An He 162A-2 and personnel of the Stabstaffel of JG 1 at Leck/Holstein in the spring of 1945, and (below) an He 162A assembly line discovered by the Allies in the former salt mine at Tarthun, near Magdeburg

Heinkel He 162A-2 Specification

Power plant: One BMW 003E-1 or -2 axial-flow turbojet with 30 sec maximum rating of 2,028 lb (920 kg) thrust, normal maximum rating of 1,764 lb (800 kg) thrust, and output of 732 lb (332 kg) thrust at 497 mph (800 km/h) at 36,090 ft (11 000 m).
Armament: Two 20-mm Mauser MG 151 cannon with 120 rpg.
Performance: Maximum speed (30 sec thrust rating), 553 mph (890 km/h) at sea level, 562 mph (905 km/h) at 19,690 ft (6 000 m), 525 mph (845 km/h) at 36,090 ft (11 000 m), (at normal max thrust), 491 mph (790 km/h) at sea level, 521 mph (838 km/h) at 19,690 ft (6 000 m), 475 mph (765 km/h) at 36,090 ft (11 000 m); flight endurance (at full throttle), 30 min at sea level, 48 min at 19,690 ft (6 000 m), 83 min at 36,090 ft (11 000 m); range at full throttle, 242 mls (390 km) at sea level, 385 mls (620 km) at 19,690 ft (6 000 m), 83 min at 36,090 ft (11 000 m); climb rate at average weight, 3,780 ft/min (19,2 m/sec) at sea level, 1,950 ft/min (9,9 m/sec) at 19,690 ft (6 000 m), 315 ft/min (1,6 m/sec) at 36,090 ft (11 000 m); take-off distance, 930 yds (850 m); take-off distance to clear 50 ft (15 m), 1,072 yds (980 m); landing distance from 50 ft (15 m), 1,040 yds (950 m).
Weights: Empty, 3,666 lb (1 663 kg); empty equipped, 3,876 lb (1 758 kg); taxying, 6,409 lb (2 907 kg); take-off, 6,184 lb (2 805 kg).
Dimensions: Span, 23 ft 7½ in (7,20 m); length, 29 ft 8⅓ in (9,05 m); height, 8 ft 6⅓ in (2,60 m); wing area, 120·56 sq ft (11,16 m²).

I applied about 20 deg of flap by pumping them down until they could just be seen from the cockpit, no flap position indicator being provided. I then set the elevator trim and moved the jet nozzle control to the S (start) position. The fuel indicator showed 450 litres (99 Imp gal). Moving on to the runway, I lined the aircraft up and opened the throttle slowly to 9,500 revs, meanwhile holding the aircraft on the brakes and checking that the temperature gauge did not exceed the maximum 600°C, although a momentary 700°C was permissible on moving the throttle or on start-up. The throttle movement from closed to full revs occupied 15 seconds if the temperature limit was observed.

The take-off was much longer than I had expected, and any attempt to pull the aircraft off prematurely under 118 mph (190 km/h) resulted in a tendency to wing dropping. Ideally the nosewheel was lifted off at about 105 mph (170 km/h)

and the aircraft allowed to fly itself off. So much for the take-off distance specified by the original requirement! Once airborne, the undercarriage was raised by pushing down the retraction lever, a handle being twisted simultaneously to raise the flaps by spring action. The total trim change proved to be only slightly nose down. With the aircraft cleaned up, I eased the throttle back to the recommended 9,200 rpm and stabilised the climbing speed at 215 mph (346 km/h). The He 162 proved very stable in the climb, and reached 5,000 ft (1 524 m) in 1½ minutes, at which I levelled out and gently brought the throttle back to 8,900 rpm which gave a cruise of 300 mph (483 km/h) with an engine temperature of 450°C.

The instrument panel was provided with a burner pressure gauge which indicated that the desirable limits were between 45 and 60. What precisely one was supposed to do outside these limits was not clear, but in my mind the upper limit was associated with use of the ejection seat. If the Germans had wanted to save more weight, this instrument would have provided a good starting point.

Stability checks showed the He 162 positive about the longitudinal and directional axes but neutral laterally. Harmony of control was excellent with the rudder perhaps just a shade too light. It was soon evident that the Germans had got the original stability problems licked, but I wondered if they had cured the sideslip trouble. Application of rudder caused large amounts of slip and skid, and considerable dipping of the nose, and no more than three-quarter rudder

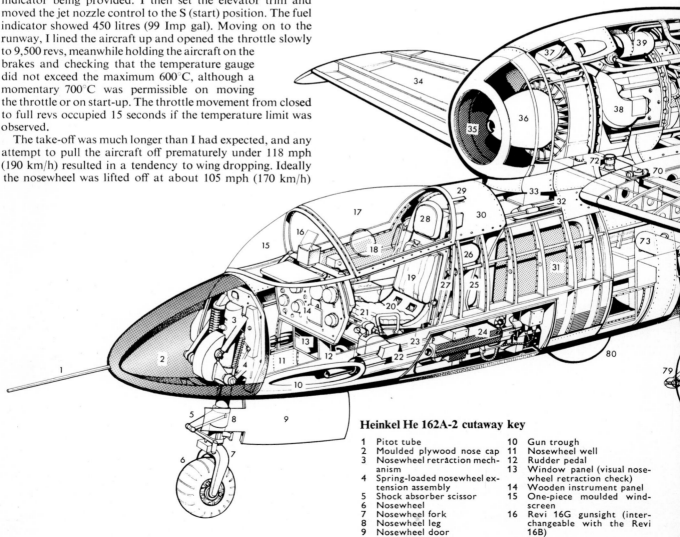

Heinkel He 162A-2 cutaway key

1 Pitot tube
2 Moulded plywood nose cap
3 Nosewheel retraction mechanism
4 Spring-loaded nosewheel extension assembly
5 Shock absorber scissor
6 Nosewheel
7 Nosewheel fork
8 Nosewheel leg
9 Nosewheel door
10 Gun trough
11 Nosewheel well
12 Rudder pedal
13 Window panel (visual nosewheel retraction check)
14 Wooden instrument panel
15 One-piece moulded windscreen
16 Revi 16G gunsight (interchangeable with the Revi 16B)

could be applied if a steady flat turn was desired; beyond this the rudders began to judder and buffet, and looking aft I could see vortices streaming back from the tops of the fins, the turn becoming jerky. The danger signals were loud and clear. On the credit side, however, the aircraft had excellent directional snaking characteristics, making it a good gun platform. From this aspect it was the best jet fighter of its time, and I was certainly in a position to judge, having flown every jet aircraft then in existence.

I then began a climb to 30,000 ft (9 144 m), and this necessitated a change of nozzle control position to H as I passed 26,000 ft (7 925 m). On the climb the fuel gauge began to drop, indicating that the two ungauged wing tanks had completely drained their contents into the main tank. Handling at 30,000 ft (9 144 m) still displayed very good stability and control characteristics, apart from that very

One of several examples of the He 162A-2 that were evaluated at various test centres in the Soviet Union

touchy rudder which had to be used sparingly. I put the nose down to commence a powered dive, at the same time moving the nozzle control to position S. There was no buffeting or vibration, and a check on the rate of roll at 400 mph (644 km/h) revealed the highest that I had ever experienced outside the realm of hydraulically-powered ailerons, and the stick

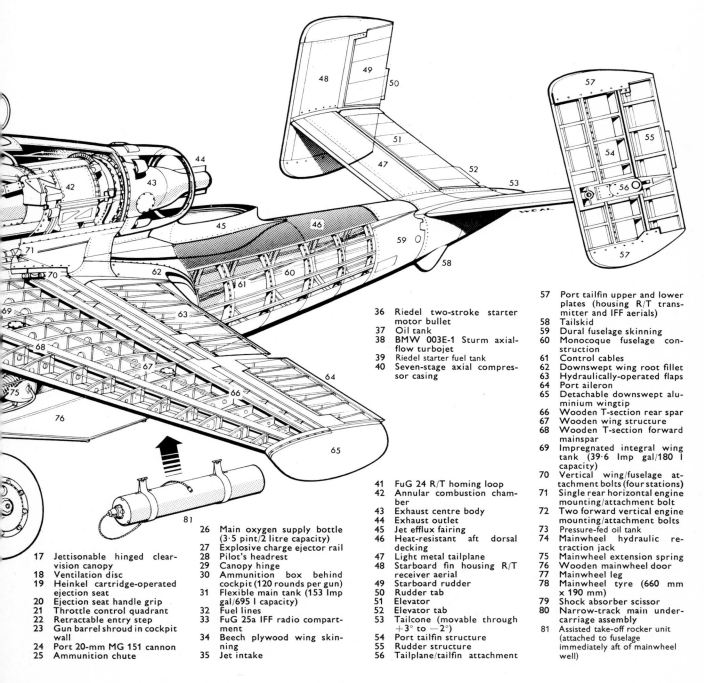

36 Riedel two-stroke starter motor bullet
37 Oil tank
38 BMW 003E-1 Sturm axial-flow turbojet
39 Riedel starter fuel tank
40 Seven-stage axial compressor casing

41 FuG 24 R/T homing loop
42 Annular combustion chamber
43 Exhaust centre body
44 Exhaust outlet
45 Jet efflux fairing
46 Heat-resistant aft dorsal decking
47 Light metal tailplane
48 Starboard fin housing R/T receiver aerial
49 Starboard rudder
50 Rudder tab
51 Elevator
52 Elevator tab
53 Tailcone (movable through +3° to −2°)
54 Port tailfin structure
55 Rudder structure
56 Tailplane/tailfin attachment

57 Port tailfin upper and lower plates (housing R/T transmitter and IFF aerials)
58 Tailskid
59 Dural fuselage skinning
60 Monocoque fuselage construction
61 Control cables
62 Downswept wing root fillet
63 Hydraulically-operated flaps
64 Port aileron
65 Detachable downswept aluminium wingtip
66 Wooden T-section rear spar
67 Wooden wing structure
68 Wooden T-section forward mainspar
69 Impregnated integral wing tank (39·6 Imp gal/180 l capacity)
70 Vertical wing/fuselage attachment bolts (four stations)
71 Single rear horizontal engine mounting/attachment bolt
72 Two forward vertical engine mounting/attachment bolts
73 Pressure-fed oil tank
74 Mainwheel hydraulic retraction jack
75 Mainwheel extension spring
76 Wooden mainwheel door
77 Mainwheel leg
78 Mainwheel tyre (660 mm x 190 mm)
79 Shock absorber scissor
80 Narrow-track main undercarriage assembly
81 Assisted take-off rocker unit (attached to fuselage immediately aft of mainwheel well)

17 Jettisonable hinged clear-vision canopy
18 Ventilation disc
19 Heinkel cartridge-operated ejection seat
20 Ejection seat handle grip
21 Throttle control quadrant
22 Retractable entry step
23 Gun barrel shroud in cockpit wall
24 Port 20-mm MG 151 cannon
25 Ammunition chute
26 Main oxygen supply bottle (3·5 pint/2 litre capacity)
27 Explosive charge ejector rail
28 Pilot's headrest
29 Canopy hinge
30 Ammunition box behind cockpit (120 rounds per gun)
31 Flexible main tank (153 Imp gal/695 l capacity)
32 Fuel lines
33 FuG 25a IFF radio compartment
34 Beech plywood wing skinning
35 Jet intake

force demanded to produce these exhilarating gyrations was delightfully light.

Levelling off at 12,000 ft (3 658 m), once again changing the nozzle position (this time to F) for high speed flight below 13,123 ft (4 000 m), I settled down to another spell of the pleasures of the phenomenal roll rate of this delightful little aeroplane, but I was careful not to impose negative *g* for more than three seconds. The thought of extinguishing the jet burner and trying the He 162 as a glider was not really to my fancy. When level speed had built up to 350 mph (563 km/h) I pulled the He 162 into a loop. It skimmed round but I had the inescapable feeling that I was playing pretty close to the minimum speed for this particular manœuvre. Finally, I tried a few stalls to get the feel of things before landing. As the stall was approached a gentle lateral lurching and some mild elevator buffet set in, being followed by a mild porpoising motion before the nose pitched down indicating stall had been reached. And so back to base.

The landing proved difficult for technical rather than aerodynamic reasons. In the first place it took a full minute to pump down the flaps, although the undercarriage came down quickly under the action of springs when a red toggle was pulled to release the up locks. In the second place, the throttle had to be shut beyond the cruising gate into the idling gate (3,000 rpm) as soon as it was certain that the runway would not be undershot, thus cutting the thrust. The approach speed had to be held at 125 mph (200 km/h) almost up to the runway threshold as there was no question of going round again once the throttle had been moved to idling, and there was therefore an inevitable tendency to arrive with excessive speed. This called for good braking, and no German aircraft that I had ever flown had brakes that came up to British standards. By *German* standards, however, the He 162's brakes were good, and I had already been favourably impressed by them during taxying, but now they proved too weak for the speed involved, and I burned up a lot of runway.

Touchdown speed was at 105 mph (170 km/h), and after two or three more flights in the He 162 I got used to judging the correct spot for closing the throttle to idling, and this expertise, coupled with the powerful elevator keeping the nosewheel off the ground down to a very low speed, greatly reduced the landing run. Stopping the engine was merely a matter of closing the throttle completely, closing the fuel cock, and switching off the fuel pump. All very simple, but there *was* a catch for the unwary. The fuel cock and the undercarriage retraction lever nestled side by side, and

requiring a downward motion to close the fuel cock *and* to retract the undercarriage was just asking for trouble!

The He 162 had no emergency systems for flaps or undercarriage, but it *was* one of the first German production aircraft to be fitted with an ejection seat. The drill for the use of this seat was simple. Firstly the canopy was jettisoned by means of pulling a cord attached to it, then the pilot placed his heels in special rests on the bottom of the seat, gripped the left handle on the seat with his left hand, and then, with his right hand, released the safety catch and squeezed the firing trigger.

My first impressions of the *Volksjäger* were not to change much, although I was to fly the little aeroplane quite frequently. It was like all the German jets — a superb aeroplane in its element but quite a handful to take-off and land. I had never met better flying controls yet they could be so easily mishandled, and such mishandling led to the disaster at Farnborough on 9 November 1945 when Flt Lt R A Marks flying an He 162 (*Werk-Nr* 120 072) lost his life. He had not had much experience with the *Volksjäger*, and as he intended to simulate my display routine I had already warned him to exercise care in the use of the rudder to assist rolling. However, his enthusiasm apparently overcame his discretion for he started a low-level roll and almost immediately one fin-and-rudder assembly collapsed. The tail unit then broke away and the aircraft tumbled vertically head-over-heels out of the sky, giving him no chance to operate the ejection seat. An unforgiving aeroplane!

In view of the fact that the He 162 never saw combat, we are left with the intriguing if purely academic question of how it would have made out if it had been used in anger. It would certainly have been an effective gun platform, and its small dimensions would have rendered it difficult to hit. Even if somewhat underpowered, it had a good performance — it could certainly have run rings around the contemporary Meteor — but it was no aeroplane to let embryo pilots loose on, and it would have demanded more than simply a *good* pilot to operate it out of a small airfield. Nevertheless, as a back-up for the formidable Me 262 it could conceivably have helped the *Luftwaffe* to regain air superiority over Germany had it appeared on the scene sooner. Personally, I shall always recall the He 162 with affection as it gave me some exhilarating hours in the air, and I cannot help but feel that the Allies were fortunate for, had another month or two and the necessary fuel been available, the He 162 might well have got in among our bombers in numbers at a time when desperate measures might just have achieved sensational results.

This He 162A-2 (Werk-Nr 120 072), built at Marienehe and presumably acquired at Leck from the inventory of Jagdgeschwader 1, *was the example of this remarkable little warplane that was being flown on 9 November 1945 at Farnborough, Hants, by Flt Lt R A Marks when, as the result of a structural failure in the tail during a low-level roll, the machine crashed, the pilot losing his life.*

JUNKERS JU 87D

STUKA! What other acronym that saw common usage in Europe during the first eighteen or so months of World War II could evoke such terror in the minds of so many? To those countless European refugees jamming the roads in frantic endeavour to escape the advancing *Wehrmacht*, Stuka was synonymous with death and destruction wrought from the sky with terrifying precision; in military circles it was the generally-accepted sobriquet of a warplane that had greater réclame than any other — the controversial Junkers Ju 87 dive bomber.

When first committed to combat, the Stuka — a derivation of *Sturzkampfflugzeug* which was a term descriptive of *all* dive bombers — was believed by its advocates, not least among whom was Ernst Udet, to be the supreme weapon; the legendary reputation that it acquired during the Polish and French campaigns lent credence to claims for its invincibility so assiduously propagated. But the Stuka was not solely a highly effective precision bombing instrument which, if not capable of "putting a bomb in a pickle barrel", was at least able to hit its target in a diving attack with an accuracy of less than 30 yards; it was a mass demoraliser, hurtling vertically earthwards with a banshee-like wail that had a devastating psychological effect.

From its inception, the *Luftwaffe* had displayed a marked predilection for the Stuka. The service was first and foremost a tool for the direct support of the ground forces and the Stuka was seen as a successor to long-range artillery. Unfortunately for the *Luftwaffe*, use of the Stuka presupposed control of the air; a desirable situation that was to be enjoyed increasingly rarely as the conflict progressed. Once control of the air could

no longer be guaranteed, the Stuka, in the form of the Ju 87, had become an anachronism. Sturdy and tractable a warplane though this angularly ugly creation of the Junkers Flugzeug- und Motorenwerke undoubtedly was, it was also the natural prey of the fighter, and the sight of the Ju 87's evil-looking shape sitting squarely in his gunsight was the dream of every fighter pilot. The career of the Ju 87 had reached its zenith over France, had entered its eclipse over the British Isles and had seen its nadir over the Soviet Union.

This was all in the past, however, by the time I finally found an opportunity to realise my ambition to fly this once much-vaunted warplane. I had gained considerable experience of dive bombing techniques with the Blackburn Skua, the Vultee Vengeance and the Douglas Dauntless, and while none of these had been a hot rod in so far as level flight performance was concerned, I was convinced that all three were a cut above the Ju 87 which, in view of its reputation, must therefore have something of which I was unaware up its sleeve.

The opportunity arose on 23 August 1945 at Husum, in Schleswig Holstein, not far from the Danish border. Some of the more obsolescent ex-*Luftwaffe* hardware had wound up at this airfield and included in this miscellany was a solitary Ju 87D-3, presumably flown in by some pilot as the Third Reich finally crumbled. A cursory inspection of this rugged-looking juggernaut revealed the fact that all gun armament had been removed — possibly for use with ground defensive positions during the last days of fighting — and that, in general, it was in pretty good shape. There was certainly no evidence to suggest that it had ever been flown operationally, and despite the anachronistic appearance of the aircraft, I formed the opinion that it could not have come off the "Weser" Flugzeugbau assembly line much earlier than the previous summer.

The Ju 87D was obviously a machine of great solidity, with its heavy cranked wings, sturdily-braced tailplane and massive fixed undercarriage. From its broad-bladed Junkers VS 11 constant-speed airscrew to the trim tabs on its big, square-cut rudder, the Junkers dive bomber gave an impression of immensity and certainly a lot of aeroplane for one engine to pull — in this case a liquid-cooled 12-cylinder Junkers Jumo 211J-1 which gave 1,420 hp at 2,600 rpm and 1,190 hp at 2,400 rpm. The cowling embodied quite an amount of armour plate to protect engine and cooler, and I was to discover liberal quantities of additional armour distributed beneath and around the two cockpits whose occupants would have had little else going for them if they had encountered a determined fighter.

Relatively few of the WW II German aircraft could be considered beautiful in the accepted sense, but the Ju 87D was undeniably *ugly* in the true sense, and it was hard to believe that

Junkers Ju 87D-3 cutaway drawing key

1 Spinner
2 Pitch-change mechanism housing
3 Blade hub
4 Junkers VS 11 constant-speed airscrew

5 Anti-vibration engine mounting attachments
6 Oil filler point and marker
7 Auxiliary oil tank (5·9 Imp gal/26,8 l capacity)
8 Junkers Jumo 211J-1 12-cylinder inverted-vee liquid cooled engine
9 Magnesium alloy forged engine mount
10 Coolant (Glysantin-water) header tank
11 Ejector exhaust stubs
12 Fuel injection unit housing
13 Induction air cooler
14 Armoured radiator
15 Inertia starter cranking point
16 Ball joint bulkhead fixing (lower)
17 Tubular steel mount support strut
18 Ventral armour (8 mm)
19 Main oil tank (9.9 Imp gal/45 l capacity)
20 Oil filling point

21 Transverse support frame
22 Rudder pedals
23 Control column
24 Heating point
25 Auxiliary air intake
26 Ball joint bulkhead fixing (upper)
27 Bulkhead
28 Oil tank (6·8 Imp gal/31 l capacity)
29 Oil filler point and marker (Intava 100)
30 Fuel filler cap
31 Self-sealing starboard outer fuel tank (33 Imp gal/150 l capacity)
32 Underwing bombs with *Dienartstab* percussion rods
33 Pitot head
34 Spherical oxygen bottles
35 Wing skinning
36 Starboard navigation light
37 Aileron mass balance
38 "Double wing" aileron and flap (starboard outer)
39 Aileron hinge
40 Corrugated wing rib station
41 Reinforced armoured windscreen
42 Reflector sight
43 Padded crash bar
44 Signal flare tube
45 Braced fuselage mainframe

46 Front spar/fuselage attachment point
47 Pilot's seat (reinforced with 4-mm side and 8-mm rear armour)
48 Inter-cockpit bulkhead
49 Sliding canopy handgrip
50 External side armour
51 Pilot's back armour (8 mm)
52 Headrest
53 Aft-sliding cockpit canopy (shown part open)
54 Radio mast cut-out
55 Anti-crash hoop (magnesium casting)
56 Radio mast
57 Radio equipment (FuGe 16) compartment
58 Additional (internal) side armour
59 Canopy track
60 Handhold/footrests
61 Braced fuselage mainframe
62 Rear spar/fuselage attachment point

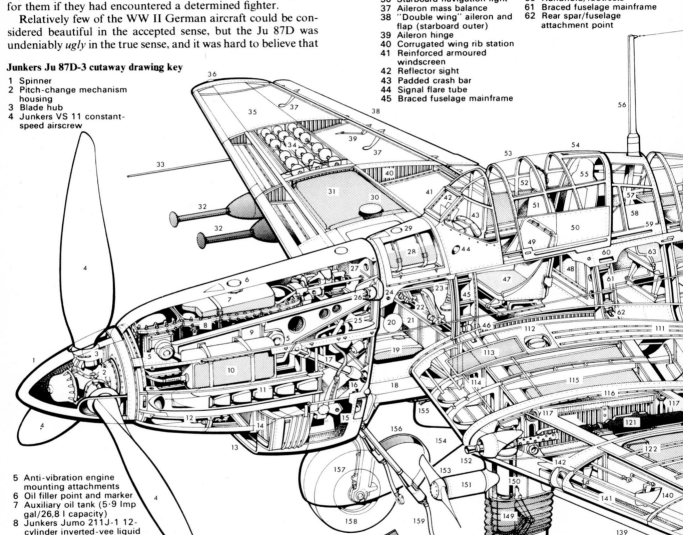

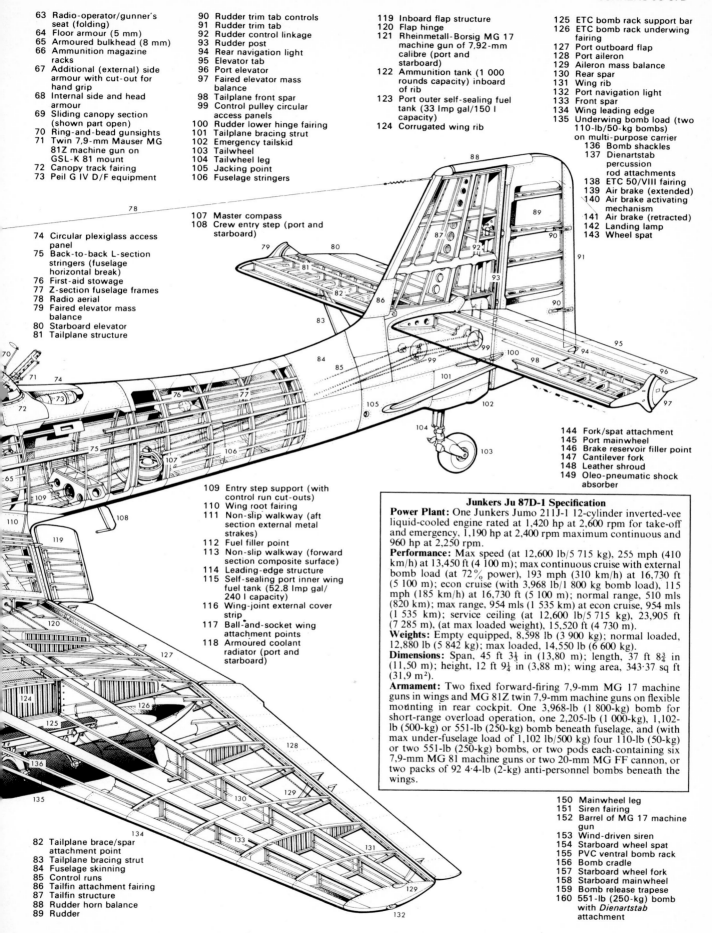

63 Radio-operator/gunner's seat (folding)
64 Floor armour (5 mm)
65 Armoured bulkhead (8 mm)
66 Ammunition magazine racks
67 Additional (external) side armour with cut-out for hand grip
68 Internal side and head armour
69 Sliding canopy section (shown part open)
70 Ring-and-bead gunsights
71 Twin 7,9-mm Mauser MG 81Z machine gun on GSL-K 81 mount
72 Canopy track fairing
73 Peil G IV D/F equipment

74 Circular plexiglass access panel
75 Back-to-back L-section stringers (fuselage horizontal break)
76 First-aid stowage
77 Z-section fuselage frames
78 Radio aerial
79 Faired elevator mass balance
80 Starboard elevator
81 Tailplane structure

90 Rudder trim tab controls
91 Rudder trim tab
92 Rudder control linkage
93 Rudder post
94 Rear navigation light
95 Elevator tab
96 Port elevator
97 Faired elevator mass balance
98 Tailplane front spar
99 Control pulley circular access panels
100 Rudder lower hinge fairing
101 Tailplane bracing strut
102 Emergency tailskid
103 Tailwheel
104 Tailwheel leg
105 Jacking point
106 Fuselage stringers

107 Master compass
108 Crew entry step (port and starboard)

109 Entry step support (with control run cut-outs)
110 Wing root fairing
111 Non-slip walkway (aft section external metal strakes)
112 Fuel filler point
113 Non-slip walkway (forward section composite surface)
114 Leading-edge structure
115 Self-sealing port inner wing fuel tank (52.8 Imp gal/240 l capacity)
116 Wing-joint external cover strip
117 Ball-and-socket wing attachment points
118 Armoured coolant radiator (port and starboard)

119 Inboard flap structure
120 Flap hinge
121 Rheinmetall-Borsig MG 17 machine gun of 7,92-mm calibre (port and starboard)
122 Ammunition tank (1 000 rounds capacity) inboard of rib
123 Port outer self-sealing fuel tank (33 Imp gal/150 l capacity)
124 Corrugated wing rib

125 ETC bomb rack support bar
126 ETC bomb rack underwing fairing
127 Port outboard flap
128 Port aileron
129 Aileron mass balance
130 Rear spar
131 Wing rib
132 Port navigation light
133 Front spar
134 Wing leading edge
135 Underwing bomb load (two 110-lb/50-kg bombs) on multi-purpose carrier
136 Bomb shackles
137 Dienartstab percussion rod attachments
138 ETC 50/VIII fairing
139 Air brake (extended)
140 Air brake activating mechanism
141 Air brake (retracted)
142 Landing lamp
143 Wheel spat

144 Fork/spat attachment
145 Port mainwheel
146 Brake reservoir filler point
147 Cantilever fork
148 Leather shroud
149 Oleo-pneumatic shock absorber

Junkers Ju 87D-1 Specification

Power Plant: One Junkers Jumo 211J-1 12-cylinder inverted-vee liquid-cooled engine rated at 1,420 hp at 2,600 rpm for take-off and emergency, 1,190 hp at 2,400 rpm maximum continuous and 960 hp at 2,250 rpm.
Performance: Max speed (at 12,600 lb/5 715 kg), 255 mph (410 km/h) at 13,450 ft (4 100 m); max continuous cruise with external bomb load (at 72% power), 193 mph (310 km/h) at 16,730 ft (5 100 m); econ cruise (with 3,968 lb/1 800 kg bomb load), 115 mph (185 km/h) at 16,730 ft (5 100 m); normal range, 510 mls (820 km); max range, 954 mls (1 535 km) at econ cruise, 954 mls (1 535 km); service ceiling (at 12,600 lb/5 715 kg), 23,905 ft (7 285 m), (at max loaded weight), 15,520 ft (4 730 m).
Weights: Empty equipped, 8,598 lb (3 900 kg); normal loaded, 12,880 lb (5 842 kg); max loaded, 14,550 lb (6 600 kg).
Dimensions: Span, 45 ft 3¼ in (13,80 m); length, 37 ft 8¾ in (11,50 m); height, 12 ft 9¼ in (3,88 m); wing area, 343·37 sq ft (31,9 m²).
Armament: Two fixed forward-firing 7,9-mm MG 17 machine guns in wings and MG 81Z twin 7,9-mm machine guns on flexible mounting in rear cockpit. One 3,968-lb (1 800-kg) bomb for short-range overload operation, one 2,205-lb (1 000-kg), 1,102-lb (500-kg) or 551-lb (250-kg) bomb beneath fuselage, and (with max under-fuselage load of 1,102 lb/500 kg) four 110-lb (50-kg) or two 551-lb (250-kg) bombs, or two pods each containing six 7,9-mm MG 81 machine guns or two 20-mm MG FF cannon, or two packs of 92 4·4-lb (2-kg) anti-personnel bombs beneath the wings.

150 Mainwheel leg
151 Siren fairing
152 Barrel of MG 17 machine gun
153 Wind-driven siren
154 Starboard wheel spat
155 PVC ventral bomb rack
156 Bomb cradle
157 Starboard wheel fork
158 Starboard mainwheel
159 Bomb release trapese
160 551-lb (250-kg) bomb with *Dienartstab* attachment

82 Tailplane brace/spar attachment point
83 Tailplane bracing strut
84 Fuselage skinning
85 Control runs
86 Tailfin attachment fairing
87 Tailfin structure
88 Rudder horn balance
89 Rudder

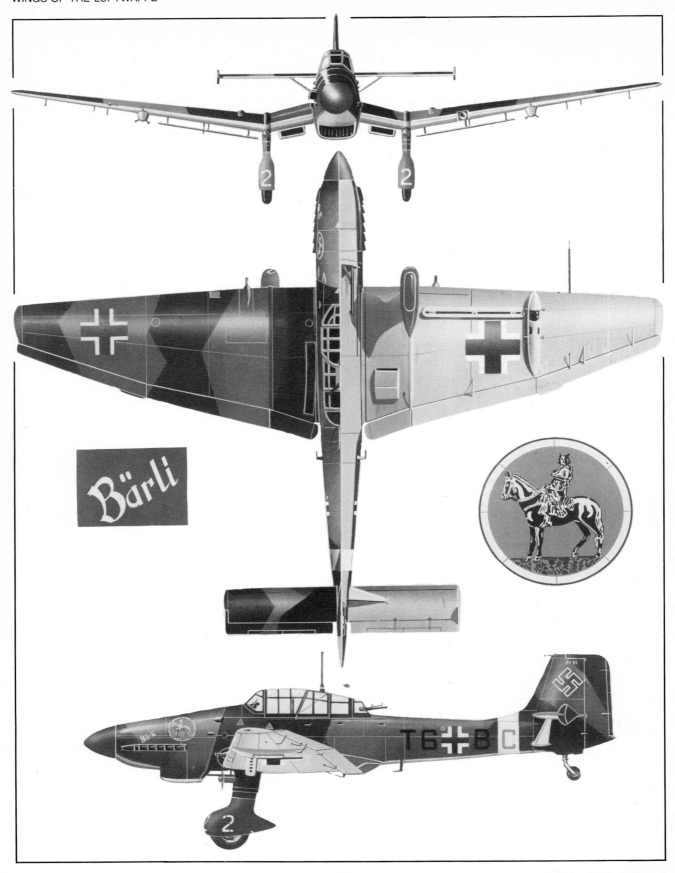

The general arrangement drawing above illustrates a Junkers Ju 87D-3 (Werk-Nr 2491) T6+BC of the Stab II Gruppe Stukageschwader 2 "Immelmann" operating in the Stalingrad area during autumn-winter 1942. The Stab II Gruppe emblem, "Der Bamberger Reiter" (The Horseman of Bamberg), was in black and white on a red disc outlined in white with the horse standing on a representation of grass. The individual aircraft name "Bärli" (the diminutive of "Little Bear") was white, the "C" code letter (indicating Stab II Gruppe) was green and superimposed on white identification band.

this sub-type of the Stuka had represented a serious attempt on the part of the aerodynamicists to *clean up* the basic design. Its predecessor, the Ju 87B, could certainly have been the product of an aerodynamicist's nightmare, with its fixed spatted undercarriage and large radiator bath looking, head on, for all the world like the extended talons and gaping maw of some monstrous bird. The Ju 87D, on the other hand, lacked some of the angularity of the earlier model but was not, in my view, much of an improvement æsthetically, and its design was *incredibly* obsolescent; small wonder that, apart from its service with one *Gruppe* led by the inveterate Hans-Ulrich Rudel which persisted in flying this aged warbird by daylight on the Eastern Front, the Ju 87 had spent much of its declining operational years in the nocturnal assault rôle with the *Nachtschlachtgruppen*.

Big enough and slow enough . . .

I clambered into the pilot's cockpit and settled down to look around, and my first impression of a very big aeroplane for one engine was reaffirmed. Following the Pilot's Notes, I placed the fuel cock in the "both tanks" position, gave a few strokes of primer, switched on the fuel booster pumps, set the throttle to figure "1" on the quadrant, switched on both magnetos and energised the inertia starter and booster coil by pushing a handle on the lower left side for 10 seconds, then pulling out the handle until the engine fired. Warm up could be made up to 1,600 rpm on the brakes but higher revs demanded that the tail be anchored in case the aircraft nosed over. After such anchoring, the engine was run up to 2,200 rpm and 1.3 *atas* of boost, and then throttled back to 1.0 *ata* for magneto checks. After the engine checks the tail anchorage was released and the aircraft was taxied with the tailwheel lock in the free position. I found that the aircraft needed controlled braking to manœuvre and was sensitive to any crosswind.

Before taking-off it was necessary to straighten out and lock the tailwheel, switch the fuel pumps on, set the flaps to take-off position, the trims to zero and the airscrew pitch lever to START. The Ju 87D-3 was fairly lightly loaded and with full

(Above) A Ju 87D-5 (T6+AS) of 8./St.G.2 operating over the Kursk salient in the summer of 1943, and (below) a Ju 87D-1 of 7./St.G.1 being "bombed up" during the summer of 1942 on the Northern Sector of the Russian Front.

(Below) Ju 87D-3s of 4./St.G.77 seen during the return to base after an operation over the Soviet Union during the winter of 1942-43. The D-3 sub-type was intended primarily for use as a schlachtflugzeug and embodied increased armour protection for the engine, radiator and crew

(Above) A Ju 87D-8 of St.G.3 operating in Italy during the summer of 1943, and (immediately below) a Ju 87D-5 in temporary white winter camouflage taking-off for a mission in the Soviet Union during the winter of 1942-43. This aircraft is believed to have belonged to Stuka-geschwader 77

(Below) A Ju 87D-3 of 4./St.G.77, the notice above the propeller spinner indicating that the aircraft had flown its 300th sortie. Beneath the starboard wing may be seen 110-lb (50-kg) bombs with Dienartstab percussion rods

power accelerated surprisingly well, unsticking at about 72 mph (116 km/h) in a distance of some 500 yards (457 m). The climb was made at 2,300 rpm and 1.15 *atas* of boost, the flaps retracting meanwhile until two signal lamps indicated that they had reached the zero position. Climbing speed could then be increased to 133 mph (215 km/h) and was eased off 6 mph (10 km/h) for every 3,280 ft (1 000 m) of altitude gained. At an altitude of 11,480 ft (3 500 m) the supercharger was moved from low gear to the automatic position, but climb throughout was laborious.

Once settled down to the cruise the feeling of vulnerability became almost oppressive, probably accentuated by the high position of the pilot's seat and the good visibility through the large glasshouse canopy. The Ju 87D was big enough and slow enough to present an ideal target to the humblest tyro among fighter pilots and it must even have come high in the popularity stakes with anti-aircraft gunners. Certainly its large ailerons failed to instil any liveliness into evasive manœuvres, and although its elevators were reasonably light the aircraft was just too stable longitudinally to be very manœuverable. It was hardly surprising that once Soviet fighters of respectable performance began to put in an appearance in quantity over the Eastern Front the Ju 87D-equipped *Stukagruppen* were decimated.

There could be no doubt that the Ju 87D needed fighter cover on its way to a target area as surely as a fish needs water, but my consuming interest was to learn how this aircraft, anachronism though it equally undoubtedly was, performed in the area in which it had displayed such astonishing bombing accuracy and precision in its heyday. So I flew out over the North Sea to put in some dive bombing practice on the mud-banks that lie off the coast.

The check list for preparing the Ju 87D to enter the dive was as follows:

Landing flaps at cruise position
Elevator trim at cruise position
Rudder trim at cruise position
Airscrew pitch set at cruise
Contact altimeter switched on
Contact altimeter set to release altitude
Supercharger set at automatic

A Ju 87D-1 of II/St.G.1 (formerly III/St.G.51) over the Soviet Union during the summer of 1942. Two 110-lb (50-kg) bombs can just be seen beneath each wing, a 551-lb (250-kg) bomb with a Dienartstab attachment being carried by the fuselage rack

Throttle pulled right back
Cooler flaps closed
Dive brakes opened

This last action made the aircraft nose over into the dive under the influence of the pull-out mechanism which was actuated by the opening of the dive brakes which also actuated the safety pilot control. The most difficult thing in dive bombing training is avoiding overestimating the dive angle which invariably feels much steeper than it actually is. Every dive bomber of WW II vintage featured some form of synthetic aid to judging dive angle, and in the Ju 87 this consisted simply of a series of lines of inclination marked on the starboard front side screen of the cockpit.

These marks, when aligned with the horizon, gave dive angles of 30 deg to 90 deg. Now a dive angle of 90 deg is a pretty palpitating experience for it always feels as if the aircraft is over

A Ju 87D-3 of the Rumanian Grupul 6 Picaj, the three-squadron dive-bombing component of the Corpul 1 Aerian which operated in concert with the Luftwaffe's Stukagruppen as part of the I Fliegerkorps in 1943

the vertical and is bunting, and all this while *terra firma* is rushing closer with apparently suicidal rapidity. In fact, I have rarely seen a specialist dive bomber put over 70 deg in a dive, but the Ju 87 was a genuine 90 deg screamer! For some indefinable reason the Ju 87D felt right standing on its nose, and the acceleration to 335 mph (540 km/h) was reached in about 4,500 ft (1 370 m), speed thereafter creeping slowly up to the absolute permitted limit of 373 mph (600 km/h) so that the feeling of being on a runaway roller-coaster experienced with most other dive bombers was missing.

As speed built up, the nose of the Ju 87 was used as the aiming mark. The elevators were moderately light in the initial stages of the dive but they heavied up considerably as speed built up. Any alterations in azimuth to keep the aiming mark on the target could be made accurately by use of the ailerons. These also heavied up as speed increased but always remained very effective. Use of the elevator or rudder trimmers in a dive or pull-out was strictly forbidden. During the dive it was necessary to watch the signal light on the contact altimeter, and when it came on, the knob on the control column was depressed to initiate the automatic pull-out at 6 *g*, a 1,475-ft (450-m) height margin being required to complete the manoeuvre. The automatic pull-out mechanism had a high reputation for reliability, but in the event of failure the pull-out could be effected with a full-blooded pull on the control column aided by judicious operation of the elevator trimmer to override the safety pilot control.

The sequence of events on selecting the dive brakes was most interesting. On extension of the brakes, red indicators protruded from each wing upper surface. This action automatically brought into play the safety pilot control and the dive recovery mechanism. The object of the latter was to return the elevator trimmer flaps to their normal position after release of the bomb,

thus initiating pull-out from the dive which had been started by the elevator trim being brought into action to nose the aircraft over. The safety pilot control was a restriction introduced into the control column movement whereby this was limited by means of hydraulic pressure to a pull of only 5 deg from the neutral position, thus obviating excessive *g* loads in pulling-out. In an emergency this restriction could be overridden to give a 13 deg movement. Once the aircraft had its nose safely pointed above the horizon from the pull-out, the dive brakes were retracted, the airscrew pitch set to take-off/climb and the throttle opened up to 1.15 *atas* of boost, although in conditions of enemy flak it was recommended that the full 1.35 *atas* be used. The radiator flaps were then opened.

When I finally turned for Schleswig, to where I was supposed to deliver the Ju 87D-3, I must confess that I had had a more enjoyable hour's dive bombing practice than I had ever experienced with any other aircraft of this specialist type. Somehow the Ju 87D did not appear to find its natural element until it was diving steeply. It seemed quite normal to stand this aircraft on its nose in a vertical dive because its acceleration had none of that uncontrollable runaway feeling associated with a 90 deg inclination in an aircraft like the Skua. Obviously, the fixed undercarriage and the large-span dive brakes of the Junkers were a highly effective drag combination.

However, the Ju 87D also had a reputation for standing on its nose in an entirely different context — during a landing! Although a somewhat ponderous aircraft, it could carry out all normal aerobatics, and it was easy and fairly pleasant to fly, but a three-point landing was desirable every time. A structural weakness in the undercarriage could lead to failure of the upper mainwheel fork and a subsequent collapse of the wheel assembly, particularly on a rough airfield surface. The leg could collapse forward or backward, and in the latter case there was a grave danger of the aircraft turning over on its back with somewhat dire results for the crew which could expect little protection from the cockpit canopy. Another weak point was the tailwheel, and the Pilot's Notes gave warning that unless a three-point landing was achieved there was danger of tailwheel damage.

Duly warned, I set about the simple preparations for landing at Schleswig which were to reduce speed to about 125 mph (200 km/h), select flaps down on the crosswind leg at approximately 112 mph (180 km/h), lock tailwheel, set airscrew pitch to fully fine and approach at 93 mph (150 km/h), progressively reducing to 75 mph (120 km/h) at hold-off. View for landing was excellent, the brakes proved powerful and could be applied almost immediately after a three-pointer, and the landing run

(Above) A close-up view of a Ju 87D-2 "Heinrich" of I/St.G.2 (circa 1942) illustrating the high position of the pilot and the large canopy which combined to give the author a "feeling of vulnerability". (Below) A Ju 87D-5 of 9./St.G.77 displaying well-worn temporary white winter finish.

(Above) A Ju 87D-1 of II/St.G.1 in flight over the Soviet Union during the summer of 1942, and (below) Ju 87D-5s of St.G.77 returning from a sortie on the Eastern Front during the winter of 1942-43

was very short indeed. The Ju 87D could, I understand, be landed with full bombload or, in an emergency, with the dive brakes extended, although to three-point the aircraft in the latter circumstances apparently required a 60-lb (27-kg) pull on the control column to overcome the safety pilot control.

The Ju 87 will always be associated with the victorious German *blitzkrieg* tactics employed in Poland and France during the first year of WW II; campaigns that fulfilled the most sanguine expectations of the Stuka's protagonists. Its first encounter with determined fighter opposition during the "Battle of Britain", which forced the withdrawal of the Ju 87-equipped *Stukagruppen* from the Cherbourg area to the Pas de Calais where they were to sit out the final phases of that epic conflict, pricked the Ju 87's bubble of success and revealed the fact that this aircraft had become an anachronism in the context of fighting in the west. But the day of the Stuka was far from over, for the Ju 87 was to enjoy further successes wherever the *Luftwaffe* succeeded in maintaining a measure of mastery in the air, the *Stukagruppen* ensuring that even the Soviet campaign initially proved a repetition of the débâcle suffered by the French.

The Ju 87 was, nevertheless, a poorly armed, somewhat cumbersome and highly vulnerable aircraft by any standard, yet it was the mount that carried the most highly-decorated Knight's Cross winner of the war — Hans-Ulrich Rudel who flew no fewer than 2,530 sorties and claimed the destruction of 519 tanks! That Rudel should have survived the war that he fought almost exclusively in this obsolescent Junkers design must speak volumes not only for his piloting skill but also for the capabilities of his rear gunner, who also won the *Ritterkreuz*, for it will always remain a mystery to me how these stalwarts escaped destruction if there were any enemy fighter pilots of even mediocre skill in the same area of sky as their Ju 87. There is no gainsaying the fact, however, that shortcomings galore though the Junkers dive bomber undoubtedly possessed, it gave resolute service from 0426 hours on 1 September 1939, when three Ju 87Bs of 3.*Staffel* of *Stukageschwader* 1 took-off from Elbing for the first bombing sortie of WW II, until the closing months of the war when the Ju 87D soldiered on with several *Nachtschlachtgruppen* and its tank-busting derivative, the Ju 87G, fought on with the specialized anti-tank *Staffeln*. □

DORNIER DO 217

TASTES in aeronautical pulchritude change with the times, but even today, when angularly ugly contours such as those of Panavia's Tornado or more bulbous forms akin to that of General Dynamics' "chinless" F-16 are considered by many the epitome of *functional* beauty, few with an eye for line would deny that the supremely graceful Dornier Do 17 shoulder-wing bomber, first revealed in 1935 and promptly dubbed the "Flying Pencil", was among the most elegant and beautiful shapes ever to have taken to the skies. Setting new standards in aerodynamic cleanliness, with its exceptionally slender, pencil-like side profile — although this slimness was seen to be illusory in planform as the near-cylindrical cross section changed rapidly to what can only be described as an inverted triangle to produce an abnormally broad centre fuselage, the section then transforming once more to an ellipse — which time and the dictates of military expediency were soon to impair, this *Schulterdecker-Kampfflugzeug* understandably generated considerable publicity when it made its international début in July 1937 at Zürich where it won the "Circuit of the Alps".

The process of prostituting purity of line for operational efficiency really began with the Do 17Z, the new forward fuselage of which had been created solely to afford the lower aft-firing gun a better field of fire and owed nothing to aerodynamic æstheticism. Nevertheless, something of the beauty of contour first displayed by that original Do 17 could still be perceived in what may be considered to have been its ultimate descendant, the Do 217. The girlish slenderness of line had translated over the intervening years to that of matronly corpulence; indeed, the deepening of the fuselage introduced with the E-series of this aeroplane was suggestive of a fairly advanced stage in pregnancy. It still looked good, however, with an aura of stolid efficiency not dissimilar to that which emanated from the Junkers Ju 88, and it was with some relish that I first clambered through the hinged crew entry trap in the underside of Do 217M-1 *Werk-Nr* 56158 at Schleswig on 24 August 1945.

I had actually flown its predecessor, the Do 17Z, the day before at Husum and had found it pleasant enough but somewhat underpowered with its BMW-Bramo 323P Fafnir nine-cylinder radials each giving out 1,000 hp for take-off and 940 hp at 13,125 ft (4 000 m) and attached to a gross weight of 18,931 lb (8 587 kg), which, in max overload condition, could rise to 19,481 lb (8 836 kg). It did not need a mathematician to assess that the Do 217M-1, with its two Daimler-Benz DB 603As each rated at 1,750 hp for take-off and 1,850 hp at 6,890 ft (2 100 m) pulling an aeroplane weighing up to 36,817 lb (16 700 kg), offered little improvement in power-to-weight ratio. The Daimler-Benz engines had, of course, only been applied to the Do 217 to safeguard against production delays that could have arisen had shortages of BMW 801D 14-cylinder radials occurred, but even with the *intended* power plant, the parallel production Do 217K-1 offered no better power-to-weight ratio.

We knew a fair amount about the Do 217M-1 as, on the night of 23-24 February 1944, an example of this type (*Werk-Nr* 56051) of 2.*Staffel* of *Kampfgeschwader* 2 that had received minor damage from anti-aircraft fire over the north-west suburbs of London — its crew promptly baling out at 10,000 feet (3 050 m) — had flown on to make an excellent pilotless belly landing in Cambridge, although this aircraft had not been restored to flying condition. The origin of the aircraft that I found at Schleswig was obscure — all indication of the unit by which it had been operated had been painted out and the aircraft had presumably been brought in to the collection field by one of our ferry people — but it is likely that it had originally been included on the strength of KG 2.

The Do 217M-1 was certainly well armed, with a 7,9-mm MG 131 machine gun in the extreme nose with a thousand rounds, a 13-mm MG 131 with 500 rounds in an electrically-operated dorsal turret, another 13-mm MG 131 with a thousand rounds in the ventral step and a pair of

7,9-mm MG 81s with 750 rpg in lateral positions. The German penchant for grouping the entire crew together in the forward fuselage had been adhered to, with the pilot and observer/bomb aimer up front, the radio operator behind the pilot and the gunner behind him. Immediately aft of the crew compartment was the fairly capacious bomb cell with stowage space for up to 5,550 lb (2 520 kg) of bombs

Decidedly underpowered

After flying the Do 217M-1 at Schleswig on both the 24th and 25th of August, I renewed my acquaintance with *Werk-Nr* 56158 almost two months later at Farnborough, whither it had meanwhile been ferried, having acquired along the way the Air Ministry number 107. It was at the RAE that, on 18 October, I undertook full handling trials with the Dornier and, on 29 December, finally delivering it to Brize Norton and an indeterminate fate, with the thought that if the Do 217M *was* — as I had anticipated on first sight — one of those underpowered twins that abounded in the early 'forties time scale, it had certainly been less lethal than some of them and at least pleasant to fly when everything was working!

That the Do 217M-1 was underpowered there was no doubt, the deep-throated, powerful roar of its DB 603s notwithstanding. Having clambered into the cabin via the footholds and handholds in the ventral trap, the thought immediately struck me that here was a cramped version of the He 177's cockpit. The layout was fairly logical and functional, but the "goldfish bowl" effect of the immense areas of transparent panelling was, like that of the larger bomber's cockpit, not a little disconcerting — a pilot at home with the "cosiness" of British or US cockpits and unused to such a surfeit of glazing would have felt decidedly naked and exposed. The pilot's control could be swung over to the observer's position so that the former could be relieved of the strain of flying the aeroplane for periods during long missions.

The starting procedure was to set both fuel cocks to flight position (FLUGSTELLUNG) and the ignition timing lever to the central position (NORMAL), booster pumps on (ZU), prime the engines via the pump and selector switch located behind the

The Do 217K-1 (at head of opposite page, above and immediately below) was the first production version of the Dornier bomber from which the stepped windscreen was eliminated. The example on the opposite page retains its radio call-sign letters and was photographed prior to delivery to the Luftwaffe

The Do 217M-1, a captured example (Werk-Nr 56527) of which is illustrated below, differed from the Do 217K-1 solely in the type of engine installed, the two models being manufactured in parallel and entering service with the Luftwaffe almost simultaneously

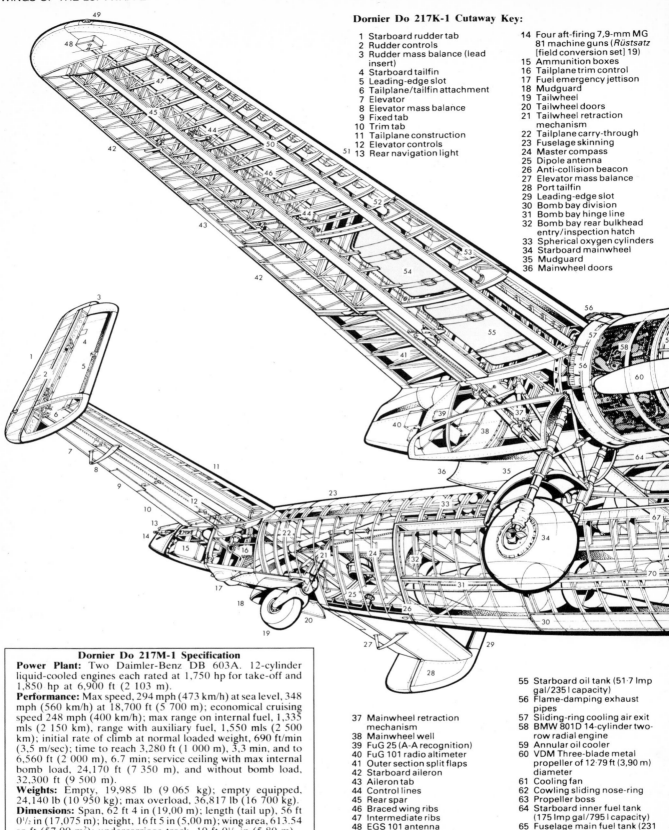

Dornier Do 217K-1 Cutaway Key:

1 Starboard rudder tab
2 Rudder controls
3 Rudder mass balance (lead insert)
4 Starboard tailfin
5 Leading-edge slot
6 Tailplane/tailfin attachment
7 Elevator
8 Elevator mass balance
9 Fixed tab
10 Trim tab
11 Tailplane construction
12 Elevator controls
13 Rear navigation light
14 Four aft-firing 7,9-mm MG 81 machine guns (*Rüstsatz* [field conversion set] 19)
15 Ammunition boxes
16 Tailplane trim control
17 Fuel emergency jettison
18 Mudguard
19 Tailwheel
20 Tailwheel doors
21 Tailwheel retraction mechanism
22 Tailplane carry-through
23 Fuselage skinning
24 Master compass
25 Dipole antenna
26 Anti-collision beacon
27 Elevator mass balance
28 Port tailfin
29 Leading-edge slot
30 Bomb bay division
31 Bomb bay hinge line
32 Bomb bay rear bulkhead entry/inspection hatch
33 Spherical oxygen cylinders
34 Starboard mainwheel
35 Mudguard
36 Mainwheel doors

37 Mainwheel retraction mechanism
38 Mainwheel well
39 FuG 25 (A-A recognition)
40 FuG 101 radio altimeter
41 Outer section split flaps
42 Starboard aileron
43 Aileron tab
44 Control lines
45 Rear spar
46 Braced wing ribs
47 Intermediate ribs
48 EGS 101 antenna
49 Starboard navigation light
50 Front spar
51 Leading-edge hot-air de-icing
52 Hot-air duct
53 Balloon-cable cutter in leading-edge
54 Starboard outer fuel tank (35 Imp gal/160 l capacity)

55 Starboard oil tank (51·7 Imp gal/235 l capacity)
56 Flame-damping exhaust pipes
57 Sliding-ring cooling air exit
58 BMW 801D 14-cylinder two-row radial engine
59 Annular oil cooler
60 VDM Three-blade metal propeller of 12·79 ft (3,90 m) diameter
61 Cooling fan
62 Cowling sliding nose-ring
63 Propeller boss
64 Starboard inner fuel tank (175 Imp gal/795 l capacity)
65 Fuselage main fuel tank (231 Imp gal/1 050 l capacity)
66 Wing spar carry-through
67 Bomb bay top hinge line
68 Load-bearing beam
69 Bomb shackle
70 Bomb bay centre hinge line
71 Typical bomb load: two 2,205-lb (1 000-kg) SC 1000 bombs

Dornier Do 217M-1 Specification

Power Plant: Two Daimler-Benz DB 603A. 12-cylinder liquid-cooled engines each rated at 1,750 hp for take-off and 1,850 hp at 6,900 ft (2 103 m).

Performance: Max speed, 294 mph (473 km/h) at sea level, 348 mph (560 km/h) at 18,700 ft (5 700 m); economical cruising speed 248 mph (400 km/h); max range on internal fuel, 1,335 mls (2 150 km), range with auxiliary fuel, 1,550 mls (2 500 km); initial rate of climb at normal loaded weight, 690 ft/min (3,5 m/sec); time to reach 3,280 ft (1 000 m), 3,3 min, and to 6,560 ft (2 000 m), 6.7 min; service ceiling with max internal bomb load, 24,170 ft (7 350 m), and without bomb load, 32,300 ft (9 500 m).

Weights: Empty, 19,985 lb (9 065 kg); empty equipped, 24,140 lb (10 950 kg); max overload, 36,817 lb (16 700 kg).

Dimensions: Span, 62 ft 4 in (19,00 m); length (tail up), 56 ft 0½ in (17,075 m); height, 16 ft 5 in (5,00 m); wing area, 613.54 sq ft (57,00 m²); undercarriage track, 19 ft 0½ in (5,80 m).

Armament: Two 7,9-mm MG 81 machine guns with 500 rpg in nose, one 13-mm MG 131 machine gun with 500 rounds in electrically operated dorsal turret, one 13-mm MG 131 machine gun with 1,000 rounds in ventral step and two 7,9-mm MG 81 machine guns with 750 rpg in lateral position. Max bomb load of 8,818 lb (4,000 kg) of which 5,550 lb (2 510 kg) carried internally.

seat, set the ignition switches to M1 + 2 and then operate the inertia starters by pulling out the handles until the engines fired and then releasing them. While the throaty DB 603s warmed up, the take-off check list was followed: Oil coolers shut; airscrews set to 12 o'clock on the indicators; flaps set to START position after selecting the upper position for electrical operation on the switch (behind the pilot's head); trimmers set at zero; tailplane incidence set at + 1 deg (nose heavy); booster pumps ON and fuel selector lever in position 1. There was a very neat 12-lamp indicator on the portside of the cockpit dash which indicated the position of the flaps, undercarriage and dive brakes.

The extensive glazing of the fuselage nose of the K- and M-series Do 217 produced something of a "goldfish bowl" effect for the pilot, the large areas of transparent panelling being seen in this photo of the Do 217K-2. The RF2C periscope with its PV1B sighting head for the tail-mounted battery of fixed guns can be seen

After the usual engine checks, I taxied out to the take-off position and made the final checks of setting the coolant radiators 10 deg open and locking the tailwheel by pulling the half-wheel type control column back beyond the mid position marked by a white line at the base of the column. With full power of 2,700 rpm and 1.4 *atas* of boost, the lightly-loaded Do 217M could be pulled off at 99 mph (160 km/h) and then held down until speed reached 124 mph (200 km/h) before retracting the undercarriage — which took a lengthy 30-40

78 Batteries (two 24-Volt)
79 Radio equipment
80 Dorsal gunner's seat support
81 Cabin hot-air
82 Dorsal gunner's station
83 Armoured turret ring
84 Aerial mast
85 Gun safety guard
86 Starboard beam-mounted 7,9-mm MG 81 machine gun (750 rounds)
87 13-mm MG 131 machine gun (500 rounds)
88 Electrically-operated dorsal turret
89 Revi gunsight
90 Angled side windows
91 Jettisonable decking
92 Bomb-aimer's folding seat
93 Navigator's table
94 Pilot's contoured seat

95 Rear-view gunsight
96 Upper instrument panel
97 Nose glazing
98 Control horns
99 Engine controls
100 One 13-mm MG 131 in strengthened nose glazing (alternatively twin 7,9-mm MG 81Z)
101 Balloon-cable cutter in nose horizontal frame
102 Cartridge ejection chute
103 Ammunition feed
104 Lotfe 7D bombsight
105 Bomb aimer's flat panel
106 Control column counterweight
107 Nose armour
108 Ventral gunner's quilt
109 Ammunition box (nose MG 131)
110 Cartridge collector box
111 Entry hatch
112 Entry hatch (open)
113 Entry ladder
114 Port mainwheel doors
115 Mudguard
116 Port mainwheel
117 Mainwheel leg cross struts
118 Port engine cowling
119 Landing light (swivelling)
120 Control linkage
121 Pitot head
122 Port navigation light
123 Port aileron
124 Aileron trim tab

72 Forward bomb doors
73 13-mm MG 131 machine gun in ventral position (1,000 rounds)
74 Ammunition ejection chute
75 Ventral gunner's station
76 Armoured bulkhead
77 Cartridge collector box

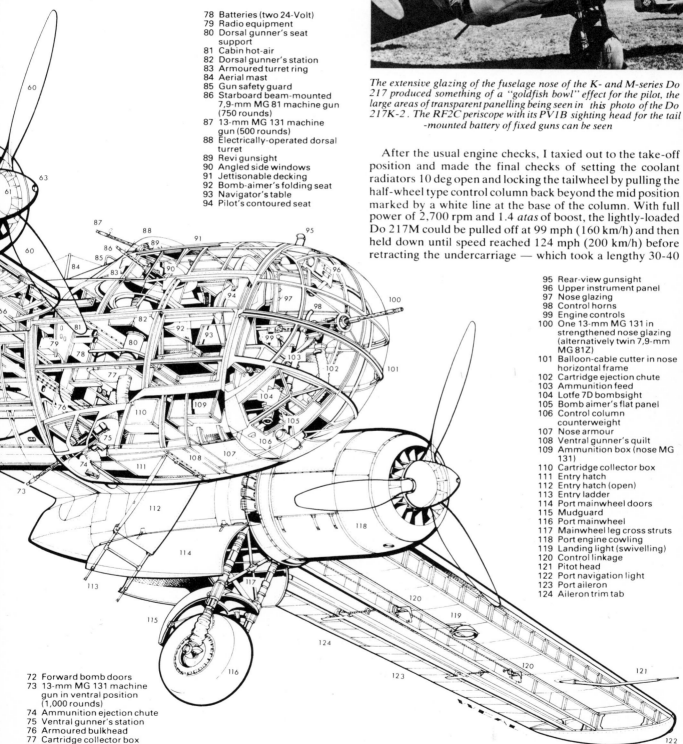

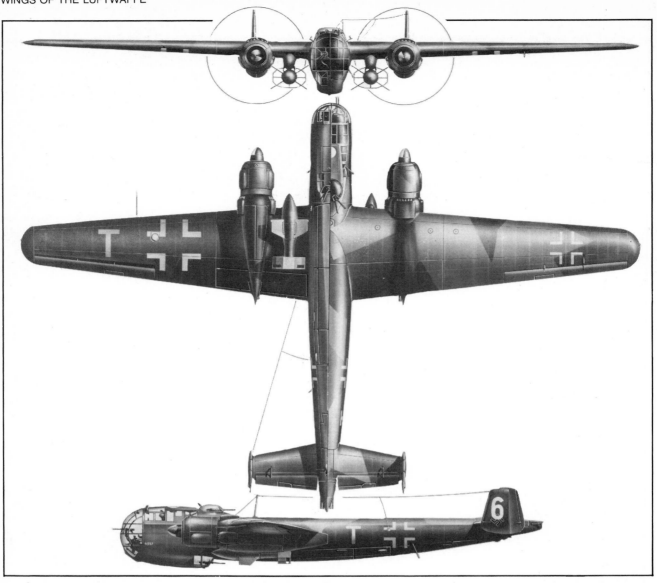

The Do 217K-2/R19 (Werk-Nr 4957) illustrated above was a Fritz X-carrying long-span version operated by III/KG 100 based at Marseilles-Istres for the anti-shipping rôle over the Mediterranean from late August 1943.

(Below) The Do 217M-1 (Werk-Nr 56158) that the author flew at the Royal Aircraft Establishment late in 1945, eventually delivering the aircraft to Brize Norton

(Above) A Do 217K-1 sporting the emblem of Luftflotte 2 on the fuselage nose, indicating that this aircraft was subordinated directly to the Luftflotte Headquarters

(Above) A standard production Do 217K-2 (Werk-Nr 4572). This model introduced extended wing outer panels and was intended specifically for operation as a carrier of FX 1400 Fritz X stand-off missiles, these being attached to special launching pylons between the fuselage and engine nacelles. The Do 217M-1 (below) was essentially similar to the K-1 apart from its engines, DB 603s supplanting the BMW 801D radials.

Dornier Do 217M-1 Cockpit Instrumentation Key:

1 Auxiliary external stores release knob (Rüstsatz 16)
2 Fuselage heating lever
3 Wing leading-edge heating lever
4 Oil cooler flaps actuating lever
5 Propeller de-icing switch
6 EiV contact breaker (Fzf)

7 Spark plug cleanser/tropical filter activation
8 Emergency-stop switch panel
9 FBG 16 remote-control panel
10 Cooler intakes emergency lever

11 Starter switch
12 Auxiliary external stores release lever (Rüstsatz 10)
13 Ignition advance levers (cold-weather starting)
14 Stores box
15 Plexiglass protective cover
16 Main line switch

17 Ignition switch
18 Emergency fuel jettison knob
19 Propeller pitch control levers
20 Throttle locking lever
21 ADb 11 junction box
22 Autopilot switch
23 SZKK 1 panel

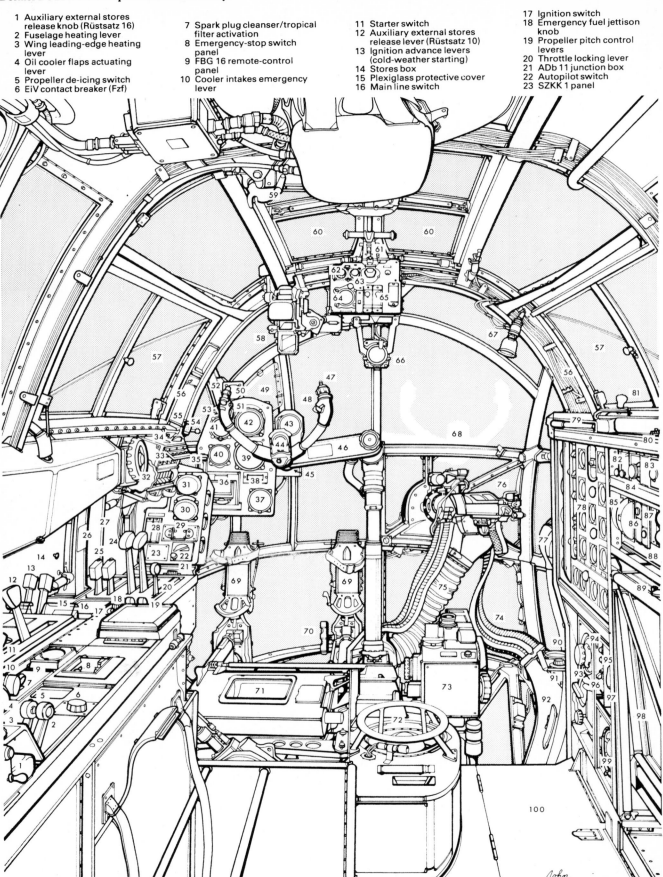

24 Throttle levers
25 Fuel cock levers
26 Operating instructions table
27 Engine data plate
28 Propeller setting switch
29 Twelve-lamp indicator
30 Dual pressure gauge
31 Dual RPM counter
32 Aileron/elevator/rudder trim knobs and indicators
33 Ultra-violet lighting/pitot head heating/instrument panel lighting switches
34 Course correction / autopilot / compass switches
35 Deviation tables
36 Directional gyro
37 Radio altimeter
38 Course setting
39 Repeater compass
40 Airspeed indicator
41 Fine-coarse altimeter
42 Artificial horizon
43 Variometer
44 Clock
45 AFN 2 radio navigation homing indicator
46 Control column swing-over arm
47 LRi 2 autopilot turn switch
48 Fixed weapon firing button
49 Clear-vision panel
50 Emergency turn-and-bank indicator
51 BK XI bomb-release button
52 FuG 16 transmission button
53 Pitot head heating indicator (obscured by control horn)
54 Lever for hinged section of blind-flying panel (Nos 43 and 45)
55 Ultra-violet light
56 No 4 fuselage frame
57 Sliding window panels
58 Stuvi 5B dive-bombing sight
59 Landing flap manual coupling lever
60 Jettisonable canopy roof section
61 Canopy jettison lever

62 Dimmer switch
63 Illuminator button
64 Trim indicator
65 Trim levers
66 Standby compass
67 Cockpit light
68 Control column swing-over position
69 Rudder pedals
70 Rudder adjustment screw
71 Pilot's seat mount
72 DÆF controls
73 Lotfe 7D bombsight
74 Ammunition feed
75 Link and casing collector chute
76 MG 81Z machine gun
77 Oxygen supply
78 Engine instrument nel/temperature/pressure gauges
79 Bomb jettison lever
80 EiV contact breaker
81 Bomb-arming crank
82 ZH- and QFF transmitter (BZA 1)
83 ADb 11 junction box
84 Wind-speed indicator (BZA 1)
85 External bomb rack switches
86 BG 25
87 ASK-N smoke discharge switchbox
88 Dimmer switches
89 Observer's seat release
90 Height-compensated airspeed indicator
91 BZA 1 true-speed indicator
92 Ammunition box
93 RAB 14d automatic sequence bomb release
94 Bomb door position indicator switch
95 Bomb door indicator lights
96 Bomb door closing switch
97 ZSK 244A ignition switch box
98 Observer's foldaway seat
99 Angled delivery setting control
100 Bomb aimer's well

seconds to come up. At 500 ft (150 m) power was reduced to 2,500 rpm and 1.3 *atas*, the flaps being raised at about 143 mph (230 km/h). With the flaps up, a climbing speed of 146 mph (235 km/h) was established and this gave a rate of climb of very moderate proportions. Indeed, the service ceiling was barely 25,000 ft (7 620 m).

I tested the aircraft in cruising flight at 18,000 ft (5 486 m) and with the tailplane incidence at +2 deg (ie, nose heavy) gave a best speed of 325 mph (523 km/h) true. It was very stable about all three axes, and the controls were well harmonised and effective, and not unduly heavy for bomber operations. At the other end of the speed range, the stall occurred at 96 mph (155 km/h) and was characterised by a gentle nose-down pitch. If the aircraft was flown for any length of time at economical cruise or flown for endurance, the ignition timing lever had to be set to the plug cleaning position from time to time for five seconds.

The fuel system incorporated a central tank, two wing-root tanks and two outboard wing tanks, giving a total capacity of 651 Imp gal (2 960 l). White warning lights came on in the cockpit when the fuel lever fell to 99 Imp gal (450 l), and the transfer pump had then to be switched on. When the warning lights came on a second time, the fuel selector lever had to be moved to position 11.

At this stage I tried out the Dornier's single-engine performance and this proved decidedly unimpressive, underlining the fact that the aircraft was definitely underpowered — above 4,920 ft (1 500 m) height could not be maintained at 2,300 rpm and 1.3 *atas*. To me it is one of the most unpleasant feelings that can be experienced in flying to have to cope with an underpowered twin on one engine in critical conditions such as exist during take-off or in a bad-weather landing. That knife-edge sensation may set the adrenalin flowing but it leaves one with an enduring and

The swollen ventral contour of the centre fuselage of the Dornier bomber suggested a relatively advanced stage in pregnancy, a characteristic seen to effect in this photo of a Do 217K-1

nasty impression of the offending aircraft. My favourite 'twins' have all been overpowered and the aircraft for which I have had the greatest abhorrence have all been *underpowered* 'twins' — the Do 217M did not qualify for inclusion in the latter category as its inadequate power was, to some extent, mitigated by redeeming features, but it was never to rank high in my book.

An unimpressive dive bomber

Reverting to normal power, I decided to chance my arm and try out the dive bombing characteristics of this somewhat ponderous aeroplane. So preoccupied with the dive bombing concept had been the *Reichsluftfahrtministerium* that one would not have been untowardly surprised if its *Technische Amt* had insisted that maritime patrol flying boats be capable of functioning as fully-fledged dive bombers. This German penchant for converting every aircraft into a dive bomber, which reached the ultimate in impracticability with the He 177, had come pretty near to this situation with the Do 217. The dive brake took the form of a rather novel extension of the extreme rear fuselage, operating somewhat after the fashion of a four-ribbed umbrella, the "ribs" forming the four sides of the extension when closed. The brake was operated by a threaded collar and spindle, movement of the collar pulling the "ribs" open against four short hinged struts.

Early trials with this brake applied to the Do 217 had proved anything but satisfactory. Apart from lack of reliability of the brake itself, its deployment exerted severe strain on the rear fuselage, sometimes resulting in distortion of the stringers and buckling of the stressed skin. On occasions, the torsion rod — which extended from the cockpit to the tail of the fuselage to which the screw jack operating the dive brake was attached — was itself distorted, jamming the brake in the deployed position after the aircraft had pulled out of a dive. Dornier had, in fact, delivered Do 217s to service units with an alternative tail cone packed in the bomb-bay so that the dive brake could be removed after delivery of the aircraft and the tail cone fitted. Nevertheless, the *Technische Amt* had elected to ignore the shortcomings of the Do 217 in the dive bombing rôle and the Do 217M-1 that we had picked up at Schleswig was fully equipped with tail brake.

First, I made a straight dive to 435 mph (700 km/h), which was the maximum permitted speed below a height of 9,840 ft (3 000 m), in order to get the feel of the controls which I found heavied up considerably. The engine revs built up to 2,750 during the dive so that there was a lot of attendant noise, and the pull-out called for a good, full-blooded heave. After climbing to regain height, I prepared for a dive using the tail-mounted braking device and automatic pull-out equipment. The latter had a three-position switch marked "Level Flight — Trim — Dive Brake". Pressing the "Trim" switch brought the starboard trim tab into play, while further selection of "Dive Brake" brought both dive trim tabs into action and opened the umbrella-style brake, as indicated by a red light on the 12-lamp indicator.

The Do 217M entered the dive automatically by this selection and had soon attained its "braked-condition" limiting speed of 357 mph (575 km/h). The feeling of solidity during the dive gave an impression of virtual non-manœuvrability. The pull-out was initiated either by pressing the bomb release knob on the control column or by selecting "Level Flight", this also retracting the dive brake. All very sedate and totally unimpressive as a precision weapon. Small

wonder that most Do 217s employed during the later stages of the war had had the dive mode deleted and a tailcone *Rüstsatz* (Field Conversion Set) applied comprising four aft-firing 7,9-mm MG 81 machine guns which could be fired by the pilot with the aid of the RF2C periscope fitted with a PV1B sighting head.

The landing pattern was entered at 155 mph (250 km/h) with about 0.65 *atas*, the oil coolers being opened fully and the coolant radiators 30 deg. The propellers were then set manually to 11.30 on the pitch indicators, which were displayed both in the cockpit and on the inboard side of each engine nacelle, and at 149 mph (240 km/h) the undercarriage was lowered, taking some 30-40 seconds to extend fully. Flaps were lowered to the START position at 146 mph (235 km/h) and fully deployed at 137 mph (220 km/h), tail incidence having to be trimmed to -4 deg (tail heavy).

The final engine-assisted approach was made at 124 mph (200 km/h) and touch-down occurred at about 99 mph (160 km/h) at a landing weight of 28,000 lb (12 700 kg) or 109 mph (175 km/h) at 31,970 lb (14 500 kg), the control column

being held back beyond neutral to keep the tailwheel locked until the landing run had been completed. There was one particular catch to watch out for on landing. When the flaps were selected DOWN with electrical operation and the tail incidence trimmer wheel began to turn, the flaps had quickly to be selected UP and the flap operation lever set to manual with the incidence trimmer wheel being moved by hand, otherwise the change of trim could not be held.

The Do 217M was no world beater by any stretch of the imagination but it was competent enough for its day. Its performance was such that its forté was obviously nocturnal operation unless it could rely on the absence of serious fighter opposition, and it was a reasonably effective maritime strike aircraft in which mode it carried the Hs 293A or *Fritz X* missiles with, presumably, sufficient success to justify its retention in production until June 1944. Writing an epitaph for this last of the Dornier bomber line to see combat, one would perhaps say that it had been a moderate aircraft which established an undistinguished but honourable operational record.

The Do 217K and M were the end products of a process of continuous evolution that began in the mid 'thirties with the extraordinarily elegant Do 17, the so-called "Flying Pencil". Demands for increased operational efficiency and capability were catered for at the expense of aerodynamic aestheticism, and the Do 217K-1 (right) and the Do 217M-1 (below) exuded matronly stolidity, the girlish slenderness of their progenitor having disappeared with the passage of time

HEINKEL HE 177

Those who witnessed the arrival at the Royal Aircraft Establishment, Farnborough, of a Heinkel He 177A-5 *Greif* (Griffin) heavy bomber, sporting crude *Armée de l'Air* roundels, AEAF striping and the legend *Prise de Guerre* on its fuselage sides, late that summer Sunday afternoon of 10 September 1944, may have been excused a surprised uplift of the eyebrows. Some strange aircraft were, from time to time, to be seen over Hampshire in the RAE circuit during those late war years, but this was as fabulous a creature as the mythical animal from which it had taken its name.

Our first information of the existence of this big Heinkel bomber had come to us from a knowledgeable *Luftwaffe* PoW, who, captured as early as 13 June 1940, had described the essential features of the aircraft with what was to prove to be considerable accuracy. Subsequently, the operational début of the new warplane had been awaited with a certain amount of trepidation, but as time passed and it failed to appear in service in the sort of quantities commensurate with the long period that was known to have elapsed since its development had begun or with the total number known to have been constructed, it had become increasingly obvious that this potentially potent aircraft was in trouble. Nevertheless, it had seemed likely that the technical defects that had delayed its service introduction would eventually be overcome and that, sooner or later, it would appear on operations.

Information gleaned from PoWs that had come into contact with the He 177 had often proved contradictory; while one had stressed the difficulties that it was encountering in its development programme, another had declaimed that it was about to provide the *Luftwaffe* with a weapon superior to anything available to RAF Bomber Command or the USAAF. Most reports suggested that the Heinkel heavy bomber was

very fast and easily handled in flight; *Reichsluftfahrtministerium* officials had been overheard expressing the view that the He 177 was fully as manœuvrable as the very much smaller and pretty nimble Ju 88; one PoW, a pilot of considerable experience, had alleged that the He 177 had performed tighter turns than the fighter variant of the Ju 88 when the two had been flown together in mock combat, and another PoW from KG 100 had asserted that the Heinkel could employ relatively small airfields, such as that at Graz, with greater facility than the Do 217 medium bomber.

This had all built up into a pretty impressive picture, and it went without saying, therefore, that we were *very* anxious to get our hands on an intact specimen of the bomber to sort fact from fiction and to evaluate its several novel and ingenious features. At 2131 hours on 21 January 1944, the first night of Operation *Steinbock*, the so-called "Little Blitz" which marked the operational début of the *Greif* over the British Isles, an example of the He 177A-5 (*Werk-Nr* 15747) had been brought down by a night fighter at Whitmore Vale, near Hindhead, Surrey, but only the tail unit, which had broken off about three feet forward of the fin, had survived relatively undamaged, the remainder of the aircraft being completely destroyed except for the outer section of the port mainplane.

The wreckage was removed to the RAE for detailed examination and revealed some information, as did the wreckage of three more He 177s shot down between 23 February and 2 March during attacks on London, but we were still anxious to secure an example of the *Greif* that we could evaluate.

After the Allied landings of June 1944, considerable interest had focussed on the Toulouse area, some of this interest certainly being generated by the fact that the principal centre in France for the overhaul and repair of the He 177 had been established at Blagnac airfield*, near Toulouse. An operation was planned for the capture of an intact specimen of the He 177 as soon as an opportunity presented itself, this being organised by one of the most widely-known and successful SOE (Special Operations Executive) operatives, G R Starr, DSO, MC, who, using the pseudonym of *Colonel Hilaire*, had been directing the operations of *Maquis* units in the Gers region for more than a year. The operation was to be undertaken by several Jedgburg units of *Maquis* in co-operation with British and US personnel parachuted into the area on 17 August 1944.

On the morning of 2 September, the RAE received a signal that the operation had been mounted and that an He 177 had been isolated on Blagnac airfield, and a "pirate" venture was promptly organised with aircraft drawn from the RAE's Wireless and Electrical Flight, a team being despatched from the RAE to Blagnac aboard a Hudson (T9433), with two Beaufighters (R2241 and KW292) as escort. The senior officer was Grp Cpt A F Hards*, the CO at Farnborough, who was to fly the Hudson back from Blagnac, and he was accompanied by Wg Cdr Roland J Falk, Chief Test Pilot and Operations Administrator at the RAE, whose task it was to fly the He 177 to Farnborough, and Sqdn Ldr Pearse who was to serve as engineer aboard the Heinkel bomber.

The Beaufighters got separated from the Hudson in inclement weather and lost contact, KW292 (flown by Sqdn Ldr E A

Towards the end of 1942, the Heinkel organisation occupied the AIA facilities at Blagnac and subsequently utilised these as a centre for repairs and modifications to the He 177s operated by KG 40 from Mérignac. The repair of major components was divided between Toulouse (wings and fuselages) and Bayonne (tail assemblies), final re-assembly being undertaken at Blagnac. In fact, during the period 1943-44, very few aircraft were repaired — actually eight — owing to a combination of the delaying tactics employed by the French labour force and RAF bombing of the installation.

Grp Cpt Hards was to lose his life on 18 January 1946 while flying a Dornier Do 335 (see page 76).

(Head of opposite page) An He 177A-3/R1 of Kampfgeschwader 40 which participated in the first operational sorties flown by the unit from Châteaudun. (Above) An He 177A-3/R2 and (below) He 177A-1s employed in the operational training rôle by the Flugzeugführerschule (B) 16 at Burg, near Magdeburg

(Above and below) The He 177A-5/R6 (Werk-Nr 412951) photographed above the Hampshire countryside while under test from Farnborough during the autumn of 1944. This particular specimen was flown quite frequently at Farnborough until November of that year and then infrequently until delivered to Boscombe Down in February 1945

Hood) exhausting its fuel and eventually making a wheels-up landing in a field after remaining airborne for seven hours, and the pilot of T9433 (Flt Lt A Martin) baling out over the coast when his Beaufighter, too, ran out of fuel after logging seven-and-a-half hours. After some difficulty in locating Blagnac because of poor visibility, the Hudson had reached its destination in 5 hr 50 min, deposited Falk and Pearse, and had taken-off again for return to Thorney Island. "Roly" Falk

had received no information about the flying characteristics of the Heinkel bomber and was warned by the French mechanics that the Germans had experienced some dangerous control problems with the aircraft, but he did not find it a particularly difficult aircraft to manage and 2 hr 45 min after taking-off from Blagnac eight days later, he delivered the prize safely to Farnborough.

It was thus that the RAE acquired He 177A-5/R6 *Werk-Nr*

412951, formerly included on the strength of *Kampfgeschwader* 40, and a fascinating aeroplane it was from some aspects for it probably embodied as much ingenuity as any German wartime aircraft. It was also the German aircraft industry's most dismal failure and was to be referred to, more or less seriously, as being deadlier to its crews than to its enemies! The Griffin of mythology would seem to have been a successful mating of the head and wings of an eagle with the body and hind quarters of a lion; Ernst Heinkel's team apparently enjoyed somewhat less success in attempting to mate a conventional structure with an innovatory power plant arrangement to create *its* Griffin, and the result was certainly never to emulate in its guardianship of the Third Reich the ferocity with which its namesake guarded the Scythian gold of Greek legend. Not that the *Greif* was a fundamentally poor design. On the contrary, it was of extremely advanced concept, but its advanced features were subject to teething troubles and the difficulties represented by these and the insufficiently energetic attempts to eradicate them were compounded by specification changes stemming from impractical operational demands, conflicting military and political policies and vacillation on the part of the *Reichsluftfahrtministerium* in its priorities.

The specification for what was to become the *Greif* was originally drawn up by the *Führungsstab der Luftwaffe* in mid-1936, Heinkel receiving instructions to proceed with a mock-up a year later, on 2 June 1937, of what was an extraordinarily advanced design prepared by the ingenious Dipl-Ing Siegfried Günter. The radical features of Günter's design included coupled engines with surface evaporation cooling and a system of remotely-controlled defensive gun bar-

bettes offering appreciably less drag than manned turrets. The difficulties that the *Greif* was to encounter from its birth with belated recognition of their causes, the monotonous series of fires in the air, aerodynamic problems and structural failures; all are today well documented and have no place in this narrative. It suffices to say that as I climbed into the He 177A-5 at Farnborough on the afternoon of 20 September 1944 for my first flight test of our latest acquisition, what I knew of the reputation of the big Heinkel gave me little cause for hilarity.

Flying from a "goldfish bowl"
I have always had a predilection for flying unconventional aircraft; a partiality for canards, tailless or all-wing designs; a penchant towards prone piloting positions, skid under-carriages and other off-beat features. In my book, the He 177 qualified for the unconventional category if only on the score of its power plant arrangement. I had flown some aircraft in my day with inadequate briefing, but until I first handled the He 177 I had never flown an aircraft without any briefing whatsoever! It was a routine that I was to become familiar with, however, when testing other ex-*Luftwaffe* aircraft.

Between its arrival from Blagnac and the commencement of flight testing from Farnborough, the Heinkel's *Armée de l'Air* roundels had given place to those of the RAF and the serial TS439 had been allocated. The He 177 stood big, as the Americans would say. Its ground stance reminded me vividly of a Stirling that had sagged at the knees; if it had been a choice between the He 177 and the Stirling as æsthetically the least appealing of bombers I think that the German contender would have won by a short head.

(Above and below) The He 177A-5/R6 at Farnborough after its arrival from Blagnac in September 1944, still sporting French roundels and the legend "Prise de Guerre". The coding F8 may just be seen on the fuselage side ahead of the roundel

Heinkel He 177A-5 cutaway drawing key

1 Starboard navigation light
2 Detachable wingtip
3 FuG 101 radio altimeter (FM)
4 Aileron control runs
5 Starboard aileron
6 Aileron trim tab
7 Spring-loaded geared tab
8 Aileron counter-balance
9 FuG 102 radio altimeter (pulsed)
10 Tab mechanism
11 Fowler flap outboard track
12 Fowler flap position (extended)
13 Aileron tab control linkage
14 Flap actuating cylinder (hydraulic)
15 Control cables
16 Main spar (outboard section)
17 Wing ribs
18 Auxiliary front spar
19 Heated leading-edge
20 Oil radiator intake
21 Starboard Hs 293 radio-controlled glide-bomb
22 Starboard outer mainwheel door (open position)
23 Starboard outer mainwheel well
24 Balloon cable-cutter in leading-edge
25 Starboard ETC weapons rack
26 Twin oil radiators (starboard engines)
27 Radiator outlet flap
28 Hot-air ducting
29 Mainwheel door actuating cylinder
30 No 8 (starboard outer) fuel tank of 246·5 Imp gal/1 120 l capacity (flexible bag)
31 Fuel filler cap
32 Fowler flap outer section
33 Auxiliary rear spar
34 Wing dihedral break point
35 Fowler flap track
36 Starboard fuel starting tank (2 gal/9 litre capacity)
37 Starboard oil tanks
38 Main hydraulic tank (starboard only) (7 gal/32 litre capacity)
39 Fuel filler cap
40 No 3 (starboard inner) fuel tank of 136·5 Imp gal/621 l capacity (metal/self-sealing)
41 Fowler flap inner section
42 Mainspar (inboard section)
43 Starboard inner mainwheel well
44 Engine supercharger
45 Nacelle fairing
46 Wing spar attachment point and fairing
47 Engine accessories
48 Daimler-Benz DB 610A-1 24-cylinder liquid-cooled engine
49 Anti-vibration side-mounting pad
50 Supercharger and wing de-icing intakes
51 Nacelle former
52 Coolant vents
53 Engine forward mounting
54 Cooling gills
55 Double-gear crank casing
56 Single propellor shaft
57 Propellor de-icing saddle tank
58 Nacelle cooling profile
59 Propellor variable-pitch mechanism
60 Propellor boss
61 Blade cuffs
62 VDM four-blade propellor (right-handed)
63 Chin intake
64 Flame damper exhaust
65 Starboard outer mainwheel leg
66 Starboard inner mainwheel leg

67 Starboard outer mainwheel
68 D/F loop in dorsal blister
69 Emergency hydraulic tank (5·5 Imp gal/25 litre)

70 No 7 fuselage frame
71 C-Stand ammunition tank (1,000 rounds)
72 Dorsal barbette remote drive motor
73 Revi gunsight with slotted 10-mm armour protection
74 Remote control sighting cupola
75 Barbette traverse control handle
76 Barbette elevation control handle
77 Main radio panel (FuG 10P: general-purpose set) (FuG 17Z: VHF communication and homing) (FuG BL 2F: Blind-approach)
78 First-aid pack
79 Navigator's take-off/landing station
80 Window
81 Gunner's seat
82 Emergency jettison panels (port and starboard)
83 Bomb-aimer's seat (raised)
84 External rear-view mirror
85 Engine control panel (starboard)
86 Internal rear-view mirror
87 Offset ring-and-bead gunsight
88 MG 81 7.9-mm machine gun (A1-Stand)
89 Circular gun mounting
90 Balloon cable-cutters in nose horizontal frames
91 Ammunition feed
92 A1-Stand ammunition tank (1,000 rounds)
93 Hinged window panel (port and starboard)
94 Pilot's seat (armour plate: 9-mm back, 6-mm seat)

95 Rudder pedals
96 Cockpit hot-air
97 Lower glazed section often overpainted/armoured
98 Lotfe 7D bombsight fairing
99 'Boxed' gunsight
100 MG 151 20-mm cannon (A2-Stand)
101 Bullet-proof glass in nose of 'bola'
102 De-icing intake
103 Ventral crew entry hatch

104 Telescopic ladder
105 Actuating arm
106 MG 151 20-mm cannon ammunition feed
107 De-icing air heater/blower
108 A2-Stand ammunition tank (300 rounds)
199 Toilet installation
110 C-Stand ammunition feed
111 Thermos flasks
112 Circular vision port
113 MG 131 13-mm machine gun (C-Stand) at rear of 'bola'
114 'Fritz X' (Kramer X-1) radio-controlled bomb

115 Cruciform main fins
116 SAP warhead
117 Tail fin structure
118 Air-brake attachment
119 Ventral bomb rack (only fitted if forward bomb-bay blanked off)
120 Forward bomb-bay (often blanked off)
121 Fuel tank retaining strap lugs
122 Internal bomb shackle
123 Bomb-bay central partition
124 No 4 (fuselage) fuel tank (334 Imp gal/1520 l) (Replaced by 759 Imp gal/3450 l tank if bomb bay blanked off) (metal/self-sealing)
125 Fuel filler cap
126 Barbette remote drive cooling duct and linkage
127 Remote control dorsal barbette (B1-Stand)

128 Twin 13-mm MG 131 guns
129 No 13 fuselage frame
130 Barbette structure
131 B1-Stand double ammunition tank (1,000 rounds per gun)
132 Central bomb bay (often blanked off)

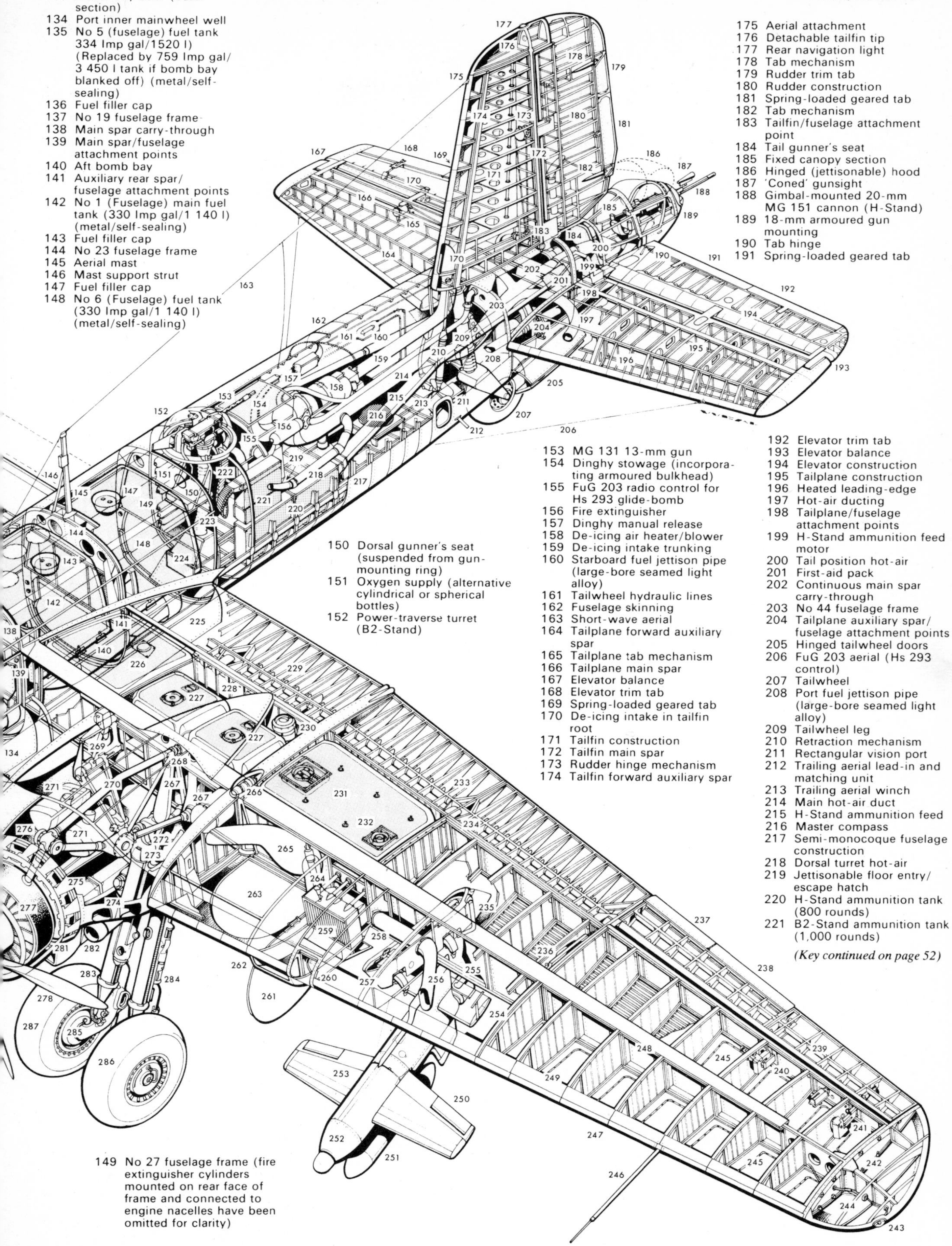

133 Bomb bay door (outer section)
134 Port inner mainwheel well
135 No 5 (fuselage) fuel tank 334 Imp gal/1520 l) (Replaced by 759 Imp gal/ 3 450 l tank if bomb bay blanked off) (metal/self-sealing)
136 Fuel filler cap
137 No 19 fuselage frame
138 Main spar carry-through
139 Main spar/fuselage attachment points
140 Aft bomb bay
141 Auxiliary rear spar/ fuselage attachment points
142 No 1 (Fuselage) main fuel tank (330 Imp gal/1 140 l) (metal/self-sealing)
143 Fuel filler cap
144 No 23 fuselage frame
145 Aerial mast
146 Mast support strut
147 Fuel filler cap
148 No 6 (Fuselage) fuel tank (330 Imp gal/1 140 l) (metal/self-sealing)

150 Dorsal gunner's seat (suspended from gun-mounting ring)
151 Oxygen supply (alternative cylindrical or spherical bottles)
152 Power-traverse turret (B2-Stand)

153 MG 131 13-mm gun
154 Dinghy stowage (incorporating armoured bulkhead)
155 FuG 203 radio control for Hs 293 glide-bomb
156 Fire extinguisher
157 Dinghy manual release
158 De-icing air heater/blower
159 De-icing intake trunking
160 Starboard fuel jettison pipe (large-bore seamed light alloy)
161 Tailwheel hydraulic lines
162 Fuselage skinning
163 Short-wave aerial
164 Tailplane forward auxiliary spar
165 Tailplane tab mechanism
166 Tailplane main spar
167 Elevator balance
168 Elevator trim tab
169 Spring-loaded geared tab
170 De-icing intake in tailfin root
171 Tailfin construction
172 Tailfin main spar
173 Rudder hinge mechanism
174 Tailfin forward auxiliary spar

175 Aerial attachment
176 Detachable tailfin tip
177 Rear navigation light
178 Tab mechanism
179 Rudder trim tab
180 Rudder construction
181 Spring-loaded geared tab
182 Tab mechanism
183 Tailfin/fuselage attachment point
184 Tail gunner's seat
185 Fixed canopy section
186 Hinged (jettisonable) hood
187 'Coned' gunsight
188 Gimbal-mounted 20-mm MG 151 cannon (H-Stand)
189 18-mm armoured gun mounting
190 Tab hinge
191 Spring-loaded geared tab

192 Elevator trim tab
193 Elevator balance
194 Elevator construction
195 Tailplane construction
196 Heated leading-edge
197 Hot-air ducting
198 Tailplane/fuselage attachment points
199 H-Stand ammunition feed motor
200 Tail position hot-air
201 First-aid pack
202 Continuous main spar carry-through
203 No 44 fuselage frame
204 Tailplane auxiliary spar/ fuselage attachment points
205 Hinged tailwheel doors
206 FuG 203 aerial (Hs 293 control)
207 Tailwheel
208 Port fuel jettison pipe (large-bore seamed light alloy)
209 Tailwheel leg
210 Retraction mechanism
211 Rectangular vision port
212 Trailing aerial lead-in and matching unit
213 Trailing aerial winch
214 Main hot-air duct
215 H-Stand ammunition feed
216 Master compass
217 Semi-monocoque fuselage construction
218 Dorsal turret hot-air
219 Jettisonable floor entry/ escape hatch
220 H-Stand ammunition tank (800 rounds)
221 B2-Stand ammunition tank (1,000 rounds)

(Key continued on page 52)

149 No 27 fuselage frame (fire extinguisher cylinders mounted on rear face of frame and connected to engine nacelles have been omitted for clarity)

He 177A-5/R6 bombers of II/KG 40 at Bordeaux-Mérignac in the spring of 1944 after the Gruppe reverted to the Atlantic reconnaissance rôle

After clambering into the cabin through the down-swinging door in the floor, I lowered myself into the first-pilot's seat, which was quite comfortably upholstered on an armour-plate frame. I took stock of the cockpit which was so big and featured such immense areas of transparent panels that I felt as though I was sitting in an outsize goldfish bowl. The control column was of the centralized type with an arm which could be swung to the opposite hand for operation by the second pilot who occupied a collapsible seat to starboard and was provided with auxiliary rudder pedals. The main flying panel was mounted vertically in front of and to the port hand of the pilot, and placed horizontally along the port wall of the cockpit was the main control panel carrying the fuel cocks, ignition switches, engine

couplers, throttles, starting levers, priming buttons, oil filter and plug cleaning levers, de-icing control and fire extinguishing levers. Three separate trim control wheels were positioned behind the throttles, engine instruments were arranged on a panel along the starboard cockpit wall beside the co-pilot, and the undercarriage, flap and fuel jettison controls were mounted in the roof.

Starting of the Daimler-Benz DB 610 24-cylinder liquid-cooled engines — two 12-cylinder DB 605s mounted side-by-side with a single gear-casing connecting the two crankcases and the two crankshaft pinions driving a single airscrew shaft gear — was by the usual hand/electric inertia starter, and taxying proved easy once one got used to the fact that the steering swing produced by one of these coupled units was considerably less than that produced by the outboard engine of a conventional four-piston engine layout. The view was good forward and while I could see the port wingtip I was unable to see its opposite number, so a little caution was called for in tight situations. The brakes were moderately good with the usual judder associated with German foot brakes, and since the large vertical tail and slab-sided fuselage were susceptible to crosswind effect, I found the aircraft a bit of a handful under such conditions.

The take-off was made with the flaps set to START using 1.3 *atas* of boost and 2,500 rpm. The boost was not automatically controlled, so I employed the technique of slowly opening the throttles with the flight engineer following with his hand at the base of the levers on the throttle quadrant. At 1.2 *atas* I released the throttles for him to take over their control and act as a constant speed unit. There was a strange hiatus in engine response on opening up, but once past this dead area of throttle travel the engine response to the throttle proved excellent. The He 177 showed no tendency to swing and the tail could be raised early in the run, showing light and effective elevator response. However, I was to learn that in crosswind take-offs the rudder was very sluggish in correcting swing, presumably due to its spring tab system.

The aircraft had to be eased off the ground at about 93 mph (150 km/h) and then held down while the massive undercarriage — each unit comprising two immense single-wheel oleo legs attached to the mainspar with the outboard legs retracting upward and outward and the inboard legs swinging upward and inward — was raised and speed built up to the single-engine failure safety speed of 112 mph (180 km/h). There was no change of trim as the undercarriage came up, and when the flaps were raised at 155 mph (250 km/h) there was again very little trim change but a definite sink could be felt.

Climb was ponderous by any standard and gave me my first

Heinkel He 177A-5 cutaway drawing key continued

222 Ammunition feed	255 Tracking flare installation
223 Flexible chute	256 Outboard leading-edge
224 Empty belt link and	hot-air
cartridge collector box	257 Port ETC weapons rack
225 Aft bomb bay door	258 Oil radiator outlet flap
(outer section)	259 Twin oil radiators (port
226 No 2 (port inner) fuel tank	engines)
(136·5 Imp gal/621 l)	260 Searchlight/landing light
(metal/self-sealing)	261 Port outer mainwheel door
227 Port oil tanks	door (open position)
228 Auxiliary rear spar	262 Oil radiator intake
229 Fowler flap construction	263 Port outer mainwheel well
(inner section)	264 Mainwheel door actuating
230 Port fuel starting tank	cylinder
(2 gal/9 litre)	265 Hot-air ducting
231 No 7 (port outer) fuel tank	266 Wing spar attachment point
(246 Imp gal/1 120 l)	and fairing
(flexible bag)	267 Individual undercarriage/
232 Fuel filler cap	main spar attachment
233 Fowler flap construction	268 Engine bearer ball socket
(outer section)	269 Hydraulic retracting jack
234 Flap hinge fairing	attachment
235 ETC rack hot-air	270 Upper engine bearer
236 Fowler flap track attachment	271 Coolant tanks
237 Spring-loaded geared tab	272 Engine support strut
238 Aileron trim tab	273 Mainwheel oleo leg pivot
239 Port aileron construction	points
240 Tab mechanism	274 Supercharger and wing
241 Aileron mechanism	de-icing intakes
242 Wingtip attachment bolts	275 Cooling gills
243 Port navigation light	276 Engine forward mounting
244 Detachable wingtip	277 Segmented annular radiator
245 Wing undersurface access/	278 VDM four-blade propellor
inspection panels	(left-handed)
246 Pitot head	279 Blade cuffs
247 Heated leading-edge	280 Propellor boss
248 Main spar (outboard section)	281 Chin intake
249 Auxiliary front spar	282 Flame damper exhaust
250 Hs293 radio-controlled	283 Port inboard mainwheel
glider-bomb	oleo leg (inward retracting)
251 1,300-lb (590-kg) thrust	284 Port outboard mainwheel
rocket motor housing	oleo leg (outward
252 1,100-lb (500-kg) warhead	retracting)
253 Wing control surfaces	285 Mainwheel axle
254 Tail-mounted aerial masts	286 Port outer mainwheel
(radio signal receivers)	287 Port inner mainwheel

(Above) An He 177A-3/R2 of Flugzeugführerschule (B) 16 and (below) an He 177A-5/R6 of II/KG 40 based at Bordeaux-Mérignac in June 1944

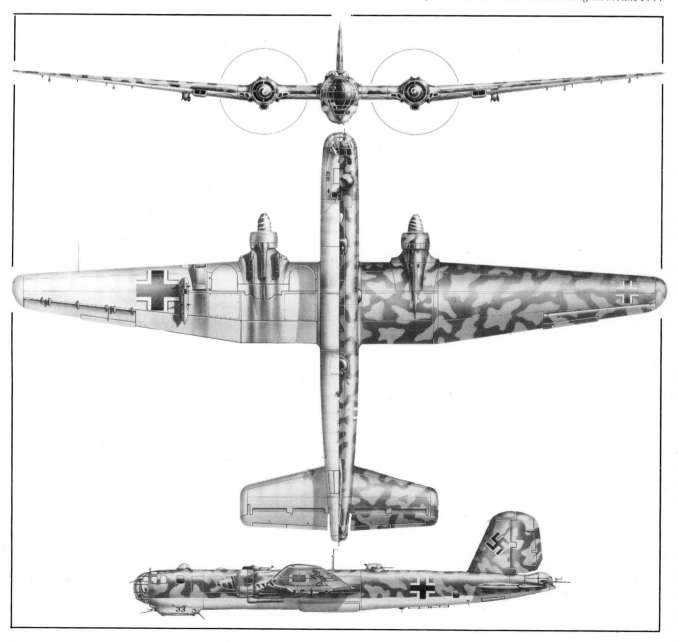

Heinkel He 177A-5 Specification

Power Plant: Two Daimler-Benz DB 610A-1/B-1 (A-1 port and B-1 starboard 24-cylinder liquid-cooled engines each rated at 2,950 hp at 2,800 rpm for take-off, 2,600 hp at 2,600 rpm at sea level and 2,750 hp at 2,600 rpm at 6,890 ft (2 100 m).

Performance: Max speed (at max loaded weight), 230 mph (370 km/h) at sea level, 270 mph (435 km/h) at 13,125 ft (4 000 m), 273 mph (440 km/h) at 18,700 ft (5 700 m), (at 80% max loaded weight), 248 mph (400 km/h) at sea level, 303 mph (487 km/h) at 18,700 ft (5 700 m); max cruise, 258 mph (415 km/h) at 19,685 ft (6 000 m), econ cruise, 210 mph (338 km/h) at 19,685 ft (6 000 m); max range with two Henschel Hs 293 missiles, 3,417 mls (5 500 km), with two Fritz X missiles, 3,100 mls (4 990 km); initial climb rate, 620 ft/min (3,15 m/sec); time to 6,560 ft (2 000 m), 8·8 min, to 13,125 ft (4 000 m), 19·8 min, to 19,685 ft (6 000 m), 36·5 min; service ceiling (with max load), 22,310 ft (6 800 m).

Weights: Empty equipped, 37,038 lb (16 800 kg); normal loaded, 59,966 lb (27 200 kg); max, 63,343 lb (31 000 kg).

Dimensions: Span, 103 ft 1¾ in (31,44 m); length, 72 ft 2 in (20,30 m); height, 20 ft 11¾ in (5,17 m); wing area, 1,097·92 sq ft (102,0 m²).

Armament: One 7,9-mm MG 81J machine gun with 2,000 rounds on spherical mounting in glazed nose, one 20-mm MG 151 cannon with 300 rounds in forward ventral gondola position, two 7,9-mm machine guns with 2,000 rpg in rear ventral gondola position, two 13-mm MG 131 machine guns with 750 rpg in remotely-controlled forward dorsal barbette, one 13-mm MG 131 machine gun with 750 rounds in electrically-operated aft dorsal turret and one 20-mm MG 151 cannon with 300 rounds in tail position. (He 177A-5/R2) Sixteen 110-lb (50-kg) SC 50, four 551-lb (250-kg) SC 250 or two 1,102-lb (500-kg) SC 500 general-purpose bombs internally, or two LMA III parachute sea mines, LT 50 torpedoes, Henschel Hs 293 or FX 1400 Fritz X missiles externally.

impression of the sensitivity of the He 177 to air turbulence. On attaining 9,840 ft (3 000 m) the change of altitude and engine power to settle into maximum continuous cruise necessitated a push force of some 20 lb (9,0 kg) before the new flight condition was trimmed out. A check of stability showed it to be positive about all axes but the controls were all remarkably light for so large an aircraft. Indeed, I had the inescapable feeling that the elevator was *dangerously* light and as I was all too well aware from intelligence reports that there had been a number of cases of He 177s breaking up in the air, I decided to treat this control very gently.

I then began a cautious exploration of the aircraft's diving characteristics. The original specification of 1936 that had given birth to the *Greif* had called for sufficient structural strength to permit medium angle diving attacks, but the Stuka mentality had been so inculcated in the minds of the *Oberkommando der Luftwaffe* that, after prototype construction had reached an advanced stage, the RLM's Technical Department had insisted that the capability to perform medium angle diving attacks was insufficient and that it was desirable that this *heavy bomber* should be capable of performing 60 deg diving attacks! In order to withstand the tremendous stresses imposed during the pull-out from such a dive on an aircraft of the He 177's size some substantial structural strengthening had been called for and the vicious upward weight spiral that had started when it had been found that the surface evaporation cooling system was impractical* took another turn.

I first eased the He 177 from a trimmed level flight speed of 186 mph (300 km/h) into a dive to 248 mph (400 km/h), this

---

The original design utilised a system of surface evaporation cooling to augment orthodox radiators, but despite an immense amount of research it had been found necessary to provide orthodox radiators large enough to offer sufficient cooling without being supplemented by surface evaporation. The larger radiators naturally raised airframe drag, reducing in consequence both speed and range. In order to maintain the specified range it had therefore become necessary to provide additional fuel cells in the wings. These, in turn, had necessitated structural strengthening with attendant increases in weight and further reductions in anticipated performance.

Heinkel He 177A-5 Greif Cockpit Equipment and Instrumentation Key:

1 Starter switch (port outer)
2 Starter switch (port inner)
3 Starter switch (starboard inner)
4 Starter switch (starboard outer)
5 Starter fuel priming button (Starboard pump)
6 Starter fuel priming button (port pump)
7 Wing de-icing lever
8 Oil filter cleaning levers (inner pair)
9 Engine OFF switch (port outer)
10 Engine OFF switch (port inner)
11 Engine OFF switch (starboard inner)
12 Engine OFF switch (starboard outer)
13 Spark plug cleaning levers (outer pair)
14 Alternative D/F position indicator (see No 81)
15 Starter fuel hand pump
16 Starter fuel pressure gauge
17 Intercom ON/OFF
18 Dive-brake trimming switch (often deleted)
19 Aileron trim handwheel
20 Elevator trim handwheel
21 Rudder trim handwheel
22 FuG 25 switch panel
23 Engine clutch (coupling) levers
24 Throttles
25 Clutch lever (port linked engines)
26 Clutch lever (starboard linked engines)
27 Frequency tuning clamp
28 Ignition switches
29 Undercarriage position indicators
30 Oxygen pressure gauge
31 Oxygen contents gauge
32 Fire extinguisher levers
33 Visual homing indicator
34 Fine-coarse altimeter (partly obscured by l/h control horn)
35 Airspeed indicator (obscured by l/h control horn)
36 B-Knopf XI pilot's bomb release button (on l/h control horn)
37 Artificial horizon
38 'Patin' radio compass (partly obscured by l/h control horn)
39 Pitot head heating indicator (obscured by l/h control horn)
40 Fowler flap warning lamp
41 Hinged instrument panel handgrip
42 Blind-approach indicator
43 Altimeter (obscured by control horn)
44 Control horn locking button
45 Chronometer
46 Variometer (partly obscured by control column arm)
47 Emergency turn-and-bank indicator
48 Internal rear-view mirrors (port and starboard)
49 Inward-hinged window panels (2)
50 Hinge levers
51 Engine fire warning lamps (port and starboard)
52 Side-window anti-glare curtains
53 Jettisonable roof panels (2)
54 Jettison levers
55 Dive-bomber sight support clamp (stowed)
56 Roof panel anti-glare curtains
57 Searchlight/landing light switch
58 Identification lights switch
59 Pilot's instrument panel illumination switch
60 Engine control panel illumination switch
61 Internal lighting switch
62 Navigator's station light switch
63 De-icing air heater/ blowers switches and indicator
64 Compass stabilizer switch
65 Auxiliary identification lights switch
66 Tail heating cut-out switch
67 Pitot head heating switch
68 Undercarriage switch
69 Main cockpit illumination
70 Fowler flap switch
71 Main auto-pilot switch
72 Signalling equipment push-button
73 Instrument panel illumination dimmer switch
74 Stuvi 5B dive-bomber sight (stowed)
75 Dive-bomber sight release lever
76 Emergency bomb-release lever
77 Emergency fuel jettison lever (port tail vent)

78 Emergency fuel jettison
  lever (starboard tail vent)
79 Smoke discharge lever
80 Auto-pilot emergency
  override button
81 Main D/F position indicator
82 Stand-by compass
83 Main circuit-breaker panel
84 MG 81 retaining clamp
85 MG 81 7,9-mm machine
  gun (A1-Stand)
86 Ring mounting with fabric
  cuff
87 Offset (horizontal)
  ring-and-bead sight
88 Cartridge casing and link
  duct
89 Ammunition feed
90 Flexible chute
91 Control column arm pivot
  point
92 Auto-pilot turn switch
93 Control column arm
  (pivots 180 deg to bomb-
  aimer's position)
94 Vertical drift guide wires
95 Propellor pitch position
  indicators (port and
  starboard) (partly obscured
  by control column)
96 Propellor pitch switches
  (on control column)
97 Directional gyro (partly
  obscured by control
  column)

98 Repeater compass (partly
  obscured by control
  column)
99 Rudder pedals
100 Pilot's oxygen supply
101 Adjustable pilot's seat
  (6-mm armour)
102 Armrest
103 Bomb-aimer's seat-back
  (lowered to form bombing
  couch)
104 Foot-rest
105 Bomb-aimer's seat cushion
106 Bomb-aimer's back-up
  rudder stirrups
107 Lotfe 7D bombsight and
  true-vision panel
108 FuG 203 control column
  (Hs 293 radio-guidance)
109 Bomb-arming lever (on
  forward face of ZSK box)
110 Aircraft true-speed indicator
111 Wind speed indicator
112 Height correction indicator
113 ZSK 244A bomb fusing
  panel
114 RAB 14d bomb-sequence
  selector panel
115 Engine control console
  lighting
116 Console lighting switch
117 Back-up throttles
118 Turn-and-bank indicator
119 Variometer

120 Air speed indicator (height
  compensated for bombing)
121 Double boost pressure
  gauges (port and starboard)
122 Reduction gear oil double
  pressure gauge (port and
  starboard)
123 Engine RPM counters
  (port engines)
124 Engine RPM counters
  (starboard engines)
125 Fuel consumption selector
  switch
126 Fuel consumption gauge
127 Oil contents gauge
128 Oil contents selector switch
129 Coolant temperature gauges
  (port)
130 Coolant temperature gauges
  (starboard)
131 External air temperature
132 Oil temperature gauges
  (port)
133 Oil temperature gauges
  (starboard)
134 Hydraulic pump pressure
  gauge
135 Fuel and oil combined
  pressure gauges (port)
136 Fuel and oil combined
  pressure gauges (starboard)
137 Hydraulic pump pressure
  gauge switch
138 Hydraulic reservoir pressure
  gauge

139 Warning klaxon OFF switch
140 Fuel warning lamp
  (reserve: red)
141 Fuel warning lamp (full:
  green)
142 Bleed tank contents gauge
143 Fuel pump automatic
  switches
144 Fuel contents gauges
  (inner wing tanks)
145 Fuel contents gauges
  (fuselage tanks)
146 Fuel contents gauges
  (outer wing tanks)
147 Undercarriage emergency
  hand pump
148 Emergency reserve hydraulic
  pressure gauge
149 Reserve-tank pump
  automatic switches
150 Reserve-tank pump manual
  switch covers (3)
151 Reserve-tank pump
  indicators (3)
152 Identification diagram and
  tables
153 Compressed air tank
  switch
154 Intercom junction panel
155 Smoke discharge equipment
  selector panel
156 Warning klaxon
157 Oxygen contents gauge
158 Oxygen pressure gauge

Changing a propeller on the port Daimler-Benz DB 610 power plant of an He 177A-5/R6 bomber of II Gruppe of Kampfgeschwader 40 at Bordeaux-Mérignac in the spring of 1944 when the unit was engaged in reconnaissance over the Atlantic

calling for a push force of about 25 lb (11,3 kg). The controls heavied up only slightly and response was still good, particularly on the elevator. I pushed the speed up to 323 mph (520 km/h) and there was very little increase in control heaviness, pull out from this trimmed speed at 2 g being possible with two fingers of one hand. From that moment on, the accelerometer became the object of my constant attention when flying the He 177!

Since the permissible pull-out acceleration was 2·3 g with a flying weight of 26·57 tons (27 tonnes), it was obviously vital to know the exact flying weight of the He 177 at all times. The aircraft had an automatic pull-out device and an acceleration warning apparatus fitted, but it really was somewhat nail-biting to have to treat a giant like this immense Heinkel bomber as though it were made of glass. The He 177 must surely remain a monument to the incredibly blind adherence of the Germans to the dive bombing mode of attack because it had served them so handsomely during the opening phases of the war; dive bombing in a Junkers Ju 87 was one thing but in a monster like the He 177 it was little short of ludicrous.

An impression of fragility

The stalling characteristics of the He 177 in the clean state were mild. There was a pronounced buffet at 115 mph (185 km/h) before the nose dropped straight at 112 mph (180 km/h). With flaps and undercarriage lowered, however, the aircraft buffeted violently at 87 mph (140 km/h) before the nose dropped at 84 mph (135 km/h). The buffet experienced in this landing configuration was so very violent that I really had some concern about possible structural damage. Somehow, the He 177

always conveyed an impression of fragility despite its size.

On the glide down to circuit altitude at 137 mph (220 km/h), I checked out the trim changes resulting from lowering the undercarriage and flaps but in neither case were there any. The glide angle with engines throttled back at 106 mph (170 km/h) was very flat, this making touch-down easy because there was very little change of attitude to be made from the powered approach. But this had its disadvantages, as I was soon to discover, because the final turn-in to land had to be made so far out from the airfield and this, combined with poor view in the turn, made it extremely difficult to line up with the runway. The final stages of the approach with power could be made at 99 mph (160 km/h), the throttles having to be eased back just a little at the runway threshold for the He 177 to land itself.

The aircraft tended to roll along the tarmac with rather less deceleration than might have been expected and firm use of the brakes was called for. Never being impressed with the brakes fitted to German aircraft I was even less so with those of the He 177. They seemed inadequate for the job of stopping such a large aeroplane and if applied harshly would judder and set up an uneven swing that could come frighteningly near to getting out of hand. The prospect of a ground loop was anything but cheering when one considered the Heinkel bomber's history of undercarriage troubles, and the PoW who, a year or two before, had claimed that the He 177 could use relatively small airfields without difficulty must truly have been stretching his imagination.

To assess the value of the *Greif* to the Third Reich as an operational aircraft is not difficult. It was Germany's only genuine production four-engined bomber, an immense amount of production capacity was devoted to building well over a thousand aircraft of this type and it need never have been built for by the time it was considered fit for operational service there was no real requirement for it. Of course, hindsight is cheap and it is to be admitted that the original requirement to which it was designed was viable enough and that it *could* have provided the *Luftwaffe* with the weapon to mount and maintain a large-scale strategic bombing offensive. The *Oberkommando der Luftwaffe* took a calculated risk, gambling that the production of shorter-range medium bombers in sufficiently large numbers might deter Britain and France from going to the aid of Poland. When it became obvious that this gamble had not come off the sands of time were running out fast. The technical concept of the He 177 was fascinating, but it had become a muddle of conflicting operational staff requirements which gave birth to the inevitable chain of teething troubles, design compromises and, in the end, mediocrity. Had real energy been displayed in erasing the shortcomings of the He 177 at a sufficiently early stage, the story could well have been very different.

During interrogation of Dr Ernst Heinkel at the end of WW II, I suggested to him that his organisation had seemed to enjoy more success with smaller aeroplanes than with large ones. His face displayed some annoyance when he replied that I must be referring to "that accursed 177". He associated Ernst Udet, the former *Generalluftzeugmeister*, in his mind with the whole disastrous story, and in particular the demand for a 60-deg diving attack capability which he blamed on Udet's influence. Heinkel himself had not been very closely involved

with the original design of the He 177. Dipl-Ing Heinrich Hertel had been Heinkel's Technical Director and Chief of Development during the initial development of the bomber but had left the Heinkel organisation in March 1939, and his departure at that juncture had not augured well for the future of the aircraft. In fact, in November 1942, Hertel had returned to Heinkel as a *Reichsluftfahrtministerium* Deputy with full powers to reorganise the development of the He 177. But it proved to be a case of closing the stable door after the horse had bolted, and Ernst Heinkel summed up his feelings when he said to me: "I even look more kindly on the He 111Z* than that 177!"

For my part, after putting in quite a few hours on the RAE's He 177A-5 on 20, 21 and 22 September 1944, and reacquainting myself with the aircraft in August 1945 when I tested another example of the He 177A-5 at Schleswig, the *Greif* went down in my book as a loser. I instinctively felt it to be unreliable and it was one of the very few German aircraft of the period that I tested that I did not *enjoy* flying. The aircraft originally acquired at Blagnac was flown quite frequently at Farnborough until November 1944, and then infrequently until 20 February 1945 when it was delivered to Boscombe Down. I was told that it was later shipped to the USA but have no idea of its ultimate fate.

*The so-called Heinkel-Zwilling (Heinkel-Twin), a product of the imagination of Generaloberst Udet and possibly the most improbable aircraft to attain service status during WW II, was a transport and glider tug created by joining two He 111H-6 fuselages, complete with stub wing centre sections, engines and tail assemblies, by means of a new constant-chord wing section which mounted a fifth engine.

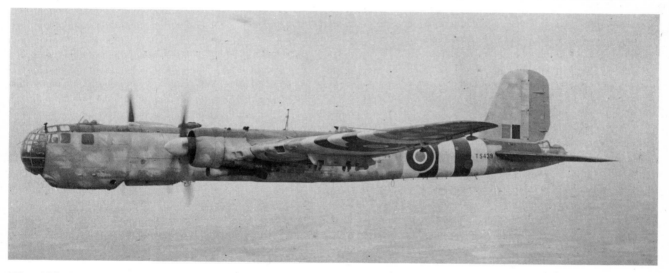

(Above) The He 177A-5/R6 under test from Farnborough in 1944, and (below) the fourth He 177A-7 after capture by US forces, this sub-type having extended wings, DB 613 engines and equipment changes to suit it for the high-altitude bombing rôle

MESSERSCHMITT ME 262

I F ASKED TO NOMINATE the most formidable combat aircraft to evolve in World War II, I would unhesitatingly propose Messerschmitt's Me 262. I say "unhesitatingly" advisedly, despite having flown the Spitfire in virtually all of its variants, the Mosquito, the Lancaster, the Mustang, and even Mitsubishi's Zero-Sen; all warplanes that might be considered as contenders for this accolade. Dubbed unofficially and not entirely appropriately the *Schwalbe*, or Swallow, a bird popularly regarded as a harbinger of summer, the Me 262 was also to receive the appellation of *Sturmvogel*, or Stormy Petrel, which was perhaps more suitable in view of the storms that it was to weather before finally succumbing to the pressure of events that it could no longer influence.

If the Me 262 was a harbinger of anything it was the future in so far as fighter design technology was concerned. It was a fantastic aeroplane from several aspects, and its eleventh hour début in the finale to the *Götterdämmerung* of Germany's Third Reich provided as dramatic a movement as any the great Wagner himself could have composed. In this case, however, the "composer" was one Professor Willy Messerschmitt, whose Bf 109 fighter, after blooding over Spain, had provided most of the vertebræ of the *Luftwaffe's* spinal column throughout the entire war. The same fertile brain had given birth to the Bf 110 and the Me 410, both very useful twin-engined combat aircraft, but its *pièce de résistance* was unquestionably the Me 262, which was both turbojet-driven and swept-winged — a truly startling combination in 1944.

This remarkable creation had stemmed from design studies initiated by Willy Messerschmitt in the autumn of 1938 for an airframe to be powered by two of the then quite revolutionary and still largely theoretical axial-flow gas turbines that were being evolved by the Bayerische Motoren-werke (BMW). It was destined to fly for the first time, however, on 18 April 1941 powered by a Jumo 210G piston engine, having lost out in the race — of the existence of which the participants were unaware — for the distinction of being the world's first twin-turbojet aircraft to get airborne, this claim to fame having been gained 16 days prior to the Me 262's piston-engined début by the rather less sophisticated — from the aerodynamic viewpoint — Heinkel He 280.

The decision to gain a working knowledge of the characteristics of the Me 262 airframe by flying it with a piston engine, if the result of *force majeure* (ie, non-availability of flight-cleared turbojets), at least permitted the proving of its several novel features, such as the mating of a near-triangular section fuselage with a wing embodying a swept outer panel and automatic leading-edge slats, without complicating matters by simultaneously testing totally new and virtually untried power plants. A full 15 months were to elapse before the Me 262 was to effect its first successful flight on turbojet power, this event in fact taking place at 08.40 hours on 18 July 1942 with *Flugkapitän* Fritz Wendel at the controls.

The vicissitudes of the Me 262 from that point until Germany's final collapse have been well documented, and it suffices to say that the attitude of high-level officialdom towards this epoch-marking warplane ran the full gamut from indecisiveness, coloured strongly by an unwillingness to relinquish the orthodox, to a desire to jettison virtually every other aircraft manufacturing programme in order to produce the maximum possible numbers of this radical aeroplane. In so far as the Me 262 itself was concerned, it was to be expanded in capability from its diurnal fair-weather air superiority rôle, for which it was primarily intended, to fighter-bomber and ground support tasks, and, in two-seat form, conversion training and nocturnal interception. Oddly enough, in view of its comparative rarity, it was with this last-mentioned version that I made my first acquaintance with the Me 262.

A sinister beauty

I had arrived with the RAE team from Farnborough at Schleswig airfield, just after the capitulation and while the last pocket of German resistance was still holding out at nearby Flensburg, and here saw for the first time Messerschmitt's much-discussed jet fighter — actually an Me 262B-1a/U1 (*Werk-Nr* 111 980), an adaptation for night fighting of the tandem two-seat training version. I was immediately struck by its beautiful yet sinister lines which

reminded me vividly of those of a shark. I was very keen to get airborne in this aircraft, but interrogation of some of the *Luftwaffe* pilots led our team to proceed with some caution.

While obviously proud of the Me 262, the German pilots were equally obviously somewhat apprehensive of it and especially of the two-seat night fighting version! As far as we could ascertain their worries were twofold. Firstly, the turbojets were unreliable and had, we were told, an overhaul life of a mere 10 hours and a total life of no more than 25 hours. This was bad enough, but all the records had been hurriedly destroyed before our arrival, and thus we had no means of knowing how many hours any engine had already run. Secondly, the single-engine safety speed on take-off was daunting; an engine failure before 180 mph (290 km/h) had been attained produced dire results. In fact, accident fatalities on Me 262s had been appalling, particularly among the night fighter boys flying the heavier model, although there had also been just as fair a share of nasty prangs with the single-seat version when laden with bombs.

Since Schleswig airfield was the RAE's collection point for preparing German aircraft for ferrying back to Farnborough, we soon had a goodly assortment of Me 262s gathered there

(Above) An Me 262A-1a of the Kommando Nowotny, the Luftwaffe's first fully-fledged Me 262-equipped interceptor unit, and (below) the Me 262C-1a Heimatschützer I (Home Protector I) taking-off with the aid of a Walter R II-211/3 rocket motor in the rear fuselage. (head of opposite page) An Me 262A-1a photographed in May 1946 after reconstruction in the USA by the Hughes Aircraft Company

and selected the least weary-looking for the first test flights. We were still anything but impressed, however, by the information gleaned from the *Luftwaffe* pilots at Schleswig, and concluded that we should augment this by getting hold of one of the Messerschmitt test pilots. In this we were extraordinarily lucky for Messerschmitt's chief research test pilot, Gerd Lindner, had fallen into Allied hands and was promptly made available to us for interrogation.

It was the end of May when I interviewed Lindner, and I was immediately impressed by the depth of his technical knowledge. He had been concerned with the Me 262 flight development programme almost from its inception as Fritz Wendel had performed only limited testing on the Me 262 in its turbojet-driven form before his retirement, and from that time Lindner had been chief pilot on the project. From May 1944, as a result of nervous tension, Lindner had undergone an enforced two-month lay-off, and two other Messerschmitt test pilots, Karl Baur and Ludwig Hoffmann, had carried on the flight development programme until his return in August, when he made the first flight tests with a 2,205-lb (1 000-kg) bomb load, and, later, the first take-offs with the so-called *Heimatschützer I* (Home Protector I) version in which a Walter R II-211/3 bi-fuel rocket motor was mounted in the tail. He had made the first *Heimatschützer* test, incidentally, only three months before our first meeting. Armed with the information culled from Gerd Lindner, flying the Me 262 did not appear too daunting.

My first cursory glance around the cockpit of the Me 262 had revealed what was, by 1945 standards, a complex but neat layout. The dashboard carried the flight instruments on the left and the engine gauges on the right. The left console carried the throttles, fuel cocks, trimmers, ancillary controls and their emergencies, while the right had the electronics, starters, and radio equipment. All this compared pretty closely with British practice. Fuel tankage was 198 Imp gal (900 l) in the forward main tank with a similar quantity in the rear main, while the forward auxiliary tank accommodated 37 Imp gal (170 l) with up to 132 Imp gal (600 l) in the aft auxiliary, this load resulting in an all-up weight of 15,322 lb (6 950 kg) for the Me 262A-1, which brought the CG to within one per cent of the aft limit. The fuel was 87 octane

petrol with a five per cent mix of lubricating oil, and the Riedel two-stroke starter motor ran on the same fuel.

Starting proved to be a two-handed job once all the necessary starting switches had been actuated. The right hand had to depress the requisite starter lever to prime the starter motor for three or four seconds before pulling the lever upwards, and if the starter motor fired then this lever was held up until 2,000 rpm were attained. Just beside the lever was a button which had to be depressed by the right thumb to engage a low-reading rev counter. Meanwhile, as the revs crept up to between 800 and 1,000 per minute, the left hand had to press the button on the throttle to inject fuel into the main engine until ignition was obtained, pressure on the button being maintained until 2,500 rpm were reached. At 2,000 rpm the throttle could be gradually advanced until the pawl dropped into the idling gate, and then the right hand could release the starter motor lever.

At this stage the ballet of the hands really had to get into its stride, for the right hand had momentarily to release the rev counter button to flit across the cockpit and switch on the fuel cock near the throttle lever, the latter meanwhile still being clutched by the left hand which was also depressing the button at its apex. Once either fuel cock was "on", the right hand had to be transferred across the cockpit once more at a rate of knots back to the rev counter button which

The general arrangement drawing on the opposite page depicts an Me 262A-1b of 3./JG 7 based at München-Riem in the early spring of 1945. The photograph immediately above depicts Me 262A-1a fighters of the Kommando Nowotny and the similar aircraft seen below are believed to have been serving with I/KG(J) 54 at Giebelstadt

(Left) An Me 262A-1a in flight, this same aircraft being illustrated at the foot of the page, and (right) a close-up view of the cockpit of the Me 262 which afforded the pilot an outstanding field of view

had to be depressed until 3,000 rpm were reached and at which, in theory, the engine could idle safely. This unbelievably complex procedure with all its demands on manual dexterity then had to be repeated for the other engine, and the contortions necessary were aided in no way by the narrowness of the cockpit and the fact that the starter levers and fuel cocks were well aft on the consoles.

Underpowered but exciting

Once the rigmarole of engine starting had been completed, and assuming that both engines *were* functioning, the process of taxi-ing could begin. This called for very restrained movement of the throttles to ensure that the limiting jetpipe temperature of 650°C (1,202°F) was not exceeded, but once 6,000 rpm were reached the governor cut in and throttle movement could be accelerated. View from the cockpit was excellent and every upper part of the aircraft was within the pilot's field of vision. The mainwheel brakes were operated, as on all German aircraft, by toe action, and the Me 262 embodied the somewhat odd feature of a hand-operated nosewheel brake, which, I assume, was needed when the aircraft was fully loaded, German brakes never seeming too positive in their action.

The take-off preparations were simple enough. The elevator had to be trimmed nose heavy, and the flaps set at 20 deg, this angle being indicated on each flap upper surface. There was an elevator trimmer gearing lever mounted on the control column, and this had a course setting for take-off and landing, and a fine setting for high-speed flight. After lining up the aircraft on the runway, the engines were opened up to 8,500 rpm on the brakes, and a check was made that the *Zwiebel* (Onion), as the exhaust cone had been dubbed, was protruding from each orifice*. Full power of 8,700 rpm was then applied and a quick check was made on jetpipe temperature, burner pressure, and fuel pressure. A five per cent drop in fuel pressure meant an aborted take-off. At full power fumes or smoke invariably penetrated the cockpit, and as the canopy had to be closed for take-off the sensation was, to say the least, disturbing. The nosewheel was raised at 100 mph (160 km/h), and the aircraft pulled gently off at

---

* This so-called "Onion" sometimes detached itself from its mounting, sealing off the exhaust orifice and producing a flame-out. The tremendous asymmetric drag thus created invariably resulted in the aircraft skidding sideways with the tailplane in the "fuselage shadow" and thus ineffective. Few pilots succeeded in recovering from the ensuing dive.

The Me 262A-1a (Werk-Nr 110 025) illustrated below belonged to the Kommando Nowotny, *the first fully-fledged Me 262A-equipped interceptor unit of the* Luftwaffe. *This view shows well the exceptionally clean lines possessed by this, the "most formidable combat aircraft to evolve in World War II".*

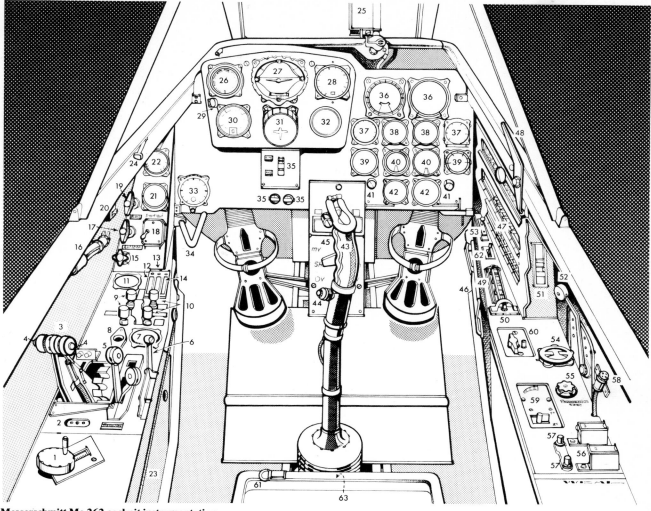

Messerschmitt Me 262 cockpit instrumentation

1 Handwheel for rudder trimming
2 Contact for pilot's gloves (electric heating)
3 Power lever
4 Pressbuttons for starting device
5 Switch lever for fuel cock battery
6 Lever for tailplane adjustment
7 Tailplane position indicator
8 Master battery cut-off switch
9 Contactor switch for landing flaps
10 Contactor switch for undercarriage
11 Pressure gauge for compressed air
12 Indicator signal for port undercarriage
13 Indicator signal for nosewheel

14 Indicator signal for starboard undercarriage
15 Oxygen valve
16 Breathing tube
17 Emergency lever for landing flaps
18 Switch box for RATOG
19 Emergency handle for undercarriage
20 Knife switch (contactor) for jet orifice adjustment
21 Oxygen flow meter
22 Oxygen pressure gauge
23 Cable line for jettisoning RATOG
24 Ventilation (air vent) lever
25 Reflex (or: reflector) sight and base
26 Airspeed indicator
27 Turn-and-bank indicator combined with artificial horizon
28 Rate-of-climb indicator

29 Indicator signal for Pitot-head heating
30 Sensitive/coarse altimeter
31 Pilot's repeater compass
32 AFN indicator
33 Board clock
34 Nosewheel brake handle
35 Fire safety cut-out switches
36 RPM indicator
37 Gas pressure indicator
38 Injection pressure indicator
39 Gas temperature indicator
40 Oil pressure indicator
41 Residual level indicator
42 Fuel supply gauge
43 Control column
44 Pneumatic (gun) loading button
45 Fuse switchbox
46 Board (document) case holder
47 Main switchboard
48 Canopy jettison lever

49 Signal flare firing gear
50 Contactor for FuG 25a detonator charge
51 Deviation table
52 Bomb load emergency release
53 Switch for window-shield heating
54 Frequency switch
55 Frequency control for air-to-air communications set
56 Starting switch
57 Changing-over (or reversing) button for RPM indicator
58 Contact for pilot's helmet leads
59 Junction box (wall socket)
60 Control unit for R/T
61 Loop for seat-type parachute
62 Selector (or throw-over) switch for signal flare ammo
63 Pilot's seat adjusting gear

124 mph (200 km/h). Once airborne, it was necessary to raise the undercarriage and reduce flap deflection by 10 deg, immediately easing the stick forward until momentum built up to that all-important single-engine safety speed of 180 mph (290 km/h). The flaps could then be fully raised. This speed must surely have been engraved on every Me 262 pilot's heart!

The take-off run was long, and the aircraft gave one the feeling that it was underpowered, as indeed was the contemporary Meteor I. If one throttle was cut at 160 mph (260 km/h) the Me 262 went into a violent diving turn. Full

rudder was required to counteract the swing and roll, and backward stick pressure had to be applied to keep the nose up. This action had to be taken within two seconds or else the situation was disastrous. The rudder force involved was high. Initial climbing speed was 286 mph (460 km/h), and from 185 mph (300 km/h) upward the Me 262 really took the bit between its teeth and became a thoroughly exciting aeroplane to fly. The Jumo 004B turbojets tended towards the temperamental above 13,125 ft (4 000 m), at which altitude the fuel pumps had to be switched on to sustain combustion, and above 29,530 ft (9 000 m) it was considered

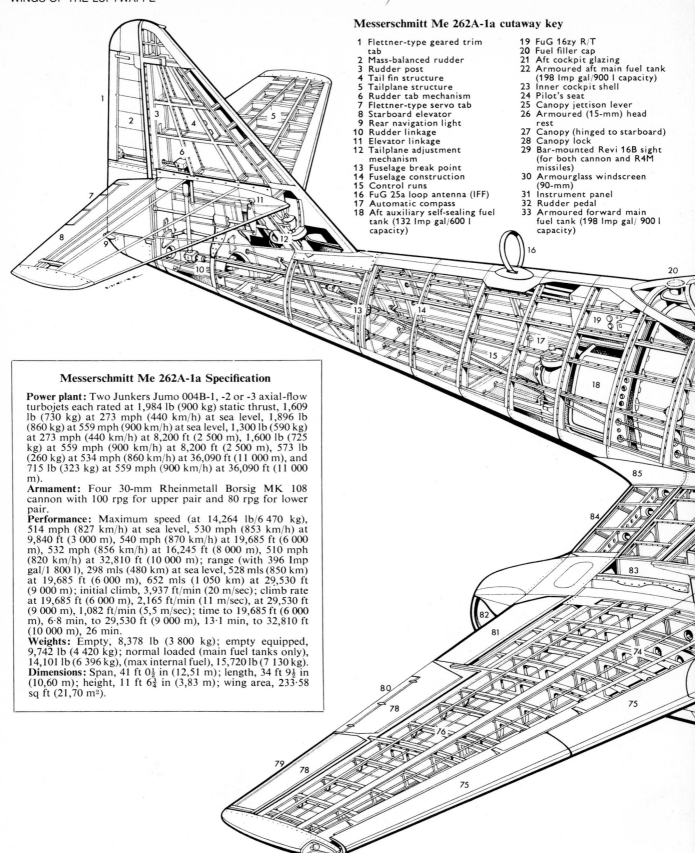

Messerschmitt Me 262A-1a cutaway key

1 Flettner-type geared trim tab
2 Mass-balanced rudder
3 Rudder post
4 Tail fin structure
5 Tailplane structure
6 Rudder tab mechanism
7 Flettner-type servo tab
8 Starboard elevator
9 Rear navigation light
10 Rudder linkage
11 Elevator linkage
12 Tailplane adjustment mechanism
13 Fuselage break point
14 Fuselage construction
15 Control runs
16 FuG 25a loop antenna (IFF)
17 Automatic compass
18 Aft auxiliary self-sealing fuel tank (132 Imp gal/600 l capacity)
19 FuG 16zy R/T
20 Fuel filler cap
21 Aft cockpit glazing
22 Armoured aft main fuel tank (198 Imp gal/900 l capacity)
23 Inner cockpit shell
24 Pilot's seat
25 Canopy jettison lever
26 Armoured (15-mm) head rest
27 Canopy (hinged to starboard)
28 Canopy lock
29 Bar-mounted Revi 16B sight (for both cannon and R4M missiles)
30 Armourglass windscreen (90-mm)
31 Instrument panel
32 Rudder pedal
33 Armoured forward main fuel tank (198 Imp gal/ 900 l capacity)

Messerschmitt Me 262A-1a Specification

Power plant: Two Junkers Jumo 004B-1, -2 or -3 axial-flow turbojets each rated at 1,984 lb (900 kg) static thrust, 1,609 lb (730 kg) at 273 mph (440 km/h) at sea level, 1,896 lb (860 kg) at 559 mph (900 km/h) at sea level, 1,300 lb (590 kg) at 273 mph (440 km/h) at 8,200 ft (2 500 m), 1,600 lb (725 kg) at 559 mph (900 km/h) at 8,200 ft (2 500 m), 573 lb (260 kg) at 534 mph (860 km/h) at 36,090 ft (11 000 m), and 715 lb (323 kg) at 559 mph (900 km/h) at 36,090 ft (11 000 m).

Armament: Four 30-mm Rheinmetall Borsig MK 108 cannon with 100 rpg for upper pair and 80 rpg for lower pair.

Performance: Maximum speed (at 14,264 lb/6 470 kg), 514 mph (827 km/h) at sea level, 530 mph (853 km/h) at 9,840 ft (3 000 m), 540 mph (870 km/h) at 19,685 ft (6 000 m), 532 mph (856 km/h) at 16,245 ft (8 000 m), 510 mph (820 km/h) at 32,810 ft (10 000 m); range (with 396 Imp gal/1 800 l), 298 mls (480 km) at sea level, 528 mls (850 km) at 19,685 ft (6 000 m), 652 mls (1 050 km) at 29,530 ft (9 000 m); initial climb, 3,937 ft/min (20 m/sec); climb rate at 19,685 ft (6 000 m), 2,165 ft/min (11 m/sec), at 29,530 ft (9 000 m), 1,082 ft/min (5,5 m/sec); time to 19,685 ft (6 000 m), 6·8 min, to 29,530 ft (9 000 m), 13·1 min, to 32,810 ft (10 000 m), 26 min.

Weights: Empty, 8,378 lb (3 800 kg); empty equipped, 9,742 lb (4 420 kg); normal loaded (main fuel tanks only), 14,101 lb (6 396 kg), (max internal fuel), 15,720 lb (7 130 kg).

Dimensions: Span, 41 ft 0½ in (12,51 m); length, 34 ft 9½ in (10,60 m); height, 11 ft 6¾ in (3,83 m); wing area, 233·58 sq ft (21,70 m²).

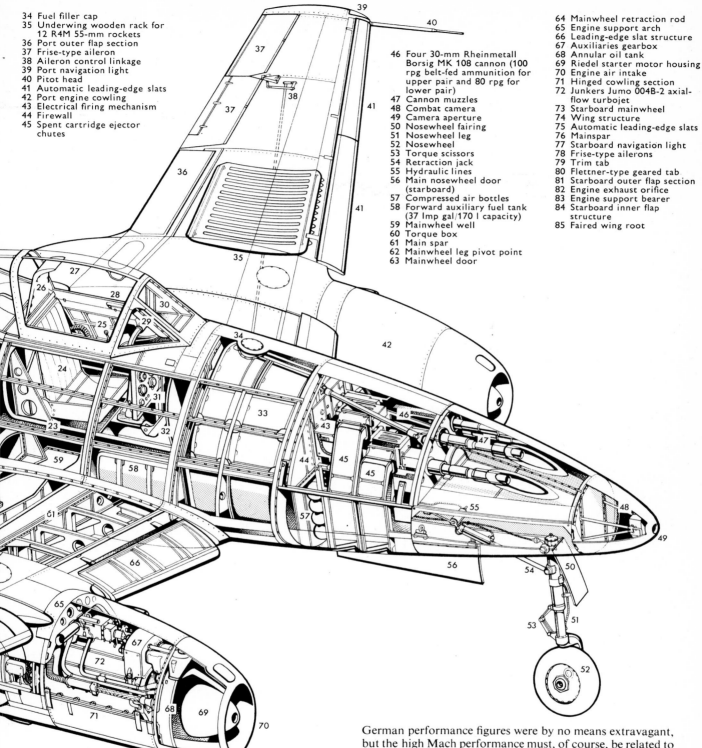

34 Fuel filler cap
35 Underwing wooden rack for 12 R4M 55-mm rockets
36 Port outer flap section
37 Frise-type aileron
38 Aileron control linkage
39 Port navigation light
40 Pitot head
41 Automatic leading-edge slats
42 Port engine cowling
43 Electrical firing mechanism
44 Firewall
45 Spent cartridge ejector chutes

46 Four 30-mm Rheinmetall Borsig MK 108 cannon (100 rpg belt-fed ammunition for upper pair and 80 rpg for lower pair)
47 Cannon muzzles
48 Combat camera
49 Camera aperture
50 Nosewheel fairing
51 Nosewheel leg
52 Nosewheel
53 Torque scissors
54 Retraction jack
55 Hydraulic lines
56 Main nosewheel door (starboard)
57 Compressed air bottles
58 Forward auxiliary fuel tank (37 Imp gal/170 l capacity)
59 Mainwheel well
60 Torque box
61 Main spar
62 Mainwheel leg pivot point
63 Mainwheel door

64 Mainwheel retraction rod
65 Engine support arch
66 Leading-edge slat structure
67 Auxiliaries gearbox
68 Annular oil tank
69 Riedel starter motor housing
70 Engine air intake
71 Hinged cowling section
72 Junkers Jumo 004B-2 axial-flow turbojet
73 Starboard mainwheel
74 Wing structure
75 Automatic leading-edge slats
76 Mainspar
77 Starboard navigation light
78 Frise-type ailerons
79 Trim tab
80 Flettner-type geared tab
81 Starboard outer flap section
82 Engine exhaust orifice
83 Engine support bearer
84 Starboard inner flap structure
85 Faired wing root

inadvisable to reduce revs below 6,000 per minute as to do so was to ensure a flame-out, and restarting could not be attempted above 13,125 ft (4 000 m)!

Our interest in the Me 262 at RAE Farnborough was threefold. Firstly, we were intrigued to discover if the performance really did match the capabilities claimed by the Germans; secondly we were anxious to discover the behaviour of the swept-wing configuration at high Mach numbers, and thirdly we wanted to know if this aircraft provided a good gun platform. We soon ascertained that the German performance figures were by no means extravagant, but the high Mach performance must, of course, be related to the contemporary state of the art, to use an Americanism. To place matters in perspective, it should be remembered that, in the same time scale, there were only two military jet aircraft in the UK, the Meteor I and the prototype Vampire. The former had a maximum safe Mach number of 0·8, and then the nose pitched up so strongly that speed fell away automatically, while the latter started trim change effects at speeds as low as Mach 0·74 with vigorous porpoising building up by Mach 0·78.

The Spitfire, on the other hand, had the remarkable maximum safe flight Mach number of 0·83, and I had dived

One of the six Me 262As assigned to the Naval Air Test Center at Patuxent River. These aircraft were allocated BuAer numbers, that illustrated being 121442. (below) An Me 262A-1 exhibited at Farnborough in the late autumn of 1945 as part of a display of captured German aircraft

one to Mach 0·86, although at that speed the aircraft was in a near vertical dive and completely out of control. Of course, the maximum safe flight Mach number is by no means that at which the aircraft can be employed tactically, or, in other words, at which combat manœuvres can be carried out. Gerd Lindner had told me that he had dived the Me 262 up to Mach 0·86, although above Mach 0·83 the research dives had been performed under strict control. Before take-off the elevator trim had been set by the aerodynamicists and not touched in flight other than in cases of dire emergency. Apparently the aircraft was dived from about 26,250 ft (8 000 m) at an angle between 20 and 25 deg until 620 mph (1 000 km/h) TAS was achieved at about 19,685 ft (6 000 m). At Mach 0·83 the nose started to drop and it was necessary to apply some 30 lb (14 kg) of pull on the stick with both hands. As the Mach number increased a violent buffeting set in, apparently coming from the aft portion of the cockpit canopy and producing an extremely alarming high-frequency banging. The aircraft meanwhile became progressively heavier in the nose, the stick pull necessary at Mach 0·86 increasing to about 100 lb (45 kg). Recovery was effected by holding the dive angle steady until the Mach number auto-

matically reduced with the decreasing altitude.

On the strength of these tests, the *Luftwaffe* pilots had been instructed not to exceed an airspeed of 596 mph (960 km/h) below 26,250 ft (8 000 m), more than 560 mph (900 km/h) being considered inadvisable above that altitude. They were also advised to set the elevator trimmer so that a slight initial push was required to enter a dive, and that the trimmer should not be used as an aid to recovery. Nevertheless, these instructions were sometimes forgotten in the heat of combat, and accidents happened.

Sinuous propensity

I carried out high Mach dives on the Me 262 up to a maximum of Mach 0·84, and these fully confirmed all Gerd Lindner's observations. The important thing, however, was that I had ascertained the tactical usability of the Me 262 up to Mach 0·82, and this capability had undoubtedly endowed Messerschmitt's fighter with a marked advantage over every other operational aircraft of WW II.

One of the flight characteristics plaguing early jet aircraft was the phenomenon known as directional snaking. Its probable cause was recognised as being airflow separation just forward of the tail section, this giving rise to a small-amplitude, short-period yawing oscillation. This compressibility effect did, of course, seriously impair the aircraft's tactical use as a stable gun platform, and we at Farnborough had experienced severe snaking trouble with the Meteor I above Mach 0·7. The attempts that were made to sort out this problem on the Meteor I make quite a saga, the problem of high Mach snaking being compounded by another undesirable form of sinuosity, rough air snaking, which seriously limited the Meteor's tactical use in the ground attack rôle.

Interrogation of Lindner had revealed an almost identical story of a lengthy trial-and-error process in attempting to eliminate the Me 262's tendency to snake. It had been ascertained that rough air snaking was due to a lack of effective fin area which was inherent in the design. Since the destabilising effect of the airscrew was missing, it had evidently seemed apparent that fin area could be reduced for a given stability, but in fact the loss of resultant damping had proved excessive. The Me 262's snaking characteristics had improved when the top third of the fin-and-rudder assembly had been removed, but the loss in rudder power had increased the single-engine safety speed to 200 mph (320 km/h), so this modification had been found unacceptable. We had had

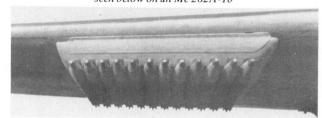

External ordnance loads sullied the aerodynamic purity of the Me 262: an SC 500 bomb and Borsig take-off assistance rockets are seen above on the Me 262 V10 and 12 R4M missiles on a wooden rack are seen below on an Me 262A-1b

(Above and below) An Me 262A-1 (Werk-Nr 111 711) which was surrendered by its pilot to US forces at Rhein-Main on 30 March 1945, and was subsequently flown by USAAF pilots for the compilation of a pilot's handbook on the type

In so far as the Luftwaffe was concerned, one of the greatest tragedies of WW II was the decision to adapt the Me 262 for the bombing rôle. Seen above is the Me 262A-2a with two 551-lb (250 kg) SC 250 bombs beneath the fuselage

similar results with an identical modification to the Meteor I, although these had not been quite so successful, as the nose of the Gloster fighter was much shorter than that of the Me 262 which acted as a counteracting fin, and made up for some of the loss of damping resulting from reduction of the tail fin area.

The high Mach snaking had been found to be due to induced rudder oscillation caused by variation in rudder hinge movement which tended to move the rudder to overbalance direction. The best way of combating this effect was by use of rudder auto stabilisation, as we discovered with the Meteor after the war had ended, but German experimentation had not progressed that far. The German development programme had gone no further than the thickening of the trailing edge of the fin-and-rudder assembly and the provision of strips of sheet metal which were bent outwards along this edge. The overall effect was better than that obtained with the Meteor I but inferior to that of the little Heinkel He 162.

The normal range of flight characteristics from aerobatic manœuvres to the stall revealed the Me 262 as a very responsive and docile aeroplane, leaving one with a confident impression of a first-class combat aircraft for both fighter and ground attack rôles. Harmony of control was pleasant,

with a stick force per *g* of 6 lb (2,72 kg) at mid CG position and a roll rate of 360 deg in 3·8 sec at 400 mph (645 km/h) at 5,000 ft (1 525 m). Maximum speed attainable in level flight on one engine was about 310 mph (500 km/h), and this called for application of one-third full rudder.

For landing the undercarriage could be lowered at 310 mph (500 km/h), but it was preferable to reduce speed to 250 mph (400 km/h) and throttle back to 5,000 rpm, thus counteracting the nose-up trim change as the wheels came down. I found it best, after lowering the undercarriage, to open up to 6,000-7,000 rpm and lower the flaps 20 deg at about 225 mph (350 km/h), turning in at 185 mph (300 km/h). When on finals it was advisable to apply full flap at 155 mph (250 km/h), reducing speed to 125 mph (200 km/h) for crossing the airfield boundary. The Me 262's landing run was long and was always accompanied by that unpleasant suspicion of fading brakes that one had with all German aircraft of the period. Lindner's distrust of the Jumo turbojets was obvious from his recommendation to approach high and steep, sideslipping in to land, but I found this technique to result in vigorous buffeting, and it was certainly not to be recommended as an operational practice.

That, then, was the Me 262, variously known as the *Schwalbe* and the *Sturmvogel*. But whatever the appellation, it was in my view unquestionably the foremost warplane of its day; a hard hitter which outperformed anything that we had immediately available but which, fortunately for the Allies, was not available to the *Luftwaffe* in sufficient numbers to affect drastically the course of events in the air over Europe. It was a pilot's aeroplane which had to be *flown* and not just heaved into the air. Basically underpowered and fitted with engines sufficiently lacking in reliability to keep the adrenalin flowing, it was thoroughly exciting to fly, and particularly so in view of its lack of an ejector seat. I was reminded vividly of this aircraft when I first flew the F-4 Phantom some 20 years later. This later-generation US aircraft offered its pilot that same feeling of sheer exhilaration, but the Phantom possessed the added attractions of safety and reliability which perhaps kept the pulse at a somewhat lower tempo than it attained when flying the Me 262 in those now-distant days of 1945.

One of the several examples of the Me 262A-1 that were assembled by the Czechoslovak aircraft industry in the immediate postwar years, this aircraft having been photographed at Olomouc in 1957

DORNIER DO 335

Whatever commodities the German aircraft industry found in short supply during the relatively brief and highly dramatic existence of the Third Reich, ingenuity was not to be numbered among them. To the conventionalist it was perhaps to seem in retrospect that German design teams had vied one with another in whimsicality; that development had been influenced more by caprice than by the normal processes of aeronautical research. It was to be mooted that German combat aircraft design revealed a less bigoted approach to the radical than that generally displayed abroad, a suggestion certainly supported by the audacity embodied by many of the progeny of German drawing boards. Indeed, today, some 30 years after the Third Reich finally expired, it may be seen clearly that a readier acceptance of the innovatory did exist in Germany; that this resulted in some of the most freakish aeroplanes of WW II, and that, much to

the confusion of the traditionalists, the majority of these freaks turned in startlingly good performances.

Among the more extravagant looking of these German digressions from what was considered the orthodox of the day was a quite remarkable and distinctly bizarre creation of the Dornier-Werke GmbH, which, during its brief existence, bore the singularly inappropriate popular appellation of *Pfeil* (Arrow). Few aircraft could have possessed more remote a resemblance to a slender pointed missile, but if hardly arrow-shaped and if æsthetically one of the least attractive fighters of its generation, it was certainly one of the fastest piston-engined fighters in the world ever to have attained production status. The Germans claimed a maximum speed in excess of 470 mph (756 km/h) for the single-seat version of the *Pfeil*, or Do 335 as it was officially known, and my experience with this fascinating warplane

(At head of page) The Do 335 V1 (CP + UA) photographed during its initial trials from Oberpfaffenhofen, and (below) the Do 335 V3 (T9 + ZH) which, the first prototype to be fitted with the definitive oil cooler and annular radiator, was transferred to the 1. Staffel of the Versuchsverband des Oberbefehlshabers der Luftwaffe *after completing the test programme at Oberpfaffenhofen.*

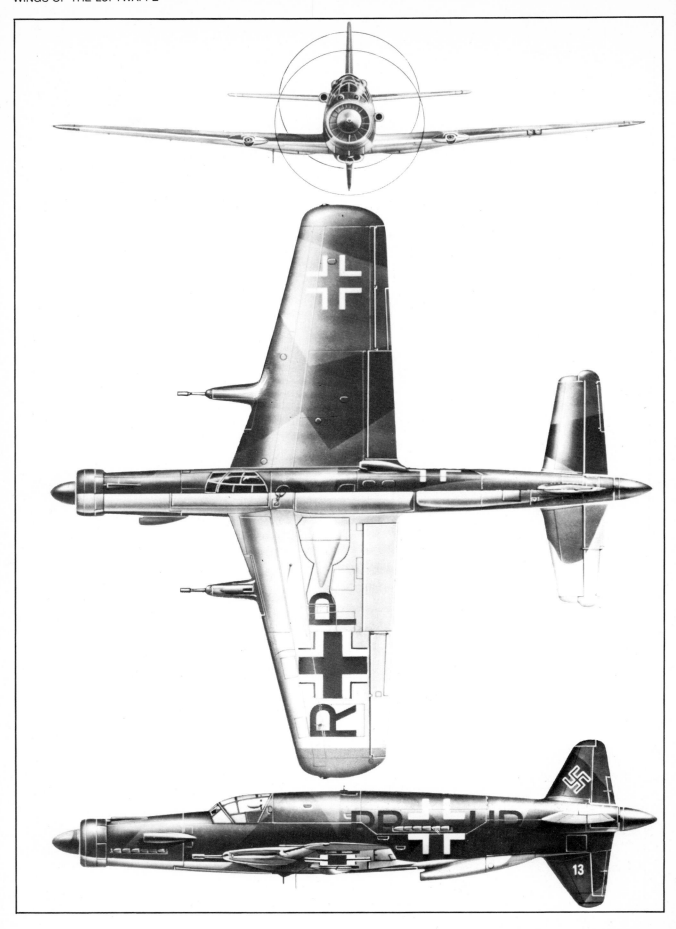

(Above and below right) The seventh pre-production Do 335A-O fighter-bomber, and (opposite page) the Do 335 V13, prototype for the Do 335B-1 day zerstörer. This differed essentially from the single-seat A-series in having an additional fuel cell substituted for the internal weapons bay and an augmented gun armament, two 30-mm MK 103 cannon being mounted in the wings, these pivoting downwards for ease of loading and maintenance. The V13 was externally similar to the V14 (prototype for the Do 335B-2) which, flight tested in France, differed only in items of equipment.

was to furnish little reason for disputing that claim.

The Do 335 was not exactly revolutionary as the tandem fore-and-aft engine arrangement — years later to be referred to as being of centre-line thrust concept — dated back to WW I, but of the several experimental twin-engined fighters flown with engines mounted fore and aft of the pilot, the Dornier warplane was the first to couple an orthodox tractor engine installation with an engine driving a pusher airscrew aft of the tail assembly. Prof-Dr Claudius Dornier first patented the arrangement in 1937, but it was not until late 1942 that the first metal was to be cut at Oberpfaffenhofen on prototypes of a warplane embodying this radical power plant arrangement, the first of these, the Do 335 V1, eventually making its initial flight on 26 October 1943. Production was too late getting into its stride to enable the Do 335, or *Ameisenbär* (Ant Eater) as it was dubbed by some pilots, to attain operational status with the *Luftwaffe*. It is therefore a matter for conjecture as to how this highly unusual warplane may have fared in combat, but although it may now seem that evaluation of the potential of the Do 335 after hostilities had terminated was of purely academic interest, at the RAE, at Farnborough during the second half of 1945 we were very interested indeed in assessing the handling qualities and performance produced by the combination of features incorporated in Dornier's strange warplane.

A massive warrior

I first saw the Dornier fighter at Farnborough during the summer of 1945 when a Do 335A-12 two-seat conversion trainer was flown in by one of our ferry team of test pilots specially selected for the task of collecting interesting captured German aircraft. My first impression was of a massive, tall aeroplane which looked as though it would need all the power that could be mustered by its two engines to move its bulk through the air. Viewing the aircraft head on, however, my impression changed to one of a sleek streamlined cigar carefully sandwiched between two neatly-cowled, highly-charged power units, the entire contraption being supported by a somewhat stalky undercarriage.

I had heard many stories, all second- or third-hand, of the Do 335's astonishingly high performance and also of its teething troubles. Particularly fascinating was the story that

when two prototypes came to grief the bodies of their pilots were found to be devoid of arms. The story, recounted to me by a German pilot, alleged that the loss of the upper limbs had resulted when the unfortunate victims had gripped two inclined levers at cockpit sill level and pulled them aft to activate the hood jettison system. This action released the hood effectively, but since the levers were *attached* to the hood, a firm grip meant, so the story went, that the hands and arms were wrenched off with the rapidly departing canopy. This story made something of an impression on me, and I clambered into the cockpit filled with curiosity. Sure enough, the notorious hood jettison levers were there.

Apart from its fore-and-aft engine arrangement the Do 335 had its share of unusual features, such as reversible pitch on the forward airscrew and an ejector seat. Of all-metal construction, the Do 335's trapezoidal stressed-skin wing featured 13 deg of taper on the leading edge, was built up around a single box spar, and carried variable-camber flaps inboard of the hydraulically-powered ailerons. The tailplane was of cruciform type and, together with the rear airscrew, would have provided a suicidal obstruction for bailing out but for the ejector seat, and even then provision was made for jettisoning the upper vertical tail surface and rear airscrew by means of explosive bolts which had to be actuated before the ejector seat was fired. The nose-mounted engine was provided with a neat annular nose radiator, the aft engine being cooled by a ventral scoop-type radiator and driving the pusher airscrew by means of a hollow extension shaft supported by three thrust races. The main fuel tank of 270·5 Imp gal (1 230 l) capacity was installed immediately aft of the cockpit and was supplemented by a pair of 68 Imp gal (310 l) self-sealing tanks in the wing centre section forward of the spar.

To the best of my knowledge, the Do 335 was only the second production piston-engined aircraft in the world to feature an ejector seat*, which, therefore, became the focal point of attention before my first flight. The drill for its use

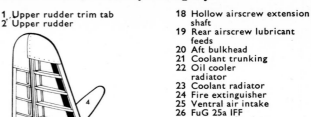

Dornier Do 335B-2 cutaway drawing key

1. Upper rudder trim tab
2. Upper rudder
18. Hollow airscrew extension shaft
19. Rear airscrew lubricant feeds
20. Aft bulkhead
21. Coolant trunking
22. Oil cooler radiator
23. Coolant radiator
24. Fire extinguisher
25. Ventral air intake
26. FuG 25a IFF
27. FuG 125a blind landing receiver

was hardly ideal for a speedy exit in an emergency. On the starboard side of the cockpit was a row of three buttons. If the first button was depressed a charge was exploded which, in theory, blew off the rear airscrew, the second button activating another charge which blew off the upper vertical tail surfaces, while the third button armed the ejector seat. The hood then had to be jettisoned manually and, finally, the seat was fired by squeezing a trigger on the arm rest. I do not know if an emergency ejection was ever made from a Do 335, and I suppose that in a real do-or-die situation one could have ejected without the preliminaries and played Russian roulette with the blades of the rear airscrew.

Although possessing lingering doubts regarding the viability of the ejection sequence, I found the Do 335 lively to fly, and right from the short take-off run under the smooth roar of the two Daimler-Benz DB 603s it afforded that

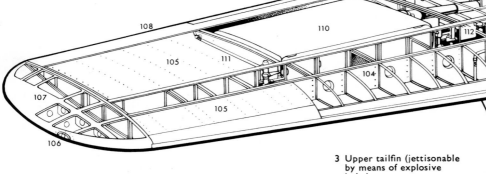

comforting feeling of being over powered, a gratifying sensation that one seldom experiences. Care had to be taken not to lift the nose too high on take-off as the ground clearance for the lower fin was strictly limited. Once airborne and the undercarriage selected UP, the pilot received an alarming thump right under his ejector seat as the nosewheel, which turned through 45 deg, retracted backwards into a bay immediately beneath the seat. The climb was very steep for such a large aircraft, and it was obviously capable of keeping right on up to well above 35,000 ft (10 670 m). Stability was

3. Upper tailfin (jettisonable by means of explosive bolts)
4. VDM airscrew of 10·83 ft (3,30 m) diameter
5. Airscrew spinner
6. Airscrew pitch mechanism
7. Starboard elevator
8. Elevator tab
9. Metal stressed-skin tailplane structure
10. Ventral rudder
11. Tail bumper
12. Tail bumper oleo shock-absorber
13. Ventral tailfin (jettisonable for belly landing)
14. Coolant outlet
15. Rear navigation light
16. Explosive bolt seatings
17. Rudder and elevator tab controls

28. Rear engine access cover latches
29. Exhaust stubs
30. Supercharger intake
31. Coolant tank
32. Engine bearer

The first ejector seat-equipped production piston-engined aircraft was the Heinkel He 219A

33 Aft Daimler-Benz DB 603E-1 12-cylinder inverted-Vee liquid-cooled engine rated at 1,800 hp for take-off and 1,900 hp at 5,905 ft (1 800 m)
34 Supercharger
35 Aft firewall
36 FuG 25a ring antenna
37 Fuel filler cap
38 Main fuel tank (270 Imp gal/1 230 l capacity)
39 Secondary ventral fuel tank
40 Two (9·9 Imp gal/45 l capacity) lubricant tanks (port for forward engine and starboard for rear engine)
41 Pilot's back armour
42 Rearview mirror in glazed teardrop
43 Headrest
44 Pilot's armoured ejector seat
45 Clear-vision panel
46 Jettisonable canopy (hinged to starboard)
47 Protected hydraulic fluid tank (9·9 Imp gal/45 l capacity)

66 Breech of nose-mounted MK 103 cannon
67 Engine bearer
68 Forward DB 603E-1 engine
69 MG 151 cannon blast tubes
70 Gun trough
71 Hydraulically-operated cooling gills
72 Coolant radiator (upper segment)
73 Oil cooler radiator (lower segment)
74 VDM airscrew of 11·48 ft (3,50 m) diameter
75 Airscrew spinner
76 MK 103 cannon port
77 Armoured radiator ring
78 Coolant tank (3·3 Imp gal/15 l capacity)
79 Exhaust stubs
80 Nosewheel oleo leg
81 Nosewheel scissors
82 Damper
83 Nosewheel
84 Mudguard
85 Retraction strut
86 Nosewheel door
87 MK 103 cannon ammunition tray

The massive broad-track undercarriage of Dornier's push-and-pull fighter is seen clearly in this view of the seventh pre-production Do 335A-0

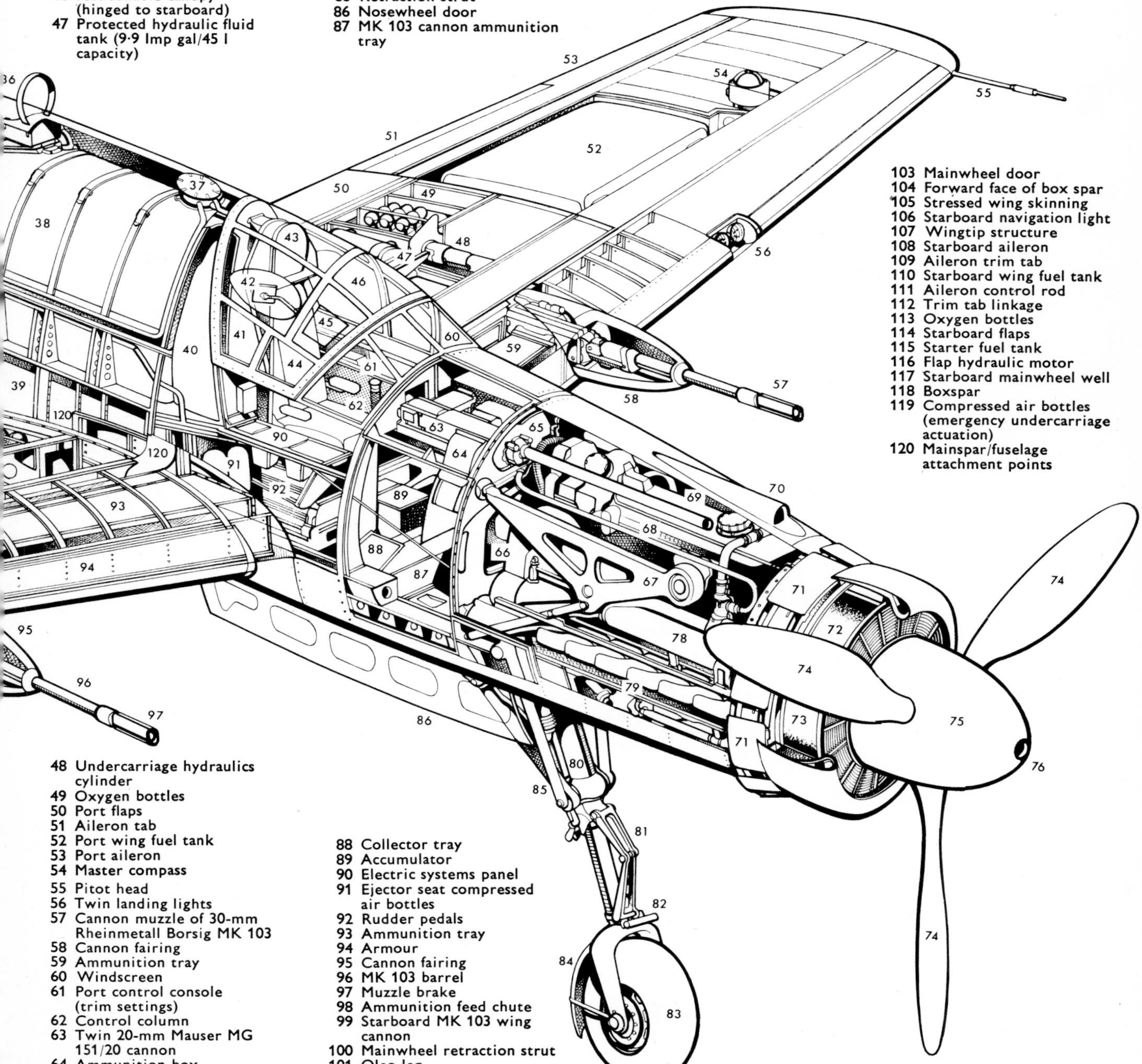

103 Mainwheel door
104 Forward face of box spar
105 Stressed wing skinning
106 Starboard navigation light
107 Wingtip structure
108 Starboard aileron
109 Aileron trim tab
110 Starboard wing fuel tank
111 Aileron control rod
112 Trim tab linkage
113 Oxygen bottles
114 Starboard flaps
115 Starter fuel tank
116 Flap hydraulic motor
117 Starboard mainwheel well
118 Boxspar
119 Compressed air bottles (emergency undercarriage actuation)
120 Mainspar/fuselage attachment points

48 Undercarriage hydraulics cylinder
49 Oxygen bottles
50 Port flaps
51 Aileron tab
52 Port wing fuel tank
53 Port aileron
54 Master compass
55 Pitot head
56 Twin landing lights
57 Cannon muzzle of 30-mm Rheinmetall Borsig MK 103
58 Cannon fairing
59 Ammunition tray
60 Windscreen
61 Port control console (trim settings)
62 Control column
63 Twin 20-mm Mauser MG 151/20 cannon
64 Ammunition box
65 Forward firewall

88 Collector tray
89 Accumulator
90 Electric systems panel
91 Ejector seat compressed air bottles
92 Rudder pedals
93 Ammunition tray
94 Armour
95 Cannon fairing
96 MK 103 barrel
97 Muzzle brake
98 Ammunition feed chute
99 Starboard MK 103 wing cannon
100 Mainwheel retraction strut
101 Oleo leg
102 Starboard mainwheel

73

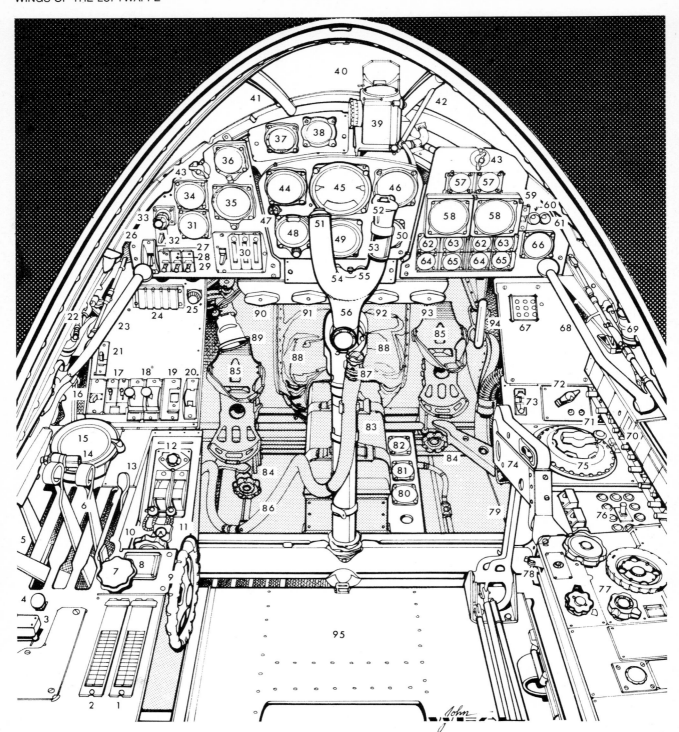

good about all axes but control harmony was poor. The powered ailerons gave a sharp rate of roll despite the 45 ft (13,70 m) plus of wing span, and aileron forces were in marked contrast to the heavy elevator and rudder forces.

The temptation to do a flat-out power run was irresistible in view of the German claim that this was the fastest piston-engined aircraft in the world, and my figures for the two-seat Do 335A showed a true airspeed of about 430 mph (692 km/h) at 18,000 ft (5 486 m) which was impressive by any standards. This inevitably led me to try the performance on each engine independently, the other being shut down and its airscrew feathered. The results of these tests were certainly not startling but revealed the fact that the Do 335 had a measurably better performance on the rear pusher airscrew

than on the front tractor airscrew, although I was keenly aware that under all conditions of flight the rear engine ran considerably hotter than the one in front.

View in the air was excellent, and I had a distinct feeling that the Do 335 was better suited to nocturnal than diurnal fighting, although I had still to see, let alone fly, the single-seat version. Landing proved to be a fairly straightforward affair at an approach speed of 115 mph (185 km/h) and at a noticeably shallow nose-up attitude. Obviously the wing incidence had been so arranged to decrease the chances of a nose-up landing attitude that would have dug the rear fin into the ground, and the stick could not be held back on the ground as the same danger would have resulted, so it was easy to see why reverse pitch was available on the front

Dornier Do 335A Cockpit Instrumentation Key:

1 Deviation tables (master compass)
2 Deviation tables (standby compass)
3 Rear engine fire-extinguisher button (covered)
4 Front engine fire-extinguisher knob
5 Fuel safety cock levers
6 Throttle levers
7 Rudder trim handwheel
8 Trim indicator
9 Elevator trim handwheel
10 Aileron trim handwheel
11 Oxygen flow valve
12 Main electrics emergency switch
13 Throttle lock
14 Compass lamp
15 Standby (emergency) compass
16 Steering switch
17 Propeller selector switches (2)
18 Propeller manual control switches (2)
19 Landing flaps switch
20 Undercarriage switch
21 Explosives charge switch (belly landing)
22 UV light
23 Canopy release lever

24 Undercarriage position indicators
25 Compass lamp dimmer switch
26 Searchlight switch
27 Identification/navigation lights switch
28 Instrument panel lighting switch
29 Pitot heating switch
30 Armament control panel (SZKK3)
31 Gyro control switch
32 Auxiliary identification lights switch
33 UV lights dimmer switch
34 External air temperature indicator
35 Radio altimeter
36 Clock
37 Oxygen pressure gauge
38 Oxygen regulator
39 Revi 16D gunsight
40 Windshield
41 Windshield frame
42 Gunsight brace
43 Hinged panel sections retaining screws
44 Airspeed indicator
45 Artificial horizon
46 Variometer
47 Pitot heating indicator

48 Altimeter
49 Master (repeater) compass
50 AFN2 radio navigation indicator
51 Bomb release button (left horn of control column)
52 Fuselage cannon firing button (right horn of control column; MG 151 firing button on forward face of horn)
53 Course setting (autopilot)
54 Autopilot switch
55 R/T transmit button
56 Control column
57 Propeller pitch indicators
58 Combined pressure/RPM indicators
59 Fuel transfer pump switch (nose auxiliary tank)
60 Rate-of-use fuel warning lamp
61 Fuel contents warning lamp
62 Coolant temperature gauges
63 Oil temperature gauges
64 Fuel pressure gauges
65 Oil pressure gauges
66 Fuel contents gauge
67 Fire warning lamps
68 Canopy emergency jettison lever
69 UV light
70 Electrics switch panel
71 Explosives charge switch (abandon aircraft)
72 BG 25a control panel
73 'Kurs' (Course) axial-switch

74 Ejector seat activating mechanism
75 ZSK 246 fuse box and selector switch
76 ASK 335 bomb release switch panel
77 FuG 16Z(Y) control panel
78 Radio selector switch
79 Provision for FBG 2 installation
80 Ejector seat system pressure gauge
81 Emergency compressed air pressure gauge
82 Pressure oil pressure gauge
83 Battery casing
84 Rudder pedal adjustment starwheels
85 Rudder pedals
86 Oxygen hose
87 Oxygen connection
88 Cannon breech cover
89 Spotlamp
90 Undercarriage emergency switch
91 Landing flaps emergency switch
92 Steering emergency switch
93 Bomb-bay doors emergency switch
94 Bomb-bay doors emergency lever
95 Ejector seat base

The second pre-production Do 335A-0 (above and below) was found intact at Dornier's Oberpfaffenhofen facility and taken to the USA for evaluation by the US Navy at Patuxent River. In 1947, this particular example was donated to the Smithsonian Institute, being returned to Germany in the seventies and restored for exhibition by Dornier

airscrew. Apparently, however, pilots were recommended to land slightly tail down and use the mainwheels and the tail bumper (which had an oleo leg and was incorporated in the lower fin) for the initial impact before allowing the nose to drop on to the forward wheel. In the event of a wheels-up landing proving necessary, incidentally, provision was made for jettisoning the lower vertical surfaces. I did not use airscrew pitch reversal on my first two landings but, for comparison purposes, used it on the following two. I estimated that the reduction in landing run was something of the order of 200 yards (183 m), or about 25 per cent of the total distance of the run without use of reverse pitch.

Getting with the single-seater

My initial flights in the Do 335A-12 left me with three compelling urges — firstly to fly the single-seat model, secondly to fly the two-seater from the rear seat, and lastly to try the "bang seat". The first two of these urges were to be gratified, and while I did not seriously want to use the ejector seat for real, it seemed to me that we might conduct static trials when flight testing of the Do 335 was completed, just to see if the upper vertical tail surfaces and the airscrew really *did* blow off. Unfortunately, circumstances were to destroy the two Do 335s that we acquired with accidents in which the ejector seats were not used.

During December 1945, word filtered through — as it did

in the most mysterious ways at the RAE — that a single-seat Do 335A was lying in a corner of an old hangar on the Rheims airfield. Naturally, we at Farnborough were interested, and I was soon on my way to Rheims with the small team of ex-*Luftwaffe* personnel that we kept on a semi-POW basis at the RAE to help service the German jets that we had there. Rheims airfield was disused but there was a combined US-French supply organisation on the airfield boundary. I was puzzled as to the reason for their disinterest in the aircraft. Or was it that they were simply unaware that it was there? For that matter, what was a Do 335 doing at Rheims? Perhaps somebody had attempted to use it for an escape to Spain and had abandoned the aircraft because of mechnical trouble for there was still considerable fuel in its tanks.

It took my German team a whole week to check over the aircraft, working under primitive conditions in freezingly cold weather, but finally we were ready for a test flight. This immediately revealed a recalcitrant hydraulic system affecting the raising and lowering of the undercarriage. We had little option but to fly the aircraft as it was, and after two short test hops we had just about enough fuel left in the tanks to get to Merville where fuel was available. I handed our prize over to a German pilot for the flight to Merville since he was more familiar with German hydraulic systems, but on arrival at his destination he found that he could not lower the nosewheel. He therefore feathered the forward airscrew and landed on the grass, the aircraft suffering relatively little damage. Nevertheless, the accident wrote *finis* to the exercise of getting a single-seat Do 335 back to Farnborough for testing, and my acquaintance with this variant of the Dornier fighter was thus restricted to a short test flight at Rheims.

On my return to Farnborough, the CO, Grp Capt A F Hards, asked me to check him out for a solo trip in our two-seat Do 335, and on 18 January 1946 he went off solo. As he returned to the airfield we could see that the rear engine was on fire and we hoped that he would land on the nearest runway. Whether he was unaware of the fire or felt it safer to attempt his first landing in this strange German bird into wind will never be known, but he continued around the circuit as if no emergency existed, heading for the duty runway. He had covered roughly two-thirds of the circuit when

(Above) The Do 335A that came to grief at Merville, in northern France, as related by the author, while being ferried by a German pilot from Rheims to Farnborough late in 1945, and (below) the Do 335A-12 flown by the author at Farnborough and in which Grp Capt Hards lost his life on 18 January 1946 after the elevator control cables burned through when a fire started in the rear engine

(Above) The Do 335 V11 prototype for the Do 335A-10 tandem-seat dual-control conversion trainer variant of the Pfeil, and (below right) the ejection seat of the Do 335 V3 which was activated after the upper vertical tail surface and rear propeller had been jettisoned by means of explosive bolts

the Dornier suddenly plunged vertically into a school-house in Cove village. The elevator control cables had obviously burned through and Grp Capt Hards had no chance to eject.

The Do 335 had certainly proved itself the most trouble-some, mechanically, of the captured German aircraft that we had tested at Farnborough, probably indicative of the fact that it had been committed to production before all its bugs had been wrung out, but despite all the trouble that it gave us I was of the opinion that it would have made a highly successful night fighter with its good stability, endurance and excellent turn of speed. As a day fighter, however, although possessing an impressive performance by piston-engined fighter standards and a pretty potent armament, it was no aircraft for dogfighting. To be fair, fighter-versus-fighter combat was never intended to be the Do 335's forté, and it certainly could have given Allied heavy bombers an unpleasant time, with its good overtaking speed, its lethal firepower, and its worthwhile endurance which would have enabled it to fly standing patrols while awaiting intruding bomber formations.

The combination of features embodied by the Do 335 *Pfeil* rendered it unique at the time of its birth and it was destined to remain so, but had the Dornier warplane not appeared at the tailend of the piston-engined fighter era it is more than likely that its configuration would have been plagiarised.

Dornier Do 335A-0 Specification

Power Plant: Two Daimler-Benz DB 603A-2 12-cylinder in-verted-Vee liquid-cooled engines each rated at 1,750 hp at 2,700 rpm for take-off and having maximum continuous ratings of 1,375 hp at 2,300 rpm at sea level and 1,390 hp at 2,300 rpm at 21,655 ft (6 600 m). Fuel capacity, 407 Imp gal (1 850 l).
Armament: Two 15-mm Mauser MG 151/15 cannon each with 200 rounds and one 30-mm Rheinmetall Borsig MK 103 can-non with 70 rounds. Provision for one 1,102-lb (500-kg) SC 500 bomb in fuselage weapons bay.
Performance: Max speed, 360 mph (580 km/h) at sea level, 437 mph (703 km/h) at 21,655 ft (6 600 m), 455 mph (732 km/h) at 23,295 ft (7 100 m); range (with 1,102-lb/500-kg bomb), 764 mls (1 230 km) at 342 mph (550 km/h) at sea level, 994 mls (1 600 km) at 393 mph (633 km/h) at 19,685 ft (6 000 m), 858 mls (1 380 km) at 437 mph (703 km/h) at 21,655 ft

(6 600 m), 1,336 mls (2 150 km) at 286 mph (460 km/h) at 19,685 ft (6 000 m); climb (at 20,944 lb/9 500 kg) to 3,280 ft (1 000 m), 1·3 min, to 6,560 ft (2 000 m), 3·0 min, to 13,125 ft (4 000 m), 6·0 min, to 19,685 ft (6 000 m), 10·0 min, to 26,247 ft (8 000 m), 14·5 min; service ceiling (at 20,944 lb/9 500 kg), 31,170 ft (9 500 m), on one engine, 14,765 ft (4 500 m), (at 18,298 lb/8 300 kg), 35,105 ft (10 700 m), on one engine, 22,310 ft (6 800 m); take-off distance to 65·6 ft (20 m), 1,050 yds (960 m); landing speed (at 19,842 lb/9 000 kg), 118 mph (190 km/h).
Weights: Empty equipped, 14,396 lb (6 530 kg); max loaded, 20,966 lb (9 510 kg).
Dimensions: Span, 45 ft 3⅓ in (13,80 m); length, 45 ft 5⅓ in (13,85 m); height, 16 ft 4⅞ in (5,00 m); wing area, 414·41 sq ft (38,50 m²).

FOCKE-WULF FW 190 & TA 152

EIN ZWEITES EISEN IM FEUER — a second iron in the fire! Such was the *raison d'être* of Dipl-Ing Kurt Tank's compact, well-proportioned and æsthetically-appealing single-seat fighter that first fired its guns in anger over the Channel Front with *II Gruppe* of *Jagdgeschwader 26 "Schlageter"* in July 1941. Several fighters were to display the hallmark of the thorough-bred during World War II — aircraft that were outstanding to varying degrees of excellence in their combat performance, their amenability to a variety of operational scenarios, their ease of pilot handling and their field maintenance tractability — but none more so than Tank's remarkable creation sporting the prosaic designation of Focke-Wulf Fw 190 but dubbed more emotively if unofficially the *Würger* (Butcher-bird — a species of shrike) by its designer himself.

Within six or seven months of its operational début, the Fw 190 was causing widespread consternation among RAF fighter squadrons based in the south of England. The Tank-designed fighter could out-perform the contemporary Spitfire on every count with the exception of the turning circle — one leading RAF pilot is recorded as having commented acidly when this attribute of his mount was stressed during a pre-operation briefing, "Turning doesn't win battles!". By April 1942, RAF combat attrition on the Channel Front reached prohibitive levels primarily as a result of the activities of its redoubtable German adversary — more than a hundred Spitfires being lost on offensive operations over Occupied Europe during the course of the month — and the Merlin 61-engined Spitfire Mk IX was still two or three months away. But while going a long way towards redressing the balance and even offering an edge in climb and performance above 26,000 feet (7 925 m), the Spitfire Mk IX was still to be left standing by the Focke-Wulf's half-roll and dive!

The Fw 190 was to reveal defects — and what fighter yet conceived has been perfect? — but it probably came as close to perfection by the standards of the day as any contemporary. Yet its gestation and, indeed, early infancy were not attended by any noticeable enthusiasm on the part of the Operations

Staff, the *Luftwaffenführungsstab*, which held the somewhat complacent opinion that a back-up for Messerschmitt's Bf 109 was unnecessary and serious consideration of a successor premature. Fortunately for the *Jagdflieger*, the *Reichsluftfahrtministerium* adopted a somewhat more far-sighted attitude, and while its Technical Department was not very favourably disposed towards a *radial*-engined fighter, the potential supply situation of the Daimler-Benz series of liquid-cooled in-line engines in the years immediately ahead motivated acceptance of Kurt Tank's proposal that the new radial air-cooled engine being developed by the Bayerische Motoren Werke should be given serious consideration as a fighter power plant.

The blending of the bulky radial engine into the contours of the new fighter was nothing short of masterly and as an exercise in the mating of compactness with functional elegance the Focke-Wulf design was a masterpiece. It was to suffer its share of vicissitudes during development — the decision to terminate development of the BMW 139 engine around which it had been designed very nearly brought about its premature demise — but it was to be recognized by the *Luftwaffe* as potentially a truly outstanding combat aircraft long before attaining maturity; a view with which the RAF was reluctantly to concur once the service had tested the mettle of the newcomer in French skies.

Indeed, as the months passed and the Focke-Wulf consolidated the ascendancy that it had established over its RAF contemporaries from the time of its operational début, morale of pilots of the Spitfire Mk V squadrons inevitably being affected, Air Ministry concern over the situation began to border on desperation which generated a crop of bizarre schemes for acquiring an example of this *bête noire* so that it could be thoroughly analysed and its Achilles Heel — for such, it was believed, must surely exist — revealed for the edification of RAF Fighter Command. Plans were, in fact, being formulated for a commando raid on a *Luftwaffe* fighter base with the object of sequestering a Focke-Wulf, when, at 2035 hours on 23 June 1942, one *Oberleutnant* Arnim Faber landed on what he took to be a *Luftwaffe* airfield on the Cherbourg Peninsula. Taxying slowly along the runway under a marshaller's orders, Faber was intensely surprised when someone leaped onto the wing of his fighter and pointed a Verey pistol at his head! The RAF finally had its Fw 190!

The Portreath and Exeter Spitfire Wings, which had been engaged in a support sweep over Brittany, had, unbeknown to them, been trailed across the Channel by Fw 190s of the *Gruppenstab* of III *Gruppe* and 7. *Staffel* of *Jagdgeschwader* 2 from Maupertus and Morlaix. Flying low, the Spitfires had been approaching Start Point on the Devonian coast when the Fw 190s had curved out of the low sun, one of them, flown by *Unteroffizier* Willi Reuschling, promptly colliding with the Spitfire flown by Wg Cdr Alois Vasatko. The ensuing combat between the surviving fighters had been brief as both RAF and *Luftwaffe* aircraft were critically low on fuel, but one of the Focke-Wulfs, its pilot apparently disorientated, had flown away in a north-easterly direction towards Exeter.

Four Spitfires had been hurriedly scrambled by the Exeter Wing, two crashing on take-off, one returning to base with R/T trouble and the other being summarily despatched by the lone Fw 190 with which contact had then been lost until it appeared barrel-rolling across RAF Pembrey, near Swansea. Lowering its undercarriage while still inverted, the fighter had landed off a steep turn. The Duty Pilot, one Sgt Jeffreys, who had followed the Focke-Wulf's antics through binoculars, grabbed a Very pistol, ran from the control tower and jumped on to the wing of the fighter as it taxied in. Arnim Faber had apparently inadvertently flown a reciprocal course, mistaken the northern coastline of the Bristol Channel for the Cherbourg Peninsula and, in the poor light, failed to realize that he was landing on an RAF airfield.

It was thus that the RAF acquired Fw 190A-3 *Werk-Nr* 5313. The depths of its pilot's despair at unwittingly providing his enemies with such a prize may be gauged from the fact that he subsequently attempted suicide, and my compassion for him was certainly to be stimulated some time later, in February 1944, when I very nearly suffered a similar experience while testing a new Typhoon from Farnborough above cloud — although no navigational error was to be involved in my case, my near close-acquaintance with a *Luftwaffe* airfield resulting from deliberate radio direction spoofing by the Germans.

Elegant lethality

The RAF took advantage of its windfall of 23 June 1942 with creditable rapidity. It was promptly transported by road from Pembrey to the Royal Aircraft Establishment at Farnborough, both airframe and engine being dismantled and thoroughly analysed before re-assembly, and on 3 July, a mere 10 days after landing at Pembrey, the Fw 190A-3 was flown at the RAE by Wg Cdr (later Gp Capt) Hugh J Wilson as MP499. Ten days later, on 13 July, this invaluable prize was delivered to the Air Fighting Development Unit at Duxford, where it was put through intensive performance trials and flown competitively against several Allied fighter types.

The AFDU trials confirmed what the RAF already knew — that the Fw 190 was a truly outstanding combat aircraft. They also produced vitally important information which went some way towards restoring the situation in so far as the RAF was

(Head of opposite page and below) Early production Fw 190A-3 fighters posing for propaganda photographs while being flown by factory test pilots and prior to delivery to the Luftwaffe in the spring of 1942

concerned and in eradicating something of the awe in which the Focke-Wulf had come to be held by Allied pilots. It was concluded that the Fw 190 pilot trying to "mix it" with a Spitfire in the classic fashion of steep turning was doomed, for at any speed — even below the German fighter's stalling speed — it would be out-turned by its British opponent. Of course, the *Luftwaffe* was aware of this fact and a somewhat odd style of dogfighting evolved in which the Fw 190 pilots endeavoured to keep on the vertical plane by zooms and dives, while their Spitfire-mounted antagonists tried everything in the book to draw them on to the horizontal. If the German pilot lost his head and failed to resist the temptation to try a horizontal pursuit curve on a Spitfire, as likely as not, before he could recover the speed lost in a steep turn he would find another Spitfire turning inside him! On the other hand, the German pilot who kept zooming up and down was usually the

recipient of only difficult deflection shots of more than 30 deg. The Fw 190 had tremendous initial acceleration in a dive but it was extremely vulnerable during a pull-out, recovery having to be quite progressive with care not to kill the speed by "sinking".

Arnim Faber's Fw 190A-3 was thoroughly wrung out and dispelled the mystique with which the Focke-Wulf had been surrounded during the first year of its operational career; the fortuitous acquisition of this one warplane probably saving the lives of countless RAF pilots. But familiarity certainly did not breed contempt, for although conversant with both attributes and shortcomings of the fighter, we were equally conversant with the fact that it had to be treated with the utmost respect as an antagonist, despite its awesome reputation by now having been placed in perspective.

By the time I arrived at Farnborough, the Fw 190A-3 that had been delivered to Pembrey had served its purpose and been

(Right) A flamboyantly decorated Fw 190A-2 of II/JG 1 operating from bases in Holland in the spring of 1942, and (below) early production Fw 190A-3s undergoing pre-delivery trials at a company test centre

Fw 190A-5 fighters undergoing servicing between sorties from an airfield in the Soviet Union during the winter of 1942-43. The unit is believed to be the II Gruppe of Jagdgeschwader 54 "Grünherz"

finally grounded — the last recorded flight having taken place on 29 January 1943 and the airframe being struck off charge eight months later, on 18 September, for firing trials. Its place in the RAE inventory had been taken by an Fw 190A-4, which, assigned the serial PE882, had landed in error at RAF West Malling during the early hours of 17 April 1943. Two other examples of the A-4 sub-type of the Focke-Wulf fighter were to fall into our hands at around this time, incidentally, both landing in error at RAF Manston during night operations, one on 20 May and the other on 20 June 1943, these acquiring the serials PM679 and PN999.

I recall clearly the excitement with which I first examined the Focke-Wulf fighter; the impression of elegant lethality that its functional yet pleasing lines exuded. To me it represented the very quintessence of aeronautical pulchritude from any angle. It was not, to my eye, *more* beautiful than the Spitfire, but its beauty took a different form — the contrast being such as that between blonde and brunette! It sat high on the ground, the oleo legs of its undercarriage appearing extraordinarily long, and it was immediately obvious that, despite the superlative job of cowling done by the Focke-Wulf designers, the big BMW 801D air-cooled radial engine was pretty obtrusive. Nevertheless, I was pleasantly surprised to find, after clambering into the somewhat narrow cockpit, that the forward view was still rather better than was offered by the Bf 109, the Spitfire or the Mustang. The semi-reclining seat — ideal for high-g manoeuvres — proved relatively comfortable and the controls fell easily to the hand, although the flight instruments were not, in my opinion, quite so well arranged as those of the contemporary Bf 109G.

In general, the cockpit layout was good and I was fascinated by the ingenious *Kommandgerät*, a sort of "brain-box" relieving the pilot of the job of controlling airscrew pitch, mixture, boost and rpm. The KG 13A control column was of standard type, including a send/receive button for the FuG 16Z radio (which had supplanted the FuG 7a of the A-3 model), a gunnery selector switch and a firing button. This particular example of the fighter (ie, PE882) was, in fact, an Fw 190A-4/U8 *Jabo* with provision for two bomb carriers beneath the wings each capable of carrying a 551-lb (250-kg) SG 250 bomb or a 66-Imp gal (300-l) drop tank and a third carrier beneath the

fuselage, the fixed armament being reduced to a pair of 20-mm MG 151 cannon in the wing roots, these being harmonized at 220 yards (200 m) rather than the usual 490 yards (450 m). The sighting view, when sitting comfortably in the normal position, was somewhat better than that of the Spitfire owing to the nose-down attitude of the Fw 190 in flight. The pilot was well protected from frontal attack by the engine and the sharply-sloping 50-mm armour-glass windscreen and from the rear by his shaped 8-mm armour seat-back and 13-mm head-and-shoulder armour, plus small 8-mm plates disposed above and below the seat-back and on each side.

All the ancillary controls were electrically operated by an array of pushbuttons whose creator had obviously never had to think in terms of those massive leather flying gauntlets issued as standard to British pilots and guaranteed to convert their hands into bunches of bananas, and a particularly good feature of the cockpit was the outstanding search view that it offered, the good all-round visibility rendering a rear-view mirror unnecessary.

Superb control harmony

My first opportunity to fly the Focke-Wulf did not arise until 4 February 1944, the actual aircraft being the previously-mentioned Fw 190A-4/U8 PE882. This fighter had seen a lot of flying from the RAE and was destined, 10 weeks later, to be transferred to No 1426 Flight at Collyweston with which it was to fly until 13 October 1944, when, after a fire in the air, it was to crash on the road between Kettering and Stamford, demolishing three walls before coming to rest in the garden of a house. On this cold February morning at Farnborough, however, the sad demise of this particular Focke-Wulf was still some way into the future, and despite the substantial number of hours that it had flown since reaching British hands, it gave every impression of youthfulness.

The BMW 801D engine was started by an inertia starter energized by a 24-volt external supply or by the aircraft's own battery. The big radial was primed internally, both fuel tanks and pumps selected ON and the cooling gills set to one-third aperture. We had found that the BMW almost invariably fired first time and emitted a smooth purr as it ran, such being the case on this particular morning, and once I had familiarized

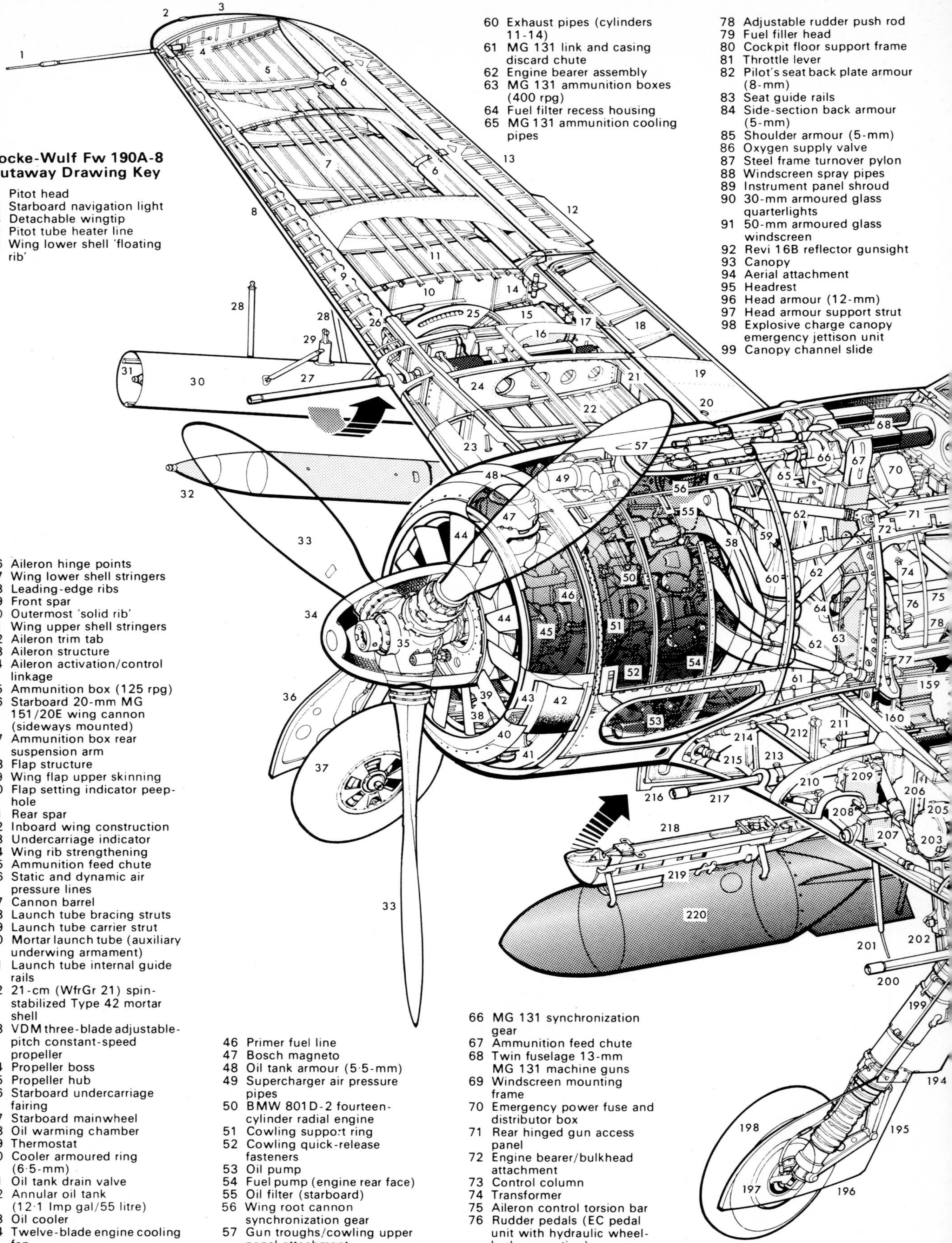

**Focke-Wulf Fw 190A-8
Cutaway Drawing Key**

1 Pitot head
2 Starboard navigation light
3 Detachable wingtip
4 Pitot tube heater line
5 Wing lower shell 'floating rib'
6 Aileron hinge points
7 Wing lower shell stringers
8 Leading-edge ribs
9 Front spar
10 Outermost 'solid rib'
11 Wing upper shell stringers
12 Aileron trim tab
13 Aileron structure
14 Aileron activation/control linkage
15 Ammunition box (125 rpg)
16 Starboard 20-mm MG 151/20E wing cannon (sideways mounted)
17 Ammunition box rear suspension arm
18 Flap structure
19 Wing flap upper skinning
20 Flap setting indicator peep-hole
21 Rear spar
22 Inboard wing construction
23 Undercarriage indicator
24 Wing rib strengthening
25 Ammunition feed chute
26 Static and dynamic air pressure lines
27 Cannon barrel
28 Launch tube bracing struts
29 Launch tube carrier strut
30 Mortar launch tube (auxiliary underwing armament)
31 Launch tube internal guide rails
32 21-cm (WfrGr 21) spin-stabilized Type 42 mortar shell
33 VDM three-blade adjustable-pitch constant-speed propeller
34 Propeller boss
35 Propeller hub
36 Starboard undercarriage fairing
37 Starboard mainwheel
38 Oil warming chamber
39 Thermostat
40 Cooler armoured ring (6·5-mm)
41 Oil tank drain valve
42 Annular oil tank (12·1 Imp gal/55 litre)
43 Oil cooler
44 Twelve-blade engine cooling fan
45 Hydraulic-electric pitch control unit

46 Primer fuel line
47 Bosch magneto
48 Oil tank armour (5·5-mm)
49 Supercharger air pressure pipes
50 BMW 801D-2 fourteen-cylinder radial engine
51 Cowling support ring
52 Cowling quick-release fasteners
53 Oil pump
54 Fuel pump (engine rear face)
55 Oil filter (starboard)
56 Wing root cannon synchronization gear
57 Gun troughs/cowling upper panel attachment
58 Engine mounting ring
59 Cockpit heating pipe

60 Exhaust pipes (cylinders 11-14)
61 MG 131 link and casing discard chute
62 Engine bearer assembly
63 MG 131 ammunition boxes (400 rpg)
64 Fuel filter recess housing
65 MG 131 ammunition cooling pipes
66 MG 131 synchronization gear
67 Ammunition feed chute
68 Twin fuselage 13-mm MG 131 machine guns
69 Windscreen mounting frame
70 Emergency power fuse and distributor box
71 Rear hinged gun access panel
72 Engine bearer/bulkhead attachment
73 Control column
74 Transformer
75 Aileron control torsion bar
76 Rudder pedals (EC pedal unit with hydraulic wheel-brake operation)
77 Fuselage/wing spar attachment

78 Adjustable rudder push rod
79 Fuel filler head
80 Cockpit floor support frame
81 Throttle lever
82 Pilot's seat back plate armour (8-mm)
83 Seat guide rails
84 Side-section back armour (5-mm)
85 Shoulder armour (5-mm)
86 Oxygen supply valve
87 Steel frame turnover pylon
88 Windscreen spray pipes
89 Instrument panel shroud
90 30-mm armoured glass quarterlights
91 50-mm armoured glass windscreen
92 Revi 16B reflector gunsight
93 Canopy
94 Aerial attachment
95 Headrest
96 Head armour (12-mm)
97 Head armour support strut
98 Explosive charge canopy emergency jettison unit
99 Canopy channel slide

100 Auxiliary tank: fuel (25·3 Imp gal/115 litre) or GM-1 (18·7 Imp gal/85 litre)
101 FuG 16ZY transmitter-receiver unit
102 Handhold cover
103 Primer fuel filler cap
104 Autopilot steering unit (PKS 12)
105 FuG 16ZY power transformer
106 Entry step cover plate
107 Two tri-spherical oxygen bottles (starboard fuselage wall)
108 Auxiliary fuel tank filler point
109 FuG 25a transponder unit
110 Autopilot position integration unit
111 FuG 16ZY homer bearing converter
112 Elevator control cables
113 Rudder control DUZ-flexible rods

114 Fabric panel (Bulkhead 12)
115 Rudder differential unit
116 Aerial lead-in
117 Rear fuselage lift tube
118 Triangular stress frame
119 Tailplane trim unit
120 Tailplane attachment fitting
121 Tailwheel retraction guide tube
122 Retraction cable lower pulley
123 Starboard tailplane
124 Aerial
125 Starboard elevator
126 Elevator trim tab
127 Tailwheel shock strut guide
128 Fin construction
129 Retraction cable upper pulley

142 Forked wheel housing
143 Drag yoke
144 Tailwheel shock strut
145 Tailwheel locking linkage
146 Elevator actuation lever linkage
147 Angled frame spar
148 Elevator differential bellcrank
149 FuG 25a ventral antenna
150 Master compass sensing unit
151 FuG 16ZY fixed loop homing antenna

170 Aileron transverse linkage
171 Ammunition box (125 rpg)
172 Ammunition box rear suspension arm
173 Aileron control linkage
174 Aileron control unit
175 Aileron trim tab
176 Port aileron structure

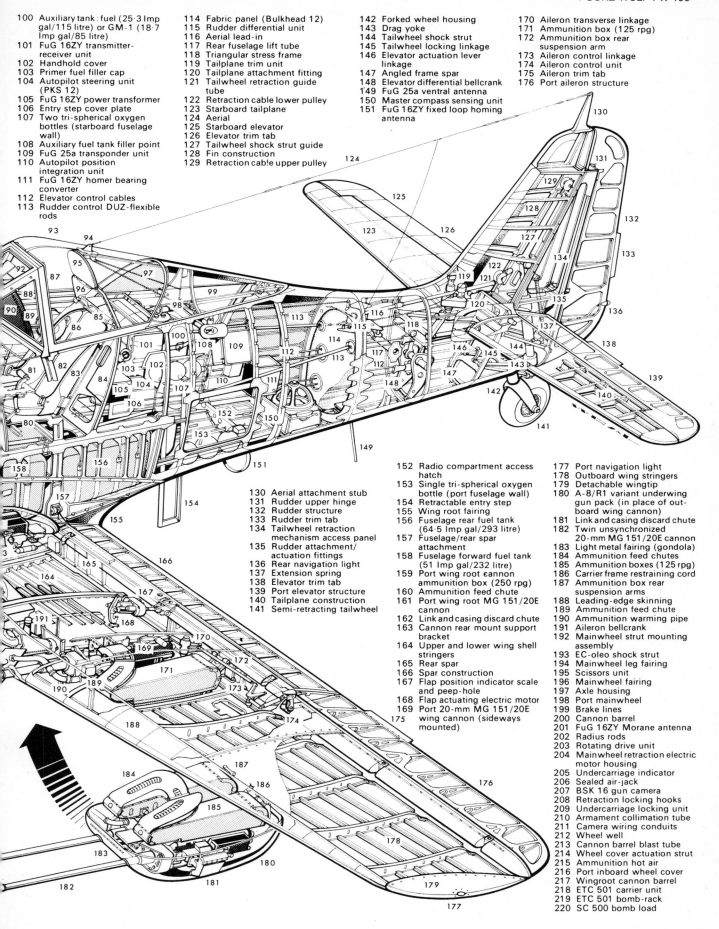

130 Aerial attachment stub
131 Rudder upper hinge
132 Rudder structure
133 Rudder trim tab
134 Tailwheel retraction mechanism access panel
135 Rudder attachment/actuation fittings
136 Rear navigation light
137 Extension spring
138 Elevator trim tab
139 Port elevator structure
140 Tailplane construction
141 Semi-retracting tailwheel

152 Radio compartment access hatch
153 Single tri-spherical oxygen bottle (port fuselage wall)
154 Retractable entry step
155 Wing root fairing
156 Fuselage rear fuel tank (64·5 Imp gal/293 litre)
157 Fuselage/rear spar attachment
158 Fuselage forward fuel tank (51 Imp gal/232 litre)
159 Port wing root cannon ammunition box (250 rpg)
160 Ammunition feed chute
161 Port wing root MG 151/20E cannon
162 Link and casing discard chute
163 Cannon rear mount support bracket
164 Upper and lower wing shell stringers
165 Rear spar
166 Spar construction
167 Flap position indicator scale and peep-hole
168 Flap actuating electric motor
169 Port 20-mm MG 151/20E wing cannon (sideways mounted)

177 Port navigation light
178 Outboard wing stringers
179 Detachable wingtip
180 A-8/R1 variant underwing gun pack (in place of outboard wing cannon)
181 Link and casing discard chute
182 Twin unsynchronized 20-mm MG 151/20E cannon
183 Light metal fairing (gondola)
184 Ammunition feed chutes
185 Ammunition boxes (125 rpg)
186 Carrier frame restraining cord
187 Ammunition box rear suspension arms
188 Leading-edge skinning
189 Ammunition feed chute
190 Ammunition warming pipe
191 Aileron bellcrank
192 Mainwheel strut mounting assembly
193 EC-oleo shock strut
194 Mainwheel leg fairing
195 Scissors unit
196 Mainwheel fairing
197 Axle housing
198 Port mainwheel
199 Brake lines
200 Cannon barrel
201 FuG 16ZY Morane antenna
202 Radius rods
203 Rotating drive unit
204 Mainwheel retraction electric motor housing
205 Undercarriage indicator
206 Sealed air-jack
207 BSK 16 gun camera
208 Retraction locking hooks
209 Undercarriage locking unit
210 Armament collimation tube
211 Camera wiring conduits
212 Wheel well
213 Cannon barrel blast tube
214 Wheel cover actuation strut
215 Ammunition hot air
216 Port inboard wheel cover
217 Wingroot cannon barrel
218 ETC 501 carrier unit
219 ETC 501 bomb-rack
220 SC 500 bomb load

myself with the self-centering tailwheel — a feature that had been criticized by some AFDU pilots — I found taxying the essence of simplicity as the fighter could be swung freely from side to side on its broad-track undercarriage. Furthermore, the brakes were very good, although view with the tail down left much to be desired.

I soon felt completely at home in the cockpit. After lining up for take-off, I moved the stick to an aft position in order to lock the tailwheel, applied 10 degrees of flap, set the elevator trimmer to neutral and the propeller pitch to AUTO and gently opened up the engine. I encountered some tendency to swing to port but easily held this on the rudder, and using 2,700 rpm and 23·5 lb (1·6 atas) boost, found the run to be much the same as that of the Spitfire Mk IX. Unstick speed was 112 mph (180 km/h) and after retracting the undercarriage by depressing the appropriate button, I reduced boost to 21·3 lb (1·45 atas) and at 143 mph (230 km/h) activated the pushbutton which raised the flaps. I then set up a climbing speed of 161 mph (260 km/h) using 2,500 rpm and this gave a climb rate of 3,150 ft/min (16 m/sec).

A remarkable aspect of this fighter was the lack of re-trimming required for the various stages of a flight. There was no aileron trimmer in the cockpit, but if the external adjustable trim tab had been inadvertently moved as a result, for example, of a member of the groundscrew pushing against it, an out-of-

trim force of considerable proportions *could* result at high speed. Decidedly the most impressive feature of the German fighter was its beautifully light ailerons and its extremely high rate of roll. Incredible aileron turns were possible that would have torn the wings from a Bf 109 and badly strained the arm muscles of any Spitfire pilot trying to follow. The ailerons maintained their lightness from the stall up to 400 mph (644 km/h), although they heavied up above that speed.

The elevators proved to be heavy at all speeds and particularly so above 350 mph (563 km/h) when they became heavy enough to impose a tactical restriction on the fighter as regards pull-out from low-level dives. This heaviness was accentuated because of the nose down pitch which occurred at high speeds when trimmed for low speeds. The critical speed at which this change in trim occurred was around 220 mph (354 km/h) and could be easily gauged in turns. At lower speeds, the German fighter had a tendency to tighten up the turn and I found it necessary to apply slight forward pressure on the stick, but above the previously-mentioned critical figure, the changeover called for some backward pressure to hold the Focke-Wulf in the turn.

At low speeds rudder control proved positive and effective, and I found it satisfactory at high speeds, seldom needing to be used for any normal manœuvre. It was when one took the three controls together rather than in isolation that one appreci-

Focke-Wulf Fw 190A-8 Cockpit Instrumentation Key

1 Helmet R/T connection
2 Primer fuel pump handle
3 FuG 16ZY communications and homing switch and volume control
4 FuG 16ZY receiver fine tuning
5 FuG 16ZY homing range switch
6 FuG 16ZY frequency selector switch
7 Tailplane trim switch
8 Undercarriage and landing flap actuation buttons
9 Undercarriage and landing flap position indicators
10 Throttle
11 Throttle-mounted propeller pitch control thumbswitch
12 Tailplane trim indicator
13 Instrument panel lighting dimmer
14 Pilot's seat
15 Throttle friction knob
16 Control column
17 Bomb release button
18 Rudder pedals
19 Wing cannon firing button
20 Fuel tank selector lever
21 Engine starter brushes withdrawal button
22 Stop cock control lever
23 FuG 25a IFF control panel
24 Undercarriage manual lowering handle
25 Cockpit ventilation knob
26 Altimeter
27 Pitot tube heater light
28 MG 131 "armed" indicator lights
29 Ammunition counters
30 SZKK 4 armament switch and control panel
31 30-mm armoured glass quarterlights
32 Windscreen spray pipes
33 50-mm armoured glass windscreen
34 Revi 16B reflector gunsight
35 Padded coaming
36 Gunsight padded mounting
37 AFN 2 homing indicator (FuG 16ZY)
38 Ultra-violet lights (port and starboard)
39 Airspeed indicator
40 Artificial horizon
41 Rate of climb/descent indicator
42 Repeater compass
43 Supercharger pressure gauge
44 Tachometer
45 Ventral stores manual release
46 Fuel and oil pressure gauge
47 Oil temperature gauge
48 Windscreen washer operating lever
49 Engine ventilation flap control lever
50 Fuel contents gauge
51 Propeller pitch indicator
52 Rear fuel tank switchover light (white)
53 Fuel contents warning light (red)
54 Fuel gauge selector switch
55 Underwing rocket (WfrGr 21) control panel
56 Bomb fusing selector panel and (above) external stores indicator lights
57 Oxygen flow indicator
58 Flare pistol holder
59 Oxygen pressure gauge
60 Oxygen flow valve
61 Canopy actuator drive
62 Canopy jettison lever
63 Circuit breaker panel cover
64 Clock
65 Map/chart holder
66 Operations data card
67 Flare box cover
68 Starter switch
69 Flare box cover plate release knob
70 Fuel pump circuit breakers
71 Compass deviation card
72 Circuit breaker panel cover
73 Armament circuit breakers
74 Oxygen supply

The Fw 190A-4/U8 flown by the author is seen below on 20 April 1943, three days after its arrival in the UK and prior to the removal of wing bomb pylons and fuselage rack, and (above) at a somewhat later stage in the RAF flight test programme after these appendages had been removed

ated the fact that the Fw 190's magic as a fighter lay in its superb control harmony. A good dogfighter *and* a good gun platform called for just the characteristics that this German fighter possessed in all important matters of stability and control. At the normal cruise of 330 mph (530 km/h) at 8,000 ft (2 440 m), the stability was very good directionally, unstable laterally and neutral longitudinally.

Some penalty is, of course, always invoked by such handling attributes as those possessed by the Fw 190, and in the case of this fighter the penalty was to be found in the fact that it was not at all easy to fly on instruments. Of course, Kurt Tank's aircraft was originally conceived solely as a clear-weather day fighter. It is significant that all-weather versions were fitted with the Patin PKS 12 autopilot. I checked out the maximum level speed of my Fw 190A-4/U8 — which, incidentally, had had its external stores carriers removed by this time — and clocked 394 mph (634 km/h) at 18,500 ft (5 640 m), and I ascertained that the service ceiling was around 35,000 ft (10 670 m), so it matched the Spitfire Mk IX almost mile per hour and foot per foot of ceiling. Here were apparently two aircraft that were so evenly matched that the skill of the pilot became the vital factor in combat supremacy. Skill in aerial combat does, however, mean flying an aircraft to its limits, and when the performance of the enemy is equal to one's own, then handling characteristics become vital in seeking an advantage. The Focke-Wulf had one big advantage over the Spitfire Mk IX in that it possessed an appreciably higher rate of roll, but the Achilles Heel that the AFDU had sought with Arnim Faber's Fw 190A-3 was its harsh stalling characteristics which limited its manoeuvre margins.

The AFDU comparisons between the Focke-Wulf and the Spitfire Mk IX — with the former's BMW 801 at 2,700 rpm and 20·8 lb (1·42 *atas*) boost and the latter's Merlin 61 at 3,000 rpm and 15 lb (1·00 *ata*) — had revealed that the German fighter was 7-8 mph (11-13 km/h) faster than its British counterpart at 2,000 ft (610 m) but that the speeds of the two fighters were virtually the same at 5,000 ft (1 525 m). Above this altitude, the Spitfire began to display a marginal superiority, being about 8 mph (13 km/h) faster at 8,000 ft (2 440 m) and 5 mph (8 km/h) faster at 15,000 ft (4 570 m). The pendulum then swung once more in favour of the Focke-Wulf which proved itself some 3 mph (5 km/h) faster at 18,000 ft (5 485 m), the two fighters level pegging once more at 21,000 ft (6 400 m) and the Spitfire

then taking the lead until, at 25,000 ft (7 620 m) it showed a 5-7 mph (8-11 km/h) superiority.

In climbing, little difference was found between the Fw 190 and the Spitfire Mk IX up to 23,000 ft (7 010 m), above which altitude the climb of the German fighter began to fall off and the difference between the two aircraft widened rapidly. From high-speed cruise, a pull up into a climb gave the Fw 190 an initial advantage owing to its superior acceleration and the superiority of the German fighter was even more noticeable when both aircraft were pulled up into a zoom climb from a dive. In the dive, the Fw 190 could leave the Spitfire Mk IX without difficulty and there was no gainsaying that in so far as manoeuvrability was concerned, the German fighter was markedly the superior of the two in all save the tight turn — the Spitfire could not follow in aileron turns and reversals at high speeds and the worst heights for its pilot to engage the Fw 190 in combat were between 18,000 and 22,000 ft (5 485 and 6 705 m), and at altitudes below 3,000 ft (915 m).

The stalling speed of the Fw 190A-4 in clean configuration was 127 mph (204 km/h) and the stall came suddenly and virtually without warning, the port wing dropping so violently that the aircraft almost inverted itself. In fact, if the German fighter was pulled into a *g* stall in a tight turn, it would flick out into the opposite bank and an incipient spin was the inevitable outcome if the pilot did not have his wits about him. The stall in landing configuration was quite different, there

Fw 190A-4/U8 PE882 under test from Farnborough after removal of the wing pylons and fuselage bomb/drop tank shackles. It was eventually to be written off on 13 October 1944 after transfer to No 1426 Flight at Collyweston.

Focke-Wulf Fw 190A-8 Specification

Power Plant: On BMW 801D 14-cylinder radial air-cooled engine rated at 1,700 hp for take-off and 1,440 hp at 18,700 ft (5 700 m). Fuel capacity, 115·5 Imp gal (524 l) in two fuselage tanks, plus 25·3 Imp gal (115 l) in optional rear fuselage tank plus provision for 66·2-Imp gal (300-l) drop tank.

Performance (Clean): Max speed, 355 mph (571 km/h) at sea level, 402 mph (647 km/h) at 18,045 ft (5 500 m); max speed with GM1 nitrous oxide boost, 408 mph (656 km/h) at 20,670 ft (6 300 m); normal cruising speed, 298 mph (480 km/h) at 6,560 ft (2 000 m); initial rate of climb, 3,450 ft/min (17,5 m/sec); time to climb to 19,685 ft (6 000 m), 9·1 min; to 26,250 ft (8 000 m), 14·4 min; to 32,800 ft (10 000 m), 19.3 min; service ceiling, 33,800 ft (10 300 m) and with GM1 boost, 37,400 ft (11 400 m); max range, 644 mls (1 035 km) at 22,970 ft (7 000 m); range with one drop tank, 915 mls (1 470 km) at 301 mph (485 km/h) at 16,400 ft (5 000 m).

Weights: Empty equipped (clean), 7,652 lb (3 470 kg); empty equipped (fighter-bomber), 7,740 lb (3 510 kg); normal loaded, 9,660 lb (4 380 kg); max take-off (fighter-bomber), 10,724 lb (4 865 kg).

Dimensions: Span, 34 ft 5½ in (10,506 m); length, 29 ft 4¼ in (8,95 m); height (over airscrew), 12 ft 11½ in (3,95 m); wing area, 196·98 sq ft (18,3 m²); undercarriage track, 11 ft 6 in (3,50 m).

Armament: Two 13-mm MG 131 machine guns with 475 rpg in fuselage; two 20-mm MG 151/20E cannon with 250 rpg in wing roots and two 20-mm MG 151/20E cannon with 140 rpg in outer wing panels.

being intense pre-stall buffeting before the starboard wing dropped comparatively gently at 102 mph (164 km/h).

For landing on this and the numerous subsequent occasions that I was to fly an Fw 190, I extended the undercarriage at 186 mph (300 km/h), lowering the flaps 10 deg at 168 mph (270 km/h), although the pilot's notes recommended reducing speed below 155 mph (250 km/h) and then applying 10 deg of flap before lowering the undercarriage. My reason for departing from the recommended drill was that the electrical load for lowering the undercarriage was higher than that required for the flaps, and German batteries were in rather short supply at Farnborough — that in the Fw 190A-4/U8 was most definitely weary — so I considered it prudent to get the wheels down before taxing the remaining strength of the battery further!

The turn onto final approach was made at 155 mph (250 km/h) and full flap was applied at 149 mph (240 km/h), speed then being eased off to cross the boundary at 124 mph (200 km/h). The view on the approach was decidedly poor because the attitude with power on was rather flat and, unlike most fighters of the period, it was not permissible to open the cockpit canopy, presumably owing to the risk of engine exhaust fumes entering the cockpit. The actual touch-down was a little tricky as a

(Above) the outstanding engine accessibility of the Fw 190 is illustrated graphically by this photograph of a captured Fw 190A-5 (Werk-Nr 150 051) in the USA. (Below) An Fw 190G-8 (Werk-Nr 181 550) captured by US forces in Sicily in 1944

An Fw 190A-5 (Werk Nr 150 051) photographed in March 1944 while being flown from US Naval Air Station Patuxent River for evaluation purposes. By this time, the guns had been removed and a non-standard aerial fitted

perfect three-point attitude was difficult to attain and anything less than perfect resulted in a reaction from the very non-resilient undercarriage and a decidedly bouncy arrival. If a three-pointer *could* be achieved, the landing run was short and the brakes could be applied harshly without fear of nosing over.

I was to fly the Fw 190 many times and in several varieties — among the last of the radial-engined members of Kurt Tank's fighter family that I flew was an Fw 190F-8 (AM111) on 28 July 1945 — and each time I was to experience that sense of exhilaration that came from flying an aircraft that one instinctively knew to be a top-notcher, yet, at the same time, demanded handling skill if its high qualities were to be exploited. Just as the Spitfire Mk IX was probably the most outstanding British fighter to give service in World War II, its Teutonic counterpart is undoubtedly deserving of the same recognition for Germany. Both were supreme in their time and

class; both were durable and technically superb, and if each had not been there to counter the other, then the balance of air power could have been dramatically altered at a crucial period in the fortunes of both combatants.

Flying the Ta 152

Having flown the BMW 801-powered Fw 190 on many occasions and in several versions, I was understandably delighted when an opportunity arose to get my hands on what was, from the production standpoint at least, the ultimate development of Kurt Tank's superb basic design, the high-flying Ta 152H-1. I recall that the sole example of this intriguing and allegedly potent fighter to be taken to the UK had been, for reasons unbeknown to me, dismantled in Germany and flown into the Royal Aircraft Establishment at Farnborough in the capacious hold of an Arado Ar

The Fw 190A-5 – the example illustrated being Werk-Nr 150 051 while under US Navy test – entered production early in 1943, differed from the A-4 that it supplanted in having lengthened engine bearers and was intended to accept a wider variety of Umrüst-Bausätze (Factory Conversion Sets)

This Ta 152H-1 was among several captured examples tested by Allied pilots at the end of the war and is seen here in front of the familiar hangars at the RAE Farnborough during a display of enemy equipment in 1945.

232B transport, whereas run-of-the-mill captured aircraft were almost invariably flown in. Oddly enough, this cotton-wool treatment of Tank's fighter continued, and I cannot recall that, after re-assembly, it was put through any specific flight testing other than that I was instructed to perform while flying it from Farnborough to Brize Norton for storage during the summer of 1945.

The original radial-engined Fw 190 had been, in my view, an aerodynamic beauty oozing lethality, but it struck me on first seeing the Ta 152H-1 standing outside Farnborough's famous 'A' shed in the company of the latest Allied fighters — the Tempest V, the Mustang III, the Spitfire 21 and the Martin-Baker M.B.5 — that Tank's design had lost much its aesthetic appeal over the intervening years, with its overly prominent proboscis and wings that seemed to stretch into infinity. If now less curvaceous, it still exuded efficiency, however, and I had little doubt that it was capable of doing all that the Germans claimed for it.

High performance at all altitudes was ensured by its 18.7 Imp gal (85 l) of nitrous oxide (GM 1) and 15.4 Imp gal (70 l) of methanol-water (MW 50), which, injected into the Jumo 213E engine according to the altitude at which the fighter was flying, boosted output mightily. Perhaps this was the clue as to why the Ta 152H-1 was never really put through its paces in the UK — we had no GM 1 or MW 50 at Farnborough! Nevertheless, lack of nitrous oxide and methanol-water notwithstanding, my adrenalin began to flow that summer morning as I eased myself into the cockpit of Ta 152H-1 *Werk-Nr* 150168 and peered along that immense nose which stretched out so far ahead of the windscreen — the only aircraft that I was ever to fly offering a comparable stretch of nose was the Blackburn Fire-

brand. The German fighter was, of course, equipped with a pressure cabin and since I had done quite a lot of high altitude flying in the pressurised Spitfire XIX on clear air tubulence investigation, the opportunity given by the flight to Brize Norton to make a comparison between the German and British fighters was irresistible.

The take-off of the Ta 152H-1 was shorter than that of the Spitfire XIX and the climb was steeper albeit somewhat slower than that of the British fighter, but once the 30,000 ft (9 145 m) mark had slipped past on the altimeter, the Tank fighter gave the impression of holding its rate of climb better than its British counterpart. In so far as manoeuvrability was concerned, the story was very much the same; the Spitfire was certainly the better of the two below 30,000 ft (9 145 m), there being little to choose between British and German fighters between that altitude and 35,000 ft (10 670 m), but above the latter altitude the Ta 152H-1 enjoyed a decided edge. I gave the German fighter its head on the way to Brize Norton and did a full throttle run at 35,000 ft (10 670 m), which, by my rough reckoning, worked out at around 425 mph (684 km/h), or about 35 mph (56 km/h) less than the Spitfire XIX was capable of, but, of course, the availability of GM 1 boost would have more than redressed the balance and the Ta 152H-1 was certainly the superior aeroplane on the score of range. In essence, however, these two potential opponents were remarkably close from many aspects, illustrating how closely parallel Britain and Germany were running in piston-engined fighter technology.

On the descent from altitude to Brize Norton, I had time to make quick checks on the stability and control of the German fighter. I found a noticeable reduction in roll rate and an increase in the stick force per *g* by comparison with its BMW

Another of the captured Tank fighters, a Ta 152H-1, shown here with the US Foreign Evaluation (FE) number 112 for trials in the USA, and with unauthentic Luftwaffe *markings applied crudely over RAF roundels and fin flash. The general arrangement drawing on the opposite page depicts the Ta 152C V7 Werk-Nr 110 007, prototype for the Ta 152C-0/R11*

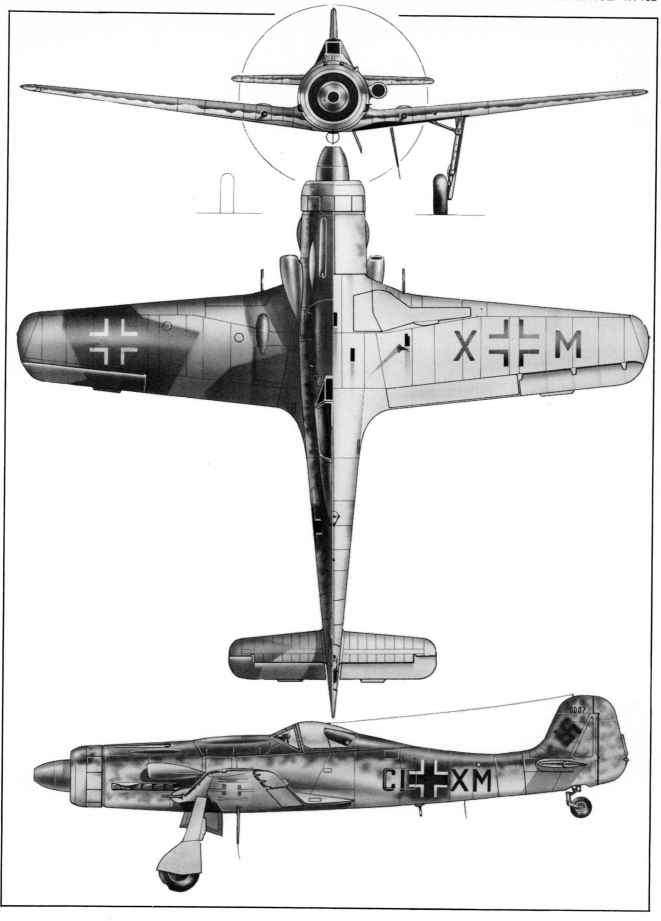

801-powered predecessors, some of the more attractive qual- ities of the original fighter having been sacrificed in order to achieve the best possible performance at extreme altitudes. I therefore expected the stability to be improved over that of the Fw 190, as indeed it was, but it was not so good that a pro- tracted flight at 45,000 ft (13 715 m) would not have been a fatiguing experience, a fact evidently recognised by the provi- sion of an autopilot.

The landing at Brize Norton from an approach at 118 mph (190 km/h) was straightforward enough, although I took the precaution of landing off a curved final to see round that fantastic nose. With its wide-track undercarriage, the aircraft felt very stable on the landing run, a characteristic for which I was to be thankful some weeks later, after the powers-that-be had decided that our Ta 152H-1 should take its place in the static park of the Exhibition of German Aircraft and Equip- ment that was being organised at Farnborough.

On 22 October 1945, I returned to Brize Norton to bring the Ta 152H-1 back to Farnborough for the exhibition, the fighter having been in storage since I had delivered it there on 18 August. Needless to say, I gave the aircraft a pretty thorough pre-flight check and engine run-up before taking-off for Farn- borough. In the event, the flight was uneventful, but once I touched down on Farnborough's main runway and began to apply the foot brakes I immediately realised that these were very weak indeed. In fact, they faded away rapidly to zero effectiveness. A slight swing started to develop and I let this go enough to steer me on to the grass in order to slow the aircraft. I

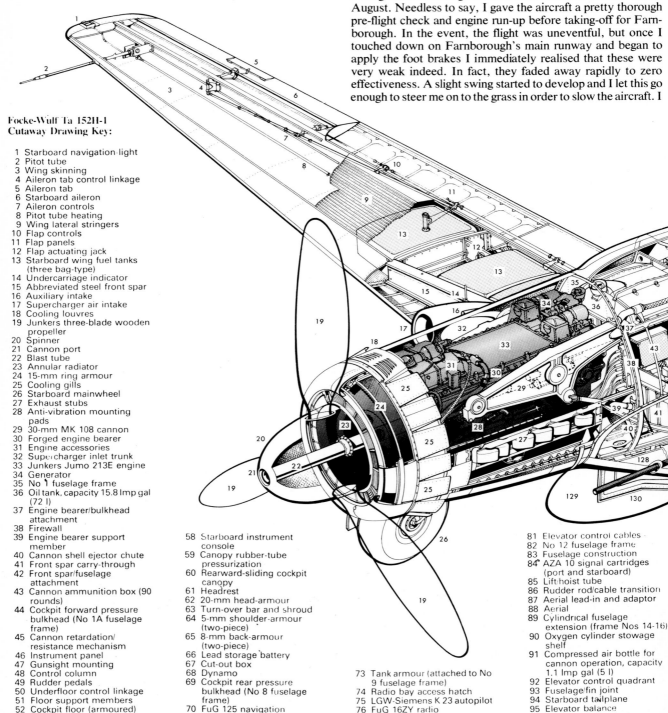

Focke-Wulf Ta 152H-1 Cutaway Drawing Key:

1 Starboard navigation light
2 Pitot tube
3 Wing skinning
4 Aileron tab control linkage
5 Aileron tab
6 Starboard aileron
7 Aileron controls
8 Pitot tube heating
9 Wing lateral stringers
10 Flap controls
11 Flap panels
12 Flap actuating jack
13 Starboard wing fuel tanks (three bag-type)
14 Undercarriage indicator
15 Abbreviated steel front spar
16 Auxiliary intake
17 Supercharger air intake
18 Cooling louvres
19 Junkers three-blade wooden propeller
20 Spinner
21 Cannon port
22 Blast tube
23 Annular radiator
24 15-mm ring armour
25 Cooling gills
26 Starboard mainwheel
27 Exhaust stubs
28 Anti-vibration mounting pads
29 30-mm MK 108 cannon
30 Forged engine bearer
31 Engine accessories
32 Supercharger inlet trunk
33 Junkers Jumo 213E engine
34 Generator
35 No 1 fuselage frame
36 Oil tank, capacity 15.8 Imp gal (72 l)
37 Engine bearer/bulkhead attachment
38 Firewall
39 Engine bearer support member
40 Cannon shell ejector chute
41 Front spar carry-through
42 Front spar/fuselage attachment
43 Cannon ammunition box (90 rounds)
44 Cockpit forward pressure bulkhead (No 1A fuselage frame)
45 Cannon retardation/ resistance mechanism
46 Instrument panel
47 Gunsight mounting
48 Control column
49 Rudder pedals
50 Underfloor control linkage
51 Floor support members
52 Cockpit floor (armoured)
53 Seat harness attachment
54 Pilot's seat (armoured)
55 Instrument panel shroud
56 Revi 16B gunsight
57 Armoured-glass windscreen

58 Starboard instrument console
59 Canopy rubber-tube pressurization
60 Rearward-sliding cockpit canopy
61 Headrest
62 20-mm head-armour
63 Turn-over bar and shroud
64 5-mm shoulder-armour (two-piece)
65 8-mm back-armour (two-piece)
66 Lead storage battery
67 Cut-out box
68 Dynamo
69 Cockpit rear pressure bulkhead (No 8 fuselage frame)
70 FuG 125 navigation equipment (only in H-1/R11 all-weather variant)
71 Distributor
72 GM 1 tank, capacity 18.7 Imp gal (85 l)

73 Tank armour (attached to No 9 fuselage frame)
74 Radio bay access hatch
75 LGW-Siemens K 23 autopilot
76 FuG 16ZY radio transmitter/receiver
77 No 10 fuselage frame
78 Rudder control rod
79 Compressed air line
80 Master compass

81 Elevator control cables
82 No 12 fuselage frame
83 Fuselage construction
84 AZA 10 signal cartridges (port and starboard)
85 Lift/hoist tube
86 Rudder rod/cable transition
87 Aerial lead-in and adaptor
88 Aerial
89 Cylindrical fuselage extension (frame Nos 14-16)
90 Oxygen cylinder stowage shelf
91 Compressed air bottle for cannon operation, capacity 1.1 Imp gal (5 l)
92 Elevator control quadrant
93 Fuselage/fin joint
94 Starboard tailplane
95 Elevator balance
96 Starboard elevator
97 Elevator tab
98 Fin construction
99 Tailwheel retraction cable
100 Rudder upper hinge

then applied full opposite rudder to prevent a ground loop developing. After a few adrenalin-pumping seconds, the Ta 152H slowed gently to a standstill. I doubt that this hydraulic fault was ever rectified as I cannot recollect the fighter ever flying again.

In my view, the Ta 152H was every bit as good as any of its Allied piston-engined counterparts and, from some aspects, better than most. It was unfortunate for the *Jagdflieger* but undoubtedly fortunate for the Allies that it arrived on the scene too late to play any serious rôle in the air war.

101 Rudder construction
102 Tailwheel leg retraction guide
103 Rudder hinge control
104 Rudder tab
105 Rear navigation light
106 Electric lead
107 Elevator torque tube
108 Tailwheel shock-absorber
109 Elevator tab
110 Elevator balance
111 Elevator construction
112 Semi-retractable tailwheel (380 x 150-mm)

126 Wing gun forward mounting
127 BSK 16 camera gun
128 Gun barrel
129 Auxiliary drop tank, capacity 66 Imp gal (300 l)
130 Port inboard undercarriage door
131 Ventral antenna

144 Fuel pump
145 VHF interference suppressor
146 Port inboard wing tank (MW 50), capacity 15.4 Imp gal (70 l)

Focke-Wulf Ta 152H-1 Specification

Power Plant: One Junkers Jumo 213E-1 12-cylinder liquid-cooled Vee in-line engine rated at 1,750 hp for take-off or 2,050 hp with MW 50 methanol-water injection and 1,320 hp at 32,810 ft (10 000 m) or 1,740 hp with GM 1 nitrous oxide boost. Six wing tanks with total capacity of 234 Imp gal (1 018 l) plus one fuselage tank of 130 Imp gal (600 l) capacity.
Performance: Max speed, 332 mph (534 km/h) at sea level or 350 mph (563 km/h) with MW 50; 465 mph (748 km/h) at 29,530 ft (9 000 m) with MW 50 and 472 mph (760 km/h) at 41,010 ft (12 500 m) with GM 1; continuous cruising speed, 311 mph (500 km/h) at 22,965 ft (7 000 m); initial rate of climb, 3,445 ft/min (17,5 m/sec) with MW 50; service ceiling, 48,550 ft (14 800 m) with GM 1; range (clean, at max continuous cruise speed), 755 mls (1 215 km) at 376 mph (605 km/h) at 32,810 ft (10 000 m); range (with 66-Imp gal/215-l drop tank, at economical cruise), 1,250 mls (2 000 km) at 293 mph (472 km/h) at 22,965 ft (7 000m).
Weights: Empty equipped, 8,642 lb (3 920 kg); normal loaded, 10,472 lb (4 750 kg); max take-off, 11,502 lb (5 217 kg).
Dimensions: Span, 47 ft 4½ in (14.440 m); length, 35 ft 1½ in (10.710 m); height, 11 ft 0¼ in (3.36 m); wing area, 250.8 sq ft (23.3 m²).
Armament: One 30-mm Mk 108 engine-mounted cannon firing through airscrew spinner with 90 rounds and one 20-mm MG 151 cannon in each inner wing with 175 rpg.

147 Port navigation light electric lead
148 Port centre wing tank (B4 fuel)
149 Mainwheel leg attachment plate (spar rear face)

113 Fin spar attachment
114 Antenna
115 D F loop
116 Retractable entry step
117 Spring-loaded hand/foothold
118 Rear fuselage fuel tank (protected), capacity 80 Imp gal (362 l)
119 Rear spar/fuselage attachment
120 Forward fuselage fuel tank (protected), capacity 51 Imp gal (233 l)
121 Wing gun breech fairing
122 Port MG 151/20 wing gun
123 Shell ejector chute
124 Port ammunition box (175 rounds)
125 Undercarriage retraction guide track

132 Undercarriage retraction strut
133 Towing lug (port and starboard legs)
134 Undercarriage leg
135 Port mainwheel (740 x 210-mm)
136 Brake cable
137 Axle
138 Port outboard undercarriage door
139 Shock-absorbers
140 Mainwheel leg fairing
141 Mainwheel leg pivot point
142 Undercarriage indicator
143 Abbreviated steel front spar

150 Flap actuating jack
151 Port outboard wing tank (B4 fuel)
152 Flap structure
153 Wing lateral stringers
154 Wing rib stations
155 Wing skinning
156 Aileron tab control linkage
157 Aileron tab
158 Port aileron
159 Full-span rear spar
160 Port navigation light

ARADO AR 234B

LIGHTNING is an appellation that has been bestowed on a variety of warplanes in a variety of languages, but to the Allies in the last few months of 1944 it seemed that none had been so dubbed more appropriately than the Arado Ar 234 which seared across the skies above Normandy and British East Coast harbours like greased lightning, performing its reconnaissance missions with complete impunity. The Ar 234 appeared truly *blitzschnell* to Allied fighter pilots assigned the impossible task of intercepting this turbojet-driven interloper; they had about as much chance of bringing their guns to bear on the elusive German newcomer to the air war arena as they had of knocking it from the sky with a volley of profane oaths. At the speeds and altitudes at which it normally performed its reconnoitring only mechanical malfunction could bring it down.

Whatever the advances and innovations introduced by the German turbojet-powered warplanes contemporary with the Arado and however sound may have been their aerodynamic design, few would have claimed them to be æsthetic standard setters. The Ar 234B *Blitz,* on the other hand, was advanced, innovatory *and* shapely, and when I saw my first Arado at the Danish airfield of Grove, between Herning and Viborg in Jutland, I was immediately impressed by its æsthetically attractive contours which were eloquent of aerodynamic efficiency. This aeroplane *looked* right and in my experience this was always a good omen with regard to flying qualities. With its slender shoulder-mounted wing, slim underslung engine nacelles and smooth fuselage profile, it exemplified careful aerodynamic design.

Powered by engines similar to those of the Me 262 but a much bigger aeroplane carrying almost twice as much fuel, the Arado reconnaissance-bomber followed in the wake of the Messerschmitt fighter in so far as development timing was concerned, but power plants apart, the two warplanes had one thing in common — both commenced their prototype lives with undercarriage layouts totally different from those with which they emerged in production configurations. From the outset of design the provision of an adequate

undercarriage had posed something of a problem for the Arado design team, for the thin, shoulder-mounted wing afforded insufficient space for the mainwheels, their legs and actuating mechanisms, and, in any case, would have demanded inordinately long oleos which it would have been necessary to compress during retraction. The fuselage, which was of minimum cross section, afforded little space for a conventional undercarriage and therefore the adoption of the unorthodox in the form of a jettisonable trolley was very much a case of *force majeure.*

This trolley employed a tricycle wheel arrangement, the nosewheel being steerable and the mainwheels being fitted with hydraulic brakes operated by the pilot's rudder pedals, a lever in the cockpit providing for the release of the trolley which it was intended should be jettisoned by the pilot at the moment of unstick. As the aircraft and trolley parted company a braking 'chute was automatically deployed to bring the latter to a standstill. For landing a centrally-mounted main skid and outrigger skids beneath the engine nacelles were provided, these skids being extended during take-off to provide the supports on which the aircraft rested on the trolley. The trolley weighed 1,325 lb (600 kg), but the skid arrangement gave a landing gear weight of only three per cent of the total all-up weight of the aircraft as opposed to the usual five per cent of wheeled undercarriage layouts.

Nobody was happy with this arrangement, however, as although the trolley-and-skid combination was eventually brought to a stage at which it functioned with reasonable efficiency, the aircraft was unable to manœuvre on its skids after landing, having to be raised on to the take-off trolley for towing to dispersal. Landing areas could well have become cluttered with immobile Ar 234s which would have made easy prey for any Allied fighters that happened to chance on them. Thus at an early stage in the development career of the aircraft some redesign was undertaken in order to provide space for a more orthodox fuselage-housed undercarriage. The fuselage cross section was marginally enlarged and much of the bay formed by the central fuselage box girder was adapted for wheel wells, the fore and aft fuselage tanks being enlarged to compensate for the loss of capacity resulting from the deletion of the central fuel cell in order to accommodate the mainwheels. The main members were single-wheel units with a somewhat complex hydraulically-operated mechanism which enabled them to pivot inwards while their oleo legs retracted forwards. A heavy nosewheel fork was attached to the fuselage beneath the pilot's seat, this unit retracting aft.

I arrived at Grove airfield early in May of 1945 with the specific purpose of discovering what sort of prizes had fallen into our hands when Germany had surrendered, and a rich haul of the most modern German aircraft indeed littered this former *Luftwaffe* base. The Germans had developed Grove — later to be known as Karup and to become an important NATO base — into a very large complex, and some of the *Luftwaffe* aircraft that we found there had arrived during the very last days of hostilities in Europe as their pilots fled the crumbling Fatherland. There was little opportunity to examine the Ar 234B closely on that occasion as what time I had available at Grove was occupied in drawing up an inventory of what was there — and an appetising list it made.

On returning to the RAE at Farnborough I learned that an Arado test pilot, one *Flugkapitän* Joachim Carl, had fallen into our hands. Carl was probably the most experienced of Ar 234 pilots and I was provided with an opportunity to interrogate him towards the end of the month. After a period as a flying instructor, Joachim Carl had begun test flying for the *Reichsluftfahrtministerium* in 1936, and had spent several years at the Rechlin test centre, test flying some 60 different types of aeroplane before being assigned to the Arado Flugzeugwerke in 1941 as a production test pilot, flying Junkers Ju 88A-4s and A-6s and then Heinkel He 177As which were licence built at Arado's Brandenburg-Neuendorf facility until, in May 1944, he was appointed chief test pilot and superintendent of Arado's Alt Lönnewitz flight test division in succession to *Flugkapitän* Selle. Selle had lost his life while testing the Ar 234 V7, a sudden fire in the port turbojet having burned through the control rods

Prior to the adoption of an orthodox undercarriage, the Ar 234 employed a rather cumbersome trolley-and-skid arrangement seen here on the Ar 243 V1 (immediately above and below) and V2 (head of page).

(Below) One of the several examples of the Ar 234B-2 taken to the USA for evaluation purposes after WW II, this particular aircraft having undergone testing by the US Navy

while the aircraft was in the landing circuit. An assembly line for the production *Blitz* had been set up at Alt Lönnewitz, and on 8 June 1944, two days after the D-Day landings in Normandy, Joachim Carl flew the first pre-series *Blitz*.

Carl had subsequently amassed considerable experience with the Ar 234B, and drawing on this I jotted down a complete set of flying instructions which it was obvious would have to suffice until we got our hands on a set of the official *Luftwaffe* pilot's notes. He seemed a knowledgeable and thoroughly competent pilot with a sound technical background, and so I had every confidence that the information that he had given me would be proven reliable.

Less a few compressor blades

Our first Ar 234B arrived at Farnborough on 6 June 1945, and as Sqdn Ldr Tony Martindale and I had been assigned the task of ferrying two such aircraft back from Grove as

soon as possible I went over that particular *Blitz* with a fine-toothed comb. My first impressions were decidedly favourable, although I admit that the pilot, seated way out in front in that extensively-glazed nose, was going to be very close to any accident. The narrow-track undercarriage and rather high tail did not strike me as a particularly auspicious marriage for crosswind operations. With these mental notes, I boarded a Wellington on 23 June to fly to Copenhagen, and the next day reached Grove.

Our two Arados were being prepared for flight by a team of *Luftwaffe* ground crew, and it was manifestly obvious that some of these POWs did not relish their task. On the afternoon of 24 June I spent an hour sitting in the cockpit of a third *Blitz* that it was intended that I should later return to pick up. I also chatted with some of the ground crew working on the Arados but, somewhat depressed, they were not very communicative, and as their POW status was still rather fresh to them I suppose that this was understandable enough.

The evening was so fine that Tony Martindale and I decided that we could perform quick handling flights around the airfield area and still leave ourselves with enough fuel for the short stage to Schleswig where the RAE had set up its collection centre for captured aircraft. My *Blitz* was the first ready so I taxied out to the end of the runway and ran up the engines to full power. All seemed well and I was just about to release the brakes for take-off when the starboard engine almost blew itself out of the airframe, spewing compressor blades out of the back end on to the runway. I shut down the port engine and vacated the cockpit like a scalded cat!

Failure or sabotage? That was the question. Suffice to say that what could have been a lengthy and inconclusive technical investigation was resolved peremptorily by the unorthodox but effective psychology employed by an officer of the RAF Regiment who interrogated the ground crew that had serviced my aircraft. In no time he had winkled out the saboteur who was promptly removed to the POW cage, the

(Above) An Ar 234B-2 Blitz being refuelled by Luftwaffe POWs at the Danish airfield of Grove, Jutland, preparatory to be ferried to Schleswig en route to the RAE at Farnborough. A total of nine Ar 234Bs was flown to the UK for evaluation, one of these being illustrated below after arrival. The general arrangement drawing on the opposite page depicts an Ar 234B-2/P Blitz of 9./KG 76 at Achmer in February 1945

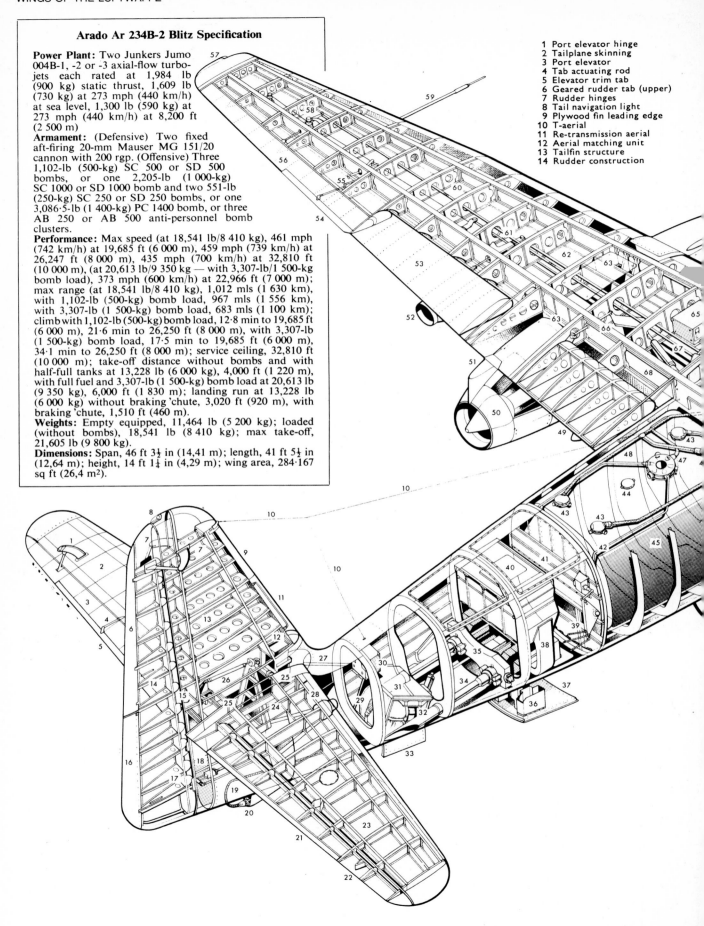

Arado Ar 234B-2 Blitz Specification

Power Plant: Two Junkers Jumo 004B-1, -2 or -3 axial-flow turbo-jets each rated at 1,984 lb (900 kg) static thrust, 1,609 lb (730 kg) at 273 mph (440 km/h) at sea level, 1,300 lb (590 kg) at 273 mph (440 km/h) at 8,200 ft (2 500 m).

Armament: (Defensive) Two fixed aft-firing 20-mm Mauser MG 151/20 cannon with 200 rgp. (Offensive) Three 1,102-lb (500-kg) SC 500 or SD 500 bombs, or one 2,205-lb (1 000-kg) SC 1000 or SD 1000 bomb and two 551-lb (250-kg) SC 250 or SD 250 bombs, or one 3,086·5-lb (1 400-kg) PC 1400 bomb, or three AB 250 or AB 500 anti-personnel bomb clusters.

Performance: Max speed (at 18,541 lb/8 410 kg), 461 mph (742 km/h) at 19,685 ft (6 000 m), 459 mph (739 km/h) at 26,247 ft (8 000 m), 435 mph (700 km/h) at 32,810 ft (10 000 m), (at 20,613 lb/9 350 kg — with 3,307-lb/1 500-kg bomb load), 373 mph (600 km/h) at 22,966 ft (7 000 m); max range (at 18,541 lb/8 410 kg), 1,012 mls (1 630 km), with 1,102-lb (500-kg) bomb load, 967 mls (1 556 km), with 3,307-lb (1 500-kg) bomb load, 683 mls (1 100 km); climb with 1,102-lb (500-kg) bomb load, 12·8 min to 19,685 ft (6 000 m), 21·6 min to 26,250 ft (8 000 m), with 3,307-lb (1 500-kg) bomb load, 17·5 min to 19,685 ft (6 000 m), 34·1 min to 26,250 ft (8 000 m); service ceiling, 32,810 ft (10 000 m); take-off distance without bombs and with half-full tanks at 13,228 lb (6 000 kg), 4,000 ft (1 220 m), with full fuel and 3,307-lb (1 500-kg) bomb load at 20,613 lb (9 350 kg), 6,000 ft (1 830 m); landing run at 13,228 lb (6 000 kg) without braking 'chute, 3,020 ft (920 m), with braking 'chute, 1,510 ft (460 m).

Weights: Empty equipped, 11,464 lb (5 200 kg); loaded (without bombs), 18,541 lb (8 410 kg); max take-off, 21,605 lb (9 800 kg).

Dimensions: Span, 46 ft 3½ in (14,41 m); length, 41 ft 5½ in (12,64 m); height, 14 ft 1¼ in (4,29 m); wing area, 284·167 sq ft (26,4 m²).

1 Port elevator hinge
2 Tailplane skinning
3 Port elevator
4 Tab actuating rod
5 Elevator trim tab
6 Geared rudder tab (upper)
7 Rudder hinges
8 Tail navigation light
9 Plywood fin leading edge
10 T-aerial
11 Re-transmission aerial
12 Aerial matching unit
13 Tailfin structure
14 Rudder construction

Arado Ar 234B-2/lr Blitz cutaway key

15 Rudder post
16 Rudder tab (lower)
17 Lower rudder hinge
18 Rudder actuating rods
19 Parachute cable
20 Cable anchor point/tailskid
21 Starboard elevator tab
22 Elevator construction
23 Tailplane construction
24 Elevator control linkage
25 Tailplane attachment points
26 Elevator rod
27 Port side control runs
28 Internal mass balance
29 Parachute release
   mechanism
30 Main FuG 16zy panel
   (BZA computer)

31 Brake parachute container
32 Starboard MG 151 cannon
   muzzle
33 Brake chute door (open)
34 Mauser MG 151/20 cannon
   (rearward firing)
35 Cannon support yoke
36 Spent cartridge chute
37 Access panel (lowered)
38 Ammunition feed chute
39 Tail surface control rods
   (starboard)
40 Ammunition box
41 Bulkhead
42 Fuel vent pipe
43 Fuel pumps
44 Fuel lever gauge
45 Rear fuel cell (440 Imp
   gal — 2 000 l capacity)
46 Fuselage frames

47 Fuel filler point
48 Fuel lines
49 Inner flap construction
50 Exhaust cone
51 Nacelle support fairing
52 RATO exhaust
53 Outer flap section
54 Aileron tab
55 Tab actuating rod
56 Port aileron

57 Port navigation light
58 Aileron control linkage
59 Pitot tube
60 Front spar
61 Outer flap control linkage
62 Wing construction
63 Nacelle attachment points
   (front and rear spar)
64 Detachable nacelle cowling
65 FuG 25a IFF unit
66 Inner flap control linkage
67 Control rods and
   hydraulic activating rod
68 Rear spar

69 Hydraulic fluid tank
   (4 Imp gal — 18 l capacity)
70 Centre section box
71 FuG 25a ring antenna
72 Suppressed D/F antenna
73 Fuel pumps
74 Fuel level gauge
75 Fuel filler point
76 Fuel lines
77 Bulkhead

78 Port control console
   (throttle quadrant)
79 Pilot entry hatch (hinged
   to starboard)
80 Periscopic sight
81 Periscopic head (rearview
   mirror/gunsight)
82 Clear vision cockpit
   glazing
83 Instrument panel
84 Rudder pedal
85 Swivel-mounted control
   stick
86 Lotfe 7K tachometric
   bombsight mounting
87 Pilot's seat
88 Starboard control console
   (oil/temperature gauges)
89 Radio panel (FuG 16zy
   behind pilot's seat)
90 Oxygen bottles
91 Nosewheel door
92 Nosewheel fork
93 Rearward-retracting
   nosewheel
94 Nosewheel well centre
   section
95 Fuselage frames
96 Forward fuel cell
   (385 Imp gal — 1 800 l
   capacity)
97 Bulkhead
98 Mainwheel door
99 Starboard mainwheel well
100 Mainwheel leg door
101 Starboard mainwheel leg
102 Forward-retracting
    mainwheel
103 SC 1000 "Hermann" bomb
    beneath fuselage
104 Engine exhaust
105 Auxiliary cooling intakes
106 Starboard Jumo 004B
    turbojet
107 Annular oil tank
108 Riedel starter motor in
    nose cone
109 Auxiliary tank (66 Imp
    gal — 300 l) beneath
    nacelle (not carried with
    SC 1000 bomb)
110 Flap outer section
    construction
111 Walter HWK 500A-1
    RATO unit
112 RATO recovery parachute
    pack
113 Aileron tab
114 Starboard aileron
    construction
115 Wing skin stiffeners
116 Starboard navigation light

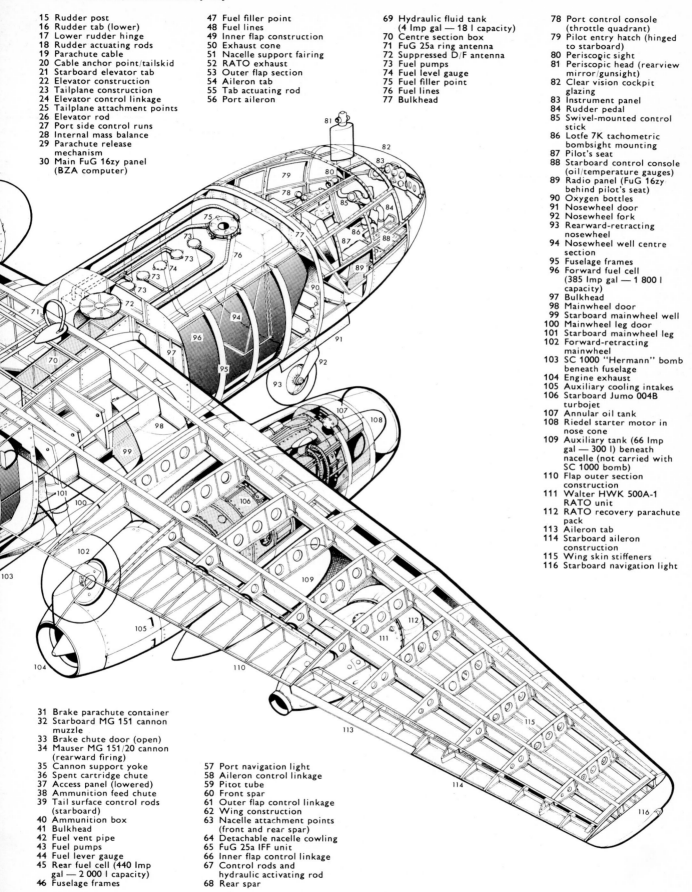

This Ar 234B-1/b (Werk-Nr 140 312), taken to Wright Field in 1945 for evaluation, was allegedly acquired at Saalbach and may be presumed to have been included on the strength of 1./FAGr.110 which performed reconnaissance missions under Luftflotte 6 during the closing months of the war in Europe

others resuming work on the two remaining aircraft under close supervision.

The next morning I clambered into Ar 234B *Werk-Nr* 140 008 which had a history of being flown operationally over the Ardennes, and took-off on an uneventful flight to Schleswig during which I found the *Blitz* a delightful aeroplane to fly. The ferry flight from Schleswig to Farnborough was made on the afternoon of the same day at an altitude of 25,000 ft (7 620 m). This took 1 hr 55 min on a dog leg course south to Gilze-Rijen in Holland and then direct to Farnborough. I flew in company with Tony Martindale whose oxygen failed over the North Sea, forcing us to drop down to 10,000 ft (3 050 m) for the last 100 or so miles of the trip. I was astonished at the ample fuel reserve that we still had on landing at our destination.

I was subsequently to fly the Ar 234B more extensively than any other high performance operational type of German aircraft, and from the outset it provided me with plenty of excitement and interest. Being a much larger aeroplane than, say, the Me 262, it was appreciably roomier and, in consequence, the controls were more rationally arranged. Starting was certainly simplified in that the necessary controls and switches were more to hand than in the Me 262, placing fewer demands on manual dexterity. Perhaps the most novel feature was the downward vision between one's feet on the rudder pedals, something that I had experienced previously only in a helicopter.

The *Blitz* was not provided with an ejection seat and an emergency escape by parachute must have presented a distinctly shaky proposition. This view is reflected somewhat by the Pilot's Notes which devote a mere 25 words to the subject with the following advice: (1) Reduce speed to 137 mph (220 km/h); (2) Uncouple the control column and throw it forward; (3) Jettison the roof hatch; (4) If possible dive sideways under the wing leading edge. The system for starting the Jumo 004B engines was in general similar to that for the Me 262's engines (see pages 61-62), and again gentle throttle handling was called for at all times to prevent a flame-out.

Take-off was made using flaps set to the START (25 deg) position; the nosewheel could be raised at 112 mph (180 km/h) and the aeroplane was pulled off gently at 124 mph (200 km/h). The elevator trimmer had to be used as speed built up and the undercarriage and flaps were raised. The trimming system was somewhat unusual in that there was an indicator gauge and an actuating lever with a twist-grip selector on top of the lever. The trimmer was set to zero for take-off and the selector arrow pointed forward (ie, nose heavy), and as speed built up the lever was pumped to give nose down trim by moving the tailplane mechanically by this pumping action.

The take-off run was long, but single-engine safety speed was 140 mph (225 km/h) when the aircraft would swing and bank, though not violently, and provided corrective action was taken within two seconds it could be held straight without loss of height. This docility was in marked contrast to the Me 262's single-engine characteristics. Flaps were raised after reaching 155 mph (250 km/h) and then speed for the initial climb built up to 248 mph (400 km/h). This was reduced to 236 mph (380 km/h) after passing through 26,245 ft (8 000 m) altitude to give optimum rate of climb. The maximum initial climb rate was 2,500 ft/min (12,7 m/sec) but had reduced to 1,800 ft/min (9,14 m/sec) by 10,000 ft (3,050 m) and to 1,000 ft/min (5,08 m/sec) by 20,000 ft (6 095 m).

These figures were certainly good for a 1945 vintage reconnaissance-bomber but the top speed of 475 mph (765 km/h) was what made *Blitz* so appropriate a name for the Ar 234B. When one recalls the comparative immunity enjoyed by our own Mosquito bomber over Germany the significance of the very much superior performance of the Arado becomes apparent. The *Blitz* handled beautifully at high altitude, its stability about all axes being positive and the harmony of control being good. These characteristics allied to the superlative view that it offered its pilot made the Ar 234B a first class platform for photography or bombing.

However, not every Ar 234B displayed these fine handling qualities; quality control was suffering adversely in the chaotic conditions prevailing in the German aircraft industry as a result of the heavy Allied bombing attacks. On the *Blitz* the extremely sharp-nosed Frise ailerons were very sensitive to rigging errors and could misbehave violently at speeds above 373 mph (600 km/h), a common fault being rapid oscillation of the ailerons accompanied by side-to-side threshing of the stick. Joachim Carl told me that he found it impossible to get the manufacturing people to tighten up tolerances sufficiently, and anything up to 10 flights were needed on each production aeroplane to get the ailerons correctly adjusted.

The *Blitz*, like all other contemporary jet aircraft, also

suffered from directional snaking, and as often as not this undesirable characteristic was aggravated by poor manufacturing standards on the rudder which sometimes came out fatter or thinner than the fin profile. The Arado company failed to tackle this problem with anything like the competence displayed by Messerschmitt in dealing with a similar affliction on the Me 262, merely rectifying the fault by off-setting the rudder hinge to one or other side, or by rigging the balance and trim tabs out in opposite directions.

German test pilots did not investigate the high Mach characteristics of the Ar 234B to any great extent, although normal production testing involved a dive from 9,840 ft (3 000 m) up to a true speed of 528 mph (850 km/h) — low altitude work that did not involve compressibility effects. The transonic region was, therefore, virtually fresh ground for us to break with the Ar 234B at the RAE, and so I embarked upon a series of dives from an altitude of 30,000 ft (9 145 m). The *Blitz* accelerated less than expected from maximum cruising speed and so a dive of some 30 deg was needed to achieve the desired entry into the compressibility region before too much altitude was lost. This also entailed using nose-down trim, as otherwise the push force to hold the dive angle became too high. At $M = 0.76$ nose heaviness set in and the elevator began to feel sloppy. These effects were accentuated until at $M = 0.82$ full backward pull on the stick was required to hold the dive angle constant and to allow the loss of altitude to have its density effect on reducing true airspeed until recovery could be effected. For its rôle as a reconnaissance-bomber, therefore, the Ar 234B had a tactical Mach number of 0·75 while its top speed at around 30,000 ft (9 145 m) was about $M = 0.72$, a useful combination exceeding that of most Allied fighters in 1944–5.

The low-speed end of the performance envelope displayed extremely docile characteristics at the stall, this being a straightforward and gentle nose drop. Stalling speed in landing condition was 112 mph (180 km/h). Landing was very easy since the view from the cockpit was superb, although once or twice I experienced heavy condensation in the cockpit which suddenly plunged the occupant into an opaque goldfish bowl. There was only one remedy for this — get on to instruments and do a fast low-level run to clear the film of moisture. Obviously this was not the situation to get into in bad weather conditions or when fuel was low. However, the German jets all had powerful heating systems and as I found

that these tended to make the cockpit excessively stuffy I did not use them at full blast, which may have accounted for my trouble.

The maximum speed for lowering the undercarriage was 248 mph (400 km/h) and then flaps to 25 deg at 199 mph (320 km/h). I found it best to apply full 45 deg flap after turning on to the final approach at about 174 mph (280 km/h), reducing speed to 130 mph (210 km/h), and, when sure of making the airfield, easing back the throttles to idling at 4,000 rpm, crossing the boundary at 124 mph (200 km/h). The landing run was lengthy as the rather ineffective brakes faded badly, having to be held on continuously throughout the ground run. All versions of the *Blitz* had a braking 'chute fitted which almost halved the landing run, but although I had my hand on the red release toggle many times I needed to use this device only once.

From Sola to Farnborough
I was able to gain far more of my *Blitz* flying experience during ferrying than testing, for our troops had come across a whole squadron of Ar 234B-2s on Sola airfield, Stavanger, and I was assigned the task of getting these aircraft back to the UK. For this I used a Siebel Si 204D as a communications hack and mobile workshop and, having loaded it with all metric tools, oils, greases, spare tyres, etc, likely to be called for during the ferrying operation, set off from Farnborough with a second pilot who was to shuttle the Siebel between Sola and Schleswig while I flew the Arados between the two bases.

Once at Sola I decided that the job called for some expert assistance, so I handpicked two German maintenance NCOs and took on strength the *Hauptmann* who had served as maintenance test pilot on the airfield. They accepted their new rôle with a certain inevitability tempered with the knowledge that their fate as my helpmates would be a good deal more agreeable than that of their comrades in the POW cage.

It had been my original intention to use the *Hauptmann* purely in an advisory capacity, then the tempting thought struck me that I might use him actually to fly some of the aircraft on the ferry route. Such a course had its risk as neutral Sweden was invitingly close for a dash for freedom, but I weighed the pros and cons and decided to minimise the risk by always flying on his tail; providing him with a course and

This photograph of the Ar 234B-1/b (also illustrated on the opposite page) emphasises the aerodynamic cleanliness of this Arado design which enjoyed the distinction of having been the first bomber to be designed specifically for turbojet power

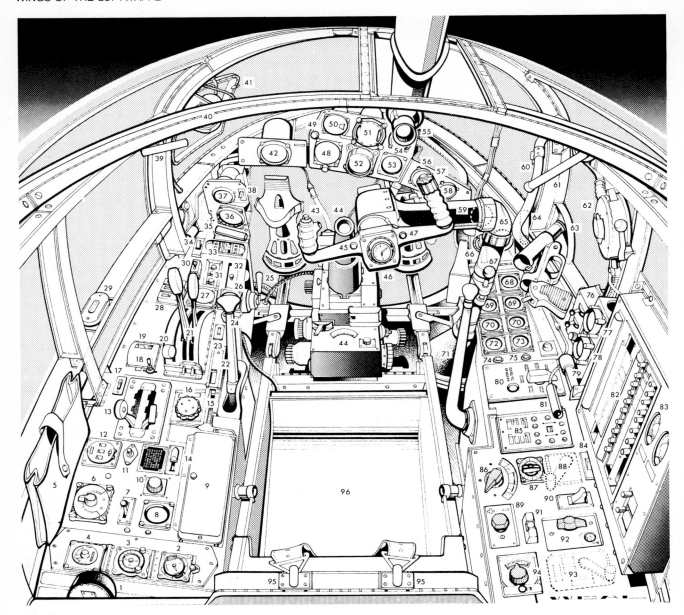

Arado Ar 234 Blitz Cockpit layout and instrumentation

1 Undercarriage warning horn
2 Contact altimeter
3 Height corrector
4 Wind corrector
5 Map (document) case
6 Rectified airspeed corrector
7 Exhaust nozzle control switch
8 Outside air temperature gauge
9 Navigation equipment stowage
10 Cockpit lights rheostat
11 RATO jettison button
12 RATO selector panel
13 Fuel cocks
14 Engine nozzle control override switch (anti-surge)
15 Tailplane position/incidence indicator
16 Rudder trim wheel and indicator.
17 Auxiliary fuel tank selector switch
18 Initial ignition switch
19 Ignition warning indicator
20 Throttle friction damper lock
21 Throttle quadrant
22 Tailplane trim actuator handle

23 Retractable landing lights (floodlights) switch
24 Emergency master electrics circuit breaker (partially obscured by 22)
25 Cockpit heating/conditioning control selector
26 Hydraulic pressure gauge (partially obscured by 22)
27 Gyro monitor (compass) switch
28 Autopilot channel selectors: Elevator/Aileron/Rudder
29 Spirit level
30 Target approach switch
31 Three-position flap selector
32 Undercarriage selector
33 Flap and undercarriage position lights (indicators)
34 Gyro horizon erection switch
35 Braking parachute streaming handle (release)
36 Incidence indicator (artificial horizon)
37 Repeater gyro horizon (rate of climb control)
38 Autopilot master switch
39 Braking parachute jettison handle

40 Standby magnetic compass (partially obscured by canopy frame)
41 Opening direct/clear-vision panel
42 Jet tailpipe pitot pressure (combined port and starboard EPR gauge)
43 Bomb release button on left-hand control column "horn"
44 Lotfe 7K tachometric bomb-sight
45 Clock illumination button
46 Clock
47 FuG 16zy (R/T) transmitter button
48 Fine-course altimeter
49 Pilot heater indicator
50 Altitude compensated airspeed indicator
51 Gyro horizon and slip indicator
52 Master compass indicator
53 FuG 16zy (AFN 2) homing indicator
54 Rate of climb and descent indicator (partially obscured by periscope eyepiece)
55 RF 2C Periscopic combined

bomb/gunsight and rear mirror
56 Port RPM gauge
57 Autopilot course-setting (turn) control: fast and slow rate (right-hand "horn")
58 Starboard RPM gauge
59 Port fuel burner pressure gauge (obscured by control column arm)
60 Oxygen hose
61 Roof canopy jettison handle
62 Oxygen regulator
63 Flare pistol mounting
64 Ultra-violet cockpit light (partially obscured by oxygen hose)
65 Starboard fuel burner pressure gauge (partially obscured by control column pivot)
66 Bomb jettison lever (partially obscured by control column mount)
67 Control column release knob (control column shown partly swivelled to expose bomb-sight)
68 Starboard oil pressure gauge (port gauge obscured by control column mount)

altitude at which to fly but ensuring that he had no maps and threatening to ram him if he deviated from course. Knowing the Ar 234B as he did he must have regarded my threat to ram him as pretty hollow since I would be highly exposed in that extensively-glazed nose. On second thoughts, he may really have believed that I had *kamikaze* tendencies.

In the event, it all worked like a charm and the task was soon completed, though the weather sometimes forced us to make an intermediate stop at Grove. Once all the Arados were assembled at Schleswig the next stage was to get them to Farnborough via, if the weather so dictated, Melsbroek, Brussels. On this leg I reckoned to let my *Luftwaffe* help-mate fly in formation on my wing, although I still had no intention of providing him with maps.

On one such trip on 3 October 1945 we took-off from Schleswig at 1715 hours with a forecast of clear weather *en route*. As it was late afternoon we planned a low-level flight to Brussels which, at fast cruise, would take an hour. Our endurance under such conditions was 1 hr 20 min, and dusk at Brussels was 1845 hours. Our route took us down the east bank of the Zuider Zee but as we reached the south bank we ran into sea fog. I switched on my wingtip lights and saw that the *Hauptmann* was still with me, so I began a gentle turn to reverse course as there was no guarantee that the weather would open up again ahead of us. Furthermore, I was not at all sure that my Teutonic companion was in good night formation flying practice; uncertainty that was to prove more than justified. On breaking clear of the fog the other Arado was no longer with me. Nor was it anywhere to be seen.

I circled a couple of times, vainly searching the sky for my wingman, and it suddenly dawned on me that I had another problem — I had not enough fuel to get back to Schleswig. The only alternative was to try to make Nordholz airfield on the North Sea coast near Cuxhaven. Nordholz had a runway long enough to take the *Blitz* but the distance was stretching it a bit and there was the possibility of sea fog there. There was really only once answer: cut one turbo-jet and hope to find Nordholz clear. Failing that there was just a chance that I could scrape into Schleswig. However, this solution brought its own problem in that on one engine my cruise speed would be so reduced that I was unlikely to make Nordholz before dusk fell at 1830 hours, and that battered airfield was certainly not manned or equipped for night flying.

It was a case of Hobson's choice and so I smartly cut one

(Above and below) The second B-series prototype, the Ar 234 V10, which was eventually used for BZA 1 bombing computer and PV1B sighting head trials.

engine and concentrated on steering accurately for Cuxhaven on the coast of the Heligoland Bight. I finally reached the coast in darkness at 1850 hours and found the weather clear, but I was not sure of the exact location of the airfield. At this moment of crisis help arrived from an unexpected source — two searchlight beams pierced the sky, met close to my aircraft and then dipped in a series of arcs, always in the same direction. It was apparent that they were guiding me to Nordholz whose runways I suddenly spotted in the light of the beams.

A quick check on my fuel made it apparent that I had no chance of reaching Schleswig. It was Nordholz or nothing. I weighed up the situation and concluded that this was no time to try a single-engine landing as I had no runway lighting and might have to make two or three passes to get lined up, if, indeed, I ever achieved that desirable situation. Fortunately the engine relight drill was delightfully simple in contrast to the ground starting. At a speed of 217 mph (350 km/h) the revs of the dead engine stabilised at about 1,200; I turned on the ignition switch with the throttle fully closed and the fuel cock off. When the revs had risen by a thousand, I opened the fuel cock and gingerly moved the throttle to the idling position, and when the revs crept up to 4,000 I switched off the ignition. So far so good, but further throttle movement gave no increase in revs.

By now the adrenalin was flowing freely and I was preparing for the final drama when, suddenly, two pairs of headlights appeared on each side of one of the runways, giving a rudimentary form of lighting in the touchdown area. With a silent blessing for small mercies, I circled and then made my approach, determined to get down on the first pass. All went smoothly and I contacted the runway in the lighted area, but then I was past the headlights and careering into the darkness. I concentrated on keeping the rudder pedals dead central as I applied the brakes, and simultaneously pulled the braking' chute release toggle. I sighed with relief as I felt

69 Port and starboard jet unit fire-warning temperature gauges
70 Jet pipe (exhaust gas) temperature gauges (port and starboard)
71 Emergency hydraulic hand-pump (see 86)
72 Front fuselage fuel tank contents gauge
73 Rear fuselage fuel tank contents gauge
74 Front tank low fuel contents warning light
75 Rear tank low fuel contents warning light
76 Riedel starter motor panel: 2-stroke engine starter switches and RPM gauge (high low range selector button)
77 Oxygen system pressure gauge
78 Oxygen flow indicator
79 Oxygen system ON/OFF cock
80 Bomb fusing box selector panel
81 Ultra-violet cockpit light
82 Main electrical switch panel

83 Voltmeters
84 Navigation lights switch (partially hidden below electrical switch panel)
85 Bomb sequence selector panel
86 Flap and undercarriage emergency hydraulic selector switch (see 71)
87 FuG 16zy frequency selector switch
88 Ventral camera doors operating handle (not fitted on bomber variant)
89 FuG 16zy receiver fine tuning (homing aerial remote-control panel)
90 FuG 16zy MCW switch (or FuG 125 "Hermine" - bearings from ground control rotating beacon)
91 FuG 25A self-destruct switch
92 FuG 25A IFF control switch
93 Camera operating panel (not fitted on bomber variant)
94 FuG 16zy volume control and homing switch (junction box)
95 Shoulder harness anchor-points
96 Pilot's seat

the aircraft gradually grind to a halt, and the jeeps that had provided the lighting now came up from behind, passing my wingtips and their drivers beckoning me to follow. The fuel gauges showed 26 Imp gal (120 l) left in the tanks, so it was even doubtful that I would be able to taxi very far!

In the warm comfort of the Officers' Mess I learned that a USAAF unit had provided my emergency runway lighting after a phone call from a British naval unit at Cuxhaven which had seen my exhaust flame, deduced that I was in trouble and displayed splendid initiative in switching on their searchlights and directing me to Nordholz. The next day I went over to Cuxhaven to thank my saviours and then, after the sea fog that had meanwhile descended on Nordholz cleared, the USAAF flew me back to Schleswig. I had made anxious enquiries about the fate of the other Arado but learned nothing until late that afternoon a phone call from a British Army unit in Holland informed me that the aircraft had landed at a small airfield called Eelde, and its pilot was being held in custody by the Dutch who seemingly had no intention of giving him up!

Next morning I set off in an Oxford for Eelde and could scarcely believe my eyes when I saw the Ar 234B on that small grass field which was liberally pitted with bomb craters. It was obvious that the *Blitz* would never be *flown* out of there. The *Hauptmann* told me that, after losing me in the turn over the Zuider Zee, he had headed north in the hope of striking the coast and getting his bearings. He had realised, as I had, that darkness was overtaking him rapidly, and when he spotted the pockmarked airfield at Eelde he had decided to take his chance while it was still daylight and put down there,

trying to steer the aircraft in a straight line that he could see existing between the craters and using the emergency braking 'chute. He was far more grateful to me for releasing him from Dutch care than for the congratulations on bringing off a remarkable landing.

There was no chance of recovering the Ar 234B from Eelde — the splendid Dutch were delighted to have an intact example of the aeroplane on their soil — and I decided to recover the Arado that I had left at Nordholz after ferrying the rest of the aircraft back to the UK. I eventually returned to Nordholz with my German maintenance team on 25 October, and by the next afternoon we were ready to fly the *Blitz* out from what was a tight runway for length. There was no question of taking-off with a full load. Indeed, the wind and temperature had to be just right to attempt a take-off with half fuel. The time of the year favoured us in so far as both of these requirements were concerned, and we did not have too long to wait.

On 27 October our calculations indicated that I should be able to get off with half fuel, but it was still critically tight. I worked out the distance at which the nosewheel would have to be off the ground if I was to clear the boundary fence, positioning one of the German NCOs at that point and another about 50 yards further on. I told the first to lay flat on his stomach and raise an arm if the nosewheel was off the ground when I reached him, the second, who I would be watching, was to repeat the signal. If the nosewheel had not left the runway this second NCO was to throw himself flat — a positive signal of affirmation or negation was vital. If he simply stood still it would mean that he had missed his companion's signal, and in the event of a negative or no signal I intended to resort to full wheel braking, the braking 'chute and the power of prayer. In the event, the nosewheel lifted dead on the mark, and the sight of the NCO's arm being thrown into the air was a joy to behold. The *Blitz* immediately grew still further in my esteem.

How then, allowing for my affection for this Arado creation, would I assess the *Blitz*? Here, once again, the German aircraft industry had produced a very superior aircraft too late and in too small numbers seriously to affect the course of the war. It was a magnificent aeroplane of which no real equivalent existed in the Allied order of battle, so it may be said without fear of contradiction that the *Blitz* was truly in a class of its own.

(Above and below) An Ar 234B-1 Blitz (Werk-Nr 121 443) photographed during evaluation by the US Navy at the Patuxent River test centre

JUNKERS JU 88

THERE IS ONE ADAGE that I have always considered singularly apposite in relation to combat aircraft: "Jack of all trades . . . master of none!" Even the most traditional of such maxims have their exceptions, however, and in so far as World War II was concerned, there were two supreme examples of exceptions to that quoted: de Havilland's superlative Mosquito and Junkers' equally outstanding 'eighty-eight'. Here were two aircraft that fulfilled multifarious rôles and excelled in all of them. Both combined æsthetic appeal with an aura of deadliness and if the Dessau-created aircraft lacked something of the ballerina-like elegance of the warplane from Hatfield, it more than compensated in functional beauty. Both displayed supreme amenability to the process of adaptation and modification to which they were subjected and both were to achieve extraordinary ubiquity. In fact, it was to be said of the German warplane that it was the very backbone of the *Luftwaffe* for much of WW II.

The Junkers Ju 88 was not *designed* as a multi-purpose aeroplane; it had been created to fulfil a 1935 demand for a so-called *Schnellbomber* — a high-speed bomber in the design of which there was no need to compromise performance by considering potential in other rôles — and its superlative versatility was to result from circumstance rather than intent. Anxious to embody state-of-the-art structural techniques with which the Dessau-based manufacturer was not fully conversant, Junkers had recruited engineers who had gained experience of light-metal stressed-skin construction in the USA, and thus the Ju 88, on which the first metal was cut in May 1936, owed virtually nothing to any design that had preceded it on the Dessau drawing boards.

Something of the outstanding potential of Junkers' new *Schnellbomber* was revealed in March 1939, when the fifth prototype, the Ju 88 V5, established a new international 1 000-km (621·3-mile) closed-circuit record by carrying a 2 000-kg (4,409-lb) payload at an average speed of 517 km/h (321·25 mph) — almost exactly the maximum attainable speed of the Hurricanes then being delivered to the RAF! Four months later, the Ju 88 V5 carried the same load over a distance of 2 000 km (1,242·7 miles) at an average speed of 500 km/h (310·7 mph); figures betokening a performance which certainly *should* have resulted in some pensive expressions on faces in the London and Paris air ministries.

The war was barely into its third week when this new warplane made its operational début, albeit a somewhat inauspicious foray despite the publicity that it was subsequently to receive. A detachment of four Ju 88A-1s deployed to Westerland, on the island of Sylt, from *Hauptmann* Helmut Pohle's Jever-based *I Gruppe* of *Kampfgeschwader* 30, took-off at 1300 hours on 26 September to attack a British flotilla including the battleships *Nelson* and *Rodney,* the battlecruisers *Hood* and *Renown,* and the carrier *Ark Royal.* Apart from a bomb which glanced off the *Hood,* failing to explode, the British vessels were unscathed, but the pilot of one of the Ju 88s, *Gefreiter* Carl Francke, who, incidentally, was a former Rechlin test pilot, thought that one of his 500-kg (1,102-lb) SC 500s *could* have hit the *Ark Royal.* This was enough for the German propagandists, who, combining wishful thinking with overly active imaginations, claimed the *destruction* of the carrier, much to the embarrassment of Francke who soon afterwards returned to Rechlin.

If this début did not appear singularly propitious, the Ju 88 soon began to show its mettle once it had overcome the teething troubles that normally accompany the phase-in of any new combat aircraft. In the case of Junkers' *Schnellbomber,* these problems centred on the slatted dive brakes hinged beneath the forward wing spar. The fuselage was already highly stressed, a condition exacerbated by actuation of the dive brakes, and limitations had to be imposed on high-speed manœuvres. Indeed, for a time all aerobatics were forbidden, but then any aerobatics by an aircraft of this size and category were something of a novelty. By the time the Ju 88 participated in the "Battle of Britain", its more serious shortcomings had been eradicated and if possessing somewhat inadequate defensive armament at that early stage in its career, it was tacitly recognised by the RAF as the most formidable warplane in its category extant.

Its capabilities in the heavy fighter, or *Zerstörer,* rôle were appreciated even before the Ju 88 was committed to opera-

A JU 88 MYSTERY

SOME MYSTERY surrounds the acquisition by the Allies of the first night fighting Ju 88 which landed at Dyce, near Aberdeen, on the afternoon of Sunday, 9 May 1943. According to Royal Observer Corps records, the aircraft, a Ju 88R-1 (*Werk-Nr* 360043 D5+EV) of 10./NJG 3, would seem to have been expected as, after making landfall some 15 miles (24 km) north of Aberdeen, it was met by Spitfires which escorted the German fighter into Dyce.

In 1974, the Federal German popular newspaper BILD am SONNTAG published an intriguing account of what it purports to be the true background. It alleges that the pilot, one *Oberleutnant* Heinrich Schmitt, son of the secretary to the then Minister for Foreign Affairs, Gustav Stresemann, had been an enemy agent since 1940, and had regularly supplied secret information to Britain through his father, who sent it from his home in Thüringen via relay-stations in Switzerland and Portugal.

Schmitt had, according to the BILD am SONNTAG account, flown to the UK at least once before his arrival in the Ju 88R-1 at Dyce. Ironically, he had been chosen to deliver a sealed package to a representative of the British High Command in 1941, landing a Do 217 at Lincoln during the night of 20-21 May, the runway lights having been switched on to guide him in. Schmitt allegedly handed the package to a waiting British officer and then immediately took-off to return to Germany.

The flight of the Ju 88R-1 to Dyce in May 1943 had begun from the airfield at Christiansand, Norway. While still within range of German radio stations, Schmitt announced that he had an engine fire and would have to ditch, and then jettisoned three life rafts. The radio station that received the emergency call marked the spot in *Planquadrat* (area) 88/41 from which the call had been transmitted, and assuming that the aircraft had gone into the sea when no further message was received, activated the search and rescue procedures.

The aircraft was presumed lost, which was precisely what Schmitt and his crew, *Oberfeldwebel* Paul Rosenberger and *Oberfeldwebel* Erich Kantwill, had intended. The aircraft then flew directly to the Scottish coastline, picked up its escort of Spitfires and then flew to Dyce, where, after landing, it was immediately surrounded by military police who had cleared the area of casual observers. The Ju 88R-1 was fitted with FuG 202 *Lichtenstein BC* which was promptly evaluated (it was adjudged to compare favourably with the British AI Mk IV, the German aerial array producing a narrower beam which enabled small target movements to be followed with greater ease), and the successful conclusion of the defection was signalled to Schmitt's father via the British secret radio station *Gustav Siegfried eins,* the code phrase being '*der Mai ist gekommen*' (May has come). The *Luftwaffe* was to learn of the desertion in the following month when both Schmitt and Rosenberger broadcast over the British radio.

tions as a bomber, and its potential as a *Nachtjäger,* too, was forseen early in the conflict, but these were of little more than academic interest when they could be procured only at the expense of the urgently-needed bomber models. In fact, bomber variants were to possess a near-monopoly on the Ju 88 assembly lines until the autumn of 1943, when operational exigencies finally dictated transfer of production accent from bomber to fighter variants.

Fortuitously and certainly fortunately, several examples of successive versions of the Ju 88 fell into Allied hands during the course of WW II, enabling something of a check to be kept on the progressive development of this remarkable warplane. A Ju 88A-1 was acquired in more or less repairable condition during the summer of 1940, and underwent some limited test flying at Farnborough in the spring of the following year. On 24 July 1941, a Ju 88A-6 landed in error on the semi-completed Lulsgate Bottom airfield, near Bristol, and less than four months later, in November, its pilot's mistake was emulated by another flying a Ju 88A-5 which he brought in to Chivenor. On 22 July 1943, a Romanian pilot defected with a newly-delivered Ju 88D-1/Trop which he flew into Limasol, Cyprus, but a more valuable acquisition had arrived at Dyce, Aberdeen [see accompanying panel], some 10 weeks earlier, on 9 May, in the form of a Ju 88R-1 night fighter of 10./NJG 3, complete with *Lichtenstein BC* radar. However, even this was not quite so valuable as the Ju 88G-1 of 7./NJG 2 which, with *Lichtenstein SN-2* and *Flensburg* equipment, was landed inadvertently at Woodbridge, Essex, on 13 July 1944, after its pilot had flown a reciprocal compass course when returning from a patrol over the North Sea.

An enjoyable introduction

My first introduction to the Junkers twin — from the viewpoint of flying the aircraft as distinct from being on the receiving end of its weaponry as had been the case on more than one occasion — came in the autumn of '43, when the opportunity arose to fly the Ju 88A-5 which had been assigned the British serial HM509, and a thoroughly enjoyable experience it was. This particular aircraft, which, as previously mentioned, had landed at Chivenor in November 1941, had seen quite a lot of flying in British hands before my chance to test the aeroplane had come along. At one time, it had even reverted to *Luftwaffe* insignia for participation in a Two Cities Film production at Fowlmere.

On clambering into the cockpit, my first impression was

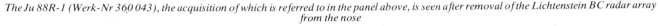

The Ju 88R-1 (Werk-Nr 360 043), the acquisition of which is referred to in the panel above, is seen after removal of the Lichtenstein BC radar array from the nose

that accommodation was very cramped for four men, though I didn't doubt that this close proximity of all crew members was good for morale in combat. The pilot was seated to port with the bomb aimer below and to starboard, the flight engineer being situated aft of the pilot and facing to the rear, with the radio operator alongside but lower in the fuselage so that he could squeeze himself into the ventral gondola to operate the lower rear gun. The bomb sight was mounted in the "beetle's eye" of optically-flat panels in the nose and every crew member had at least one gun under his control. There was a 7,9-mm MG 81 projecting through the starboard windscreen panel for the pilot, this being used either as a fixed or free-mounted weapon; the bomb aimer had a pair of free-mounted MG 81s firing through the "beetle's eye"; there was a 13-mm MG 131 firing aft from the rear of the cockpit for the flight engineer and the radio operator was provided with either a 13-mm MG 131 or a pair of MG 81s which he fired from the tail of the gondola. Of course, as these weapons had to be operated independently, no great weight of fire could be brought to bear.

Once settled in the pilot's seat, I found that, owing to my somewhat limited stature, I had to raise it fully to obtain a good view and even then there seemed to be an awful lot of metal framing for the optically-flat transparent panels which gave the aircraft its greenhouse-style crew compartment. There was also considerable fore and aft adjustment on the pilot's seat — a thoroughly commendable feature in my view since I had found that some British aircraft and almost all US aircraft had a seat-to-pedal relationship conceived purely for the king-sized pilots and totally disregarding the requirements of the pint-sized! The cockpit layout was a decided improvement on that of, say, the He 111 as regards instrument and control grouping, with the exception of the throttles which were located too far to the rear and too low. Thus, I found that after pulling the throttle levers for the first part of the movement in opening up power, I had to turn my hand through 180 degrees for the remaining part of the movement.

Starting the Junkers Jumo 211G-1 engines was, as usual, either by hand or by means of electrically-energised inertia starters, and these power plants were satisfyingly easy to get running. Rated at 1,200 hp for take-off and 1,210 hp at 820 ft (250 m) at 2,400 rpm like the earlier B-1s, the Jumo 211G-1s were essentially interim engines pending availability of the somewhat more powerful Jumo 211J which differed primarily in having a strengthened crankshaft, a fully-shrouded DVL supercharger impeller, modified boost and injection

pump controls, a pressurized coolant system and an induction air intake beneath its rear end. The developed engine was destined for installation in the Ju 88A-4 but delays in bringing the Jumo 211J to production status had resulted in the interim Ju 88A-5 with a similar airframe to that of the A-4 mated with the lower-powered engines.

Ground handling proved extremely easy due to the Ju 88's unusually good brakes. One had to ensure that the lockable tailwheel was disengaged before taxying and the oil and coolant radiators were normally opened fully. After lining up for take-off by taxying a dozen yards or so to ensure that the tailwheel was straight, this was locked in position, an inter-

(Above) A Ju 88A-6/U with FuG 200 Hohentwiel radar and drop tanks photographed at Farnborough in August 1945. This version lacked the ventral gondola and was used in the maritime rôle. (Immediately below) The Ju 88A-6 which landed in error at Lulsgate Bottom photographed in June 1942 while being flown (as EE205) by the RAE.

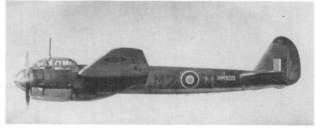

(Immediately above right) The Ju 88A-5 that landed in error at Chivenor seen flying (as HM509) in August 1942 while being tested by the Aircraft and Armament Experimental Establishment. (Below) The first of the Junkers twins to be acquired by the Allies and evaluated as AX919. This Ju 88A-1 (Werk-Nr 7036), taken on charge by the RAE in late August 1940, is seen here in April 1941, by which time the ventral gondola had been removed.

Junkers Ju 88G-7b Specification

Power Plant: Two Junkers Jumo 213E 12-cylinder inverted-vee liquid-cooled engines each rated at 1,750 hp at 3,200 rpm for take-off and 1,320 hp at 31,990 ft (9 750 m); 1,580 hp available for climb and combat at 3,000 rpm at sea level and 1,275 hp at 31,330 ft (9 550 m). With MW 50 (water-methanol) injection: 1,608 hp at 29,855 ft (9 100 m).

Performance: (At 28,900 lb/13 110 kg) Max speed, 270 mph (435 km/h) at sea level, 363 mph (584 km/h) at 33,465 ft (10 200 m), with MW 50 boost, 389 mph (626 km/h) or, without flame dampers, 402 mph (647 km/h) at 29,855 ft (9 100 m); initial climb, 1,655 ft/min (8,4 m/sec); time to 32,315 ft (9 850 m), 26·4 min; endurance (including one hour at emergency power with MW 50 boost and remainder at max continuous power), 3·72 hrs at 29,855 ft (9 100 m), (with 198 Imp gal/900 l drop tank at max econ power), 5·2 hrs.

Weights: Normal loaded, 28,900 lb (13 110 kg), (with 198 Imp gal/900 l drop tank), 30,480 lb (13 826 kg); max overload take-off, 32,350 lb (14 674 kg).

Dimensions: Span, 65 ft 10½ in (20,08 m); length, 51 ft 0⅛ in (15,55 m), (with FuG 218 with Morgenstern array and rear-facing FuG 220), 54 ft 1½ in (16,50 m); height, 15 ft 11 in (4,85 m); wing area, 586·6 sq ft (54,50 m²).

Armament: Four fixed forward-firing 20-mm MG 151 cannon with 200 rpg, two fixed upward-firing 20-mm MG 151 cannon with 200 rpg and one aft-firing 13-mm MG 131 machine gun on flexible mounting with 500 rounds.

Junkers Ju 88G-1 Cutaway Drawing Key

1 Starboard navigation light
2 Wingtip profile
3 FuG 227 'Flensburg' radar receiver antenna
4 Starboard aileron
5 Aileron control runs
6 Starboard flaps
7 Flap-fairing strip
8 Wing ribs
9 Starboard outer fuel tank (91 Imp gal/415 l capacity)
10 Fuel filler cap
11 Leading edge structure
12 Annular exhaust slot
13 Cylinder head fairings
14 Adjustable nacelle nose ring
15 Twelve-blade cooling fan
16 Propeller boss
17 Variable-pitch VS 111 wooden propeller
18 Leading-edge radar array
19 FuG 220 'Lichtenstein' SN-2 intercept radar array
20 Nose cone
21 Forward armoured bulkhead
22 Gyro compass
23 Instrument panel
24 Armour-glass windscreen
25 Folding seat
26 Control column
27 Rudder pedal/brake cylinder
28 Control runs
29 Pilot's armoured seat
30 Sliding window section
31 Headrest
32 Jettisonable canopy roof section
33 Gun restraint
34 Wireless operator/gunner's seat
35 Rheinmetall Borsig MG 131 machine gun (13-mm calibre)

36 Radio equipment (FuG 10P HF, FuG 16ZY VHF, FuG 25 IFF)
37 Ammunition box (500 rounds of 13-mm)
38 FuG 220 'Lichtenstein' SN-2 indicator box
39 FuG 227 'Flensburg' indicator box
40 Control linkage
41 Bulkhead
42 Armoured gun mount
43 Aerial post traverse check
44 Fuel filler cap
45 Whip aerial
46 Forward fuselage fuel tank (105 Imp gal/480 l capacity)
47 Fuselage horizontal construction joint
48 Bulkhead
49 Fuel filler cap
50 Aft fuselage fuel tank (230 Imp gal/1 045 l capacity)
51 Access hatch
52 Bulkhead
53 Control linkage access plate
54 Fuselage stringers
55 Upper longeron
56 Maintenance walkway
57 Control linkage
58 Horizontal construction joint
59 Z-section fuselage frames
60 Dinghy stowage
61 Fuel vent pipe
62 Master compass
63 Spherical oxygen bottles
64 Accumulator

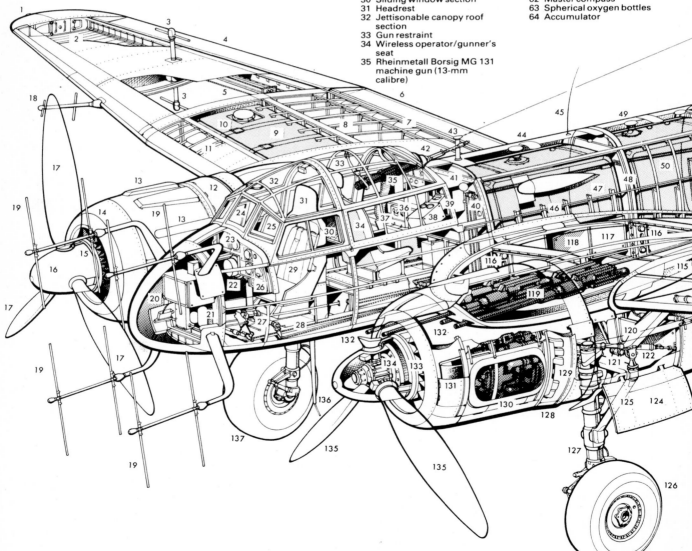

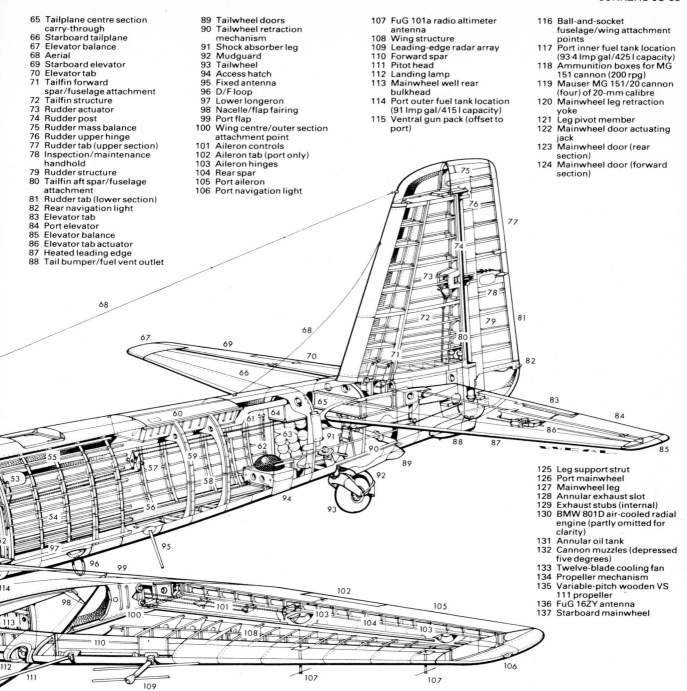

65 Tailplane centre section carry-through
66 Starboard tailplane
67 Elevator balance
68 Aerial
69 Starboard elevator
70 Elevator tab
71 Tailfin forward spar/fuselage attachment
72 Tailfin structure
73 Rudder actuator
74 Rudder post
75 Rudder mass balance
76 Rudder upper hinge
77 Rudder tab (upper section)
78 Inspection/maintenance handhold
79 Rudder structure
80 Tailfin aft spar/fuselage attachment
81 Rudder tab (lower section)
82 Rear navigation light
83 Elevator tab
84 Port elevator
85 Elevator balance
86 Elevator tab actuator
87 Heated leading edge
88 Tail bumper/fuel vent outlet

89 Tailwheel doors
90 Tailwheel retraction mechanism
91 Shock absorber leg
92 Mudguard
93 Tailwheel
94 Access hatch
95 Fixed antenna
96 D/F loop
97 Lower longeron
98 Nacelle/flap fairing
99 Port flap
100 Wing centre/outer section attachment point
101 Aileron controls
102 Aileron tab (port only)
103 Aileron hinges
104 Rear spar
105 Port aileron
106 Port navigation light

107 FuG 101a radio altimeter antenna
108 Wing structure
109 Leading-edge radar array
110 Forward spar
111 Pitot head
112 Landing lamp
113 Mainwheel well rear bulkhead
114 Port outer fuel tank location (91 Imp gal/415 l capacity)
115 Ventral gun pack (offset to port)

116 Ball-and-socket fuselage/wing attachment points
117 Port inner fuel tank location (93·4 Imp gal/425 l capacity)
118 Ammunition boxes for MG 151 cannon (200 rpg)
119 Mauser MG 151/20 cannon (four) of 20-mm calibre
120 Mainwheel leg retraction yoke
121 Leg pivot member
122 Mainwheel door actuating jack
123 Mainwheel door (rear section)
124 Mainwheel door (forward section)

125 Leg support strut
126 Port mainwheel
127 Mainwheel leg
128 Annular exhaust slot
129 Exhaust stubs (internal)
130 BMW 801D air-cooled radial engine (partly omitted for clarity)
131 Annular oil tank
132 Cannon muzzles (depressed five degrees)
133 Twelve-blade cooling fan
134 Propeller mechanism
135 Variable-pitch wooden VS 111 propeller
136 FuG 16ZY antenna
137 Starboard mainwheel

(Below) The Ju 88G-1 (Werk-Nr 712273), originally 4R+UR, which is also illustrated on pages 111 and 112

lock preventing operation of the hydraulics until the locking procedure had been completed. The flaps could then be lowered one-third of their travel and the cooling gills reduced to one-third open. Rudder and aileron trimmers were set to zero and the elevator trim set just slightly nose heavy.

Differential throttling was difficult on take-off owing to the position of the throttle levers and there was therefore a tendency to swing if the throttles were opened too quickly. In order to obtain rudder control as rapidly as possible, the stick

had to be pushed well forward to raise the tail, a process demanding application of considerable force, and as a consequence of the use of this technique the take-off run in fully loaded condition called for quite a lot of runway. Unstick occurred at 80 mph (130 km/h) and single-engine safety speed was 140 mph (225 km/h).

The climb out tended to be somewhat leisurely with a full load on, but the aircraft handled beautifully. Speed in the cruise regime was high and the rudder and ailerons were very

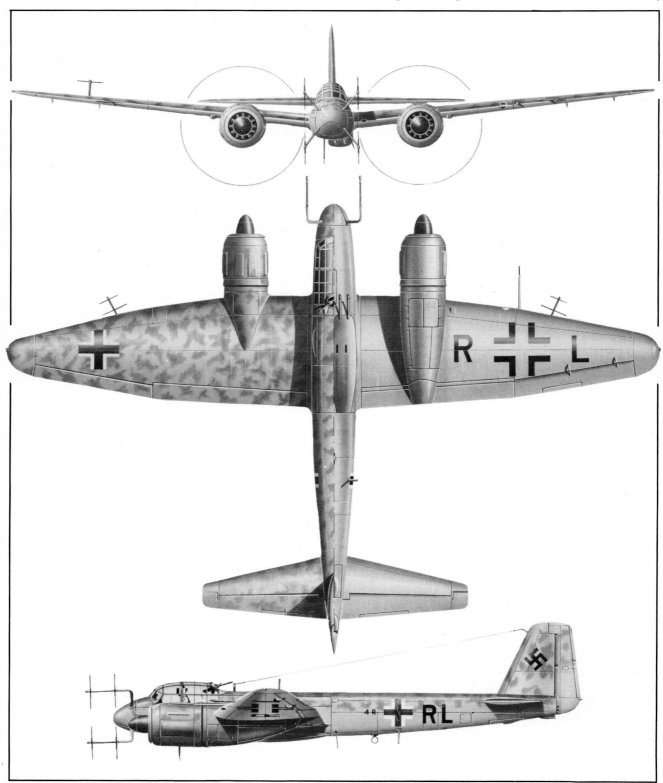

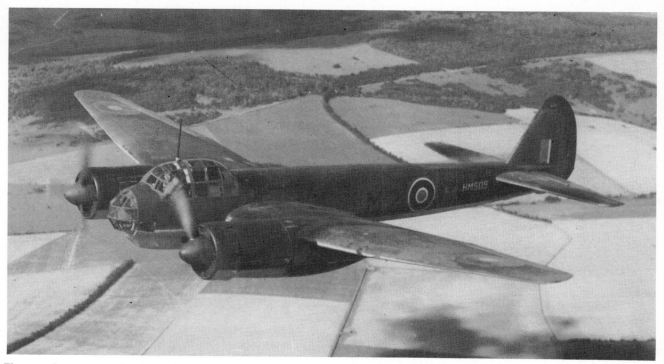

The general arrangement drawing on the opposite page illustrates an example of the Ju 88G-1 operated by 3./NJG 2 during the winter of 1944-45, seen above is the Ju 88A-5 that landed in error at Chivenor and was subsequently flown as HM509, and depicted below is a captured example of the final production night fighter version of the Junkers aircraft, the Ju 88G-7c, which featured FuG 240 Berlin N-1a centimetric radar

light throughout the entire speed range. The elevator was somewhat heavier but the automatic tail incidence control assisted any big movements required. When the actuating lever for the slatted wing-mounted dive brakes was moved forward in the cockpit, the elevators were automatically trimmed to put the aircraft into a dive and on pulling the lever back to retract the brakes the aircraft was automatically brought out of the dive. The experience of performing a dive-bombing attack with a machine of the size of the Ju 88 was something more than awe-inspiring, but the aircraft handled so beautifully that one did not have to be particularly intrepid to attempt such and, indeed, the automatic dive entry and pull-out took all the pain out of the manœuvre. But for this automatism a dive could well have been difficult to cope with as the propellers had to be constantly adjusted during the dive to prevent over-speeding and the elevators, had they not been under assistance, would have called for some pretty

strenuous effort on the part of the pilot to effect a pull-out.

The Ju 88 had the reputation of being somewhat difficult to land, but I certainly did not find it so. The probable explanation for this slur on the character of what was from almost every aspect a superlative pilot's aeroplane was that it offered a very much higher performance than any of its contemporaries when first introduced into the inventory of the *Luftwaffe* whose pilots had to learn to cope with something rather hotter than they had been used to.

Before making my first landing in the Ju 88, I checked out the stalling characteristics with undercarriage and flaps lowered. The stall occurred at 92 mph (148 km/h) with very little warning and involved a sharp wing drop. This, of course, gave a clue as to why a landing could have its exciting moments. I lowered the undercarriage at 140 mph (225 km/h) and then moved the flap lever from neutral to the first rear position, this having the effect of lowering the flaps to the first stage

(Above and below) The Ju 88R-1 which landed in mysterious circumstances at Dyce on 9 May 1943 (see page 104) photographed during trials as PJ876. This aircraft was used extensively for radio and radar investigation flights from Farnborough and Hartford Bridge, and was restored to (non-flying) exhibition standards at RAF St Athan during 1975 and is currently included in the collection of historic aircraft maintained at that station

(Above and below right) The Ju 88G-1 (Werk-Nr 712273) which was landed in error at Woodbridge in July 1944 and subsequently proved invaluable in the development of countermeasures for Germany's then latest radar devices. It is seen here flying as TP190.

without any noticeable change of trim. I then turned on to the final approach at 120 mph (193 km/h), lowered the flaps fully and experienced a strong nose-up trim change, but because of the automatic tail incidence control this only called for a reasonable push force. The final stage of the approach was made at 110 mph (177 km/h), the throttles had to be banged back on crossing the runway threshold and a considerable round-out had to be made to get the tail down. I soon discovered that it was not advisable to get the tail down too early as a swing could develop during the landing run as the rudder became blanked by the fuselage.

Although I was never to experience an emergency in the Ju 88, I recall well the instructions for action in the event of an hydraulic emergency, although the likelihood of such seemed somewhat remote in view of the fact that there were two engine-driven hydraulic pumps. However, if it did become necessary to use the hand pump, the undercarriage doors had first to be lowered and then, at a speed below 137 mph (220 km/h) the landing gear could be lowered by three minutes of hard pumping — even this effort lowered only the main-wheels as the tailwheel could not be operated by the emergency system.

The nocturnal predator

More than 18 months elapsed before, on 1 May 1945, I had a chance to fly one of the night fighter descendants of Junkers' *Schnellbomber* in the form of the Ju 88G-1 (*Werk-Nr* 712273 4R+UR) which had been landed in error by one Ltn Maeckle at Woodbridge during the previous July. This had been the first intact example of an aircraft equipped with SN-2 radar and the *Flensburg* and *Naxos* homing devices to find its way into Allied hands. The FuG 220 *Lichtenstein* SN-2 was a radar operated on a frequency of 90 megacycles — part of the spectrum not covered by the *Window* that RAF bombers had been dropping — and the FuG 227 *Flensburg* and the FuG 350 *Naxos* were radar receivers tuned to the frequencies of the RAF bombers' *Monica* tail-warning and H2S radar sets respectively. Small wonder at the elation with which the RAF greeted *this* windfall! Within 10 days the RAF was dropping a new type of *Window* which had as great a disruptive effect on SN-2 as the original *Window* had had on the *Lichtenstein BC* a year earlier, and the *Monica* sets were soon afterwards removed from RAF bombers.

The Ju 88G-1, which now sported the British serial TP190, differed appreciably from the A-series aircraft that I had flown earlier, quite apart from the alterations dictated by its changed rôle. The steady weight escalation of the night fighting version as a result of the constant demand for the installation of additional equipment had resulted in some stability

shortcomings and these had been eradicated in the G-series by adopting the larger and more angular vertical and horizontal tail surfaces of the Ju 188 bomber, while the liquid-cooled Jumo 211 engines with their annular radiators had given place to BMW 801D air-cooled radials.

There were, of course, also numerous minor changes to the cockpit. The pitch change control, for example, now utilised press switches on the throttles, there was a lot more armour around and much, much more equipment, the latter including FuG 10P HF and FuG 16ZY radio, FuG 25 IFF, an FuG 101a radio altimeter, an FuBl 2 airfield blind approach receiver, FuG 120a *Bernadine* which automatically recorded on a paper chart ground beacon bearings, and a PeGe 6 radio compass. But for all the alterations, the added weight and the increased power, the handling characteristics were little changed from those of the Ju 88A-5.

I was to fly TP190 again six months later, on 17 October, but by that time I had also flown the very much later Ju 88G-6c. On 2 June 1945, just after the German capitulation, I was assigned the task of flying back from Eire a Ju 88G-6c (*Werk-Nr* 621642) which had landed one bleak rainy morning by half light on the Irish Army Air Corps' small grass airfield at Gormanstown, on the East coast above Dublin. Its pilot proved to be a German who had emigrated to South Africa prior to WW II. Pressure had been brought to bear on him to return to Germany after he had received his call-up papers and ignored. Now when final defeat was certain, he and his crew had fled Germany, had picked up the Irish coastline with the aid of their radar, letting down through a 400-ft (120-m) ceiling in pouring rain and locating Gormanstown. The landing on a 900-ft (275-m) strip of wet grass was no mean feat, and now I was faced with the task of flying the night fighter out of this tiny Irish field.

After interrogating the *Luftwaffe* crew on the general layout of the aircraft, I ascertained that it had Jumo 213A engines, which, offering 1,750 hp plus 237 lb (107 kg) of residual exhaust thrust for take-off, drove automatic constant-speed propellers. In the event, as the aircraft was light on fuel, I did not experience too much trouble in getting it off the grass strip, although it was decidedly tight and I had to run the engines up to almost full power on the brakes, comforted by the thought that, as there was no runway as such, I could afford to allow the Junkers to swing a little during the take-off run. As a precaution, I made rendezvous with a flight of Spitfires off Anglesey and they escorted me back to Farnborough. After all, this was an operational *Luftwaffe* night fighter in full war paint and the fighting in Europe was barely over. It would have been really ironic to have been piloting the last German aircraft to be shot down over Britain! All went well, however, and the boys at the RAE got what they were really after — the airborne radar.

Before finally terminating my association with the Junkers, I was to fly another Ju 88G-6 (*Werk-Nr* 621965) at Farnborough and this gave me an opportunity which I had not really had before of confirming the high speed performance of the aircraft — I came up with a corrected figure of 400 mph (644 km/h) at 30,000 ft (9 145 m). Indeed, she was for her age a very fast lady.

Shortly after the Irish episode I made acquaintance with the Ju 188A, which, too, was powered by the Jumo 213A engines, these having automatic engine controls which meant elimination of the boost gauges and the propeller pitch controls. I found very little difference between the flying characteristics of the Ju 188A and those of the Ju 88G-6, although the view provided the pilot of the bomber was somewhat improved. The German penchant for placing their pilots in greenhouses was still very much in evidence, but with the Ju 188 they were obviously getting rather better at it — or was it

that I was simply being converted to the philosophy?

In the final analysis of which was the finest German combat aircraft of WW II, the Ju 88 must inevitably be compared with the Fw 190. It therefore makes it all the more interesting that these two outstanding aircraft should have been joined in unholy matrimony in a *Huckepack* (Pick-a-back) combination under the *Beethoven* programme, the Ju 88 forming the lower component being referred to as a *Mistel* (Mistletoe), the parasitic evergreen's connection being obvious. Although I had (what I now view as the singular) good fortune *never* to fly in this contraption, I taxied in both upper and lower components. Seated in the cockpit of the Ju 88H — which featured an elongated rear fuselage — it felt as though one was sitting beneath a bacon slicer as the propeller of the Fw 190A forming the upper component was just above one's head. On the other hand, sitting in the cockpit of the Fw 190A gave the impression of having landed on top of someone else by mistake, his aircraft being impaled on one's undercarriage legs! Of course, no pilot was carried by the lower component of the *Huckepack* combination on operational flights, but I metaphorically doff my hat to those Fw 190 pilots who actually flew this weird and wonderful contrivance.

Assessing the Ju 88 is not in the least difficult because its record speaks for itself. It was, in terms of operational effectiveness, the outstanding German bomber, long-range heavy fighter and night fighter of WW II; it performed all three primary rôles with remarkable efficiency and added to its startlingly broad repertoire the tasks of anti-shipping strike and torpedo aircraft, reconnaissance and tank busting. It was a pilot's aeroplane first and last; it demanded a reasonable degree of skill in handling and it responded splendidly when such skill was applied. There was a number of very good German aircraft but, with the exception of the Fw 190, none aroused my profound admiration as did Junkers' 'eighty-eight'.

(Above and below) Two further photographs of the Ju 88G-1 that landed in error at Woodbridge in July 1944. A photograph of this aircraft taken shortly after its arrival at Woodbridge and prior to the substitution of RAF insignia for the original Luftwaffe insignia may be found at the head of page 103

FOCKE-WULF FW 189

For some indefinable reason certain aircraft fire the imagination of certain pilots. Such pulse-quickeners are not necessarily æsthetically-appealing hot rods flaunting artistic contours that owe nothing to utilitarian considerations, or way out aberrations from the mainstream of aeronautical design, bristling with innovatory features. Such racier forms of seductive hardware are, it is to be admitted, usually the stuff of which dreams are made. But there are also the quieter seducers; those aeroplanes offering little in terms of conventional beauty, exoticism or scintillating performance; that possess an aura which, defying analysis, renders them quite irresistible to some. To me, one such aeroplane was Germany's "eye in the sky", the Focke-Wulf Fw 189.

This product of the drawing board of Dipl-Ing Kurt Tank had little claim to glamour. Indeed, by some standards it was considered a caprice of aeronautical design, with its match-stick-like tailbooms, tiny power plant and bulbous nose; a supreme example of utilitarianism overcoming aeronautical artistry. Yet, as the old adage asserts: "Handsome is as handsome does"; the Fw 189 was to prove itself supremely versatile, outstandingly reliable and almost universally popular with its pilots.

Designed specifically for tactical reconnaissance and army co-operation at a time when few endeavouring to fulfil such requirements were thinking further ahead than the classic single-engined strut-braced high-wing monoplane formula, the Fw 189, with its extensively-glazed central fuselage nacelle, twin tailbooms and two low-powered engines, was, as an approach to its intended rôle, nothing if not novel. But Tank went further, proposing the development of interchangeable fuselage nacelles each catering specifically for rôles ranging from crew training to close support; all utilising the same power plant, wings, tailbooms, tail assembly and undercarriage.

There was, of course, a measure of opposition in the *Reichsluftfahrtministerium* to the adoption of so unconventional an approach to meeting the future requirements of the *Aufklärungsstaffeln (H)*; conventionalists convinced that the twin-boom configuration would be prone to distortion under the stresses of violent manœuvres, would lack the ruggedness of the more orthodox single-engined high-wing monoplane and would never compete on the score of low-speed, low-altitude manœuvrability. Nevertheless, the Fw 189 won out against its more conventional competitor, the Arado Ar 198, and confounded the sceptics by going on to become one of the most successful aircraft ever to be employed on a large scale by the *Luftwaffe* of Germany's Third Reich.

Christened *Eule* (Owl) by Kurt Tank and his team as an allusion to its "large head and large eyes", this appellation was to prove singularly appropriate several years later when the Fw 189 was to become truly a "nocturnal bird of prey", sprouting *Lichtenstein* C-1 radar and an MG 151 *"schräge Musik"* gun mounting, and serving in the night fighting rôle with NJG 100. It was the onomatopœic sobriquet of *"Uhu"* for the Fw 189 that was to become popular in service, however, and when in 1941 the existence of this rather odd-looking aeroplane was first publicly revealed, it was referred to by the

(Above and immediately below) An early production Fw 189A-1 photographed prior to acceptance by the Luftwaffe in February 1941 and still displaying the radio call-sign letters 'SI-EM' on the sides of the tailbooms

(Below) This photograph of an Fw 189A-1 of 5.(H)/12 shows the centre-hinged two-piece canopy hatch in the open position. The emblem of the unit consisted of a pipe-playing red-suited negro boy clinging to a vertical rope

press department of the RLM as *"Das Fliegende Auge"* (The Flying Eye).

The Fw 189 had been designed primarily to meet a requirement for a tactical reconnaissance aircraft carrying three crew members, offering all-round defensive cover and possessing a somewhat better performance than anything previously envisaged for a warplane in this category. The first prototype, the Fw 189 V1, which commenced its flight test programme in July 1938 with its designer, Kurt Tank, at the controls, proved to be an all-metal low-wing cantilever monoplane with three-spar stressed-skin wings, interchangeable oval-section tailbooms projecting forward to carry small 12-cylinder inverted-vee Argus air-cooled engines and terminating in stressed-skin

vertical fins, and a central fuselage nacelle sporting enough transparent panelling for any self-respecting hothouse.

The series production aircraft changed little from that first prototype and began to enter service with the *Aufklärungsstaffeln (H)* as the Fw 189A-1 during the summer of 1941, but had still to be committed to the operational inventory of the *Luftwaffe* when, on 22 June of that year, the assault on the Soviet Union was launched. It was on the Soviet front that this Focke-Wulf aircraft was to serve almost exclusively and with considerable distinction, proving itself capable of fulfilling missions under the most adverse of conditions and displaying sufficient agility to thwart all but the most determined fighter attacks, its defensive armament being adequate to deter even these. It was found to be able to absorb substantial punishment and yet remain airborne and, on occasions, it even survived Soviet *Taran* or ramming attacks, regaining its base with substantial portions of wing or tail missing. In short, its reputation was enviable. Small wonder that I was anxious to find out for myself what made this unusual aircraft tick and, in any case, I had always had a penchant for twin-boom aeroplanes.

An Owl in the air

At the end of WW II there were not many Fw 189s lying around in Germany, despite the fact that over 800 had been built, but there was still the odd example to be found here and there, presumably having been used for such non-operational purposes as staff communications flying. I propelled myself towards the first of these aircraft that I came across on Flensburg airfield with the ulterior motive of making it my personal hack for the many trips that I was then making between the UK and the Continent. I suspect that this particular aeroplane had been used right up to the end of the fighting by Admiral Karl Doenitz's staff. In the event, I was soon to trade my Fw 189 for a Siebel Si 204D as a cross-channel transport owing to the strictly limited internal capacity of the Focke-Wulf. However, by that time I had gained considerable respect for the Fw 189 as a functional aircraft with a high degree of mechanical reliability.

I should perhaps make it clear that I did not specifically put the Fw 189 through its paces as part of a Royal Aircraft Establishment test programme, using it solely as a practical vehicle of transportation, and my observations on the characteristics of Kurt Tank's tactical reconnaissance and army co-operation aircraft are gleaned from such flying.

My first impression on climbing into the cockpit was that the view must surely be terrific as one was literally cocooned in glass, but a disappointment was in store for, in flight, the view forward was to prove somewhat poor. The cockpit layout was

Focke-Wulf Fw 189A cockpit drawing key

1 Mainspar carry-through
2 Dorsal gun position shell-collector box
3 Seat support frame
4 Fuel contents gauge (port tank)
5 Fuel contents gauge (starboard tank)
6 Fuel and oil pressure gauge (port)
7 Fuel and oil pressure gauge (starboard)
8 Elevator trim indicator
9 Rudder trim indicator
10 Propeller setting switch
11 Flap positioning switch
12 Oxygen diaphragm
13 Oxygen pressure gauge
14 Oxygen monitor (pilot)
15 Landing lamp switch
16 Entry hatch locking mechanism (port)
17 Compass deviation cards
18 Fuel mixture control
19 Throttle levers
20 Master battery cut-out
21 Flap and undercarriage warning lamps
22 Oil temperature gauge (starboard)
23 Oil temperature gauge (port)
24 Ignition switches
25 Fuel safety cock lever (port)
26 Fuel safety cock lever (starboard)
27 Undercarriage lever
28 Pilot's seat
29 Hinged direct-vision panel
30 Ring-and-bead gunsight
31 Pilot's armoured headrest
32 Hinged entry panels (lower section)
33 Fixed side panels
34 Hinge line
35 Hinged entry panels (upper section)
36 SKK 20-2
37 Pitot-tube heating indicator
38 Fuel contents warning lamps (port and starboard)
39 Pilot's leather crash pad
40 Airspeed indicator
41 Altimeter
42 Rate-of-climb indicator
43 Emergency canopy jettison handle
44 Grab handle
45 Instrument panel lighting switch
46 Navigation light automatic switch
47 Pitot-tube heating automatic switch
48 R/T headset sockets
49 Main instrument panel wiring conduit
50 Fire extinguisher buttons (port and starboard)
51 Turn-and-bank indicator

52 Artificial horizon
53 Radio-navigation indicator
54 Rudder trimming switch
55 Pilot's repeater compass
56 Manifold pressure gauge (port and starboard)
57 Cockpit illumination dimmer switch
58 Navigator's leather crash pad
59 Optically flat nose panels
60 Machine gun firing button
61 Bomb release button
62 Charger switch (reverse face of control horn)
63 Clock

64 Elevator trimming switch
65 Cut-out switch
66 Control column
67 Rudder pedals (mounted on cantilever beams)
68 Direct-reading compass*
69 RPM indicator (port)*
70 RPM indicator (starboard)*
71 GV 219d bomb sight
72 FuG 25 radio control unit
73 G 4 D/F control unit
74 Remote-control unit and key
75 Navigator's map case
76 Entry hatch locking mechanism (starboard)

77 Flare cartridges (four)
78 Navigator's seat (rotating)
79 Picture-interval regulator
80 Picture-overlap control
81 Bomb release switch panel (with smokescreen apparatus)
82 Seat adjusting lever
83 Ignition switch box
84 Cockpit heating control

_____

* mounted on canopy frame (forward of fuselage step)

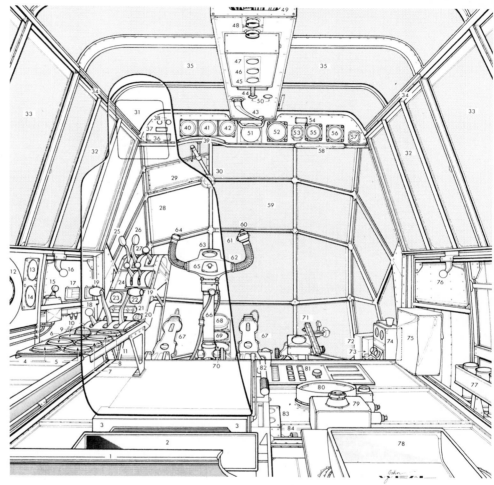

An Fw 189A-2 of 1.(H)/31 operational on the Eastern Front during the summer of 1942. The emblem on the engine cowling is that of 1.(H)/31 and comprises a sword superimposed by an eagle with forked lighting emanating from its claws.

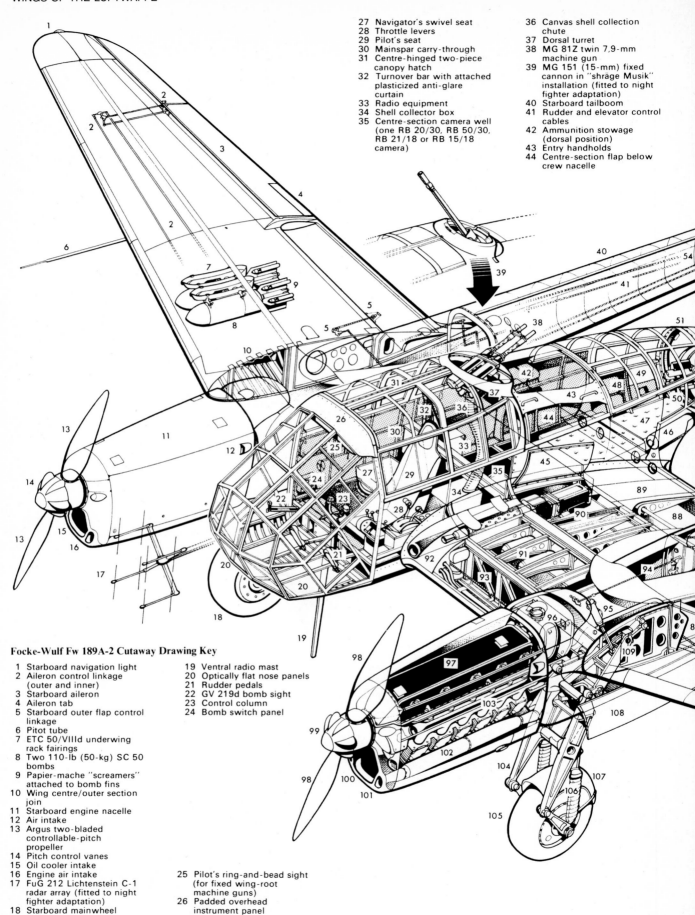

27 Navigator's swivel seat
28 Throttle levers
29 Pilot's seat
30 Mainspar carry-through
31 Centre-hinged two-piece canopy hatch
32 Turnover bar with attached plasticized anti-glare curtain
33 Radio equipment
34 Shell collector box
35 Centre-section camera well (one RB 20/30, RB 50/30, RB 21/18 or RB 15/18 camera)

36 Canvas shell collection chute
37 Dorsal turret
38 MG 81Z twin 7,9-mm machine gun
39 MG 151 (15-mm) fixed cannon in "shräge Musik" installation (fitted to night fighter adaptation)
40 Starboard tailboom
41 Rudder and elevator control cables
42 Ammunition stowage (dorsal position)
43 Entry handholds
44 Centre-section flap below crew nacelle

Focke-Wulf Fw 189A-2 Cutaway Drawing Key

1 Starboard navigation light
2 Aileron control linkage (outer and inner)
3 Starboard aileron
4 Aileron tab
5 Starboard outer flap control linkage
6 Pitot tube
7 ETC 50/VIIId underwing rack fairings
8 Two 110-lb (50-kg) SC 50 bombs
9 Papier-mache "screamers" attached to bomb fins
10 Wing centre/outer section join
11 Starboard engine nacelle
12 Air intake
13 Argus two-bladed controllable-pitch propeller
14 Pitch control vanes
15 Oil cooler intake
16 Engine air intake
17 FuG 212 Lichtenstein C-1 radar array (fitted to night fighter adaptation)
18 Starboard mainwheel

19 Ventral radio mast
20 Optically flat nose panels
21 Rudder pedals
22 GV 219d bomb sight
23 Control column
24 Bomb switch panel

25 Pilot's ring-and-bead sight (for fixed wing-root machine guns)
26 Padded overhead instrument panel

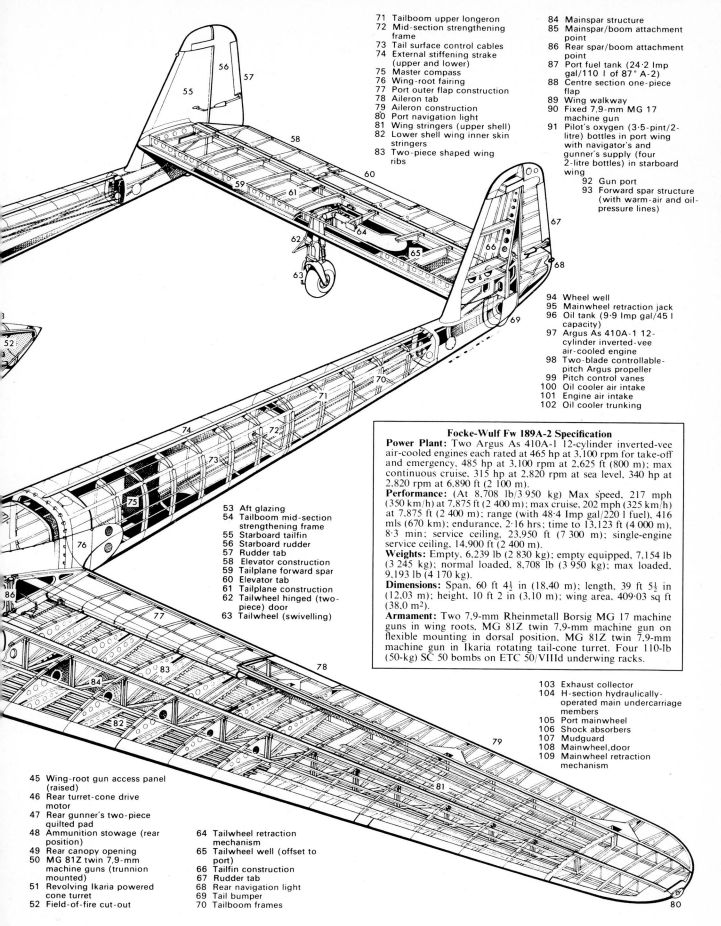

71 Tailboom upper longeron
72 Mid-section strengthening frame
73 Tail surface control cables
74 External stiffening strake (upper and lower)
75 Master compass
76 Wing-root fairing
77 Port outer flap construction
78 Aileron tab
79 Aileron construction
80 Port navigation light
81 Wing stringers (upper shell)
82 Lower shell wing inner skin stringers
83 Two-piece shaped wing ribs

84 Mainspar structure
85 Mainspar/boom attachment point
86 Rear spar/boom attachment point
87 Port fuel tank (24·2 Imp gal/110 l of 87° A-2)
88 Centre section one-piece flap
89 Wing walkway
90 Fixed 7,9-mm MG 17 machine gun
91 Pilot's oxygen (3·5-pint/2-litre) bottles in port wing with navigator's and gunner's supply (four 2-litre bottles) in starboard wing
92 Gun port
93 Forward spar structure (with warm-air and oil-pressure lines)

94 Wheel well
95 Mainwheel retraction jack
96 Oil tank (9·9 Imp gal/45 l capacity)
97 Argus As 410A-1 12-cylinder inverted-vee air-cooled engine
98 Two-blade controllable-pitch Argus propeller
99 Pitch control vanes
100 Oil cooler air intake
101 Engine air intake
102 Oil cooler trunking

53 Aft glazing
54 Tailboom mid-section strengthening frame
55 Starboard tailfin
56 Starboard rudder
57 Rudder tab
58 Elevator construction
59 Tailplane forward spar
60 Elevator tab
61 Tailplane construction
62 Tailwheel hinged (two-piece) door
63 Tailwheel (swivelling)

Focke-Wulf Fw 189A-2 Specification

Power Plant: Two Argus As 410A-1 12-cylinder inverted-vee air-cooled engines each rated at 465 hp at 3,100 rpm for take-off and emergency, 485 hp at 3,100 rpm at 2,625 ft (800 m); max continuous cruise, 315 hp at 2,820 rpm at sea level, 340 hp at 2,820 rpm at 6,890 ft (2 100 m).

Performance: (At 8,708 lb/3 950 kg) Max speed, 217 mph (350 km/h) at 7,875 ft (2 400 m); max cruise, 202 mph (325 km/h) at 7,875 ft (2 400 m); range (with 48·4 Imp gal/220 l fuel), 416 mls (670 km); endurance, 2·16 hrs; time to 13,123 ft (4 000 m), 8·3 min; service ceiling, 23,950 ft (7 300 m); single-engine service ceiling, 14,900 ft (2 400 m).

Weights: Empty, 6,239 lb (2 830 kg); empty equipped, 7,154 lb (3 245 kg); normal loaded, 8,708 lb (3 950 kg); max loaded, 9,193 lb (4 170 kg).

Dimensions: Span, 60 ft 4½ in (18,40 m); length, 39 ft 5½ in (12,03 m); height, 10 ft 2 in (3,10 m); wing area, 409·03 sq ft (38,0 m²).

Armament: Two 7,9-mm Rheinmetall Borsig MG 17 machine guns in wing roots, MG 81Z twin 7,9-mm machine gun on flexible mounting in dorsal position, MG 81Z twin 7,9-mm machine gun in Ikaria rotating tail-cone turret. Four 110-lb (50-kg) SC 50 bombs on ETC 50/VIIId underwing racks.

103 Exhaust collector
104 H-section hydraulically-operated main undercarriage members
105 Port mainwheel
106 Shock absorbers
107 Mudguard
108 Mainwheel,door
109 Mainwheel retraction mechanism

45 Wing-root gun access panel (raised)
46 Rear turret-cone drive motor
47 Rear gunner's two-piece quilted pad
48 Ammunition stowage (rear position)
49 Rear canopy opening
50 MG 81Z twin 7,9-mm machine guns (trunnion mounted)
51 Revolving Ikaria powered cone turret
52 Field-of-fire cut-out

64 Tailwheel retraction mechanism
65 Tailwheel well (offset to port)
66 Tailfin construction
67 Rudder tab
68 Rear navigation light
69 Tail bumper
70 Tailboom frames

(Above) A pre-production Fw 189A-0 delivered to the Luftwaffe in the autumn of 1940, and (below) a general arrangement drawing of an Fw 189A-2 of 1.(H)/31 operational on the Eastern Front in the summer of 1942

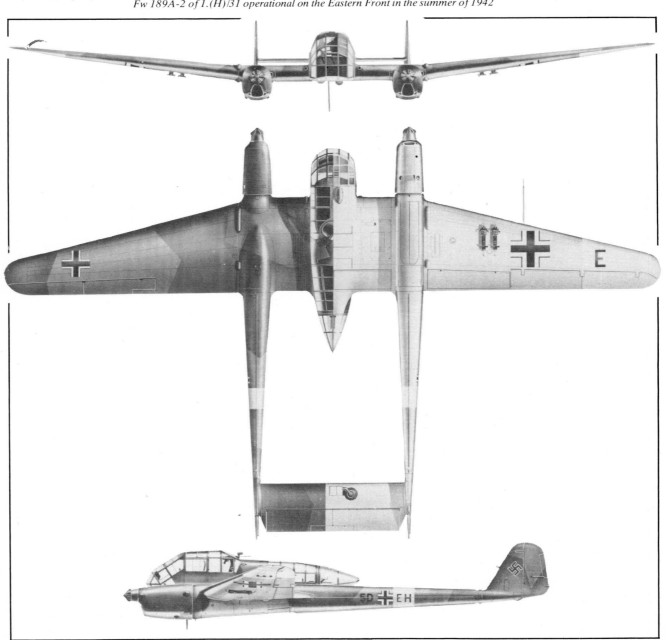

basically simple and after ensuring that the canopy hatches were secured, the fuel safety cock levers checked, the main power supply switched on and that temperature and pressure gauges were working, the single cockpit switch automatically controlling the Argus two-bladed vane-operated controllable-pitch airscrews was set to START. Engine starting was easy and reliable, which must have been a boon during cold-weather operations on the Eastern front, and the air-cooled Argus As 410A-1 engines warmed up fairly quickly. The flaps were lowered to the START position, the rudder and elevator trim tabs were set at mid position, and the throttle lever was pushed to the final notch, the take-off being made with 1·4 atas of boost and 3,100 rpm. The take-off itself was straightforward and commendably short, with only a slight tendency to swing to port, minimum lift-off speed being 68 mph (110 km/h).

Shortly after lift-off it was necessary to tread lightly on the brakes and push the undercarriage retraction lever to the EIN position, the gear being raised before 99 mph (160 km/h) was reached. Climb at the best indicated speed of 112 mph (180 km/h) with 1·2 atas and 2,820 rpm was.a steady plod and by the time 10,000 ft (3 280 m) was reached I had usually had enough, but once settled into cruising flight at 1·15 atas and 2,820 rpm, the Fw 189 gave a delightful armchair ride at a speed of about 180 mph (290 km/h). The indicated throttle settings had to be adhered to implicitly as the carburettors were of the differential (or economiser) type and the use of settings between those given for takeoff, climb, cruise, etc, resulted in the cutting-in of the carburetter high-speed auxiliary jets and uneconomically high fuel consumption. Actually I rarely cruised as high as 10,000 ft (3 280 m) as the Fw 189 was essentially a low-level aircraft and was very stable even in the bumpy air encountered close to the ground.

One drawback that I encountered with the Fw 189 while using it for cross-channel operations was a certain unpleasantness in bad visibility despite those immense areas of glass. In fact, view ahead through the sloping glass panels left something to be desired as these tended to produce a refraction effect and distorted vision in consequence.

With an engine out

From the beginning of my association with the Fw 189 I was particularly interested in the single-engine capabilities of the aircraft as I had many flights to make across the North Sea and the Focke-Wulf impressed one as a lot of aeroplane for one small Argus to pull along. Furthermore, the life history of the engines in captured German aircraft was always very much an unknown quantity owing to the Teutonic thoroughness with which all documentation had been destroyed by the *Luftwaffe*. I hasten to add that I was to fly many hours behind Argus engines, in both the Fw 189 and the Si 204D, and was to ex-

In the Fw 189 "one was literally cocooned in glass". (Above) A view of the fuselage nacelle from the tail showing the revolving Ikaria powered cone turret and (below) the completely glazed fuselage nacelle nose.

perience only one failure, this being the result of fouled spark plugs in the Siebel.

The procedure in the event of an engine failure was the usual one of throttling the engine in question to idle, closing the fuel safety cock lever, switching off the ignition and feathering the airscrew. With the rudder trim correctly adjusted, the controllability of the aircraft under asymmetric power proved to be of a very high standard. In fact, the Fw 189 was remarkably easy to fly on one engine at a somewhat unimpressive rate of progress, particularly if the way home lay across enemy territory. Horizontal flight and reasonably tight turns were possible at normal all-up weight at all altitudes up to 14,900 ft (2 400 m) which was the single-engine service ceiling and at which the indicated speed was of the order of 99 mph (160 km/h) as compared with about 112 mph (180 km/h) at ground level. It was even possible to overshoot on one engine with the undercarriage extended provided speed was not allowed to fall too low, the undercarriage immediately being retracted and the flaps, which were lowered only when about 100 ft (30 m) from the ground, being returned to the "take-off" position.

Although the distorted view forward was annoying, the landing characteristics of the Fw 189 were extremely good. On the approach the aircraft was trimmed somewhat tail-heavy, the approach itself being made at about 112 mph (180 km/h). The hydraulically-operated undercarriage, which was lowered below 99 mph (160 km/h), came down rather slowly and there was always an odd little kick as the tailwheel emerged under the influence of its rubber pulleys. If the throttle was pulled back and revs sank below 1,000 rpm with the undercarriage still retracted a warning horn was activated but this could be overriden by means of a press button on the control column if a landing was not intended.

The lengthy landing flaps, running between the ailerons and tailbooms and right across the centre section, were lowered to START position and the aircraft lost speed very quickly, the deceleration rate being around 1,100 ft/min (5,5 m/sec), giving the low landing speed of 75 mph (120 km/h) and, provided a three-point contact was achieved, a very short landing run. If the Fw 189 was landed on the mainwheels on rough grass a nasty porpoising motion could be induced which made one pray that the tailbooms were not, in fact, as frail as they looked!

In retrospect, it may be seen that the concept of the Fw 189 was a very sound one for a nation that regarded aeroplanes as essentially tools of a mighty army that was going to war with continental enemies whose fragile air support was in marked

(Above and below) The Fw 189 saw operational service almost exclusively with the Aufklärungsstaffeln (H) and their successors, the Nahaufklärungs- gruppen, on the Eastern Front, but a few were operated in North Africa and the Fw 189A-1 (SI+EG) illustrated by these photographs is seen at the factory in desert finish in October 1941, prior to acceptance by the Luftwaffe.

(Above) Four Fw 189A-1s photographed early in 1941 at Focke-Wulf's Bremen factory while awaiting acceptance testing prior to delivery to the Aufklärungsstaffeln (H) in which they were supplanting the obsolete Henschel Hs 126

(Immediately above and below) Fw 189A-2s operating on Germany's Eastern Front during the winter of 1942-43

contrast with that of the *Wehrmacht*. In developing the OV-10 Bronco for the counter-insurgency rôle (which embraces tactical reconnaissance and army co-operation tasks) some 30 years after Kurt Tank and his team turned their attention to providing this radical answer to the *Luftwaffe* requirement, the US design team at Colombus was to come up with some remarkably similar answers to those that gave birth to the Fw 189, a fact which, in itself, testifies to the advanced thinking of the Focke-Wulf Flugzeugbau in those mid 'thirties days at Bremen.

I shall always remember with affection that Fw 189A-1 which I used and enjoyed so much. It bore the *Werk-Nr* 0173, and later, in 1960, when I undertook some test flying for Focke-Wulf at Bremen, I made an attempt to trace the history of this particular machine but to no avail. At the time, the battered hangars of the factory still bore mute testimony to the devastation of Allied bombing and the records office was presumably just a hole in the ground. Of course, relatively few Fw 189s were built at Bremen, most production having taken place in the former Aero factory in Prague, Czechoslovakia, and in French factories in the Bordeaux area. If the history of *Werk-Nr* 0173 before it came into my hands is obscure, no mystery surrounds the subsequent fate of the aircraft. After we had no

further use for it as a hack at the RAE, I flew the Fw 189 to RAF Brize Norton for storage and there it was to be destroyed in a gale — a sad end to a likeable friend.

HEINKEL HE 111

From whatever aspect the Heinkel He 111 is viewed it must be admitted that its creators, the brothers Siegfried and Walter Günter, were responsible for a classic aeroplane. Not only was it fully representative of the latest aerodynamic refinements and structural techniques at the time of its début; it coupled beautiful handling characteristics with a performance enabling it to display a clean pair of heels to most contemporary fighters. By any standard, this product of the Ernst Heinkel AG must be adjudged one of the most outstanding warplanes of the mid 'thirties, although by the time I first made contact with the sleek cigar-shaped bomber the late 'thirties were about to translate to the early 'forties and, while still a formidable weapon, the He 111 had lost a little of the potency that it had enjoyed when first delivered to the *Kampfgeschwader*.

I do not have to tax my memory to recall my first sight of the Heinkel He 111. It was 28 October 1939 when He 111Ps of *Kampfgeschwader* 26 were carrying out the first raids on British territory, attacking shipping in the Firth of Forth and Scapa Flow, one of their number belonging to *Stab/KG* 26 being forced down near Dalkeith by Spitfires. By sheer coincidence, some days later I was travelling from Edinburgh to London to join my unit and in the next compartment was the pilot of the luckless He 111 under armed escort. Since I spoke German and was in uniform, I did not have much difficulty in getting permission to speak to him. Naturally enough, he was pretty dejected and not too inclined to be conversational, but he was, at the same time, anxious to analyse why he had been shot down and was obviously reaching the conclusion that the He 111's defensive armament was incorrectly distributed.

During his subsequent sojourn in London, this *Luftwaffe* pilot may well have seen other He 111s fall victim to RAF fighters and have ruefully confirmed the basic weakness of the aesthetically attractive Heinkel that was to cost the *Luftwaffe* dear — its inadequate defensive armament. Perhaps its back-

ground of simultaneous development for both commercial and military rôles had had a bearing on its defensive inadequacies, but more likely the Günter brothers had not foreseen or catered for the radically new combination of high performance, eight-gun armament and small head-on profile that was to provide their bomber's principal opposition, at least over the British Isles, in the shape of the Spitfire and Hurricane, and had concentrated instead on achieving maximum performance.

I had always admired the aerodynamically efficient and shapely Heinkel bomber which appeared to combine grace with sturdiness, and I was particularly impressed by its almost completely glazed and exquisitely streamlined fuselage nose, but on climbing into the cockpit of an He 111H-1 for the first time I was immediately made aware of the fact that the cult of streamlining was not without its snags. German designers were apparently irresistibly attracted to the idea of depositing their pilots in greenhouses, a penchant which could produce its problems, and in the case of the He 111 the pilot had so much curved glass in front of him that his view ahead was rather akin to looking down a glass tunnel.

In bad weather the surfeit of transparent panels was downright dangerous and the fact that this was recognised was to be seen from the provision made for elevating the pilot's seat and controls for landing and taxying, allowing his head to emerge through a sliding panel in the upper decking where it was in part protected from the slipstream by a small retractable windscreen. This instant Tiger Moth transformation in a frontline bomber always symbolized for me the eccentricities of functional design that the German aircraft industry seemed to come up with from time to time, and which, surprisingly enough, seemed to be accepted by the *Luftwaffe*.

The first Heinkel bomber that I had the opportunity to fly was an He 111H-1 (*Werk-Nr* 6353) which had been built at Oranienburg and taken on charge by the *Luftwaffe* on 22

August 1939. While participating in an anti-shipping operation with II/KG 26 on 9 February 1940, it had made a forced landing on moorland at North Berwick Law after its oil tanks had been punctured by a Spitfire of No 602 Squadron. It had been repaired and on 14 August 1940 had embarked upon a new career bedecked with RAF roundels as AW177, touring RAF airfields in the "circus" to familiarise allied pilots with enemy aircraft. This career was to last for more than three years, the much-flown aircraft finally being destroyed on 10 November 1943 after it spun in from low altitude at Polebrook when its pilot had attempted to evade a captured Ju 88 that was inadvertently using the same runway for landing but from the *opposite* direction.

The pilot of the He 111 was seated to port and in order to afford him maximum possible forward view, the Ikaria universal mounting for the 7,9-mm MG 15 nose gun was offset to starboard, resulting in the decidedly odd asymmetric effect so characteristic of the aeroplane. The flying controls were conventional enough and an arm at the top of the control column could be swung over to enable a member of the crew sitting on the right of the pilot to control the elevators and ailerons. No dual engine or rudder controls were provided, but the elevator and rudder trimmer controls were on the pilot's right and so could be reached by the navigator as could also the coolant radiator control handles. The throttles, supercharger control levers and airscrew pitch control levers were all on the pilot's

left. The pitch levers moved in the conventional sense and if pulled right back they feathered the airscrews. The mixture strength and boost pressure were automatically controlled. With the supercharger levers in the high gear position (ie, rearward), the high gear was automatically engaged at 11,500 ft (3 500 m) and disengaged below that altitude. Nevertheless, it was recommended that the levers be pushed to their forward position below 11,500 ft (3 500 m).

The layout of the flight instruments on a panel suspended from the roof was something of a mess in so far as instrument flying was concerned for it offered no logical scan pattern. However, this fault was common enough in aircraft of the period before a logical approach to the problem came up with the T pattern that was to be universally adopted. The engine instruments, on the other hand, were well grouped to the right of the flight instruments and gave all the information required at a glance.

The 24-volt electrical system, like that of all German aircraft of the WW II period, was more advanced than British equivalents, with its panel of circuit breaker buttons, master switch and a layout that was later to be emulated in Allied aircraft. The hydraulic system operated the undercarriage, flaps, coolant radiators, pilot's seat-and-controls elevating gear and the wheel brakes. Hand pumps were provided for the emergency lowering of the undercarriage and flaps.

The fuel system comprised a main and a reserve tank in each

(Head of opposite page) An He 111H-11 of Kampfgeschwader 55 engaged in the "Little Blitz" in the spring of 1944. (Above) An He 111H-4 of 5./KG 26 flying over the Mediterranean in 1941, and (below) an He 111H-2 of the Aufklärungsgruppe of the Oberbefehlshaber der Luftwaffe

wing, the former being of 154 Imp gal (700 l) capacity and the latter of 220 Imp gal (1 000 l) capacity. Each of the Jumo 211A-1 engines took fuel from its adjacent main tank, and transfer from the reserve to the main tank was by means of an electrically-driven transfer pump when the contents of the latter tank dropped to 44 Imp gal (200 l). Red warning lights came on automatically if the contents of the main tank fell as low as 22 Imp gal (100 l). In the event of a power system failure, the transfer of fuel from one tank to the other could be effected by a hand pump on the right of the pilot. However, the low capacity of the hand pump (delivering only 49·5 Imp gal/225 l per hour from 60 double strokes of the pump per minute) was such that the engines had to be throttled right back and thus the aircraft could only maintain an altitude of less than 9,840 ft (3 000 m). No provision was made for the cross-feeding of the tanks. Each engine had a 22 Imp gal (100 l) oil tank immediately

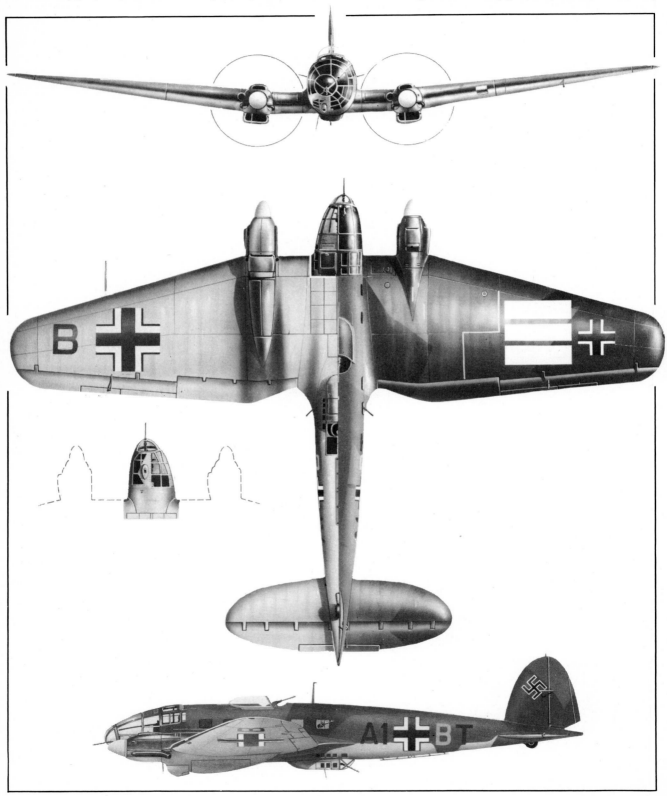

(Opposite page) This general arrangement drawing depicts an He 111H-2 operated by III/KG 53 during the ''Battle of Britain''. The white bars on the upper wing surfaces were intended as an aid to formation flying. (Above) An He 111H-2 of the Aufkl.Gr.Ob.d.L.

(Immediately above) An He 111H-4 with external bomb carrier on the port side of the centre fuselage only, the starboard internal bomb cells being retained, and (below) an He 111H-6 of Kampfgeschwader 26 taking-off on a sortie

Heinkel He 111H-3 cutaway drawing key

1 Starboard navigation light
2 Starboard aileron
3 Wing ribs
4 Forward spar
5 Rear spar
6 Aileron tab
7 Starboard flap
8 Fuel tank access panel
9 Wing centre section/outer panel break line
10 Inboard fuel tank (154 Imp gal/700 l capacity) position between nacelle and fuselage
11 Oil tank cooling louvres
12 Oil cooler air intake
13 Supercharger air intake
14 Three-blade VDM airscrew
15 Airscrew pitch-change mechanism
16 Junkers Jumo 211D-1 12-cylinder inverted-vee liquid-cooled engine
17 Exhaust manifold
18 Nose-mounted 7,9-mm MG 15 machine gun
19 Ikaria ball-and-socket gun mounting (offset to starboard)

46 Bomb flares
47 Unarmoured bulkhead
48 Rear fuselage access cut-out
49 Port 7,9-mm beam MG 15 machine gun
50 Dinghy stowage
51 Fuselage frames
52 Stringers
53 Starboard tailplane
54 Aerial
55 Starboard elevator
56 Tailfin forward spar
57 Tailfin structure
58 Rudder balance
59 Tailfin rear spar/rudder post
60 Rudder construction
61 Rudder tab
62 Tab actuator (starboard surface)
63 Remotely-controlled 7,9-mm MG 17 machine gun in tail cone (fitted to some aircraft only)
64 Rear navigation light
65 Elevator tab
66 Elevator structure
67 Elevator hinge line
68 Tailplane front spar
69 Semi-retractable tailwheel

Heinkel He 111H-16 Specification

Power Plant: Two Junkers Jumo 211F-2 12-cylinder inverted-vee liquid-cooled engines each rated at 1,350 hp for take-off and 1,060 hp at 17,390 ft (5 300 m).
Performance: Max speed (without bombs and with half fuel), 227 mph (365 km/h) at sea level, 248 mph (399 km/h) at 6,560 ft (2 000 m), 255 mph (410 km/h) at 13,125 ft (4 000 m), 270 mph (434 km/h) at 19,685 ft (6 000 m); max speed in max loaded condition), 217 mph (349 km/h) at sea level, 236 mph (380 km/h) at 6,560 ft (2 000 m), 242 mph (390 km/h) at 13,125 ft (4 000 m), 252 mph (405 km/h) at 19,685 ft (6 000 m); normal range with max bomb load, 1,212 mls (1 950 km) at 205 mph (330 km/h) at sea level, 1,200 mls (1 930 km) at 230 mph (370 km/h) at 6,560 ft (2 000 m), 1,280 mls (2 060 km) at 239 mph (384 km/h) at 16,405 ft (5 000 m); time to 6,560 ft (2 000 m) at max loaded weight, 8·5 min, to 13,125 ft (4 000 m), 23·5 min, to 19,685 ft (6 000 m), 42·0 min; service ceiling (at max loaded weight), 21,980 ft (6 700 m), (without bomb load and with half fuel), 27,885 ft (8 500 m).
Weights: Empty equipped, 19,136 lb (8 680 kg); max loaded, 30,865 lb (14 000 kg).
Dimensions: Span, 74 ft 1¾ in (22,60 m); length, 53 ft 9½ in (16,40 m); height, 13 ft 1½ in (4,00 m); wing area, 931,07 sq ft (86,50 m²).
Armament: (Defensive) One 20-mm MG FF cannon with 180 rounds in fuselage nose (additional 7,9-mm MG 15 machine gun optional), one 13-mm MG 131 machine gun with 1,000 rounds in dorsal position (electrically-operated dorsal turret mounted in He 111H-16/R1), two 7,9-mm MG 81 machine guns with 1,000 rpg in rear of ventral gondola and one 7,9-mm MG 15 or MG 81 with 1,000 rounds or two 7,9-mm MG 81 machine guns with 500 rpg in each of two beam positions. (Offensive) Total of 32 110-lb (50-kg) or eight 551-lb (250-kg) bombs internally, or 16 110-lb (50-kg) bombs internally and one 2,204-lb (1 000-kg) bomb on external PVC rack, or one 4,410-lb (2 000-kg) bomb and one 1,102-lb (500-kg) bomb externally.

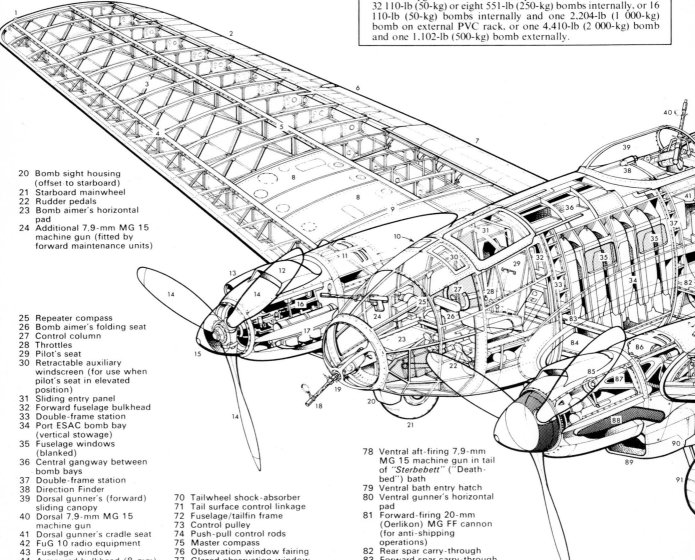

20 Bomb sight housing (offset to starboard)
21 Starboard mainwheel
22 Rudder pedals
23 Bomb aimer's horizontal pad
24 Additional 7,9-mm MG 15 machine gun (fitted by forward maintenance units)

25 Repeater compass
26 Bomb aimer's folding seat
27 Control column
28 Throttles
29 Pilot's seat
30 Retractable auxiliary windscreen (for use when pilot's seat in elevated position)
31 Sliding entry panel
32 Forward fuselage bulkhead
33 Double-frame station
34 Port ESAC bomb bay (vertical stowage)
35 Fuselage windows (blanked)
36 Central gangway between bomb bays
37 Double-frame station
38 Direction Finder
39 Dorsal gunner's (forward) sliding canopy
40 Dorsal 7,9-mm MG 15 machine gun
41 Dorsal gunner's cradle seat
42 FuG 10 radio equipment
43 Fuselage window
44 Armoured bulkhead (8-mm)
45 Aerial mast

70 Tailwheel shock-absorber
71 Tail surface control linkage
72 Fuselage/tailfin frame
73 Control pulley
74 Push-pull control rods
75 Master compass
76 Observation window fairing
77 Glazed observation window in floor

78 Ventral aft-firing 7,9-mm MG 15 machine gun in tail of "Sterbebett" ("Death-bed") bath
79 Ventral bath entry hatch
80 Ventral gunner's horizontal pad
81 Forward-firing 20-mm (Oerlikon) MG FF cannon (for anti-shipping operations)
82 Rear spar carry-through
83 Forward spar carry-through
84 Oil cooler

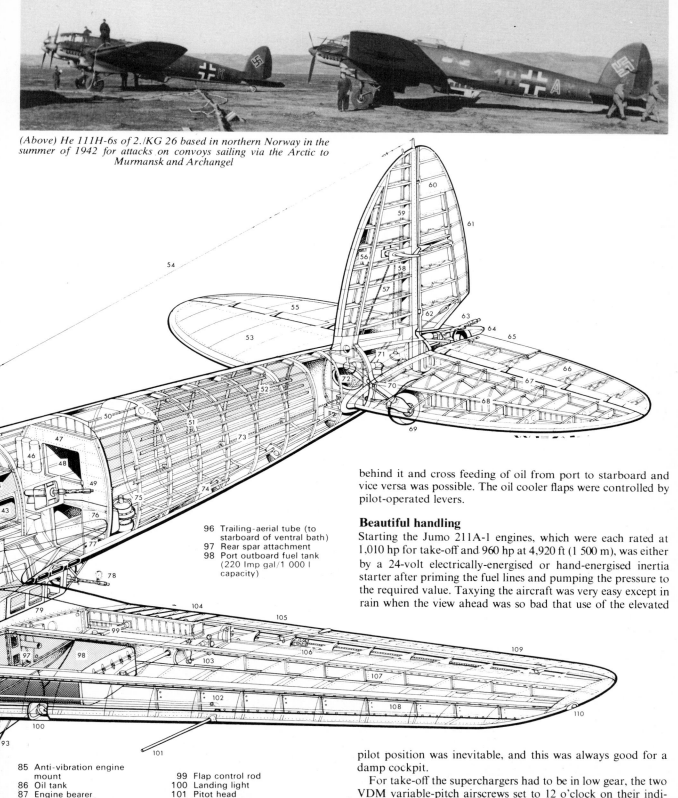

(Above) He 111H-6s of 2./KG 26 based in northern Norway in the summer of 1942 for attacks on convoys sailing via the Arctic to Murmansk and Archangel

96 Trailing-aerial tube (to starboard of ventral bath)
97 Rear spar attachment
98 Port outboard fuel tank (220 Imp gal/1 000 l capacity)

85 Anti-vibration engine mount
86 Oil tank
87 Engine bearer
88 Exhaust flame-damper shroud
89 Radiator air intake
90 Radiator bath
91 Port mainwheel
92 Mainwheel leg
93 Retraction mechanism
94 Mainwheel door (outer)
95 Multi-screw wing attachment

99 Flap control rod
100 Landing light
101 Pitot head
102 Pitot head heater/wing leading-edge de-icer
103 Flap and aileron coupling
104 Flap structure
105 Aileron tab
106 Tab actuator
107 Rear spar
108 Forward spar
109 Port aileron
110 Port navigation light

behind it and cross feeding of oil from port to starboard and vice versa was possible. The oil cooler flaps were controlled by pilot-operated levers.

Beautiful handling

Starting the Jumo 211A-1 engines, which were each rated at 1,010 hp for take-off and 960 hp at 4,920 ft (1 500 m), was either by a 24-volt electrically-energised or hand-energised inertia starter after priming the fuel lines and pumping the pressure to the required value. Taxying the aircraft was very easy except in rain when the view ahead was so bad that use of the elevated pilot position was inevitable, and this was always good for a damp cockpit.

For take-off the superchargers had to be in low gear, the two VDM variable-pitch airscrews set to 12 o'clock on their indicators, all trimmers set neutral and one-third flap lowered. The pilot's seat was usually lowered from its elevated position for take-off, although in the raised position its wind deflector was very effective and the position was not unduly draughty up to about 200 mph (320 km/h). The take-off run at 1·35 *atas* of boost and 2,400 rpm proved to be short and straightforward with little tendency to swing. This power could be held for one

Heinkel He 111H-1 cockpit drawing key (opposite)

1 Aileron trimmer
2 Ammeter
3 Starter battery selector switch } Reverse side shown
4 Starter switch (port) }
5 Starter switch (starboard)
6 Fuel tank selector levers (transfer controls)
7 Oil cooler flap controls
8 Fuel cock (injection) levers
9 Combined directional gyro/repeater compass/ auto-pilot switch
10 Emergency auto-pilot override
11 Cut-out and plug-clearing control
12 Airscrew-pitch control lever (port)
13 Airscrew-pitch control lever (starboard)
14 Magneto switches
15 Automatic stabilizer cut-out
16 Undercarriage selector lever
17 Hydraulic locking lever
18 Flap lever
19 Supercharger control levers
20 Light dimmer switch
21 Flap indicator
22 Undercarriage position (four-lamp) indicator
23 Airscrew-pitch indicator (starboard)
24 Airscrew-pitch indicator (port)
25 Throttle levers
26 Cylinder priming pumps
27 Oxygen apparatus
28 Alternative/back-up basic instrument panel (shown in dotted lines)

29 Repeater compass
30 Altimeter
31 Pitot-head heating indicator
32 Visual homing indicator
33 Visual homer
34 Turn and bank indicator
35 Directional gyro
36 Fine-coarse altimeter
37 Blind-approach indicator
38 Air speed indicator
39 Artificial horizon
40 Rate-of-climb indicator
41 Pilot's sliding side-panel
42 "Siglas" curved roof-panels
43 Sliding entry panel (open)
44 Pilot's auxiliary windscreen (raised)
45 Sliding entry panel operating handle
46 Panel lighting dimmer
47 Oil and fuel pressure gauges (starboard)
48 Oil and fuel pressure gauges (port)
49 Fuel contents warning light (starboard)
50 Roof box panel with external air-temperature gauge
51 Fuel selector switch (starboard)
52 Fuel contents gauge (starboard)
53 Fuel contents gauge (port)
54 Fuel contents warning light (port)
55 Fuel selector switch (port)
56 Emergency bomb-jettison lever
57 Sliding entry panel locking handle
58 Artificial horizon
59 Visual homing indicator
60 Turn-and-bank indicator

61 Pitot-head heating indicator
62 Blind-approach indicator
63 Airspeed indicator
64 Rate-of-climb indicator
65 Altimeter
66 Repeater compass (magnetic)
67 Directional gyro
68 Engine rev counter (port)
69 Engine rev counter (starboard)
70 Boost pressure gauge (port)
71 Boost pressure gauge (starboard)
72 Oil temperature gauge (port)
73 Oil temperature gauge (starboard)
74 Coolant temperature gauge (port)
75 Coolant temperature gauge (starboard)
76 Oil and fuel pressure gauge (port)
77 Oil and fuel pressure gauge (starboard)
78 "Siglas" curved side-panel (fixed)
79 Bombardier's sliding side-panel
80 Signal flares pouch
81 "Patin" radio compass
82 D/F frame aerial rotating handle
83 Navigator/bombardier's folding seat (used during take-off and landing)
84 Bombardier's horizontal-pad frame (canvas quilt deleted for clarity)
85 "Siglas" optically-flat floor-panel (hinged to open)
86 Bomb sight

87 Signal flare pistol stowage clip
88 "Ikaria" ball-and-socket nose MG mounting
89 "Siglas" nose cupola offset to starboard
90 "Siglas" curved panel windscreen sections
91 Bombardier's anti-glare screen (folded)
92 Pilot's anti-glare screen (folded)
93 Automatic-pilot turn switch
94 Chronometer
95 Control column swing-over arm
96 Control column
97 Pilot's intercom switch-box
98 Rudder pedals (support frames deleted for clarity)
99 "Siglas" optically flat lower side-panels
100 Harness attachment point
101 Seat-raising lever
102 Elevator trim control
103 D/F controls
104 Radiator position control (port)
105 Oil cooler intake flap position controls
106 Radiator position control (starboard)
107 Undercarriage and flaps emergency hand-pump
108 Manual fuel-system priming levers (two) on forward face of box
109 Manual fuel-transfer control lever on forward face of box
110 Cockpit heating control
111 Rudder trim control
112 Seat-raising pivot member and control conduit
114 Seat frame
115 Seat actuating cylinder

Not shown: Two-row main electrical control switch panel on bulkhead behind pilot's seat

[Top row, left (inboard) to right (outboard)]

Airscrew pitch-change gear (port)
Airscrew pitch-change gear (starboard)
Undercarriage horn indicator
Trim indicator
Temperature and contents gauges
Starting booster coil

Fuel transfer pump
Directional gyro
Course motor
Course magnet
Economical flight switch

[Bottom row, left (inboard) to right (outboard)]:

Radio systems
Starboard generator
Remote-controlled main switch
Port generator

Removable armament } Boxed
Bomb armament }
Distribution switch for lights and pitot heating

He 111H-16s of I/KG 27 with external ETC 2000 racks and temporary winter camouflage engaged in a sortie over the Eastern Front during the winter of 1942-43. Bombing was, in fact, virtually a secondary task for this and other He 111H-equipped units at this time as their primary rôle was the aerial supply of the beleaguered German forces in Stalingrad

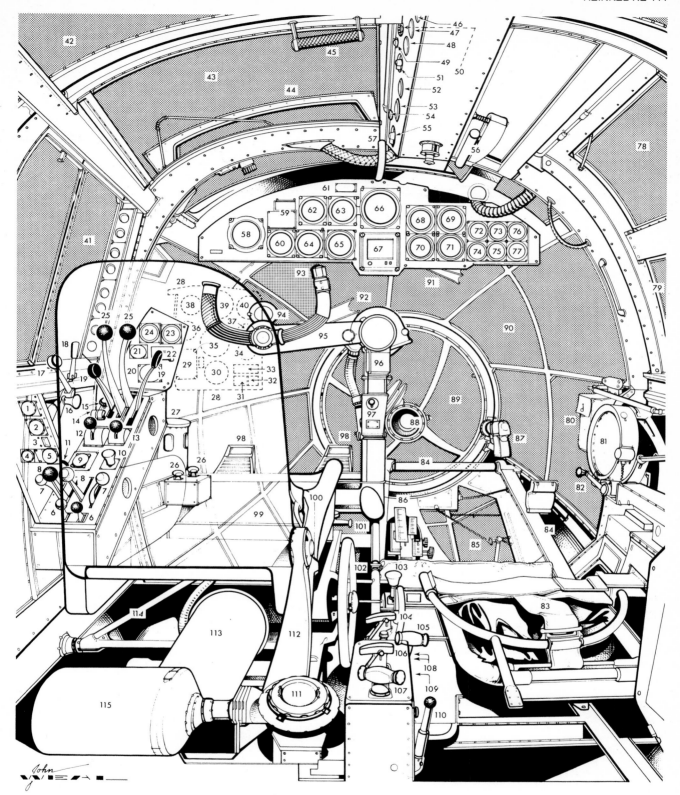

minute while raising the undercarriage and flaps, and then had to be reduced to 1·15 *atas* and 2,300 rpm for the climb. The rate of climb was very good for the period and certainly considerably superior to that of the contemporary Wellington with much the same bomb load, while the service ceiling of the He 111 was at least 5,000 ft (1 525 m) greater than that of the British bomber.

The Heinkel handled beautifully, being very stable around all axes and offering good harmony of control. All the control surfaces were mass-balanced and carried trim tabs controlled by the pilot. Except for the rudder, each control surface had setback hinges. The ailerons had two independent large-span tabs, one being for trimming and the other being an automatic servo device. The tailplane could be adjusted on the ground for three separate positions covering 3·2 deg difference in incidence. An automatic pilot was fitted which controlled the rudder only,

(Above and immediately below) The He 111H-1 (Werk-Nr 6353), formerly of II/KG 26, which was acquired by the RAF after making a forced landing at North Berwick Law on 9 February 1940, being taken on charge as AW177 and flying until 10 November 1943 when it was finally destroyed

and once engaged the aircraft could be turned at three different rates in either direction by use of a switch on the control column. To the left of the pilot was a throw-out knob which disconnected the auto-pilot in an emergency.

The in-flight limitations were clearly displayed on a metal plate in the cockpit, and showed the maximum permissible

". . . the pilot had so much curved glass in front of him that his view ahead was rather akin to looking down a glass tunnel."

speed to be 298 mph (480 km/h) and the maximum permissible acceleration at 24,251 lb (11 000 kg) to be 2·7 *g* with maximum bank in turns of 65 deg. The normal crew of four was booked for a busy time, particularly in the target zone. The pilot sat in the front port seat with the navigator/bomb aimer to star-board. The latter moved into a prone position in the nose for the actual bombing run or in the event of fighter attack when he became the nose gunner. He was also taught enough to enable him to fly the aircraft home with the help of the auto-pilot in the event of the pilot becoming a casualty. If the pilot was incapable of landing the aircraft the crew presumably baled out over friendly territory.

The rear compartment was joined to the cockpit by a narrow catwalk between the racks of eight 551-lb (250-kg) bombs which were stowed vertically in two rows, and there were usually four gun positions in the centre fuselage, all mounting single 7,9-mm MG 15s, the dorsal and ventral positions having been augmented at an early phase in the hostilities by a pair of side mountings over the wing trailing edge to provide addi-tional protection from beam attacks, a fifth member usually being added to the crew complement to operate the additional weapons. As the air war progressed the number of defensive weapons and their calibre steadily increased, and some air-craft were even to be fitted with a remotely-controlled 7,9-mm MG 17 machine gun in the tail cone as a "dissuader", others being experimentally fitted with a grenade launching tube in this position, grenades being ejected hopefully in the path of pursuing fighters. So the hard lesson learned by such as the

He 111 pilot downed in October 1939 after attacking shipping in the Firth of Forth was not entirely disregarded.

Landing preparations were begun at a speed of 125 mph (200 km/h) which was the maximum permissible speed for lowering the undercarriage, the engine speed not being above 1,700 rpm. Once the undercarriage was down the flaps were lowered and their action depressed the ailerons without any marked change of trim. The approach was made at 90 mph (145 km/h) and speed had to be kept up all the way to the hold-off to avoid a tendency on the part of the port wing to drop. The landing run was somewhat lengthy, probably a tribute to the clean lines of the aircraft.

Two or three years after flying the He 111H-1 that eventually met its end at Polebrook in November 1943, I had an opportunity to fly examples of the later He 111H-6 at Schleswig, on the Baltic Coast. Apart from having the uprated Jumo 211F-1 engine which, with a strengthened crankshaft, a fully-shrouded DVL supercharger impeller and other changes, offered 1,400 hp for take-off and 1,200 hp at 16,405 ft (5 000 m), the H-6 differed little from its predecessors and displayed no noticeable change in handling characteristics.

To assess the He 111 fairly it should be compared with its contemporaries of the mid and late 'thirties, and in such a comparison it probably stands supreme in the list of medium bombers as regards performance and versatility, but it was vulnerable to fighter attack and can hardly be regarded as a pilot's delight owing to the poor view that it offered forward from the pilot's seat in that "hall of mirrors" of a fuselage nose. Indeed, the curved transparent panels tended to emulate mirrors in sunlight, seriously inconveniencing the pilot, while in bad weather conditions . . . !

As a postscript, I should perhaps add that I almost experienced my first combat in WW II with an He 111 in the autumn of 1940 while flying a Gloster Gladiator on a training flight over Somerset. I was flying in formation with another Gladiator, both of our aircraft being armed in case of a chance encounter with the opposition, when we saw two He 111s close together heading in the direction of Bristol. We came up from behind, I personally experiencing that mixture of elation and apprehension that I was to learn always immediately preceded combat. We had a slight height advantage and were closing slowly from dead astern when I became aware of puffs of anti-aircraft fire. Suddenly there was a blinding flash and our Gladiators were flying through the debris of what seconds before had been a pair of Heinkels. The two aircraft had been flying extremely closely to each other; one had evidently suffered a direct hit in the bomb-bay and both had gone up! I shall never know whether I was cheated or spared, but I certainly felt that I did not deserve that the holes in my Gladiator's fabric should be earned thus.

He 111P-1 bombers awaiting delivery to the Luftwaffe in 1939. The singularly inappropriate radio call sign on the fuselage of the second aircraft is noteworthy. (Below) An He 111H-6 with a pair of practice LT F5b torpedoes on PVC fuselage racks

(Below) An He 111H-16 (Werk-Nr 8433) acquired by Allied forces and taken to the USA for evaluation by the USAAF at Wright Field, Ohio

JUNKERS JU 52/3M

ANGULARLY UGLY and incredibly cumbersome! How well I recall my reaction on first seeing an example of Dipl Ing Ernst Zindel's Junkers Ju 52/3m transport sporting Deutsche Lufthansa markings and sitting on the apron at Tempelhof airfield, Berlin over 40 years ago, in the summer of 1936. To my then-youthful eyes, this fantastic amalgam of corrugated skinning, trailing flappery and heavily-braced undercarriage, not to mention a trio of air-cooled radial engines, which, as I was to discover, possessed all the

A former DLH Ju 52/3m-Z serving with the Luftwaffe. Note the long-chord central engine cowling and spinners. (Head of page) Ju 52/3m g5e and g7e transports of 3.Staffel of K.Gr.z.b.V.9 on Germany's Eastern Front during the summer of 1942

discordance of a phalanx of over-revving lawnmowers, demonstrated a total disregard for the most elementary aerodynamic considerations! Yet this æsthetically-unappealing contraption possessed, so I was told at the time, very considerable commercial respectability; I was, of course, quite unaware that, probably at that very point in time, this respectability was being somewhat tarnished in Spanish skies by a less pacific and even more hideous version, with an immense dustbin accommodating a bomb-aimer-cum-gunner appended between the rearmost legs of its undercarriage tripods.

No one with any sense of the æsthetic could have considered this product of the Dessau factory of the Junkers Flugzeug-und Motorenwerke AG to be remotely handsome. Even ruggedly functional seemed an epithet of downright flattery and small wonder that, during WW II, the Allies were to refer to Junkers' "Iron Annie" as the "Corrugated Coffin". To us it seemed that when employed as a troop transport this lumbering monstrosity must surely frighten its inmates silly. It appeared to be so extraordinarily vulnerable; one could imagine it falling victim to a farmer's shotgun.

But were we maligning this ugly duckling? Was it in truth an extraordinarily well camouflaged swan? I began to doubt the validity of my first reactions when, as the fighting in Europe finally petered out, I discovered the very real affection for the *"Tante Ju"* ("Auntie Ju") possessed by the *Wehrmacht* as a whole, and began to appreciate the fact that this transport had probably played a greater rôle in shaping the course of WW II than any combat aeroplane. Puzzled that so much affection could be generated by and importance attached to an aircraft that I had viewed as an antiquated freak so many years before, I became quite anxious to make the acquaintance of the Ju 52/3m in the air. In any case, I must confess that I had always had something of a soft spot for trimotors, a configuration that seemed to go hand in hand with the high reliability tag.

There were, of course, many of the Junkers trimotors scattered around Germany at the time of the capitualtion and no small number of these were being used by the Allies for hack work. At the Royal Aircraft Establishment unit at Schleswig we had a selection of about a half-dozen and they always

(Above right) A Ju 52/3m g5e with the ring-mounting for the forward 7,9-mm MG 15 machine gun hinged upward and (immediately below) a Ju 52/3m g3e of the Flugzeugführerschule (C) at Lechfeld in the summer of 1938. Note the semi-retracted ventral gun "dustbin"

(Below) Heating the port engine of a Ju 52/3m of a blind flying school preparatory to taking-off on a training mission during the winter of 1942-43

One of the several examples of the angularly ugly but extraordinarily successful Junkers trimotor transport, a Ju 52/3m g6e, that were used by the Royal Aircraft Establishment as hacks, this one having been photographed at Farnborough in August 1945

seemed to be in use, and as soon as I found a spare moment between ferrying more exotic ex-*Luftwaffe* aeroplanes back to Farnborough, I seized the opportunity to indulge in a little nostagia with the Ju 52, for the cockpit immediately transported me back to the days of my boyhood. It was roomy, remarkably antiquated and had that strong smell of paint which, for some indefinable reason, I had always associated with German aircraft of 'thirties vintage. The view through the windscreen was reminiscent of that from the driver's cab of the old double-decker buses that plied the streets of London in the early years of the previous decade, but the cockpit layout was a *mess* — switches and knobs everywhere. How could such a basic aircraft have such a complicated cockpit?

Akin to a Wurlitzer organ

The drill for starting up the 725 hp BMW 132A-3 nine-cylinder radials was rather like playing a Wurlitzer organ. First, the main battery had to be switched on and then the ignition set to the SPÄT (retarded) position, the master ignition knob being pulled out. The three sets of ignition switches were next set to 1 + 2; the fuel switches were set to the priming position and the mixture levers under the throttles were moved down to the RICH position. The three sets of oil cooler levers were moved down to the CLOSED position and the priming pump was then actuated for the middle engine.

After this dazzling prelude, the handle for the requisite inertia starter was depressed for 10-20 seconds and then pulled up. As soon as the engine fired, the ignition had to be set to the FRÜH (advanced) position and the engine allowed to tick over at 700-800 revs until oil pressure registered. The revs could be gradually increased to 1,000-1,200 provided that the oil pressure did not rise above 7 *atas*. As soon as oil

temperature reached 30°C, the revs could be brought up to 1,400 and thus bring in the generator on the centre engine. With an oil temperature of 40°C, the oil coolers had to be set OPEN. The two outboard engines were normally started as soon as the oil pressure registered on the centre engine. When all three had warmed up, the compressed air valve was turned on for brake operation and taxying could commence.

The rigmarole to get this early 'thirties transport aircraft to actually move certainly led me to appreciate the refinements that had been embodied by aircraft designed a decade later. Even relatively simple devices, such as automatic boost control and thermostatically-controlled radiator shutters, cut down the cockpit drill enormously, and the complex procedure called for by the old Junkers trimotor was perhaps best compared with the effort needed to operate a manual gear change after years of driving a car with an automatic shift.

Before lining up for take-off, the elevator trimmer was set to neutral and then the flap/trim combination engaged by raising the knob beside the trimming wheel. This latter action was necessary because of the very large trim change associated with movement of the huge flaps which formed the typical Junkers "double-wing" arrangement. The flap setting for take-off was 25 degrees. The boost cut-out control was set to EIN for normal operation, thus restricting take-off power to 2,050 rpm. In emergency, the throttles could be pushed through the gate to give 2,150 rpm for a maximum period of three minutes.

The aircraft had a tendency to swing to port on take-off, but this could easily be corrected with rudder movement, and lift-off at a weight of 22,156 lb (10 500 kg) was effected at 68 mph (110 km/h) after a run of 1,150 ft (350 m) in zero wind. The flaps were raised in two stages on the climb-out and the flap/trim combination disengaged. The climb itself was made at 96 mph (155 km/h) with 1,800 rpm and could most politely be described as laborious. I was once to have occasion to take a Ju 52/3m up to 10,000 ft (3 050 m) and it took all of 18 minutes to get there!

However, if the Junkers climbed like the venerable old lady that she was, she also possessed all the docility associated with the venerable, being beautifully stable and virtually capable of being flown hands-off in anything but really turbulent air. On attaining cruise altitude, the brake valve was turned off and rpm reduced to 1,600 which produced a speed of 124 mph (200 km/h) at 3,000 ft (915 m) or 118 mph (190 km/h) at 7,500 ft (2 285 m). The loss of the centre engine in cruise had only the effect of reducing speed by some 12 mph (20 km/h), but the loss of an outboard engine produced a drop of around 19 mph (30 km/h) because of the offset rudder needed to counteract swing. This offset was trimmed out by pulling forward the appropriate trimmer lever — right lever for dead starboard engine and left lever if the opposite engine failed.

As I have already commented, the handling of the Junkers trimotor under virtually all conditions was very (old) ladylike, and I flew the Ju 52/3m in quite a lot of bad weather, but if there was a fair amount of turbulence one had to work fairly hard on the controls, although the rudder could be set on autopilot to take the strain out of the footwork. Unfortunately, the cockpit was decidedly noisy and inclined to be rather draughty.

The landing procedure was basically a matter of pulling back the throttles, with the slight complication of engaging the flap/trim combination and winding on full flap (40 deg) at 93 mph (150 km/h). The trimmer wheel was wound back to lower the flaps and, at the same time, this made the aircraft tail heavy to counteract the nose down pitch caused by the downcoming flaps. Another little chore to while away the time on the approach at 80 mph (130 km/h) was to turn on the brake valve.

Touch-down was a clattering, jangling affair no matter how delicate one strove to make it, but the landing run in zero wind was a mere 1,050 ft (320 m). After arrival I always got something of a kick from taxying the Ju 52/3m because of its unique braking system. To operate the left brake the port throttle had to be pulled fully back and, similarly, the starboard throttle for the right brake. Application of both brakes demanded that only the centre throttle lever be pulled fully back. It goes without saying that this Heath Robinsonish system took some getting used to — on first acquaintance one tended to pirouette around the perimeter track like an aged ballerina.

Slow and noisy though the Junkers undoubtedly was, it was also supremely reliable, a quality which, coupled with rugged construction, simplicity of operation and ease of maintenance in the field, made up the magic recipe that resulted in the fantastic longevity of the Ju 52/3m. Its capacity was, of course, comparatively limited and this imposed certain restrictions on its use, but despite being obsolescent when the first shots of WW II were fired, it soldiered on in the infinite variety of tasks performed by the *Transportverbänden* and for which only this remarkable old trimotor was readily available. Commenting on the Spanish Civil War, Adolf Hitler once remarked: "Franco ought to erect a monument to the glory of the Ju 52. It is this aircraft that the Spanish Revolution has to thank for its victory!" While the effect of the Ju 52/3m on the outcome of the Spanish conflict is a matter for conjecture*, there can be little doubt that WW II would have followed a somewhat different pattern had not this inoffensive-appearing transport been available in quantity to the *Luftwaffe*.

As a postscript to this assessment of the Ju 52/3m, some mention should perhaps be made of its offspring, the Ju 352,

---

**The intervention of the Junkers trimotors enabled the Nationalist forces to consolidate their initially precarious positions and launch a drive northwards from Seville*

A Ju 52/3m g6e abandoned on a desert airstrip in North Africa by the retreating Wehrmacht and captured by the Allied forces. Many such aircraft were repaired and pressed into service by the Allies

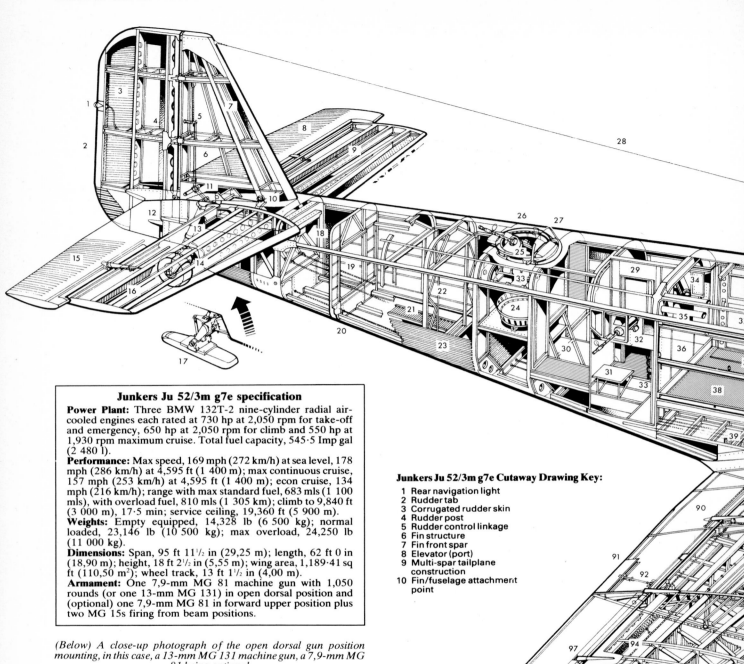

Junkers Ju 52/3m g7e specification

Power Plant: Three BMW 132T-2 nine-cylinder radial air-cooled engines each rated at 730 hp at 2,050 rpm for take-off and emergency, 650 hp at 2,050 rpm for climb and 550 hp at 1,930 rpm maximum cruise. Total fuel capacity, 545·5 Imp gal (2 480 l).

Performance: Max speed, 169 mph (272 km/h) at sea level, 178 mph (286 km/h) at 4,595 ft (1 400 m); max continuous cruise, 157 mph (253 km/h) at 4,595 ft (1 400 m); econ cruise, 134 mph (216 km/h); range with max standard fuel, 683 mls (1 100 mls), with overload fuel, 810 mls (1 305 km); climb to 9,840 ft (3 000 m), 17·5 min; service ceiling, 19,360 ft (5 900 m).

Weights: Empty equipped, 14,328 lb (6 500 kg); normal loaded, 23,146 lb (10 500 kg); max overload, 24,250 lb (11 000 kg).

Dimensions: Span, 95 ft 11½ in (29,25 m); length, 62 ft 0 in (18,90 m); height, 18 ft 2½ in (5,55 m); wing area, 1,189·41 sq ft (110,50 m²); wheel track, 13 ft 1½ in (4,00 m).

Armament: One 7,9-mm MG 81 machine gun with 1,050 rounds (or one 13-mm MG 131) in open dorsal position and (optional) one 7,9-mm MG 81 in forward upper position plus two MG 15s firing from beam positions.

Junkers Ju 52/3m g7e Cutaway Drawing Key:

1 Rear navigation light
2 Rudder tab
3 Corrugated rudder skin
4 Rudder post
5 Rudder control linkage
6 Fin structure
7 Fin front spar
8 Elevator (port)
9 Multi-spar tailplane construction
10 Fin/fuselage attachment point

(Below) A close-up photograph of the open dorsal gun position mounting, in this case, a 13-mm MG 131 machine gun, a 7,9-mm MG 81 being optional

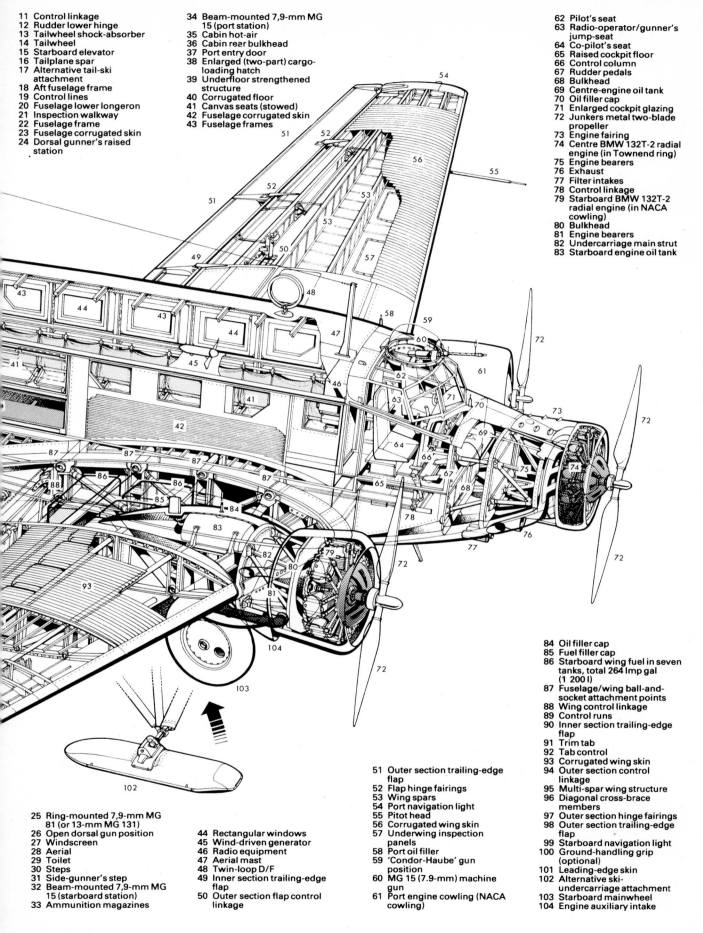

11 Control linkage
12 Rudder lower hinge
13 Tailwheel shock-absorber
14 Tailwheel
15 Starboard elevator
16 Tailplane spar
17 Alternative tail-ski attachment
18 Aft fuselage frame
19 Control lines
20 Fuselage lower longeron
21 Inspection walkway
22 Fuselage frame
23 Fuselage corrugated skin
24 Dorsal gunner's raised station

34 Beam-mounted 7,9-mm MG 15 (port station)
35 Cabin hot-air
36 Cabin rear bulkhead
37 Port entry door
38 Enlarged (two-part) cargo-loading hatch
39 Underfloor strengthened structure
40 Corrugated floor
41 Canvas seats (stowed)
42 Fuselage corrugated skin
43 Fuselage frames

62 Pilot's seat
63 Radio-operator/gunner's jump-seat
64 Co-pilot's seat
65 Raised cockpit floor
66 Control column
67 Rudder pedals
68 Bulkhead
69 Centre-engine oil tank
70 Oil filler cap
71 Enlarged cockpit glazing
72 Junkers metal two-blade propeller
73 Engine fairing
74 Centre BMW 132T-2 radial engine (in Townend ring)
75 Engine bearers
76 Exhaust
77 Filter intakes
78 Control linkage
79 Starboard BMW 132T-2 radial engine (in NACA cowling)
80 Bulkhead
81 Engine bearers
82 Undercarriage main strut
83 Starboard engine oil tank

84 Oil filler cap
85 Fuel filler cap
86 Starboard wing fuel in seven tanks, total 264 Imp gal (1 200 l)
87 Fuselage/wing ball-and-socket attachment points
88 Wing control linkage
89 Control runs
90 Inner section trailing-edge flap
91 Trim tab
92 Tab control
93 Corrugated wing skin
94 Outer section control linkage
95 Multi-spar wing structure
96 Diagonal cross-brace members
97 Outer section hinge fairings
98 Outer section trailing-edge flap
99 Starboard navigation light
100 Ground-handling grip (optional)
101 Leading-edge skin
102 Alternative ski-undercarriage attachment
103 Starboard mainwheel
104 Engine auxiliary intake

25 Ring-mounted 7,9-mm MG 81 (or 13-mm MG 131)
26 Open dorsal gun position
27 Windscreen
28 Aerial
29 Toilet
30 Steps
31 Side-gunner's step
32 Beam-mounted 7,9-mm MG 15 (starboard station)
33 Ammunition magazines

44 Rectangular windows
45 Wind-driven generator
46 Radio equipment
47 Aerial mast
48 Twin-loop D/F
49 Inner section trailing-edge flap
50 Outer section flap control linkage

51 Outer section trailing-edge flap
52 Flap hinge fairings
53 Wing spars
54 Port navigation light
55 Pitot head
56 Corrugated wing skin
57 Underwing inspection panels
58 Port oil filler
59 'Condor-Haube' gun position
60 MG 15 (7.9-mm) machine gun
61 Port engine cowling (NACA cowling)

(Above) A factory-fresh Ju 52/3m g6e transport prior to delivery to the Luftwaffe in 1941. During the course of the year, production of this sub-type gave place to that of the Ju 52/3m g7e with an enlarged starboard loading hatch and an autopilot

which represented an attempt to modernise the basic formula first established at Dessau as the 'thirties dawned. The Ju 352, to which the appellation of *Herkules* was unofficially assigned by its manufacturer, was an outstandingly practical transport aircraft. It was appreciably larger and more powerful than its parent, and offered a very much better performance. Intended from the outset to make maximum possible use of non-strategic materials, the Ju 352 had a very capacious fuselage, but what rendered it quite extraordinary in my view was its so-called *Trapoklappe* — an hydraulically-operated loading ramp which, hinged at the front and embodying a central stairway, not only touched the ground when lowered but continued under power to raise the fuselage to a horizontal position! Theoretically, it was possible for any wheeled vehicle up to the size of a large *Kübelwagen* to

drive up the *Trapoklappe* into the freight hold.

Incredibly enough, this ramp could be lowered in flight with no uncontrollable trim change or adverse turbulence effects. Indeed, during a flight demonstration of German aircraft at Farnborough in 1945, the Ju 352 was flown past with the ramp lowered and a flight engineer sitting on the lowest step of the ramp stairway smoking a cigarette! What a gimmick and what an aeroplane. Unfortunately for the *Luftwaffe*, production of the Ju 352 never really had a chance to get off the ground. Just as deliveries were getting into their stride in the summer of 1944, the worsening war situation dictated the abandoning of production with barely more than 40 delivered — too few to make any operational impact in the unglamorous sphere of military transport operations. *Sic transit gloria!*

The Junkers trimotor achieved fame during the Spanish Civil War, Adolf Hitler once commenting that "Franco ought to erect a monument to the glory of the Ju 52. It is this aircraft that the Spanish Revolution has to thank for its victory!" The aircraft illustrated above and below are Ju 52/3m g4e bombers of the Spanish Nationalist Grupo de Bombardeo Nocturno 2-G-22 which flew its last bombing sortie on 26 March 1939

HEINKEL HE 219

IF IT MAY BE SAID that aircraft can appear disconsolate or forlorn, then the big, ungainly fighters standing around at Grove, in South Jutland, on that early May morning of 1945 may certainly have been so described, with their sombre grey dapple night fighting finishes contributing to the general atmosphere of dejection that permeated this immense and formerly important *Luftwaffe* base near the Danish-German border. To reach Grove, I had overflown the last pockets of' German resistance in Schleswig-Holstein — desperate and useless if valiant last stands marking the final death throes of the Third Reich — and the scene that had greeted me was one of utter despondency. Such apathy had descended on the German troops during the preceding weeks that barely more than a gesture had been made towards adhering to their High Command's instructions that all equipment be destroyed rather than allowed to fall into Allied hands.

Grove was certainly the most sophisticated *Luftwaffe* night fighter base that we had come across, with excellent ground radar, and it was from here that elements of *Nachtjagdgeschwader* 1 had been operating the reportedly formidable Heinkel He 219, the second *Luftwaffe* aircraft to have had bestowed upon it unofficially the onomatopœic sobriquet of *Uhu* (Owl). There were certainly quite a lot of the Heinkel fighters around, with a dozen or so in various stages of repair in the hangars and many others parked on the hard standings or in dispersal areas. Admittedly, only seven of the He 219s appeared to be airworthy, quite a number having apparently suffered depredations resulting from the need to cannibalise in order to keep at least a proportion of NJG 1's inventory operational, for if the *Luftwaffe* suffered no shortage of aircraft in those final weeks of WW II, it was appallingly short of spares.

German combat aircraft were rarely noteworthy for their æsthetic qualities but more for a certain functional efficiency associated with the nation that conceived them. There were, of course, the exceptions, such as the Heinkel He 111, surely among the most shapely aeroplanes in its category, and the Messerschmitt Bf 110, which presented such pleasing purity of line before the exigencies of the times dictated its festoon-ing with radar antennæ, gun panniers, mortar shell launching tubes and drop tanks. But the He 219 was an unprepossessing beast at first sight, with its angularly ugly slab-sided fuselage flanked by immense engine nacelles and standing high on a stalky tricycle undercarriage, and odd-looking nose section which, resembling the head of some monstrous pre-historic lizard, sprouted a mini-forest of radar antennæ, or *Maikäfer-fühler* (Cockchafer-feelers) as they were unofficially known.

To my eye, the Heinkel had fewer pretentions to aeronautical beauty than any aircraft in the fighter category that had gone before, yet, bizarre though its appearance undoubtedly was, this unattractive creation had acquired the reputation of being the most effective nocturnal interceptor employed operationally by *any* of the combatants — surely proof positive of the validity of the adage "Handsome is as handsome does" in so far as aircraft are concerned.

In the space of but a few short years, night fighting, which had developed barely noticeably since WW I and relied on searchlights, flares or moonlight combined with more than a modicum of luck, had been raised to something approaching a fairly exact science, and many viewed the He 219 as the most adept practitioner of this science during the final year or so of the European portion of WW II. It certainly possessed every conceivable nocturnal intercept mod con. Its FuG 220 *Lichtenstein* SN-2 radar — sometimes coupled with the newer FuG 218 *Neptun* — was reasonably effective; its armament was formidable with the battery of forward-firing cannon eventually consisting of four 30-mm and two 20-mm weapons frequently supplemented by a pair of obliquely upward-firing 30-mm cannon in a *"schräge Musik"* installation; its de-icing was comprehensive and it was provided with such refinements as an auto-pilot, effective blind-landing aids and ultra-violet lighting, while the two crew members, who enjoyed adequate armour protection, were seated on ejection seats. This last-mentioned innovation was a development which the Heinkel fighter had the distinction of introducing into operational service. If no contender for the beauty stakes, the He 219 was certainly a very potent package.

It is strange to reflect that, apart from Northrop's P-61

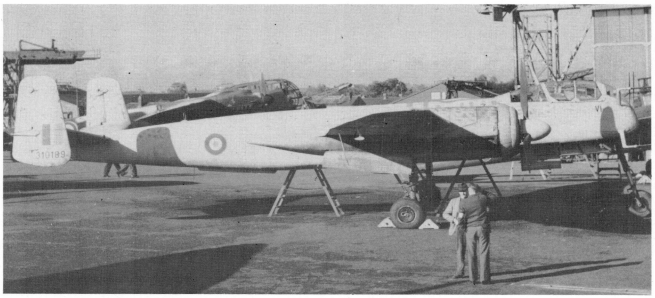

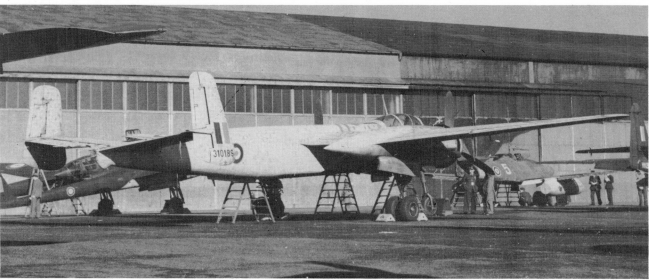

(Head of opposite page) The He 219A-053 which was completed to A-5/R1 standards with Lichtenstein C-1 and SN-2 radar, and (above and below) the He 219 V11 (Werk-Nr 310 189) after modification to A-5/R2 standard as seen at Farnborough

Black Widow, every night fighter that saw service during WW II was an improvisation; an aircraft designed for a rôle other than that of nocturnal interception to which it came by chance. Of course, the annals of aviation have seen many aircraft that have found their true métier in rôles unforseen at their conception, but the He 219 was perhaps an outstanding case in point. Having begun life on the drawing boards at Rostock-Marienehe as a private venture study in the *Kampfzerstörer* category — an all-singing all-dancing multi-purpose creation for a spectrum of rôles from long-range heavy fighter to torpedo-bomber — the project was rich in innovative features, such as remotely-controlled defensive barbettes. Indeed, it would seem that the combination of radical features proposed by the Heinkel team was *too* rich for the *Technischen Amt,* and the project drawings would undoubtedly have continued to gather dust on the drawing office shelves after rejection by the RLM in 1940 had it not been for a chance visit to Marienehe a year or so later by *Generalmajor* Kammhuber, the *General der Nachtjagd.* Un-

der his auspices the Heinkel project was reworked for the nocturnal rôle and took on tangible form as the He 219.

It is unlikely that any previous aircraft suffered a more checkered development and production career nor a more auspicious operational début. It has been said, and apparently with a certain amount of justification, that Heinkel's fighter found its principal opponents in the *Generalluftzeugmeister, Generalfeldmarschall* Erhard Milch, and the *Reichsluftfahrt-ministerium* in Berlin rather than in the night skies

Heinkel He 219A-5 Cutaway Key:

1 FuG 212 Lichtenstein C-1 antenna
2 FuG 220 Lichtenstein SN-2 antenna
3 Armoured nose
4 Curved one-piece windscreen
5 Windscreen washer/wiper
6 Handhold
7 Inner armourglass windscreen
8 Revi 16B gunsight
9 Armoured visor (deleted on late production models)
10 Control column
11 Revi 16A-N overhead gunsight (schräge Musik)
12 Folding headrest
13 Pilot's compressed-air ejection seat
14 Port instrument console
15 Footholds
16 Crew entry ladder (hinged rearwards)
17 Nosewheel leg
18 Nosewheel doors
19 Compressed air bottles
20 Nosewheel retraction gear
21 Ejection seat mounting
22 Radar operator's ejection seat
23 Flare pistol port
24 Hinged headrest
25 Aerial mast
26 FuG 212 radar screen
27 FuG 220 radar screen
28 Fuselage frame (No 9)
29 Port wing root cannon port
30 Forward fuel tank (244 Imp gal/1 110 litres)
31 Fuel filler cap
32 Suppressed D/F aerial
33 Main spar connection joint
34 Flame damper tube
35 Liquid coolant tank

55 Main undercarriage well
56 Inboard flap section
57 Mainwheel doors
58 Undercarriage pivot point
59 Firewall
60 Starter fuel tank
61 Centre fuel tank (110 Imp gal/500 litres)
62 Fuel filler cap
63 Fuselage frame (No 17)
64 Wing/fuselage aft attachment point
65 Port 20-mm MG 151 cannon
66 Wing/fuselage main attachment point
67 Ammunition troughs (300 rpg; wing root and ventral port rear cannon)

77 VDM constant-speed airscrew
78 Armoured-front annular radiator
79 Flame damper tube
80 Supercharger intake trunking
81 Port wing heating unit
82 Flap actuating jack
83 Aileron control quadrant
84 Landing light

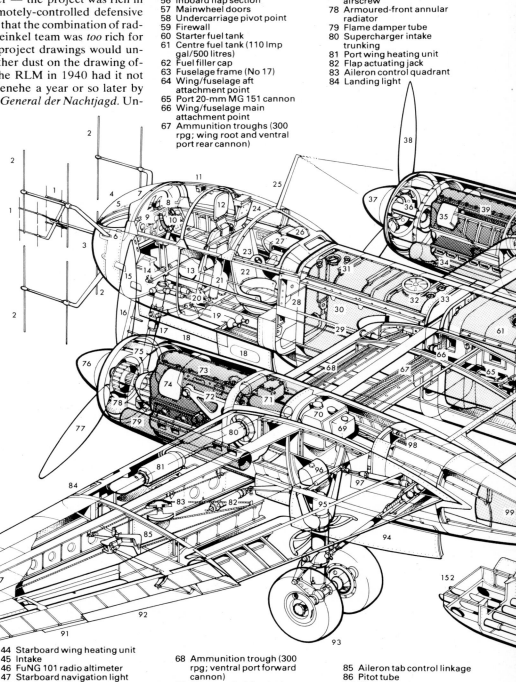

36 Airscrew shaft
37 Airscrew boss
38 VDM constant-speed airscrew
39 Daimler-Benz DB 603E engine
40 Supercharger
41 Oil tank
42 Airscrew de-icing tank
43 Main wing spar

44 Starboard wing heating unit
45 Intake
46 FuNG 101 radio altimeter
47 Starboard navigation light
48 Starboard aileron
49 Wing construction
50 Aileron tab
51 Flap construction
52 Flap actuator
53 Underwing inspection panels
54 Nacelle fuel tank (86 Imp gal/390 litres)

68 Ammunition trough (300 rpg; ventral port forward cannon)
69 Airscrew de-icing tank
70 Oil tank
71 Engine accessories
72 Engine bearer
73 Daimler-Benz DB 603E engine
74 Liquid coolant tank
75 Controllable radiator gills
76 Airscrew boss

85 Aileron tab control linkage
86 Pitot tube
87 Main wing spar
88 Wing skinning
89 Port navigation light
90 Port aileron
91 Fixed trim tab (port side only)
92 Auxiliary aileron tab
93 Twin mainwheel undercarriage

94 Mainwheel doors
95 Mainwheel leg
96 Starter fuel tank
97 Undercarriage retraction jack
98 Pressure-oil tank (port nacelle only)
99 Nacelle fuel tank (86 Imp gal/390 litres)
100 Starboard undercarriage
101 Rear fuel tank (218 Imp gal/990 litres)
102 Fuel filler cap
103 Fuselage frame (No 20)
104 Ammunition feed channel
105 Ammunition tanks (100 rpg)
106 Twin oblique-mounted 30-mm MK 108 cannon (schräge Musik)
107 Electrical supply cables (starboard fuselage wall)
108 Compressed air cylinders
109 Maintenance platform
110 Ventral antenna
111 FuG 25A (IFF) aerial

112 Service entry hatch
113 Walkway
114 Main electrical compartment
115 Crew escape dinghy
116 D/F loop (homing approach)
117 BLO 30/U fuselage heating and tailplane de-icing unit
118 Heating ducts
119 Fuselage frame (No 31)
120 Tail unit control linkage
121 Intake
122 Tailplane construction
123 Aerials
124 Tailfin construction

125 Starboard rudder
126 Rudder tab
127 Rudder control hinge
128 Elevator construction
129 Elevator trim tab
130 Flettner auxiliary tab
131 FuG 220 tail-warning antenna
132 Trailing-aerial tube
133 Tail navigation light
134 Perspex tail cone
135 Tail bumper
136 Fuselage frame (No 33)/tailplane attachment

137 Port elevator
138 Rudder tab hinge fairing
139 Port rudder
140 Built-in aerial (port tailfin leading-edge)
141 Tailfin skinning

142 Ventral weapons tray
143 Fuselage frame (No 20)
144 Ventral maintenance hatc
145 Main junction boxes
146 Weapons access hatches
147 Ammunition feed chutes
148 Rear (inboard) 20-mm MG 151 cannon
149 Forward (outboard) 20-mm MG 151 cannon
150 Blast tubes
151 Gun sighting/correction hatch
152 Cannon ports

Heinkel He 219A-7/R2 Specification
(Factory figures)

Power Plant: Two Daimler-Benz DB 603E 12-cylinder inverted-vee liquid-cooled engines rated at 1,800 hp at 2,700 rpm for takeoff, 1,900 hp at 5,905 ft (1 800 m) and 1,550 hp at 22,965 ft (7 000 m). Climb and combat: 1,580 hp at 2,500 rpm at sea level, 1,650 hp at 5,905 ft (1 800 m) and 1,440 hp at 23,200 ft (7 070 m).

Performance: Max speed, 286 mph (460 km/h) at sea level, 298 mph (480 km/h) at 6,560 ft (2 000 m), 332 mph (535 km/h) at 13,125 ft (4 000 m), 363 mph (585 km/h) at 19,685 ft (6 000 m); range at max cruise, 1,150 mls (1 850 km) at 255 mph (410 km/h) at sea level, 1,168 mls at 263 mph at 6,560 ft (2 000 m), 1,200 mls (1 930 km) at 292 mph (470 km/h) at 13,125 ft (4 000 m), 1,243 mls (2 000 km) at 317 mph (510 km/h) at 19,685 ft (6 000 m); climb rate at sea level, 1,968 ft/min (10,0 m/sec), at 6,560 ft (2 000 m), 1,693 ft/min (8,6 m/sec), at 13,125 ft (4 000 m), 1,417 ft/min (7,2 m/sec); service ceiling, 32,150 ft (9 800 m); take-off distance to clear 50 ft (15 m), 1,148 yds (1 050 m); landing distance from 50 ft (15 m), 897 yds (820 m).

Weights: Empty, 18,398 lb (8 345 kg); max loaded, 33,289 lb (15 100 kg).

Dimensions: Span, 60 ft 8⅓ in (18,50 m); length (including antennæ), 53 ft 7¼ in (16,34 m); height 13 ft 5⅔ in (4,10 m); wing area, 478·99 sq ft (44,50 m²).

Armament: Two 20-mm MG 151 cannon with 500 rpg in ventral tray, two 20-mm MG 151 cannon with 400 rpg in wing roots and two 30-mm MK 108 cannon with 100 rpg mounted at angle of 65 deg in *schräge Musik* installation.

The FuG 220 Lichtenstein SN-2 aerial array of the He 219 V11 alias A-5/R2 at Farnborough. The circular aperture in the centre of the nose was the cockpit heater air intake.

above the German capital. The inclusion of details of the resolute and extraordinary opposition that the He 219 encountered in German official circles despite its undeniable qualities is beyond the scope of this account, and it suffices to say that this opposition undoubtedly worked to the advantage of RAF Bomber Command. No less extraordinary was the operational début of the Heinkel night fighter which took place on the night of 11-12 June 1943, while a number of early pre-production examples were undergoing operational evaluation with the *I Gruppe* of *Nachtjagdgeschwader* 1 at Venlo in the Netherlands.

On this occasion, the first pre-production He 219A-0 readied for operational testing was flown on a live intercept mission by *Major* Werner Streib, the *Gruppenkommandeur*. During the course of the sortie, *Major* Streib was allegedly responsible for the destruction of five RAF bombers, but on

the final approach to Venlo after completing the mission, he discovered that his flaps were inoperative. The aircraft left the runway at high speed during the ensuing landing and broke up, though neither Streib nor his radar observer, *Unteroffizier* Fischer, suffered any injury. German records indicated that during the 10 days following Streib's signal success, the handful of available pre-production He 219s flown by his *Stabschwarm* accounted for 20 more RAF aircraft — including a half-dozen previously invulnerable Mosquitos — during the course of six sorties.

An outstanding cockpit

When I first encountered the He 219 at Grove, slightly less than two years after its auspicious début at the hands of *Major* Streib, my primary concern was the Arado Ar 234B and I could spare no time for more than a cursory examination of the Heinkel fighter on the ground. Five He 219s were eventually flown to the Royal Aircraft Establishment's captured enemy aircraft collecting point at Schleswig airfield for ferrying to Farnborough, however, and I was soon to have an opportunity to fly three of these. The aircraft flown to the UK comprised four examples of the first production model, the He 219A-2, and a single He 219A-5, which was, in fact, the He 219 V11 rebuilt to A-5 standards after suffering extensive damage in an accident. Although we carried out no specific performance or handling tests on the He 219 at Farnborough, we did some tests on certain items of its equipment which were of particular interest and I made a number of ferry flights with the aircraft during the course of which there was plenty of opportunity to assess its flying qualities.

From the pilot's viewpoint, the most impressive feature of the He 219 was its cockpit, which, at a considerable height from the ground, was reached by means of a single-sided ladder which, after the crew members were aboard, was released by a member of the ground staff to pivot upward and rearward for stowage in a slot on the underside of the fuselage. The canopy was a large, one-piece affair which hinged to starboard and offered an excellent all-round view. The cockpit itself was roomy and comfortable, and the flight instruments were arranged in the classic 'T' formation, with the engine instruments grouped to the right of the main panel. The pilot and radar operator were seated back to back on compressed-air ejection seats and, as already indicated, ev-

---

Heinkel He 219A Cockpit Instrumentation Key:

1 Heated flying-suit plug-in
2 Demolition charge fuse
3 Compressed air tank filler
4 Cooling gills emergency adjustment levers
5 Pressure-oil double (port & starboard) pressure gauge
6 Trim control knobs
7 FuG 17 (R/T) control box
8 Intercom junction box
9 Revi gunsight dimmer switch
10 Ventilation control lever
11 RPM correction setting
12 Fuel tank switch levers (with oil filter activation and motor cut-out)
13 Throttle levers (with thumb operated airscrew pitch control switch)
14 Locking lever (undercarriage ground brake)
15 Map case
16 Cockpit heating switch regulator
17 Rudder ground lock handle
18 Magneto switches
19 Flap position indicator
20 Airscrew automatic pitch engage switches
21 Electrical power override button
22 Flap emergency lowering lever
23 Undercarriage switches

24 Flap switches
25 Armoured visor lowering lever
26 Indicator light panel (12)
27 Undercarriage emergency lever
28 Nosewheel emergency lowering lever
29 Inner (armoured) windscreen washer
30 Armoured visor (early models)
31 Inner (armoured) windscreen (later variants)
32 Revi 16B gunsight
33 Windscreen wiper
34 Revi anti-glare screen switch
35 Revi night-filter screen switch
36 Panel lights
37 ASI
38 Fine/coarse altimeter
39 Emergency turn & bank indicator
40 Pitot tube indicator
41 Autopilot emergency switch
42 Turn & bank indicator/artificial horizon
43 Pilot's repeater compass
44 Variometer
45 F 307 indicator
46 Windscreen clean/demist manual control
47 RPM gauge (port)
48 RPM gauge (starboard)

49 Manifold double (port & starboard) pressure gauge
50 FuNG 101 (radio altimeter) indicator
51 Airscrew feathering indicator lamps
52 Airscrew pitch double (port & starboard) indicator
53 Engine fuel pressure gauge (port)
54 Engine fuel pressure gauge (starboard)
55 Transmit button (left control horn)
56 Fuselage gun firing-button (right control horn)
57 Wing gun firing-trigger (rear face of horn)
58 Control column
59 Rudder pedals
60 Pilot's ejector seat
61 Course setting
62 Clock
63 Oxygen supply meter
64 Oxygen pressure gauge
65 Standby compass
66 Canopy jettison handle
67 Rotary (change-over) switch
68 Coolant supply warning lamps
69 Coolant temperature gauge (port)
70 Coolant temperature gauge (starboard)

71 Engine oil temperature gauge (port)
72 Engine oil temperature gauge (starboard)
73 Compass deviation card holder
74 SZKK6 ammunition counters
75 Safety switches
76 Phosphorescent lights
77 Starboard console lights
78 Ejection seat instruction plate
79 Landing light switch
80 Navigation lights switch
81 Phosphorescent lights switch
82 Gyro control monitoring switch
83 Dimmer switch
84 Autopilot engage switch
85 Pitot heating switch
86 Pilot's ejection seat lever
87 Fuel pump switches (4)
88 Battery switches (2)
89 Fuel contents warning lamps
90 Fuel gauge (forward tank)
91 Fuel gauge (centre tank)
92 Fuel gauge (rear tank)
93 Compressed-air pressure gauge
94 Phosphorescent lighting rheostats (3)
95 Pilot's oxygen supply
96 Fuel emergency jettison levers
97 Electric starter switches
98 Auxiliary starter switches

(Above) The He 219 V16 alias He 219 A-016 which served as the prototype for the He 219 A-5 but lacked the redesigned aft cockpit canopy that was to be standardised by the A-5 sub-type. Initially flown with DB 603 A engines, this aircraft was subsequequently re-engined with the more powerful DB 603 E, and armament comprised a pair of 20-mm MG 151 cannon in the wing roots, twin 30-mm MK 108 cannon in a "schräge Musik" installation and two additional Mk 108s mounted in a ventral tray

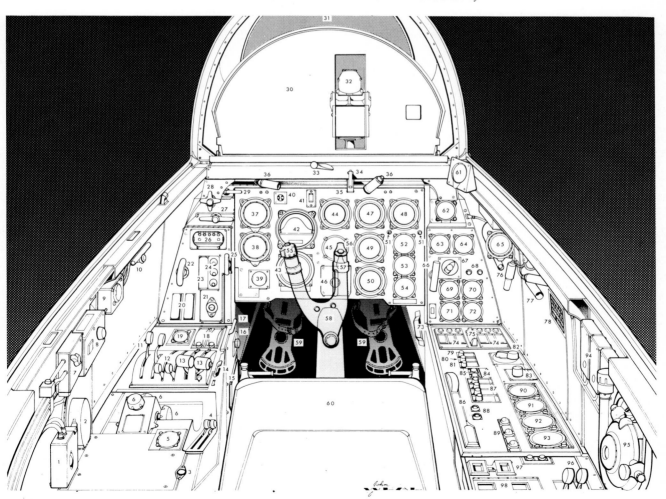

ery item of equipment that a night fighter could have at this point in time was included. Indeed, that the *Reichsluft-fahrtministerium* recognised the merits of the He 219 cockpit is indicated by the fact that, at one stage, serious considera-tion was apparently given to the possibility of grafting the entire nose on to the Junkers Ju 388.

The He 219 was always intended for the Daimler-Benz DB

603G engine rated at 1,900 hp for take-off and 1,560 hp at 24,200 ft (7 375 m), but non-availability of this power plant when the first production airframes began to roll off the Vienna-Schwechat assembly line in the autumn of 1943 necessitated the substitution of the DB 603A rated at 1,750 hp for take-off, 1,850 hp at 6 890 ft (2 100 m) and 1,625 hp at 18,700 ft (5 700 m), this model being designated He

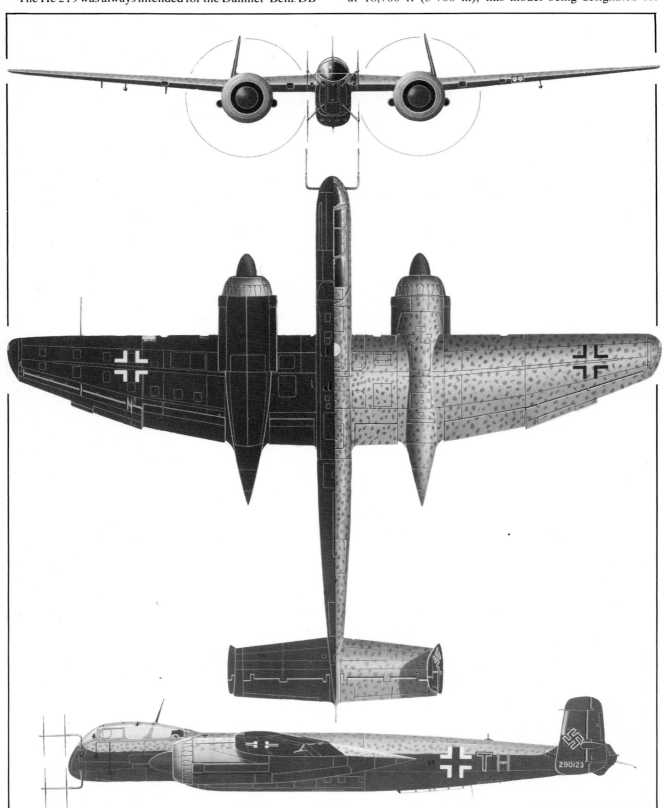

(Opposite page) The general arrangement drawing depicts an He 219A-2/R1 of 1./NJG 1 at Knokke in the spring of 1945. This aircraft (Werk-Nr 290 123) had been modified with a revised aft cockpit section similar to that standardised for the He 219A-5. (Above and below) One of the He 219A-5s that were taken to the USA for evaluation at Wright Field

219A-2. It was this version of the Heinkel fighter that I was to fly on several occasions, these flights including the ferrying of an He 219A-2 (*Werk-Nr* 290 126) from Farnborough to Brize Norton on 21 August 1945, delivering another A-2 (*Werk-Nr* 310 109) to Abingdon nine days later and then to Brize Norton on the following day and, finally, on 19 October, collecting a third A-2 (*Werk-Nr* 310 106) from Tangmere and ferrying it to Farnborough. I found no opportunity to fly the later DB 603G-powered He 219A-5* but imagine that it did not display any markedly different handling or performance characteristics to those of the A-2.

Starting of the DB 603A engines was simple. The petrol cocks were selected to tanks Nos 2 and 3 (which were the centre and rear of the three fuselage tanks) and the fuel pump for the requisite engine was turned ON. The throttle was opened about a quarter of its travel when a noticeable resistance could be felt, the magneto switches then being set to positions M1+2. Normally, the external electrically-operated inertia starters were used, although a similar internal system was available. The starter handle was depressed for 10-20 seconds, released and then pulled out for engagement, simultaneously being turned to the left to prime the engine if cold. Once an engine fired the revolutions were kept below 1,200 until oil and fuel pressures registered when it

could be warmed up at 1,500 rpm for three minutes before power checks were made. Ignition tests were made at 2,000 rpm.

Before commencing taxying all trimmers were set to ZERO, the cooling gills were opened and the ejection seat air pressures checked, that for the pilot's seat being 1,138 lb/sq in (80 kg/cm²) and that for the radar operator being 711 lb/sq in (50 kg/cm²). The Heinkel was very easy to handle during taxying but the brakes — which were very effective — had to be used generously in crosswinds. Pre-take-off checks included setting the airscrew pitch at 12.15 o'clock on the indicators and lowering the flaps to the START position. The take-off run was a lengthy 1,700 yards (1 555 m) using full take-off power of 2,700 rpm and 1.4 atas (20·6 lb) of boost.

I have read German reports that, fully loaded, the He 219 enjoyed an ample surplus of power and that an engine cutting immediately after take-off or during the approach presented little danger. There was, it is said, an instance of a pilot making an emergency take-off on one engine with his undercarriage locked in the "down" position and with flaps fully ex-

It was originally intended that the He 219A-5 would standardise on the DB 603E engine but the DB 603A was retained by initial production machines while some later examples were fitted with the DB 603Aa or DB 603G as Umrüst-Bausätze (Factory Conversion Sets)

tended! If there is any truth in this last report, I can only say that for this extraordinary feat the aircraft must have been equipped with JATO and have had a very long runway indeed! In my view, the Heinkel fighter — certainly in its He 219A-2 version — was decidedly *underpowered*. An engine failure on take-off must have been a *very* nasty emergency to handle at night as, below 137 mph (220 km/h), the aircraft was difficult to hold straight and, combined with the sink as the undercarriage came up, this meant that there was a critical area between 50 ft (15,20 m) and 300 ft (91,50 m) on climb-out.

Unstick speed was 106 mph (170 km/h) and it was possible to commence raising the undercarriage at 50 ft (15,20 m) but not lower because of the previously-mentioned sink. As speed built up to 155 mph (250 km/h) the flaps could be raised at 500 ft (152 m), this being accompanied by a noticeable sink, and the aircraft could then be settled in a steady climb at 186 mph (300 km/h) with 2,500 rpm and 1.3 *atas* (19·1 lb) of boost. Once settled in the climb, the excellent stability characteristics of the He 219 became evident. The best rate of climb was obtained by letting the initial speed of 186 mph (300 km/h) decay slowly as altitude was gained until it dropped back to 174 mph (280 km/h) at 32,810 ft (10 000 m). The rate of climb was certainly unimpressive.

A good all-weather aeroplane

When the required cruise altitude was attained, the cooling gills were closed and the engines throttled back to 2,300 rpm and 1.2 *atas* (17·6 lb). If flying for endurance then power was further reduced to 2,000 rpm and 1.05 *atas* (15·4 lb). A full power run at 20,000 ft (6 096 m) revealed somewhat sluggish acceleration and a top speed of 378 mph (608 km/h), which was somewhat below the German handbook figures.

Operation of the fuel system required tanks 2 and 3 to be used initially until half-empty (ie, about 220 Imp gal/1 000 litres remaining), thereafter switching to the forward or No 1 tank until its contents were exhausted. The cabin heating and de-icing systems were extremely effective and the auto-pilot was easy to operate and appeared reliable. The He 219 was, without a doubt, an excellent all-weather aeroplane.

Landing preparations were straightforward. The cowling gills were opened, the airscrew pitch set to 12 o'clock and, at 186 mph (300 km/h) the flaps were lowered to START. The undercarriage was lowered at 168 mph (270 km/h) and the final turn-in made at 155 mph (250 km/h). Full flap and fuel pumps were selected on the final approach and speed held at 140 mph (225 km/h), reducing to 124 mph (200 km/h) near the airfield boundary. The touch-down at 99 mph (160 km/h) was very easy with the tricycle undercarriage, but the nosewheel could not be held off the ground for very long and so the landing was fast and strong braking was called for. It was vital that, before landing, a check was made of the brake pressure which should have been at least 853 lb/sq in (60 kg/cm^2). If below that figure, a button alongside the gauge had to be pressed until the pressure built up and maintained itself. The landing run in zero wind was about 710 yards (650 m).

It was apparent in the landing condition that the lateral control afforded by the spring tab ailerons was sluggish in effect and hence turns with the flaps fully lowered were not to be recommended. In gusty conditions the Heinkel was unpleasant to handle laterally on the final approach.

From my experience with the He 219A-2, I would say that this Heinkel fighter's reputation was somewhat overrated. It was, in my view, basically a good night fighter in concept but it suffered from what is perhaps the nastiest characteristic that any twin-engined aircraft can have — it was underpowered. This defect makes take-off a critical manœuvre in the event of an engine failing and a landing with one engine out can be equally critical. There certainly could be no overshooting with the He 219 in that condition. Furthermore, it appeared to be short on performance to deal with the Mosquito, a task which was, in part, its *raison d'être*, but it was surely a very unpleasant handful for any four-engined bomber to encounter and one is led to wonder what changes might have taken place in the night skies of Germany had the *Generalluftzeugmeister* not been so resolutely opposed to this Heinkel creation or had the Heinkel organisation proven capable of delivering the He 219 to the *Nachtjagdflieger* in quantity.

The ungainly appearance of the He 219A-5 is accentuated in side elevation, as is to be seen from this photograph, but it was reputedly a very effective nocturnal interceptor, if lacking the necessary performance to deal with the Mosquito

MESSERSCHMITT BF 109G

LONGEVITY OF SERVICE has never characterised the fighter. Indeed, until the last decade or so it was possible to count the years in the firstline lifespan of the average fighter aircraft on the fingers of one hand. The tempo of fighter development has always been faster than that of any other operational aeroplane type, the pace accelerating in war when survival has at times rested in some measure on the outcome of the struggle to exceed or at least match the performance capability of whatever fighters the enemy has been able to field.

Tending to prove the rule have been the few noteworthy exceptions to be found in the annals of fighter development, perhaps the most outstanding of these being Professor Willy Messerschmitt's Bf 109 which, in its multifarious forms, survived a long drawn-out civil war and an entire full-blown world war. Few if any fighters have bettered its durability. In pre-WW II years a nimbus seemed to envelop the Bf 109; it was surrounded by a carefully-fostered mystique. The German Propaganda Ministry assiduously created a myth of invincibility around the fighter; a myth to which the *Luftwaffe* itself was to fall victim as a result of the ease with which the Bf 109 overcame most of its adversaries in the pre-Battle of Britain phases of WW II.

There was, in fact, nothing mysterious about the Bf 109. It was simply a well-conceived, soundly-designed fighter that maintained during maturity the success that attended its infancy; its fundamental concept facilitated the introduction of progressively more powerful armament and engines which enabled it to stay in the forefront of fighters for three-quarters of a decade. Probably the most efficient of this long-lived breed was the G-series, or *Gustav* as it was widely but unofficially known, although there are undoubtedly a number of former fighter jockeys who would be prepared to dispute this point with the writer, alleging that the F-series had carried the Bf 109 to the zenith of its development cycle. However, it should be

borne in mind that the demands of the air war were constantly changing; that speed and flexibility of rôle assumed increasing importance whereas these qualities had previously been mitigated to some extent by greater emphasis on handling and manœuvrability. Higher weight and power loadings that had become acceptable in consequence were reflected by *Gustav*, and if not a *great* fighter from the pilot's viewpoint the Bf 109G was of vital importance to the *Luftwaffe* on every front to which the service was committed and a warplane deserving of respect.

One of the first German combat aircraft that we received at the RAE Farnborough was a Messerschmitt Bf 109 — an E-3 of II/JG 54 that had fallen intact into French hands after its pilot had landed at Woerth, Bas-Rhin, believing himself to be over German territory. This reached us in mid-May 1940, and we subsequently received a steady enough supply of successive variants to keep a check on the Messerschmitt's performance progress *vis-à-vis* its British contemporaries. A comparison chart reveals a see-saw battle for supremacy until late 1942 when the Spitfire IX widened the performance gap so much that the Bf 109 disappeared from the chart to be replaced by the Focke-Wulf Fw 190A. The *Gustav* began to appear in really substantial numbers, therefore, at a time when the Bf 109's star on the western front at least was waning.

Sinister appearance

Inevitably a *Gustav* reached us at Farnborough. To be precise it was a Bf 109G-6/U2 (*Werk-Nr* 41 2951) which had landed at Manston in error on 21 July 1944, and like all its predecessors, it was put through the testing hoop to probe its strong points and weaknesses. The Bf 109 always brought to my mind the adjective "sinister". It has been suggested that it evinced characteristics associated with the nation that conceived it, and to me it looked lethal from any angle, on the ground or in the air; once I had climbed into its claustrophobic cockpit it *felt*

149

(Above and below) The Bf 109G-6/U2 Werk-Nr 41 2951, which, having landed in error at Manston on 21 July 1944, was allocated the serial TP814 and was flown at Farnborough by the author a month later, on 25 August. It was subsequently used for tactical trials by the Air Fighting Development Unit but crashed during a take-off from Wittering on 23 November 1944

lethal! The cockpit was small and narrow, and was enclosed by a cumbersome hood that was difficult to open from the inside and incorporated rather primitive sliding side panels. The windscreen supports were slender and did not produce serious blind spots, but space was so confined that movement of the head was difficult for even a pilot of my limited stature. The armourglass of the windscreen gave the impression of being slightly smoked and was obviously of much poorer quality than that of earlier Bf 109s that we had tested, this sign of deterioration in quality indicating the 1944 production vintage of the particular aircraft.

The blind flying panel appeared somewhat better equipped than that of the contemporary Fw 190. The auxiliary services were mostly electrical apart from the undercarriage and radiator, which were hydraulically operated, and the flaps which were directly connected to a manually-operated hand-wheel and, in consequence, tediously slow to lower.

The engine starting system was of the inertia type whereby a flywheel was wound up by one of the groundcrew turning a handle until sufficient revs were obtained to engage the starter clutch control by the pilot pulling out a handle positioned beside his left knee. The Daimler-Benz DB 605A engine emitted a pleasantly powerful throaty roar as it warmed up at 1,900 rpm while the magneto, fuel pumps and pressures, and temperatures were checked. Its response to throttle movement was particularly good. The forward view for taxying was terrible but at least the aircraft was easily steerable owing to its positive toe pedal-operated wheel brakes, and using 15 deg of flap and 1.3 *ata* boost the take-off was commendably short and certainly superior to that of the Spitfire IX in distance of run. The strong swing to port could easily be held on rudder, but it was advisable to raise the tail as quickly as possible owing to the poor forward view. This could be done fairly coarsely without fear of the airscrew hitting the ground as the high thrust line of the inverted-vee engine gave ample clearance. The *Gustav* had to be flown off as any attempt to pull it off the ground early resulted in aileron snatching as the wing slats opened unevenly.

The mainwheels retracted quickly but airscrew pitch changing was slow. The flaps were raised manually by means of the outer of two concentrically-mounted wheels to the pilot's left, the inner wheel adjusting tailplane incidence. Thus the wheels could be moved together to counteract the change in trim as the flaps came up. The position of the wing flaps was indicated on the portside flap and of the coolant radiator flaps by two small rods projecting through the wings.

The Bf 109G-6 climbed well and at a steep angle, the actual rate of climb being of the order of 3,800 ft/min (19,3 m/sec) at sea level. Stability proved excellent in the longitudinal and lateral planes but was almost neutral directionally. Control harmony was poor for a fighter, the rudder being light, the ailerons moderately light and the elevators extremely heavy. This elevator heaviness was perhaps a necessity in view of the high wing loading of the Bf 109G as over-application of longitudinal control in manoeuvres easily induced the slats to open, which, in turn, gave rise to aileron snatching and completely ruined sighting on any aircraft being attacked.

Another shortcoming was the lack of any rudder trimming device. This meant that it was necessary to apply moderate right rudder during the climb and considerable left rudder during a dive. Thus, although the Bf 109G pilots tended to use a bunt into a steep dive as an escape manoeuvre in dogfights, they had some very heavy rudder and elevator control forces to contend with as speed built up and pull-outs at low altitude had to be made with considerable circumspection. This manoeuvre was employed against early marks of Spitfire and Hurricane which could not follow without the Merlin engine cutting in the bunt, but with the availability of the negative-*g* carburettor, some RAF fighting pilots, finding a Messerschmitt on their tails, took to deliberately diving to ground level in an attempt to lure their antagonist to disaster.

At its rather disappointing low-level cruising speed of 240 mph (386 km/h) the *Gustav* was certainly delightful to fly, but the situation changed as speed increased; in a dive at 400 mph (644 km/h) the controls felt as though they had seized! The

(Above right) A Bf 109G-2 (Werk-Nr 10639) apparently shipped to the UK after capture in Sicily, arriving at Liverpool on 26 December 1943 and subsequently flown as RN228. (Below) A Bf 109G-14/U4, one of the final G-series production models, some (including that illustrated here) receiving a wooden tail assembly (signified by the U4 suffix)

Messerschmitt Bf 109G-14/U4 Cutaway Drawing Key

1 Starboard navigation light
2 Starboard wingtip
3 Fixed trim tab
4 Starboard Frise-type aileron
5 Flush-riveted stressed
   wing-skinning
6 Handley Page leading-edge
   automatic slot
7 Slot control linkage
8 Slot equalizer rod
9 Aileron control linkage
10 Fabric-covered flap section
11 Wheel fairing
12 Port fuselage machine-gun
   ammunition-feed fairing
13 Port Rheinmetall Borsig
   13-mm MG 131 machine gun
14 Engine accessories
15 Starboard machine-gun
   trough
16 Daimler Benz DB 605AM
   twelve-cylinder inverted-vee
   liquid-cooled engine

17 Detachable cowling panel
18 Oil filler access
19 Oil tank
20 Propeller pitch-change
   mechanism
21 VDM electrically-operated
   constant-speed propeller
22 Spinner
23 Engine-mounted cannon
   muzzle
24 Blast tube
25 Propeller hub
26 Spinner back plate
27 Auxiliary cooling intakes
28 Coolant header tank
29 Anti-vibration rubber
   engine-mounting pads
30 Elektron forged engine
   bearer
31 Engine bearer support strut
   attachment
32 Plug leads
33 Exhaust manifold fairing strip
34 Ejector exhausts
35 Cowling fasteners
36 Oil cooler
37 Oil cooler intake
38 Starboard mainwheel
39 Oil cooler outlet flap
40 Wing root fillet
41 Wing/fuselage fairing
42 Firewall/bulkhead
43 Supercharger air intake
44 Supercharger assembly

45 20-mm cannon magazine
   drum
46 13-mm machine-gun
   ammunition feed
47 Engine bearer upper
   attachment
48 Ammunition feed fairing

49 13-mm Rheinmetall Borsig
   MG 131 machine gun
   breeches
50 Instrument panel
51 20-mm Mauser MG 151/20
   cannon breech
52 Heelrests
53 Rudder pedals
54 Undercarriage emergency
   retraction cables
55 Fuselage frame
56 Wing/fuselage fairing
57 Undercarriage emergency
   retraction handwheel
   (outboard)
58 Tail trim handwheel (inboard)
59 Seat harness
60 Throttle lever
61 Control column
62 Cockpit ventilation inlet
63 Revi 16B reflector gunsight
   (folding)
64 Armoured windshield frame
65 Anti-glare gunsight screen
66 90-mm armourglass
   windscreen
67 'Galland'-type clear-vision
   hinged canopy
68 Framed armourglass
   head/back panel
69 Canopy contoured frame
70 Canopy hinges (starboard)
71 Canopy release catch
72 Pilot's bucket-type seat
   (8-mm back armour)

73 Underfloor contoured fuel
   tank (88 Imp. gal/400 l of 87
   octane B4)
74 Fuselage frame
75 Circular access panel
76 Tail trimming cable conduit
77 Wireless leads
78 MW 50 (methanol/water) tank
   (25 Imp. gal/114 l capacity)
79 Handhold
80 Fuselage decking
81 Aerial mast
82 D/F loop
83 Oxygen cylinders (three)

84 Filler pipe
85 Wirelss equipment packs
   (FuG 16ZY communications
   and FuG 25a IFF)
86 Main fuel filler cap
87 Aerial
88 Fuselage top keel (connector
   stringer)
89 Aerial lead-in
90 Fuselage skin plating
   sections
91 'U'-stringers
92 Fuselage frames
   (monocoque construction)
93 Tail trimming cables

94 Tailfin root fairing
95 Starboard fixed tailplane
96 Elevator balance
97 Starboard elevator
98 Geared elevator tab
99 All-wooden tailfin
   construction
100 Aerial attachment
101 Rudder upper hinge bracket
102 Rudder post
103 Fabric-covered wooden
   rudder structure
104 Geared rudder tab
105 Rear navigation light
106 Port elevator
107 Elevator geared tab
108 Tailplane structure
109 Rudder actuating linkage
110 Elevator control horn
111 Elevator connecting rod
112 Elevator control quadrant
113 Tailwheel leg cuff
114 Castoring non-retractable
   tailwheel
115 Lengthened tailwheel leg
116 Access panel

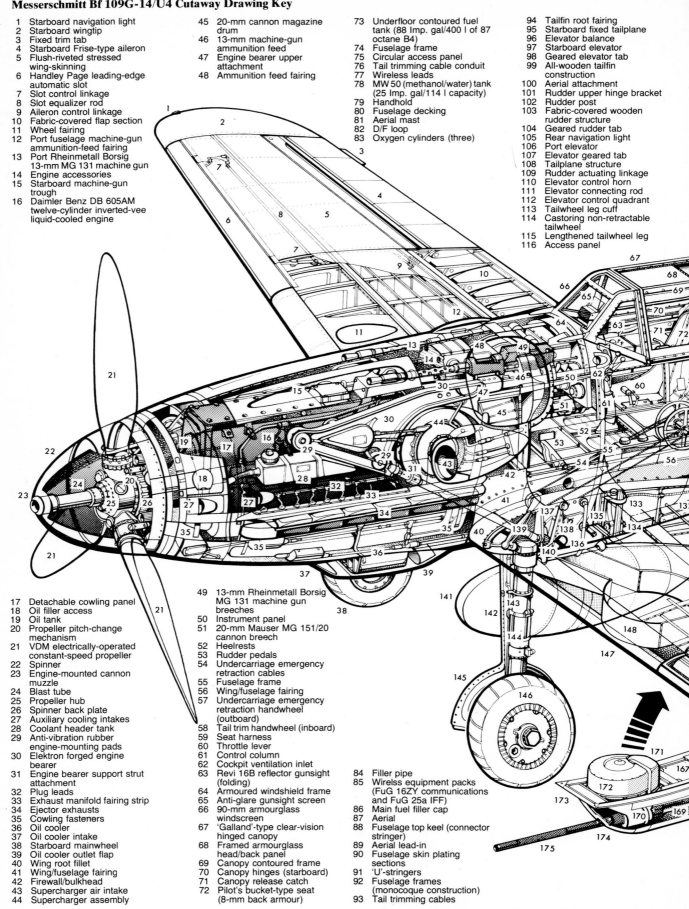

117 Tailwheel shock-strut
118 Lifting point
119 Rudder cable
120 Elevator cables
121 First-aid pack
122 Air bottles
123 Fuselage access panel
124 Bottom keel (connector stringer)
125 Ventral IFF aerial
126 Master compass
127 Elevator control linkage
128 Wing root fillet

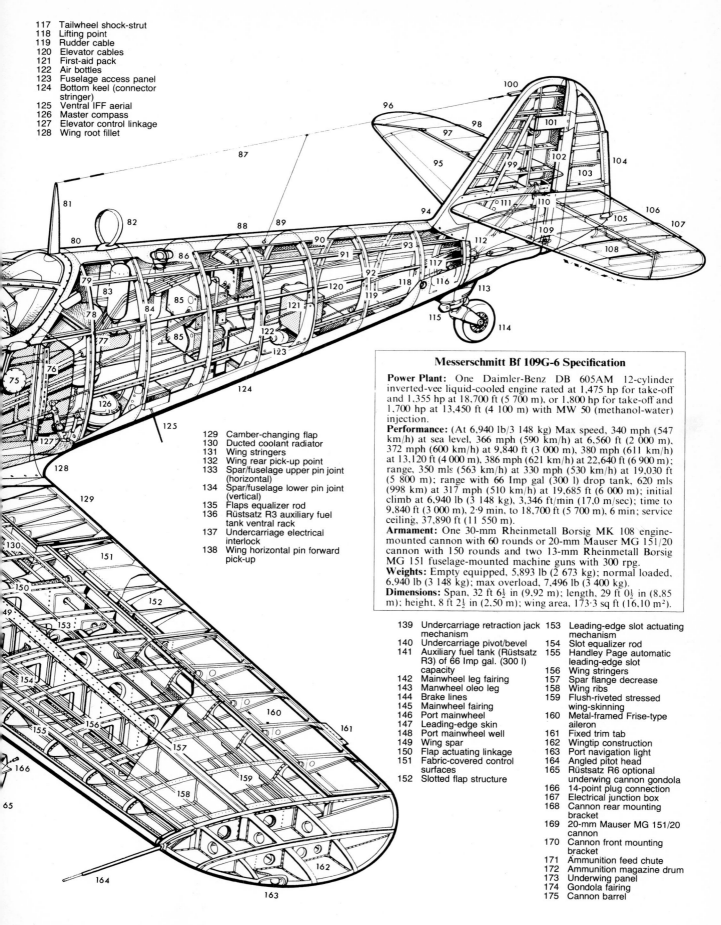

129 Camber-changing flap
130 Ducted coolant radiator
131 Wing stringers
132 Wing rear pick-up point
133 Spar/fuselage upper pin joint (horizontal)
134 Spar/fuselage lower pin joint (vertical)
135 Flaps equalizer rod
136 Rüstsatz R3 auxiliary fuel tank ventral rack
137 Undercarriage electrical interlock
138 Wing horizontal pin forward pick-up

Messerschmitt Bf 109G-6 Specification

Power Plant: One Daimler-Benz DB 605AM 12-cylinder inverted-vee liquid-cooled engine rated at 1,475 hp for take-off and 1,355 hp at 18,700 ft (5 700 m), or 1,800 hp for take-off and 1,700 hp at 13,450 ft (4 100 m) with MW 50 (methanol-water) injection.
Performance: (At 6,940 lb/3 148 kg) Max speed, 340 mph (547 km/h) at sea level, 366 mph (590 km/h) at 6,560 ft (2 000 m), 372 mph (600 km/h) at 9,840 ft (3 000 m), 380 mph (611 km/h) at 13,120 ft (4 000 m), 386 mph (621 km/h) at 22,640 ft (6 900 m); range, 350 mls (563 km/h) at 330 mph (530 km/h) at 19,030 ft (5 800 m); range with 66 Imp gal (300 l) drop tank, 620 mls (998 km) at 317 mph (510 km/h) at 19,685 ft (6 000 m); initial climb at 6,940 lb (3 148 kg), 3,346 ft/min (17,0 m/sec); time to 9,840 ft (3 000 m), 2·9 min, to 18,700 ft (5 700 m), 6 min; service ceiling, 37,890 ft (11 550 m).
Armament: One 30-mm Rheinmetall Borsig MK 108 engine-mounted cannon with 60 rounds or 20-mm Mauser MG 151/20 cannon with 150 rounds and two 13-mm Rheinmetall Borsig MG 151 fuselage-mounted machine guns with 300 rpg.
Weights: Empty equipped, 5,893 lb (2 673 kg); normal loaded, 6,940 lb (3 148 kg); max overload, 7,496 lb (3 400 kg).
Dimensions: Span, 32 ft 6½ in (9,92 m); length, 29 ft 0½ in (8,85 m); height, 8 ft 2½ in (2,50 m); wing area, 173·3 sq ft (16,10 m²).

139 Undercarriage retraction jack mechanism
140 Undercarriage pivot/bevel
141 Auxiliary fuel tank (Rüstsatz R3) of 66 Imp gal. (300 l) capacity
142 Mainwheel leg fairing
143 Manwheel oleo leg
144 Brake lines
145 Mainwheel fairing
146 Port mainwheel
147 Leading-edge skin
148 Port mainwheel well
149 Wing spar
150 Flap actuating linkage
151 Fabric-covered control surfaces
152 Slotted flap structure

153 Leading-edge slot actuating mechanism
154 Slot equalizer rod
155 Handley Page automatic leading-edge slot
156 Wing stringers
157 Spar flange decrease
158 Wing ribs
159 Flush-riveted stressed wing-skinning
160 Metal-framed Frise-type aileron
161 Fixed trim tab
162 Wingtip construction
163 Port navigation light
164 Angled pitot head
165 Rüstsatz R6 optional underwing cannon gondola
166 14-point plug connection
167 Electrical junction box
168 Cannon rear mounting bracket
169 20-mm Mauser MG 151/20 cannon
170 Cannon front mounting bracket
171 Ammunition feed chute
172 Ammunition magazine drum
173 Underwing panel
174 Gondola fairing
175 Cannon barrel

Bf109G-2 (Werk-Nr 10639) RN228 photographed at the end of February 1944. It was eventually flown by the Enemy Aircraft Flight at the Central Fighter Establishment at Tangmere

Messerschmitt Bf 109G-6 Cockpit Instrumentation Key:

1 Undercarriage emergency lowering handwheel
2 Tailplane trim wheel
3 Seat height adjustment handle
4 Tailplane incidence indicator
5 Fuel injection primer pump
6 Fuel cock lever
7 Throttle
8 Throttle-mounted propeller pitch control thumbswitch
9 Dust filter handgrip
10 Canopy lever
11 Undercarriage switches
12 Undercarriage position indicators
13 Start plug cleansing switch
14 Starter switch
15 Panel light
16 Main line switch
17 Ignition switch
18 Frame struts
19 Armoured glass windscreen
20 Revi 16B reflector gunsight
21 Armament switch
22 Ammunition counters
23 Clock
24 Repeater compass
25 Artificial horizon/turn-and-bank indicator
26 Fine and coarse altimeter
27 Airspeed indicator
28 Gunsight padding
29 Manifold pressure gauge
30 Tachometer
31 AFN 2 Homing indicator (FuG 16ZY)
32 Mechanical propeller pitch indicator
33 Tumbler switch
34 Combined coolant exit and oil intake temperature indicator
35 Fuel warning lamp
36 MK 108 cannon breech
37 Rudder pedals
38 Firing trigger
39 Gun charging knob
40 Control column
41 Pilot's seat
42 Undercarriage emergency release
43 Electric fuel contents gauge
44 Dual oil and fuel pressure gauge
45 Auxiliary fuel contents indicator
46 Panel light
47 Coolant radiator control
48 Oxygen supply indicator
49 Oxygen pressure gauge
50 Radio switch panel
51 Oxygen supply
52 Radio tuner panel

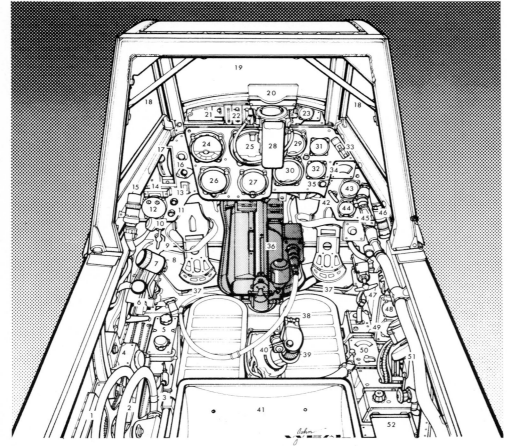

highest speed that I dived to below 10,000 ft (3 048 m) was 440 mph (708 km/h) and the solidity of control was such that this was the limit in my book. However, things were very different at high altitude, and providing the *Gustav* was kept where it was meant to be (ie, above 25,000 ft/7 620 m) it performed efficiently both in dogfighting and as an attacker of bomber formations. To give some idea of its performance, I measured 384 mph (618 km/h) in level flight at 23,000 ft (7 010 m), which conformed pretty well with the officially claimed maximum speed of 386 mph (621 km/h) at 22,640 ft (6 900 m).

I was particularly interested in the operation of the slats, the action of which gave rise to aileron snatching in any high-*g* manoeuvres such as loops or tight turns, so I did a series of stalls to check their functioning more accurately. The stall with the aircraft clean, with half fuel load and the engine throttled right back occurred at 105 mph (168 km/h). This was preceded by elevator buffet and opening of the slats about 20 mph (30 km/h) above the stall, these being accompanied by the unpleasant aileron snatching as the slats opened unevenly. The stall itself was fairly gentle with the nose dropping and the port wing simultaneously dropping about 10 degrees. In the landing configuration the stall occurred at 99 mph (160 km/h) with identical symptoms apart from heavier elevator buffeting.

A number of dummy attacks on a co-operative Lancaster and a friendly skirmish with a Mustang flown by one of the RAE pilots revealed the fact that the slipstream of these aircraft caused the intermittent operation of the Bf 109G's slats so that accurate sighting became an impossibility. After an hour's flying I still had 26 Imp gal (120 l) remaining of the 88 Imp gal (400 l) with which I had taken-off, and as I came in to land at Farnborough I found that the approach was steeper than that of the Spitfire but elevator feel was very positive and gave delightfully accurate control at 118 mph (190 km/h).

A substantial change of altitude was called for on the flare or round-out before touchdown, and even after ground contact the lift did not spill rapidly, and ballooning or bouncing could easily be experienced on rough ground. Once the tailwheel was firmly on the ground the brakes could be applied quite harshly, thus giving a short landing run, but care had to be taken to prevent any swing as the combination of narrow-track under-carriage and minimal forward view could easily result in directional problems.

No sinecure

By mid-1944, with the European war in its final phase, time had undoubtedly begun to catch up with Willy Messerschmitt's fighter, and in European skies at least it provided its pilots with no sinecure. If you happened to be flying a Hurricane and encountered *Gustav* you had something of a headache, and survival rested on the exploitation of the superior manoeuvrability of the British fighter. If you were jockeying a Spitfire V you certainly had to have your wits about you, particularly above 20,000 ft (6 095 m), and again had to rely on manoeuvrability to get you out of trouble, but if you happened to be behind the gunsight of a contemporary series Spitfire, such as the Mk IX or XIV, then it was a different story.

The Air Fighter Development Squadron flew the Bf 109G-6 for tactical trials with a Spitfire LF IX, a Spitfire XIV and a Mustang III (P-51C) and found that the first-mentioned type had a slight speed advantage up to 16,000 ft (4 877 m) when using 18 lb (8,16 kg) boost, the situation being reversed between this altitude and 20,000 ft (6 096 m) at which the Spitfire LF IX regained the speed advantage to the extent of some 7 mph (11 km/h). Using 25 lb (11,3 kg) of boost the Spitfire proved to be about 25 mph (40 km/h) faster below 15,000 ft (4 570 m) and around 7 mph (11 km/h) faster above this altitude, while climb was superior to that of *Gustav* at all altitudes and particularly

A Bf 109G-6/R6 serving with II Gruppe of Jagdgeschwader 26 in France in the autumn of 1943. Intended for the zerstörer rôle, the Bf 109G-6/R6 carried two 20-mm MG 151 cannon in underwing gondolas

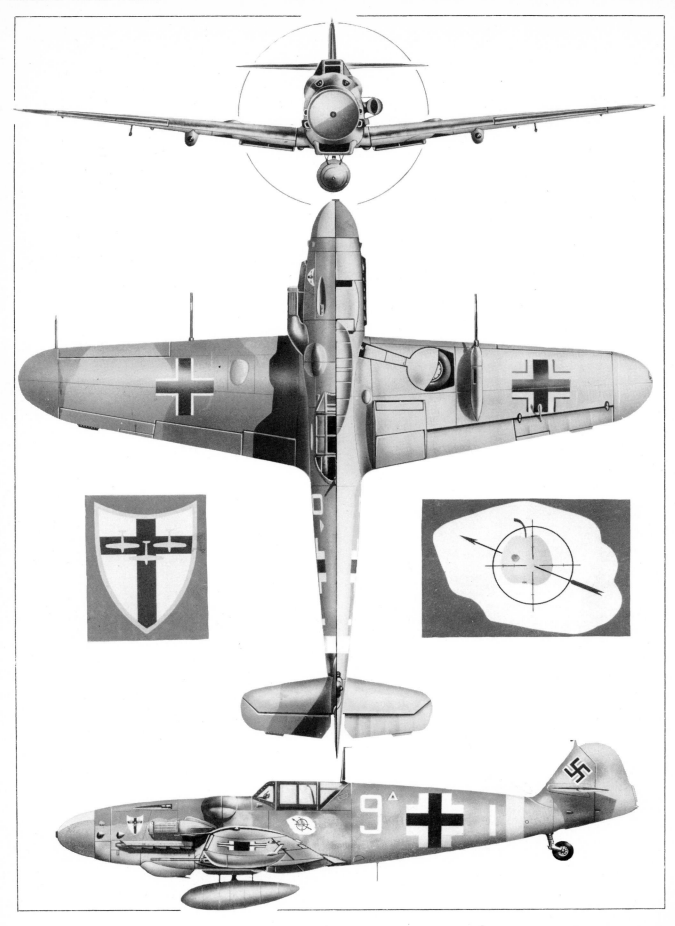

The general arrangement drawing on the opposite page depicts a Bf 109G-6/R6 with tropical filters belonging to 7./JG 27, the emblem of III Gruppe being illustrated on the left and that of 7.Staffel on the right. (Above) A Bf 109G-5 of 7./JG 27 flying over the Eastern Mediterranean late 1943

below 13,000 ft (3 960 m). The Bf 109G could leave the Spitfire LF IX behind in a dive without any difficulty, but when both aircraft were pulled up into a climb from a dive their performance was almost identical, the Spitfire slowly pulling away as soon as climbing speed was attained. The roll rate and turning circle of the British fighter was very much superior at all speeds.

In so far as the Spitfire XIV was concerned, using 18 lb (8,16 kg) of boost this was found to be 25 mph (40 km/h) faster than the *Gustav* at altitudes up to 16,000 ft (4 877 m), at which the advantage to the British fighter was reduced to 10 mph (16 km/h), speed superiority then increasing progressively with altitude until, at 30,000 ft (9 144 m), the Spitfire XIV was 50 mph (80 km/h) faster. At the rated altitude of the Bf 109G-6 (ie, 16,000 ft/4 877 m) there was little to choose between the two fighters in climbing performance, but at all other altitudes the Spitfire could show the German fighter a clean pair of heels. Comparative dives revealed that the Bf 109G-6 had a slight initial advantage but this was lost at speeds in excess of 380 mph (610 km/h) indicated, and when both aircraft were dived with engine throttled back and then pulled into climbing attitude their rate of climb was identical, but when using maximum power in the dive the Spitfire XIV easily left the *Gustav* behind in the subsequent climb.

The Mustang III possessed a clear speed advantage at all altitudes, this ranging from around 30 mph (48 km/h) at the Bf 109G-6's rated altitude to some 50 mph (80 km/h) at 30,000 ft (9 144 m). The *Gustav* offered a marginally better climb rate up to 20,000 ft (6 096 m) but between this altitude and 25,000 ft (7 620 m) the Mustang had a very slight advantage. When dived and then pulled up into a climb there was little to choose between US and German fighter, but the Mustang could steadily outdive the Bf 109G-6 and had no difficulty in out-turning the Messerschmitt.

One of my rashest ventures was to fly the Bf 109G-12 tandem two-seater from the rear cockpit with no one in the forward cockpit. I was interested to ascertain what sort of view the instructor had for landing. The answer was none! I had to make three very frightening attempts before regaining *terra firma*. The periscopic sight in the rear cockpit was of no use whatsoever in the vital final stage of flare, touch-down and landing run. One can only assumed that *Luftwaffe* instructors finding themselves in a Bf 109G-12 acquired a fatalistic acceptance of an inevitable reliance on their pupils for the finale of each training flight. I would certainly not recommend the

One of the author's most frightening experiences was, as recounted on this page, landing the two-seat Bf 109G-12 (illustrated above and below) from the rear cockpit. These photographs depict a prototype of this tandem-seat model

ultimate solution that I adopted of a split-S turning dive at the runway and then a burst of power to avoid cratering the tarmac, and making tail-up contact on the mainwheels. After the tail dropped it was anybody's guess as to the direction in which the aircraft was heading. I certainly had not the vaguest idea.

This then was *Gustav*. By the time the evolution of Willy Messerschmitt's basic design had reached the G-series it was no longer a *great* fighter, but it was still a sound all-rounder and the Bf 109G had greater flexibility from some aspects than preceding sub-types. Allied bomber formations were certainly finding *Gustav* a formidable antagonist for it had heavy firepower, a reasonable overtaking speed and presented a very small target profile to the gunners, and if the Bf 109G could no longer take on the later Allied fighters on even terms during the last year of the war, this reflected no discredit on the design team that had conceived it.

MESSERSCHMITT BF 110

THE ELDERLY Hawker Hart biplane, with a fellow Fleet Air
Arm pilot at the controls, was cruising sedately on a
training flight over the tranquil English countryside near
Salisbury. It was the fateful June of 1940, and the RAF was
frantically preparing for the showdown with the *Luftwaffe*
that it knew to be imminent, but on that pleasant summer day,
with the quiet Wiltshire landscape below bathed in sunlight,
all seemed well with the world. Suddenly, a shark-like Messerschmitt Bf 110 overtook the Hart from behind and out of the
sun, its pilot coolly ranging his aircraft alongside, and almost
before the unwary FAA pilot knew what was happening, the
Messerschmitt's rear gunner had blasted the trainer into
oblivion.

This, my first encounter, albeit at a distance, with Willy
Messerschmitt's strategic fighter of formidable repute, impressed me profoundly. The rakish lines of the intruder were suggestive of all the predatory characteristics associated with the
shark but, more important, that unhappy incident ensured
that I took truly to heart three points that were vital for survival

in the aerial arena of the first half of the 'forties, or at any other
time of hostilities for that matter. A pilot cannot afford to relax
at any stage of a flight however serene his surroundings may
seem; his neck must acquire a measure of elasticity in order to
maintain a continuous 360 deg look-out, and he must never
forget the old World War I maxim of "Beware of the Hun in
the sun!" On reflection, I may owe a lot to *that* particular Bf 110.

The *Zerstörer*, or destroyer, category of warplane, a term
for the strategic fighter as represented by the Messerschmitt
Bf 110 borrowed from naval parlance, was particularly favoured
by *Reichsmarschall* Hermann Göring, the *Oberbefehlshaber*
of the *Luftwaffe*; the Bf 110-equipped *Zerstörergruppen* were
the élite of the air arm of which he had been the principal
architect. German propagandists had made far-reaching claims
for the capabilities of the Bf 110, claims in which the *Reichsmarschall* undoubtedly believed implicitly, and when first
deployed operationally there was every reason to suppose that
it would fulfil the most sanguine expectations of its creators.
Over Poland, the Bf 110 enjoyed considerable success in combat

(Head of opposite page) Bf 110C-4 (Werk-Nr 2177) which was forced down at Goodwood on 21 July 1940. Originally flown by 4.(F)/14, this aircraft was repaired from parts salvaged from another crashed example and flown as AX772. (Above) A Bf 110C-4 serving with 7.Staffel of Jagdgeschwader 5 "Eismeer", this being essentially a single-seat fighter unit with a zerstörer staffel attached

with the appreciably more manoeuvrable if slower PZL P.11 single-seaters, and the disastrous armed reconnaissance sortie over the Schillig Roads, the Jade Estuary and Wilhelmshaven performed on 18 December 1939 by 24 Wellingtons of the RAF, when nine of the bombers fell victim to the Bf 110Cs of 1. and 2.*Staffeln* of *Zerostörergeschwader* 76, appeared to substantiate the boastful claims made by *Reichsmarschall* Göring and must have been a great morale-raiser for the crews of the *Luftwaffe* strategic fighter units.

Thus, the Bf 110 was to enjoy an awe-inspiring reputation by the time it was committed to the "Battle of Britain". There had not been time to thoroughly analyse the results of combat in French skies during May-June 1940, in which the *Zerstörergruppen* had encountered relatively modern and reasonably well-armed single-seat fighters, although under conditions of

(Above right) A Bf 110G-4b/R3 serving as a test-bed for the revised G-4d/R3 type SN-2 aerial array and (below) a Bf 110G-4b/R3 exhibited at Farnborough in October 1945

Luftwaffe aerial supremacy; encounters which had necessitated a reappraisal of the tactics employed by the *Zerstörer* formations and had revealed some of the weaknesses in the strategic fighter concept. The strategic fighter had to be something of a compromise between conflicting requirements and the Bf 110 was such a compromise, if a remarkably successful one. The concept demanded heavy firepower and sufficient fuel for long range, which, at that point in time, dictated a relatively large aircraft of twin-engined configuration. It had to possess performance comparable with that of the more specialised defensive fighter by which it was likely to be opposed, and as one of its primary tasks was the defence of bomber formations, a high degree of manoeuvrability was mandatory. Some of these desirable attributes conflicted in their achievement with others, the range requirement with its weight penalty being achieved only at the expense, for example, of manoeuvrability.

In the "Battle of Britain" the Bf 110 fell far short of anticipation and its limited success was to lead to a widespread belief that it was an unsuccessful design. This was, in fact, far from the case, for the Messerschmitt strategic fighter was *not* the indifferent warplane that its showing during the "Battle" led many to believe. It was a very effective warplane but inadequate understanding on the part of the *Führungsstab* of the limitations of the strategic fighter category led to its incorrect deployment with the result that the *Zerstörergruppen* suffered some 40 per cent attrition within less than three weeks of the launching of *Adlerangriff*.

A soundly designed warplane

Having attempted to present the rationale for the Bf 110's relatively poor showing in British skies during the summer of 1940, which resulted in this elegant warplane being adjudged unfairly by many aviation historians as unsuccessful. I would make the point that, apart from the débâcle of the *Zerstörergruppen* during the "Battle of Britain", the Bf 110 served with a fair degree of distinction throughout the whole of WW II as both diurnal and nocturnal interceptor, as an intruder and fighter-bomber, and in a variety of other operational rôles, the basic design proving amenable to power plant changes and to accommodating armament, avionics and other equipment far beyond anything envisaged at the time of its conception. By any standards, therefore, the Bf 110 must be deemed a success, and I was certainly never to meet a German pilot that disliked it — an accolade indeed.

I had always admired the sleek, business-like appearance of the Bf 110, and as soon as I flew this warplane so much vaunted

by Göring I felt that tingling sensation that I associated with an aircraft of considerable operational competence. The first example of this æsthetically-appealing aircraft that I was to fly was the DB 601A-powered Bf 110C, although I was to discover that the basic handling characteristics remained relatively unchanged with the installation of the appreciably more powerful DB 605 engines and the accompanying structural beefing-up that characterised the Bf 110G series that I was to fly later.

The pilot's cockpit was entered from the port side by means of a ladder normally accommodated entirely within the fuselage in a slot aft of the port wing trailing edge, a button aft of the slot being pressed and the ladder springing out to the extended position. The Perspex canopy over the forward seat was formed by three parts, the upper part hinging aft and the side panels folding down, and it could not be locked from the outside. I had always been intrigued to ascertain exactly how a pilot vacated the Bf 110 in an emergency as it did not look in the least simple, yet Rudolf Hess, Hitler's deputy, had apparently achieved this operation with ease after making his notorious solo night flight from Munich to the outskirts of Glasgow. After studying the problem I had to admit that I was little the wiser and concluded that an element of luck entered into a successful bale-out from the aircraft. The cockpit upper panel could be jettisoned by unlocking it and allowing it to swing up into the airstream, but thereafter the pilot apparently had to roll on to the wing and risk getting blown back against the rather considerable empennage.

The flying controls were conventional enough, apart from the automatic leading-edge slats opposite the ailerons. The slotted flaps were hydraulically operated with a position indicator graduated from 0 deg to 50 deg, and a compressed air system was provided for emergency use. The main undercarriage members operated on similar systems, the tailwheel being fixed, and the wheel brakes were hydraulic. The rudder trimmer control was somewhat unusual in that it comprised a lever moving over a notched quadrant, and when moved to port it resulted in a turn to port, and vice versa. The cockpit layout was good and the blind flying panel almost contained the six essential instruments. I say *almost* advisedly as the repeater compass had been displaced to port to make way for a cannon rounds indicator. Obviously, an Armament Officer with a strong personality had stalked the halls of the *Reichsluftfahrtministerium*.

There were many excellent features of German aircraft cockpit layouts that had been standardised, such as systems

This Bf 110C-4 was apparently captured by the Allies in France in 1944, its original identity and the circumstances of its acquisition being unknown

These photographs of the Bf110C-4, which was flown in the UK for some four years as AX772, capture the supreme elegance of this Messerschmitt fighter, which, despite its poor showing in 1940 during the "Battle of Britain", in fact served with a measure of distinction throughout World War II

AX772, illustrated by these photographs taken on 28 March 1942, was originally shot down at Goodwood on 21 July 1940 and was repaired by means of the cannibalization of another example brought down near Wareham 10 days earlier. It flew at Farnborough for the first time on 15 February 1941 and was finally placed in storage in November 1945

Messerschmitt Bf 110G-4b/R3 cutaway drawing key

1 The Hirschgeweih (Stag's Antlers) array for the FuG 220b Lichtenstein SN-2 radar
2 Single-pole type antenna for the FuG 212 Lichtenstein C-1 radar
3 Camera gun
4 Cannon muzzles
5 Cannon ports
6 Blast tubes
7 Starboard mainwheel
8 Armour plate (10-mm)
9 Twin 30-mm Rheinmetall Borsig MK 108 (Rüstsatz/ Field Conversion Set 3) with 135 rpg
10 Armoured bulkhead
11 Supercharger intake
12 Position of nacelle-mounted instruments on day fighter model
13 Exhaust flame damper
14 Auxiliary tank
15 Three-blade VDM airscrew
16 Leading-edge automatic slat
17 Pitot tube

18 FuG 227/1 Flensburg homing aerial fitted to some aircraft by forward maintenance units (to home on Monica tail-warning radar emissions)
19 Stressed wing skinning
20 Starboard aileron
21 Trim tab
22 Slotted flap
23 Hinged canopy roof
24 Armoured glass windscreen (60-mm)
25 Instrument panel
26 Cockpit floor armour (4-mm)
27 Twin 20-mm Mauser MG 151 cannon with 300 rounds (port) and 350 rounds (starboard)

35 Aerial mast
36 Upward-firing cannon muzzles
37 Two 30-mm MK 108 cannon in schräge Musik (oblique music) installation firing obliquely upward (optional installation supplied as an Umrüst-Bausatz/Factory Conversion Set)
38 Ammunition drums
39 Aft cockpit bulkhead
40 FuG 10P HF R/T set
41 FuB1 2F airfield blind approach receiver

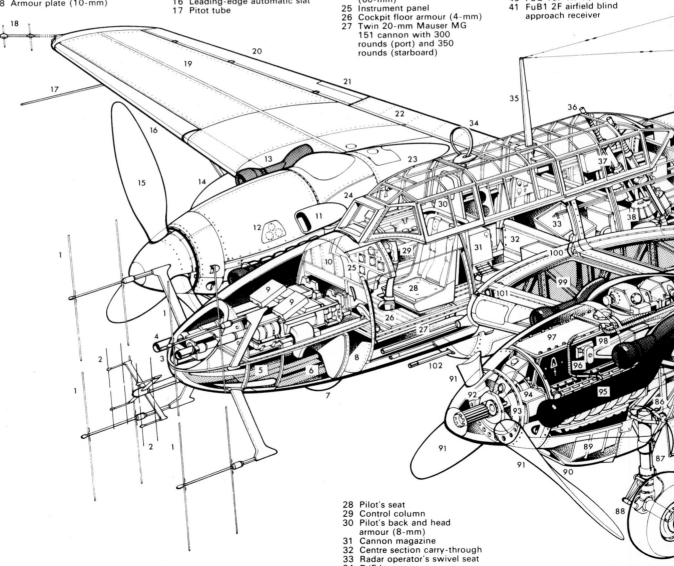

28 Pilot's seat
29 Control column
30 Pilot's back and head armour (8-mm)
31 Cannon magazine
32 Centre section carry-through
33 Radar operator's swivel seat
34 D/F loop

identification colour schemes. Another was the type of airscrew pitch indicators which were numbered like a clock face, rendering it very simple to set the pitch on any German aircraft. For take-off, for example, the clock pointers were always set at 12 o'clock by moving the electrically-actuated pitch control levers. On the early Bf 110s the clock-type pitch indicators were also mounted on each engine nacelle where they could be seen from the pilot's seat, while the later Bf 110G series had the indicators mounted only on the nacelles and not in the cockpit. All engine instruments were on the starboard of the dashboard, and mixture strength and boost pressure were controlled automatically. There was, however, one unusual engine control in the form of two handles on the cockpit ledge to starboard of the pilot. When pulled upwards these retarded the ignition so

Messerschmitt Bf 110G-4c/R3 Specification

Power Plant: Two Daimler-Benz DB 605B-1 12-cylinder inverted-Vee liquid-cooled engines each rated at 1,475 hp for take-off and 1,355 hp at 18,700 ft (5 700 m) driving three-blade controllable-pitch fully-feathering VDM airscrews. Normal fuel capacity 279 Imp gal (1 270 l) distributed between four wing tanks (two on each side of the fuselage fore and aft of the mainspar) with provision for two 66 Imp gal (300 l) drop tanks.
Performance: (At 20,701 lb/9 390 kg) Max speed, 311 mph (500 km/h) at sea level, 342 mph (550 km/h) at 22,900 ft (6 980 m); max continuous cruise, 317 mph (510 km/h) at 19,685 ft (6 000 m); max range (internal fuel), 560 mls (900 km), (with two 66 Imp gal/300 l drop tanks), 808 mls (1 300 km); max climb rate, 2,170 ft/min (11 m/sec); service ceiling, 26,250 ft (8 000 m); max ceiling, 36,090 ft (11 000 m).
Weights: Empty equipped, 11,230 lb (5 094 kg); normal loaded, 20,701 lb (9 390 kg); max take-off, 21,799 lb (9 888 kg).
Dimensions: Span, 53 ft 3¼ in (16,25 m); length (excluding radar antennæ), 39 ft 6¼ in (12,07 m); (including antennæ), 42 ft 9¾ in (13,05 m); height, 13 ft 8½ in (4,18 m); wing area, 413·33 sq ft (38,4 m²).
Armament: Two 30-mm Rheinmetall Borsig MK 108 cannon with 135 rpg and two 20-mm Mauser MG 151 cannon with 300 rounds (port) and 350 rounds (starboard), and one 7,9-mm MG 81Z twin machine gun on flexible mount with 800 rounds or twin 20-mm MG 151 or MG FF cannon in "shräge Musik" installation.

42 Handhold
43 Oxygen bottles
44 Aerials
45 Master compass
46 Starboard tailfin
47 Rudder balance
48 Rudder
49 Tab

50 Starboard elevator
51 Starboard tailplane
52 Variable-incidence tailplane
53 Elevator tab
54 Centre section fairing
55 Rear navigation light

56 Port elevator
57 Port tailfin
58 Rudder
59 Hinged tab
60 Tailwheel
61 Fuselage frames
62 Control lines
63 Dipole tuner
64 Batteries

65 Transformer
66 Slotted flap
67 Fuel tank of 57·3 Imp gal (260,5 l) capacity
68 Oil tank of 7·7 Imp gal (35 l) capacity
69 Ventral antenna
70 Coolant radiator
71 Radiator intake
72 Hinged intake fairing
73 Aileron tab
74 Aileron construction
75 Wingtip
76 Flensburg aerial (see 18)
77 Port navigation light
78 Leading-edge automatic slat
79 Wing ribs
80 Mainspar
81 Underwing auxiliary fuel tank (66-Imp gal/300-l capacity)
82 Landing light

83 Undercarriage door
84 Mainwheel well
85 Supercharger intake
86 Undercarriage pivot point
87 Mainwheel leg
88 Mainwheel
89 Oil cooler
90 Oil cooler intake
91 VDM airscrew
92 Pitch-change mechanism
93 Armoured ring (5-mm)
94 Coolant tank
95 Exhaust flame damper
96 Anti-vibration engine mounting pad
97 Daimler-Benz DB 605B-1 12-cylinder inverted-Vee engine (rated at 1,475 hp for take-off and 1,355 hp at 18,700 ft/5 700 m)
98 Forged engine bearer
99 Fuel tank (82·5-Imp gal/375-l capacity)
100 Fuselage/mainspar attachment point
101 Fuselage/forward auxiliary spar attachment point
102 Waffenwanne 151Z, a ventral tray housing a pair of 20-mm MG 151 cannon (optional)

that any oil could be burned off the sparking plugs.

The fuel system comprised a main and reserve tank in each wing, both inboard of the engine with the former forward of the single spar and the latter behind it. Each main tank held 82·4 Imp gal (375 l) and each reserve tank contained 57 Imp gal (260 l). The operation of the fuel system was virtually the same as that for the Heinkel He 111 except that there was no hand-operated transfer pump. There was a 8·8 Imp gal (40 l) oil tank in each wing, directly behind the engine bulkhead, but there was no provision for pumping oil from one tank to the other in the event of one engine failing. The inertia starters for the Daimler-Benz DB 601 12-cylinder liquid-cooled inverted-Vee engines could be energised by hand, electrically from the 24-volt aircraft battery or electrically from a ground starter.

Each engine required about eight strokes of the primer pump, and then the fuel pressure had to be pumped up by handles on the pilot's portside, this tedious pumping action having to be continued until the engines fired. These handles were omitted from the later Bf 110G series. Once started the engines were warmed up at 1,900 rpm and the magnetos and fuel pumps tested. When the oil temperature reached 104°F (40°C) the throttles could be opened to the full-throttle ground-running conditions of 2,200 rpm at 1·3 *atas* of boost.

Pleasant characteristics
Taxying the Bf 110 was very easy, with good view and ground handling even in a crosswind when differential throttling and braking could cope with all conditions. Take-off at 2,600 rpm and 1·3 *atas* of boost was normally effected without recourse to flaps in the earlier production models, but the take-off run was long and 20 deg of flap was recommended for the Bf 110G series. During the initial portion of the run directional control

Messerschmitt Bf 110C cockpit drawing key

1 Oil cooler flap levers
2 Fuel cock levers
3 Seat adjustment handle
4 Throttle levers
5 Electrical system cut-out switch
6 Fuel system priming pump levers (Deleted from Bf 110G cockpit)
7 Magneto switches
8 Undercarriage and flap emergency operation switches
9 Flap control switches
10 Air pressure gauge
11 Airscrew pitch control levers
12 Undercarriage controls
13 Undercarriage position indicator
14 Cockpit illumination
15 Repeater compass
16 D/F control
17 Control column gun button
18 Altimeter
19 Cannon rounds indicator
20 Machine gun rounds indicator with cocking switch below
21 Front cockpit locking lever
22 Reflector sight mounting
23 Turn-and-bank indicator
24 Artificial horizon
25 Port coolant temperature gauge
26 Fuel contents gauge
27 Starboard coolant temperature gauge
28 Coolant radiator flap position selector (port)
29 Fuel gauge contents tank selector switch
30 Coolant radiator flap position selector
31 Airspeed indicator
32 Rate-of-climb indicator
33 Port airscrew pitch indicator (Fitted to engine nacelle of Bf 110G)
34 Starboard (ditto)
35 Port revolutions counter
36 Starboard revolutions counter
37 Port boost gauge
38 Starboard boost gauge
39 Rudder pedals
40 Compass
41 Oxygen pressure gauge
42 Cockpit illumination
43 Dimmer switch
44 Rudder trimming control lever
45 Starter handles
46 Oxygen control
47 Spark plug cleaning handles
48 Selector lever for tank-replenishing pump
49 Switch for tank-replenishing pump
50 Switch for booster fuel pump

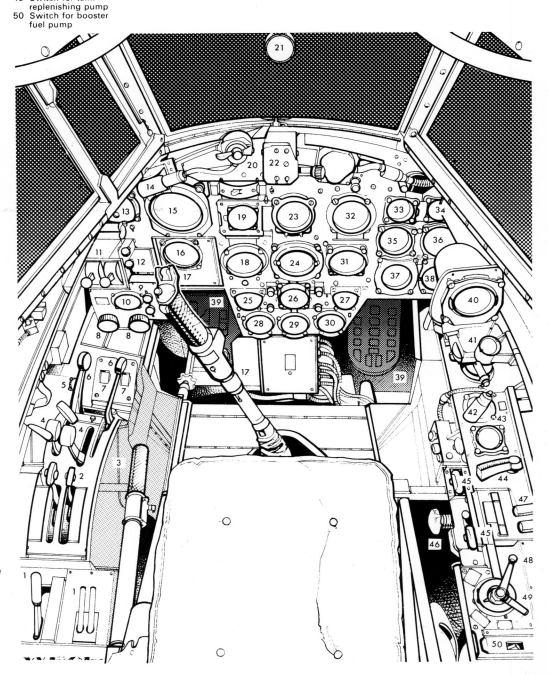

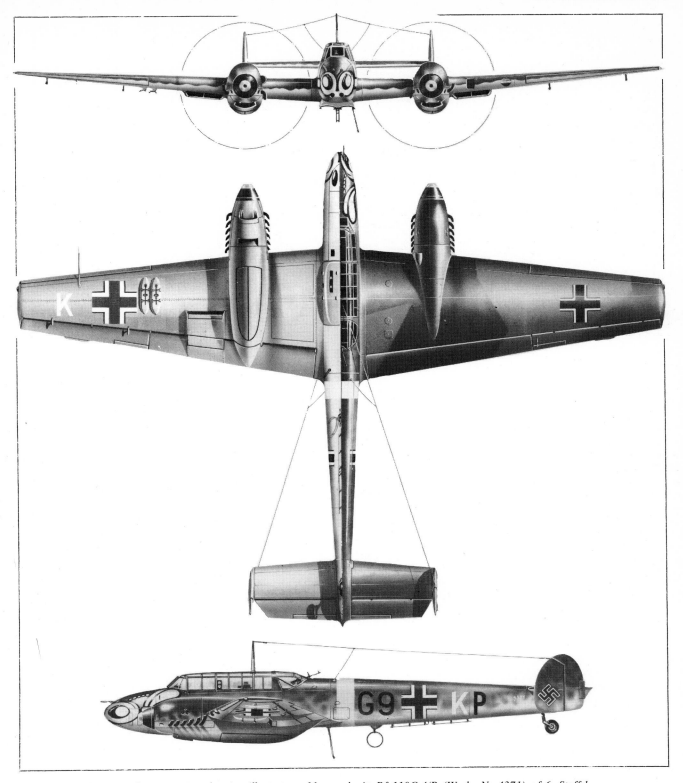

This general arrangement drawing illustrates a Messerschmitt Bf 110C-4/B (Werke-Nr 4371) of 6. Staffel, Zerstörergeschwader 1 operating over the Eastern Front during the autumn of 1942

was poor, but improved once 120 mph (193 km/h) was attained, this probably being aggravated by the tail heaviness of the aircraft since, with the tail on the ground, the rudders were, of course, considerably blanked by the fuselage and engines. Even with the stick well forward the tail was slow to rise. The take-off of the Bf 110G, with its more powerful DB 605s at 2,800 rpm and 1·42 *atas* of boost coupled with the use of flaps, was markedly improved over that of the Bf 110C.

Once off the ground the flaps were retracted at 500 ft (150 m), this amount of altitude being necessary for safety because of the considerable nose-down change of trim that accompanied upward flap movement. Speed was then built up to 150 mph (240 km/h) which gave a steep angle and a very good rate of climb at 2,300 rpm and 1·2 *atas* of boost, this being further improved on the Bf 110G at 2,600 rpm and 1·3 *atas* of boost. The controls were fairly light, well harmonised and very

A Bf 110G-4c/R3 which had the single FuG 220b Lichtenstein SN-2 radar installation and Rüstsatz 3 which comprised the replacement of the standard four 7,9-mm MG 17 machine guns by a pair of 30-mm MK 108 cannon. For much of the war, the Bf 110 provided the backbone of Germany's nocturnal fighter defence. A diurnal G-series version, the Bf 110G-2, is illustrated at the head of page 172, this example serving with III Gruppe of Zerstörergeschwader 26

effective up to 250 mph (400 km/h), but above that speed they began to heavy up, particularly the elevator, and in this respect the Bf 110 was reminiscent of its single-engined stablemate, the Messerschmitt Bf 109 (see pages 149-157). Stability was good fore and aft and directionally, but neutral laterally. Manœuvrability proved surprisingly good for so large (by contemporary standards) a fighter, but the Bf 110 suffered from the same serious fault as the Bf 109 — the automatic slats kept popping out unevenly in tight turns, sighting being ruined by the resultant lateral wobble.

The landing pattern was normally entered at 155 mph (250 km/h) and the undercarriage was fully lowered before the flaps were actuated. The first movement of the flaps caused a large change of nose-up attitude which had to be counteracted by a heavy forward force on the elevators. There was little point in trimming out this force as further flap movement caused a reversal of attitude change with the end result seeing little change of trim required. The ailerons began to droop as the flaps moved, a sudden lightening of their control being evident but no loss in effectiveness being apparent. The approach attitude at 100 mph (160 km/h) was steepish but the view from the cockpit was excellent. As with the Bf 109, care had to be taken not to hold off too high as the automatic slats were activated as the speed decayed and this could cause a wing to drop. The landing run was short as the brakes could be used heavily without any tendency for the tail to rise.

The single-engined performance of the Bf 110 with its fully-feathering airscrews was good except that a landing could be made only with a maximum of 25 deg of flap, otherwise use of more than 1,600 rpm from the one engine would result in an uncontrollable swing and bank. This restricted use of flap meant, of course, that a severe nose-up change of attitude had to be trimmed out and the pilot was faced with a few crisis seconds during which he had to work hard to prevent a loss of approach speed which could present him with some nasty control problems.

In so far as performance was concerned, during tests with a Bf 110G (*Werk-Nr* 73 0301) at the RAE, I clocked a maximum speed of 368 mph (592 km/h) at 19,000 ft (5 790 m), the maximum permissible indicated airspeed as shown on a plate in the cockpit being 435 mph (700 km/h). Cruise proved to be 305 mph (491 km/h) at 18,000 ft (5 485 m), that altitude being attained in 7·3 minutes. Performancewise the Bf 110 was certainly significantly superior to what I suppose can be considered as its

nearest British counterpart, the Beaufighter, and it was certainly appreciably more manœuvrable than the heavier and larger Bristol aeroplane with its substantially greater wing loading, and in consequence there can be little doubt that the Messerschmitt made the better day fighter. In the nocturnal rôle, the Beaufighter, with its superior radar and firepower, came into its own.

This then was the Messerschmitt Bf 110 — a versatile and effective combat aircraft in its heyday which placed Germany out in front in strategic fighter development, but like so many of the aircraft with which the *Luftwaffe* opened WW II, its production life was extended beyond anything that could reasonably be expected to maintain it in the top league. Indeed, the last Bf 110G did not roll off the assembly line until March 1945, some three years after it had been anticipated that it would be supplanted by the Me 210, and even the successor of this unfortunate design — the Me 410, a real knife-edger if I ever flew one — did nothing to reduce the importance of Messerschmitt's first "twin" in the operational inventory of the *Luftwaffe*.

It was singularly fortunate for the *Luftwaffe* that it possessed so tractable an aeroplane, and it is perhaps unfair but understandable that the Bf 110 be associated most widely with the "Battle of Britain" and judged on its showing in that epic conflict. It should be borne in mind, however, that the *Führungsstab* had never envisaged deploying Hermann's "Destroyer" other than in conditions of local *Luftwaffe* superiority if not supremacy; a situation such as that in which the Bf 110 found itself over Southern England had not been foreseen. No designer, however talented, had come up with a magic formula enabling a large and heavy twin-engined long-range fighter to compete in terms of agility with contemporary single-engined short-range single-seaters. The forward-firing armament of the Bf 110 was certainly lethal but lacking the manœuvrability of its RAF opponents, it could bring this armament to bear only if it could employ the element of surprise or if it encountered an unwary novice — a commodity of which admittedly RAF Fighter Command was in no short supply at that stage of the conflict. Its acceleration and speed were inadequate to enable it to avoid combat if opposed by superior numbers of interceptors, and its single aft-firing 7,9-mm weapon was inadequate to protect it from attack from astern. But if the Bf 110 received a mauling in the "Battle of Britain" it gave a good account of itself on many battlefronts in the years that followed.

MESSERSCHMITT ME 163

FIFTY-FIVE DEGREES of wing sweep; a pilot lying prone beneath the intake ducting for the turbojet; a speed roughly one-and-a-quarter times that of sound; a jettisonable take-off trolley and a pair of skids intended to absorb the impact of landing speeds of the order of 160 mph (257 km/h) — all pretty exotic stuff in so far as the UK was concerned 30 years ago! These were but some of the remarkable characteristics of an aeroplane on the RAE drawing boards at Farnborough in 1947. The project was exotic in the strictest definition of the adjective; it was alien in that it had been conceived by aerodynamicists introduced from abroad, and certain of its more esoteric features were decidedly *foreign* by British standards of the day. Designed by Dr Hans Multhopp, formerly in charge of Focke-Wulf's advanced studies, and one Dr Winter, a former wind tunnel expert from a German research establishment, this project had been conceived around Rolls-Royce's first and newly type-tested axial-flow turbojet, the AJ65 Avon.

It was as a result of this RAE supersonic project that, on the clear morning of 15 November 1947, precisely 32 days after the Bell X-1 had exceeded Mach unity for the first time, I was to be found struggling to extricate myself from the wrecked cockpit of a Messerschmitt Me 163B a few yards from the boundary fence at Wittering airfield, Northants. At first sight, there would seem to be little connection between the project on the Farnborough drawing boards and this audacious little wartime rocket-driven point defence interceptor, popularly known as the *Komet*. There *was* one

important connection, however, and that was the item on which it landed — a *skid*! The arguments put forward by Doctors Multhopp and Winter for a landing skid were fundamentally sound in so far as a research vehicle such as that on the RAE drawing boards was concerned. The faster the aircraft the more difficult the task of providing an adequate undercarriage, and in the RAE project there was little room for a conventional undercarriage owing to the high concentration of the component parts of the aircraft. Thus, the proposal to take-off with the aid of a jettisonable trolley and extend a pair of flush-fitting skids for landing provided a simple and logical answer to the space problem. It was anticipated that, upon release, the skids would drop and lock into position by means of a combination of their weight and the aerodynamic forces acting on them.

Calculations indicated that the approach speed of the projected research aircraft would be around 180 mph (290 km/h) and actual touch-down speed would be 160 mph (257 km/h), but little experience was available in the UK on high-speed skid-type landing, and probably the most important aspect of my test programme with the Me 163B was that of building up experience in skid landing technique. This was envisaged as a prelude to a specific group of tests that were to provide the finale to the programme. These tests were to involve a series of fast landings to obtain information on the ease of approach and touchdown at high speeds, but since the Me 163B had a touchdown speed of about 110 mph (177 km/h) it was obvious that we would have to increase

(Above) An Me 163B-1a commencing a so-called "sharp start" at Bad Zwischenahn. For take-off, the aircraft was trimmed tail heavy and the wheels were jettisoned at an altitude between 15 and 30 ft. (Immediately below left) An Me 163B being towed to take-off point by a light three-wheeled tractor known as a Scheuschlepper

(Above) The landing skid of the Me 163B in the extended position, and (below) an Me 163A (left) in company with its redesigned and larger derivative, the Me 163B.

this speed in a series of graduated steps. I was building up experience to this end and had been making encouraging progress in landing technique until that morning of 15 November.

The sensational Komet

My association with Dr Alexander Lippisch's remarkable creation had begun more than two years earlier, in the month of May 1945 at Husum, a dozen or so miles from the Danish border, where I came across some Me 163Bs of the II *Gruppe* of *Jagdgeschwader* 400, fuel shortages having prevented this *Gruppe* from flying the *Komet* operationally. To my mind, few aircraft can be genuinely described as "sensational", an epithet that can only be bestowed on an aeroplane combining four qualities — unusual design, outstanding performance, high efficiency in its intended rôle, and applied skill to fly it. Lippisch's rocket-driven interceptor was undoubtedly *sensational*. I learned more of the Me 163B at Bad Zwischenahn, Oldenburg, which had been the base of the *Erprobungskommando* (Test Detachment) 16 responsible for *Komet* tactical testing, and here I interrogated a number of *Luftwaffe* instructors who provided intriguing details of the training curriculum that had been evolved for the *Komet*. These details of the training programme, accompanied by some lurid information concerning the hazards that accompanied it, largely confirmed what I had already heard from that indomitable German woman pilot, Hanna Reitsch; a far from comforting saga for one booked to fly the Me 163B. I hasten to add that it was not the aircraft itself that presented so daunting a picture but the lethal propensities of the highly volatile fuels that its rocket motor consumed so voraciously.

Basically, the Me 163B was a single-seat tailless interceptor driven by a Walter HWK 509A bi-fuel rocket motor which theoretically provided 3,748 lb (1 700 kg) of thrust while burning immense quantities of hydrogen peroxide (with 20 per cent phosphate or oxyquinoline as a stabiliser) known as *T-Stoff,* with a solution of hydrazine hydrate in methanol, or *C-Stoff,* as a catalyst. The wing, which was swept 23·3 deg on the quarter-chord line, was of wooden construction with 8-mm plywood skinning covered by doped fabric, and featured a fixed leading-edge slot some 7 ft (2,13 m) in length which terminated about 1 ft (30 cm) from the wingtip. Lateral and longitudinal control were provided by differentially-operated fabric-covered elevons, and large longitudinal trimmer flaps were fitted inboard of the elevons and behind the landing flaps. The fuselage was an oval-section stressed-skin light alloy structure, and a two-wheel take-off trolley was attached to the rear portion of the landing skid housing by two lugs which engaged mechanical catches.

At Bad Zwischenahn I familiarised myself with the *Komet* training programme which was initiated with some flights in a *Stummel-Habicht*, a special clipped-wing version of the well-known *Habicht* (Hawk) glider, followed up by gliding flight in a water-ballasted Me 163A and then powered flight in the same type before conversion to the very much more potent Me 163B. I determined to follow this routine as closely as possible, remembering that so highly experienced a pilot as Hanna Reitsch had come a serious cropper* while flying an unpowered Me 163B. Having completed quite a bit of flying on German gliders, I looked around for a flyable Me 163A. There was one in good shape at Bad Zwischenahn,

*Hanna Reitsch was assigned to flight acceptance tests of unpowered pre-production Me 163Bs at Obertraubling, but during the fifth such flight the take-off trolley adhered to the aircraft, and every effort to jettison the trolley proved abortive. Finally, she attempted to land the aircraft with the trolley still in position. The aircraft stalled in from about 100 ft (30 m), striking the ground with tremendous force, and Hanna Reitsch suffered six fractures of the skull and displacement of the upper jawbone.

but the airfield itself was by now in pretty bad condition and so I persuaded a German instructor to fly it under tow behind a Messerschmitt Bf 110 to Fassberg while I flew another Bf 110 alongside so that I could watch the whole flight at close quarters.

After our arrival at Fassberg I spent the entire afternoon flying the Me 163A, and finally felt sufficiently confident to tackle the Me 163B. However, no Me 163B was immediately available as the RAE technical boys insisted that the aircraft chosen for trials be loaded into the hold of an Ar 232 transport and flown to Farnborough where it was to be prepared for testing. I had no means of knowing at that time that almost 14 months were to elapse between my cavorting above Fassberg in an Me 163A and finally getting my hands on an Me 163B! However, the characteristics of these tailless Lippisch-designed aeroplanes were not easily forgotten. I had learned much from flying the unpowered Me 163A, and I looked forward with considerable anticipation to flying its powered descendant.

During the interim 14 months, some practical information on the somewhat remarkable characteristics of the HWK 509A rocket motor had been provided the RAE boffins by visits to the engine test stands at the Hellmuth Walter Werke in Kiel, and the outcome was the decision to *abandon* powered flying for our tests. I was not consulted in this

(Above and below) The Me 163B flown in towed and gliding flight by the author, the Walter rocket motor having been removed and an auto-observer inserted in its place to record test data

Messerschmitt Me 163B-1a Cutaway Drawing Key:

1 Generator drive propeller
2 Generator
3 Compressed air bottle
4 Battery and electronics packs
5 Cockpit ventilation intake
6 Solid armour (15-mm) nose cone
7 Accumulator pressuriser
8 Direct cockpit air intake
9 FuG 25a radio pack
10 Rudder control assembly
11 Hydraulic and compressed air points
12 Elevon control rocker-bar
13 Control relay
14 Flying controls assembly box
15 Plastic rudder pedals
16 Radio tuning controls
17 Torque shaft
18 Port T-stoff cockpit tank (13 Imp gal/60 l capacity)
19 Control column
20 Hinged instrument panel

21 Armourglass windscreen brace
22 Revi 16B gunsight
23 Armourglass internal windscreen (90-mm)
24 Armament and radio switches (starboard console)
25 Pilot's seat
26 Back armour (8-mm)
27 Head and shoulder armour (13-mm)
28 Radio frequency selector pack
29 Headrest
30 Mechanically-jettisonable hinged canopy
31 Ventilation panel
32 Fixed leading-edge wing slot
33 Trim tab
34 Fabric-covered starboard elevon
35 Position of underwing landing flap
36 Inboard trim flap
37 FuG 16zy radio receiving aerial

38 T-Stoff filler cap
39 Main unprotected T-Stoff fuselage tank (229 Imp gal/1,040 l capacity)
40 Aft cockpit glazing
41 Port cannon ammunition box (60 rounds)
42 Starboard cannon ammunition box (60 rounds)
43 Ammunition feed chute
44 T-Stoff starter tank
45 Rudder control upper bell crank
46 C-Stoff filler cap
47 HWK 509A-1 motor turbine housing
48 Main rocket motor mounting frame
49 Rudder control rod
50 Disconnect point
51 Aerial matching unit
52 Fin front spar/fuselage attachment point
53 Tailfin construction
54 Rudder horn balance
55 Rudder upper hinge
56 Rudder frame
57 Rudder trim tab

58 Rudder control rocker-bar
59 Linkage fairing
60 Fin rear spar/fuselage attachment point
61 Rocket motor combustion chamber
62 Tailpipe
63 Rudder root fairing
64 Rocket thrust orifice
65 Vent pipe outlet
66 Hydraulic cylinder
67 Lifting point
68 Tailwheel fairing
69 Steerable tailwheel
70 Tailwheel axle fork
71 Tailwheel oleo
72 Tailwheel steering linkage
73 Coupling piece/vertical lever
74 Wingroot fillet
75 Combustion chamber support brace
76 Gun-cocking mechanism
77 Trimp flap control angle gear (bulkhead mounted)
78 Worm gear
79 Trim flap mounting
80 Port inboard trim flap
81 Elevon mounting
82 Rocker-bar
83 Elevon actuation push-rod
84 Port elevon
85 Wing rear spar

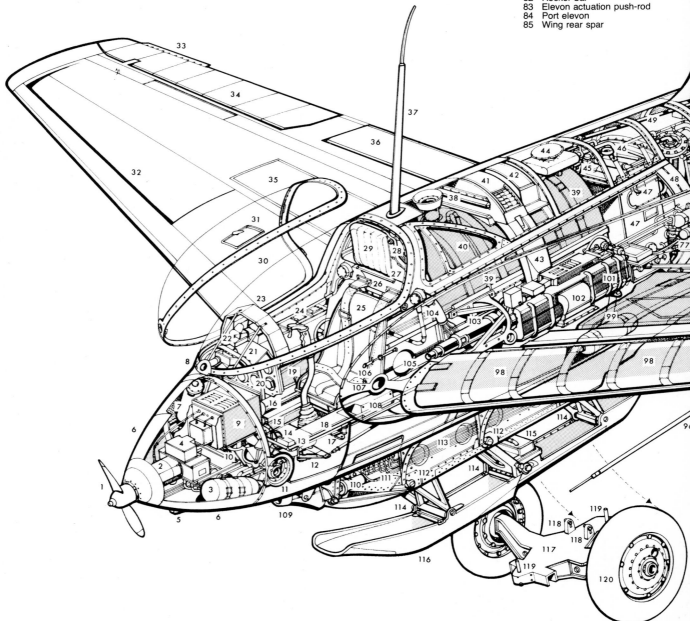

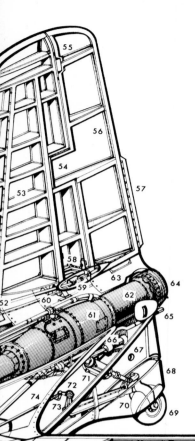

86 Trim tab
87 Elevon outboard hinge
88 Wingtip bumper
89 Wing construction
90 Fixed leading-edge wing slot
91 Elevon control bell crank
92 Position of port underwing landing flap
93 Push-rod in front spar
94 Front spar
95 FuG 25a aerial
96 Pitot head
97 Wing tank connecting-pipe fairing
98 C-Stoff leading-edge tank (16 Imp gal/73 l capacity
99 Gun-cocking compressed air bottle
100 Main C-Stoff wing tank (38 Imp gal/173 l capacity)
101 Port 30-mm MK 108 short-barrel cannon
102 Expanding shell and link chute
103 Gun forward mounting frame
104 Pressure-tight gun-control passage
105 Blast tube
106 Gun alignment mechanism
107 Cannon port
108 FuG 25a IFF pack
109 Tow-bar attachment point
110 Compressed-air ram for landing skid
111 Hydraulics and compressed-air pipes
112 Landing skid pivots
113 Landing skid keel mounting
114 Landing skid mounting brackets
115 Trolley jettison mechansim
116 Landing skid
117 Take-off trolley frame
118 Take-off trolley retaining lugs
119 Take-off trolley alignment pins
120 Low-pressure tyre

Head-on and rear views of the Me 163B employed in 1946-47 for trolley-and-skid take-off and landing trials at Wisley and Wittering

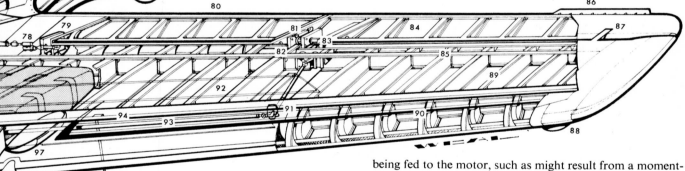

decision, but I was present at a demonstration in Kiel, and was suitably impressed when, after the shattering roar of a test run, Dr Walter took two glass rods, placed a droplet of *T-Stoff* on one and an equally minute quantity of *C-Stoff* on the other. He then inclined the rods until the droplet of *T-Stoff* fell to the floor, the *C-Stoff* following it. There was immediately a violent explosion, despite the tiny quantities of fuel and catalyst involved, both rods being shattered in Dr Walter's hands. I might not have agreed with the boffins' decision not to risk powered trials in the air, but at least now I understood it!

Certainly the *Komet* had a black accident record, for the slightest irregularity in the set ratio of *C-Stoff* to *T-Stoff*

Messerschmitt Me 163B-1a Specification

Power plant: One Walter HWK 509A-1 or -2 bi-fuel rocket motor with a maximum thrust rating of 3,748 lb (1 700 kg).
Armament: Two 30-mm Rheinmetall Borsig Mk 108 cannon with 60 rpg.
Performance: Maximum speed, 516 mph (830 km/h) at sea level, 593 mph (955 km/h) between 9,850 and 29,500 ft (3 000 and 9 000 m); time to 29,500 ft (9 000 m), 2·6 min, to 39,370 ft (12 000 m), 3·35 min; max powered endurance, 7·5 min; powered endurance after climb to 29,500 ft (9 000 m) at 497 mph (800 km/h), 2·5 min; initial climb rate, 15,950 ft/min (81 m/sec); normal radius of action, 22 mls (35·5 km) at 497 mph (800 km/h); take-off distance to clear 49 ft (15 m), 700 yd (640 m).
Weights: Empty equipped, 4,206 lb (1 908 kg); max loaded, 9,502 lb (4 310 kg).
Dimensions: Span, 30 ft 7⅓ in (9,33 m); length, 19 ft 2⅓ in (5,85 m); height (on trolley), 9 ft 0⅔ in (2,76 m); wing area, 199·13 sq ft (18,50 m²).

being fed to the motor, such as might result from a momentary interruption in the flow of one or other, could produce an explosion leaving little of the aeroplane or its unfortunate occupant. Even a bad bump on landing could produce equally disastrous results from the dregs of the temperamental rocket fuels remaining in the tanks. But there were hazards other than those stemming from the fuels. Trimmed tail heavy, the Me 163B took-off with the twin-wheel trolley attached to the housing of the skid which was extended, the lugs connecting the trolley being automatically disengaged when the pilot retracted the skid. It was standard practice to jettison the trolley at an altitude of 20–30 ft (7,0–9,0 m), but if the pilot miscalculated, the trolley *could* bounce up and hit the fuselage or even hook on to the skid. If the jettisoning gear malfunctioned, the pilot had to abandon the aircraft as the chance of making a successful landing with the trolley in position was negligible, as Hanna Reitsch had discovered to her cost.

Landing speed was high, and the landing was effected, of course, power off, so considerable judgment was called for; if the pilot failed to touch down within a reasonable distance of a cross marked on the runway and skidded on to rough ground, the chances were that the aircraft would turn turtle, and if the remaining fuel dregs failed to explode, it was more than likely that they would seep into the cockpit and eat through the *Asbestos-Mipolamfibre* protective overall worn by the luckless pilot. If neither of these unpleasant consequences of a heavy landing occurred, the pilot could still suffer "*Komet* back" — severe spinal injuries resulting from impact forces.

According to German sources, 80 per cent of all *Komet* losses resulted from accidents during take-off or landing, 15 per cent were the result of either fire in the air or loss of control in a dive, and only five per cent were combat casualties. Baling out at speeds in excess of 250 mph (400 km/h) was impossible as above this speed the hood could not be safely jettisoned. It was with this sobering store of background information that I first took to the air in an Me 163B on 10 October 1946, though, admittedly, the *Komet* in which I found myself seated had none of those appalling rocket fuels sloshing about in tanks around me, and the aircraft, which now sported the RAF serial VF241, had had its Walter rocket motor removed and an auto-observer inserted in its place to record the test data.

Delightful handling characteristics

The decision had been taken to use a Spitfire IX as a tug, and in order to avoid the risk of damaging the landing skid on the Farnborough runways, the flight test programme was begun from the grass airfield at Wisley. As I had already flown the Me 163A, albeit more than a year earlier, it had been decided to launch me straight into the test programme, and the first flight that I made on tow was to 16,000 ft (4 875 m) for static lateral stability measurements. During take-off, the Spitfire could unstick before the *Komet* so its pilot was instructed to hold his aircraft on the ground until I became airborne. There was severe bumping during the take-off run owing to the non-resilient nature of the trolley, and since headroom in the cockpit was decidedly limited and the seat could only be adjusted on the ground, I had every reason to be thankful to nature for having endowed me with optimum stature to prevent a severe beating around the head and yet still enable me to see through the windscreen.

The directional control was good as the tailwheel was steerable, no flap was used during take-off, and elevator trim was neutral. After unsticking, I pulled the *Komet* up quickly through the tug's slipstream to about 20 ft (6,0 m), having meanwhile retracted the skid and jettisoned the take-off trolley by raising the lever on the left-hand side of the instrument panel, skid retraction and trolley jettisoning being indicated on a dial alongside the lever. The Spitfire had now unstuck and its pilot held us at a low altitude until the speed built up to 170 mph (274 km/h). I already knew from my earlier Me 163A experience that the best position to hold on tow was a relatively shallow angle above the tug. If too high a position was adopted, a severe pitching oscillation was set up, or, alternatively, the tug was lost to view as the downward visibility from the *Komet* was extremely poor.

Once in free flight the *Komet* handled beautifully, with delightful harmony of control and thoroughly satisfactory stability characteristics. Indeed, it was difficult to detect any facet of handling that characterised this aircraft as being tailless. The landing process was complicated by the inadequate view from the cockpit which necessitated a wide circuit of the field as the glide angle was very flat. The flaps were lowered on the final approach, but the selector lever and handpump were awkwardly positioned on the left side of the cockpit floor. The lever had to be turned through 180 deg before the handpump could be operated, and six full strokes of the latter were necessary to lower the flaps completely. The effect of the flaps was to steepen the glide considerably at an approach speed of 130 mph (210 km/h), and once sure of getting into the field, I lowered the skid and flew it on to the ground after a low hold-off.

My first touchdown was at about 115 mph (185 km/h), the tailwheel making contact first before the *Komet* pitched forward on to the skid without any bounce. As the speed dropped off on the slide along the grass surface, the wings could be kept level by coarse use of the ailerons, and eventually one wingtip dropped on to the ground, but the aircraft continued to run straight until it finally came to a standstill about 400 yd (366 m) from the point of touching down. I had exercised the greatest care to ensure that I did not stall the aircraft on to the ground. Many a *Luftwaffe* pilot had been lifted out of a *Komet* with a broken back as a return for attempting a stall-in style of landing or for landing with the undercarriage lever down and not in neutral (in the "down" position the skid oleos were under pressure and therefore rigid), or, worst of all, landing with the skid retracted.

My flight had lasted 25 minutes, and a considerable period

An Me 163B-1a taken to the USA for evaluation. Although all the principle allies acquired several specimens of the Messerschmitt rocket-propelled fighter, none attempted flight testing under power, confining themselves to investigation of the characteristics of the aircraft in gliding flight

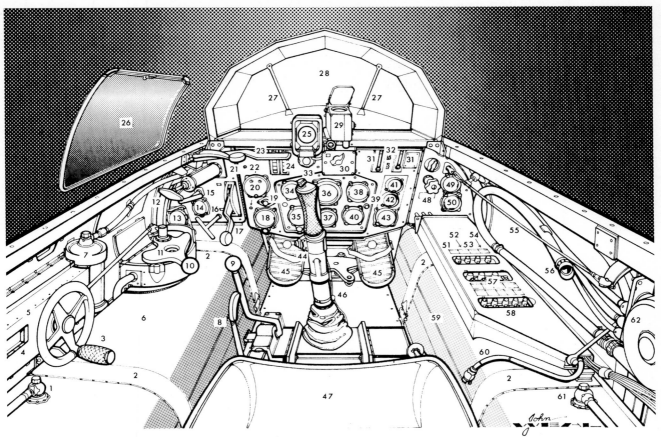

Messerschmitt Me 163B Cockpit Instrumentation Key

1	Fuel feed pipe	17	Landing skid operating
2	Tank restraining straps		quadrant
3	Trim handwheel	18	Clock/stopwatch
4	Trim adjustment indicator	19	Main line switch
5	Trim control box	20	Undercarriage position
6	Port 'T-Stoff' fuel tank		indicator
7	Oil pressure reservoir	21	Canopy latch
8	Flap selector lever	22	Hinged instrument panel
9	Flap manual pump		retaining screws
10	Throttle lever	23	Canopy release
11	Starter switch	24	Undercarriage (left) and
12	Emergency undercarriage		landing skid (right) indicators
	jettison cock	25	Compass
13	Hydraulic accumulator air	26	Clear vision panel
	pressure gauge	27	Inner screen stays
14	Undercarriage emergency	28	90-mm armoured glass inner
	jettison pressure gauge		screen
15	Emergency fuel jettison	29	Revi 16 reflector gunsight
	pull-out handle		(unpadded)
16	Tow-tug release handle	30	FuG 25a control unit

31	Ammunition counters	48	Oxygen regulator
32	Gun switches	49	Oxygen pressure gauge
33	Firing button (on control	50	Oxygen indicator
	column)	51	Bank-and-turn indicator
34	Altimeter		(artificial horizon) control
35	Airspeed indicator		switch
36	Artificial horizon	52	Port MK 108 cannon control
37	RPM counter		switch
38	Variometer	53	Starboard MK 108 cannon
39	Fuel contents warning light		control switch
40	Temperature gauge	54	Main line switch control
41	Thrust indicator (0 to 6 kg/cm²	55	Emergency canopy release
	: redlined at 3)		mechanism
42	Thrust indicator (0 to 25	56	Pilot's oxygen tube
	kg/cm² : redlined at 18.5)	57	FuG 25 control switches
43	Consumption indicator	58	FuG 16ZY control switches
44	Gun charging knob	59	Starboard 'T-Stoff' fuel tank
45	Plastic rudder pedals	60	Helmet R/T connection
46	Control column	61	Fuel feed pipe
47	Pilot's adjustable seat	62	Oxygen supply

of time was to elapse before I was once again to get airborne in the *Komet*. An extensive test programme was planned by the RAE, but, in the event, this was to be curtailed considerably as a result of maintenance difficulties. The principal problem was associated with the hydraulic system for the skid and tailwheel. In fact, on my first flight I had experienced some difficulty in getting the landing skid down, and it had been discovered that the hydraulic accumulator had failed. It was the difficulty in acquiring a replacement that was the real problem, and this was to cost us almost a year of inactivity with the Me 163B.

An imaginative project

While our *Komet* was sitting around awaiting the arrival of a replacement hydraulic accumulator, Doctors Multhopp and Winter were busy at their drawing boards at the RAE, creating on paper what, had it been smiled upon by fate, could well have been just as radical an aircraft in so far as the annals of aviation were concerned as had been Dr Lippisch's *Komet*, which, it was envisaged, was to play a rôle, if a minor

one, in bringing this imaginative project to fruition. The radical aeroplane being designed at Farnborough by the German aerodynamicists was intended to attain Mach 1·24 at 36,000 ft (10 975 m).

The project was extremely advanced, and, in the light of present-day knowledge, perhaps *too* advanced, but in those far-off days of 1947, the design of this transonic research vehicle was being actively pursued, and our *Komet* had its part to play in the development programme, its task being the creation of a pool of expertise in high-speed skid landing techniques. However, it was not until 30 September 1947 that the *Komet,* VF241, could be flown again, and before getting down to the most important aspect of its flight test programme, the handling trials interrupted during the previous year by the failure of the hydraulic accumulator had to be completed. Therefore, I continued stability tests from a towed ascent to 18,000 ft (5 485 m), stalling trials and high-speed dives being performed during subsequent flights, all of which revealed some interesting features worth recording.

The stall was an abrupt and severe one, except with the CG in the forward position when it could not be stalled owing to lack of elevon power. In any other loading condition there was no advance warning of a stall other than a sudden silence accompanied by sloppiness of control. The port wing dropped sharply, followed by the nose, and the subsequent spiral dive was steep, but recovery was straight-forward. Stalling speeds were measured with a trailing static and venturi pitot head, so that for these tests I had 100 ft (30 m) of rubber tubing trailing beneath the aircraft, and something like an 11-lb (5-kg) practice bomb attached to the end of it. This little lot was neatly packaged for take-off and released in flight, and was intended to be jettisoned at the end of the tests, being lowered gently to the ground at

the end of a drogue parachute.

I certainly had my share of troubles with this equipment. On one occasion the lot fell off during take-off as a result of excessive bumping during the run, and on another occasion both tubing and "bomb" wrapped themselves around the fuselage and fin during the spiral dive resulting from a stall. In an effort to unwind the tubing, I held the *Komet* in the dive after recovery, pulled the aircraft up into a roll and held it momentarily in the inverted position with a fair amount of negative *g*, and then operated the jettison release. All this worked like a charm except that the drogue parachute caught up on the tailwheel, and there it remained firmly for the landing.

The upper end of the speed scale could be explored to only a limited degree as the *Komet* was unpowered, and we did not normally tow above 20,000 ft (6 095 m) owing to the risk of overheating the Spitfire's engine. However, even without power, the *Komet* accelerated smoothly and rapidly in a dive, and we therefore made one special tow to 25,000 ft (7 620 m). During the subsequent dive I attained 440 mph (708 km/h) at 17,000 ft (5 180 m) which was equivalent to Mach 0·8. At this Mach number the elevon control forces were still moderate, and there were none of the signs of the onset of compressibility that I had anticipated, *Luftwaffe* pilots having all told me that the *Komet* buffeted badly and then dropped its nose violently in a "graveyard dive" at Mach 0·84.

I had by now reached what had become the primary purpose of testing the Me 163B, the building up of touch-down speeds on the landing skid in a series of graduated stages. I would join the airfield circuit in the direction of landing, aiming to cross the airfield boundary at an altitude of 1,640 ft (500 m) and at a speed of 155 mph (250 km/h), lowering the skid, which did not alter the trim, and at the same time turning the flap selector lever to the "down" position. At this slow glide speed the stability had deteriorated, and all the controls were very light, but this was compensated to some extent by the effectiveness of the rudder. I then flew round the airfield in a wide curve, swinging out just before turning on to the final leg of the approach, giving myself a gentle turn-in so as not to lose too much height. View was poor and the glide was very flat until the flaps were lowered on the final leg which I aimed to commence at about 650 ft (213 m) at a speed of 135 mph (217 km/h), pumping down the flaps as desired to steepen the gliding angle.

Lowering the flaps gave a nose-up change of trim for the first one-third of their travel and then a nose-down change for the remainder, the total effect being slightly nose down. I always wound on tail-heavy trim as the flaps were lowered, having found that this helped to reduce any sink if they had to be raised late on approach. If I was too high on the approach I had to lose this by weaving and not by slipping it off because control was insufficiently effective to make this a safe manoeuvre at low speed. For the same reason, the aircraft gave a rough ride in gusty weather, and large amounts of elevon movement aided by rudder were necessary to keep level. These points had been stressed by *Luftwaffe* pilots, and they had certainly not been guilty of exaggerating them.

In spite of the apparent deterioration in stick free stability at low speeds, the landing process on the *Komet* was very much easier than on other tailless aircraft that had been flown in the UK. On many such aircraft there is a tendency to fly off once the hold-off has been initiated, the pilot then having to push the stick forward to get the aircraft on to the ground. This is due to a deterioration in longitudinal stability near the stall, resulting in a stick free reversal which is sometimes quite severe, and the pilot does not become aware of this until the aircraft is rising. On the *Komet* our

Me 163B-1a interceptors belonging the Jagdgeschwader 400 in the autumn of 1944 at the start of this innovative little interceptor's brief and largely abortive operational career

tests showed that there was an increase in stick fixed stability as the stall was approached, and the superior behaviour of the aircraft during landing was probably due to this factor which, in large measure, resulted from the leading-edge slots delaying the onset of the tip stall. A low "daisy-cutter" hold-off was the thing to aim for, and then a gentle lowering on to the grass surface. Measurements of the landing run averaged 400 yd (365 m) on dry grass, but this distance almost doubled on wet grass.

Fast landings and finis

The stage was now set for the fast landing trials. It was decided, however, that Wisley might prove on the tight side for these, and the decision was taken, therefore, to transfer the *Komet* test programme to Wittering. During the war years, Wittering had been one of three special emergency landing strips for bombers returning from the continent so badly damaged that a crash landing seemed probable. The grass strip had originally been five miles long, but by the time I arrived at Wittering with the *Komet* two-fifths of this had been restored to the farmers.

I flew VF241 on tow from Wisley to Wittering, a distance of 120 miles (193 km) covered in 35 minutes at an altitude of 3,500 ft (1 067 m), on 1 November 1947, dividing my time during the trip between estimating, not without some apprehension, the fatigue strength of the towline and despairing at the pocket handkerchief size of the English fields over which we were passing. Nevertheless, Wittering was reached in safety, and I left the *Komet* there for a few days to be prepared for the fast landing tests. I returned to Wittering on 13 November, commencing the trials that afternoon. The first landing was made without using landing flaps, a touch-down speed of 133 mph (214 km/h) being recorded, and I experienced no difficulties of any kind. A second landing made without flaps that evening recorded a 136 mph (219 km/h) touchdown, but the landing was rough, presumably, I assumed, owing to the somewhat rutted surface of the airfield rather than the higher touchdown speed as the increment in this had been very small.

The next day was unsuitable for flying, but the morning of 15 November dawned clear. During discussion of the earlier results it had been concluded that the application of slight flap might prove necessary to get a steeper angle of approach and thus build up speed on the approach and attain a higher touchdown speed without excessive float on hold-off. It should be remembered that the landing flaps functioned more in the fashion of dive brakes than as lift devices, and, indeed, only gave a measured increase in maximum lift coefficient of 0·1. This technique certainly worked, but perhaps it was a little *too* effective for after my next flight I touched down at 158 mph (254 km/h).

Actual contact with the airfield was not hard, but the run-out was too much for the hydraulic skid which collapsed and smashed up into the fuselage, ramming the oleo legs through the cockpit floor and jamming the rudder bar fully over to port. Simultaneously, my legs were pushed up and jammed beneath the instrument panel, and as the *Komet* veered to port in a gentle curve which became more pronounced as the left wing dropped and ploughed into the ground, the instrument panel and instruments and fittings broke loose and peppered me. After a run of 610 yd (558 m), the aircraft finally came to a standstill just short of the airfield side of the boundary fence. It took quite a while to free me from the wreckage of the cockpit. My primary concern was not for the cuts and abrasions that I had suffered but for my spine. To say that it had taken a severe jolting would have been an understatement, and, indeed, I was subsequently to discover that I was heavily bruised from the base of my spine to the hairline of my neck. The damage to the skid was irreparable, and thus RAE trials with the *Komet* came to an abrupt end. This accident did not mean the end of the RAE transonic research aircraft project, the scheme really foundering in the post-war financial lull affecting aircraft research and development.

Although I was destined never to fly the Me 163B under rocket power, I had acquired a thorough first-hand knowledge of the aircraft's inherent flying characteristics, and I had interrogated so many *Komet* pilots that I feel capable of giving a fair estimate of this warplane's operational worth. Its most startling performance characteristic was its "rocket-like" climb to 40,000 ft (12 190 m) in something short of four minutes at a speed of 435 mph (700 km/h), placing it well above enemy bomber formations with impunity. It possessed no pressure cabin, so 40,000 ft (12 190 m) was near enough its operational ceiling, but even 30,000 ft (9 145 m) gave sufficient excess of height to set up a fast dive without power straight through the intruding bomber stream, blasting away with its pair of 30-mm MK108 cannon each of which was provided with 60 rounds. With a tactically usable speed of Mach 0·82, the *Komet* could not be touched by Allied escort fighters as it flitted through the bomber formations, banging away with its Rheinmetall-Borsig "power hammers". But the closing speed of the *Komet* with its bomber prey was very high, while the minimum distance at which it stood any chance of hitting a target of the size of the B-17 Fortress was 650 yd (595 m). Since the *Komet* pilot had to break off the attack at a distance of some 200 yd (183 m) from the bomber in order to avoid

collision, he was left with something less than three seconds in which to operate his slow-firing cannon.

After this pass came the critical moment for the *Komet* pilot as he had to relight the Walter rocket to zoom up to altitude for his next pass which could be a repeat of the dive from above or a firing run on the climb through the bomber formation. The total time available at full throttle was 230 seconds, and two minutes had to elapse between an engine cut and relight, so the *Komet* pilot's cockpit stopwatch was vital for his survival. Furthermore, he had to ensure that he had sufficient fuel remaining in his tanks to be able to accelerate away from possible pursuit by escort fighters after making his final firing pass. With such a restricted endurance and range, the Me 163B obviously had to be under constant radar control from its base, and the *Komet*, of course, possessed no night flying capability, being very much a fair weather fighter.

To sum up, the *Komet* was of dubious operational effectiveness, and was probably more lethal to its pilots than to its enemies, and, on balance, its operational record hardly justified the tremendous research effort that carried it to service status. There is no gainsaying, however, that the Me 163B was a brilliant conception. Given more breathing space for development than a wartime environment permitted, the Walter rocket motor could probably have been brought to higher stages of reliability and flexibility, and the *Komet* could have proved the grave embarrassment to the Allied daylight bombing offensive that had been feared when Allied intelligence first reported its existence.

Postscript

As a postscript to my association with the Me 163B, I was involved in the return of a specimen of this aircraft to its country of origin. The RAF had, in November 1964, handed over a *Komet* airframe to the Germans, but it lacked a rocket motor, and no such power plant had apparently survived in Germany. At the time, I was naval attaché in Bonn, and the Germans, knowing of my work on the Me 163B, asked if I could help them to obtain a rocket motor. I vaguely recalled having seen, in 1949, the Walter motor from VF241 lying in the corner of a hangar at the RAE, together with bits and pieces of V 1 and V 2 missiles, and the battered remains of the Caproni-Campini C.C.2. Could that rocket motor still be gathering dust at Farnborough? Investigation elicited the fact that it was, and the RAE generously handed it over.

Thus, eventually a complete Me 163B, refurbished in *Luftwaffe* finish of the period *sans*, of course, the swastikas (concerning which some sensitivity remains to this day) and sporting the unofficial crest of 7.*Staffel* of *Jagdgeschwader* 400, was finally unveiled on 2 July 1965 in the museum in Munich, and I was invited to attend the ceremony. It was a nostalgic gathering which included the designer of the *Komet*, Dr Alexander Lippisch, Dr Willy Messerschmitt whose rôle in the story of the Me 163B had been that of a somewhat unwilling foster parent, Dr Helmuth Walter who had been responsible for the power plant of the *Komet*, Rudolf "Pitz" Opitz who had taken over responsibility for the Me 163B flight development programme from Heini Dittmar who had suffered spinal injuries, performed the first powered flight with the Me 163B and later became *Kommandeur* of II/JG 400, and Wolfgang Späte, the former *Kommodore* of JG 400. Only Heini Dittmar, who had died some years earlier in a flying accident, and Hanna Reitsch were missing from the *Komet* "inner circle".

It is improbable that such a reunion will ever take place again, as many of those present are now dispersed all over the globe, but this small and exclusive band was there almost in its entirety to pay its respects to what was perhaps Germany's most incredible aeroplane, an example of which had finally returned home to rest in a place of honour.

The author (right) talking to former Messerschmitt chief test pilot, Fritz Wendel, during the unveiling of a restored Me 163B in Munich in July 1965. Rudolf "Pitz" Opitz, who was responsible for much of the flight testing of the Me 163, may just be seen (facing the camera) behind the author